Record
of the
Courts
of
CHESTER COUNTY
PENNSYLVANIA

- 1681-1697 -

By:
The Colonial Society of Pennsylvania

Southern Historical Press, Inc.
Greenville, South Carolina

This volume was reproduced from
An personal copy located in the
Publisher's private Library

All rights reserved. No part of this publication may be reproduced, stored in a retrieval system, transmitted in any form, posted on to the web in any form or by any means without the prior written permission of the publisher.

Please direct all correspondence and orders to:

www.southernhistoricalpress.com
or
SOUTHERN HISTORICAL PRESS, Inc.
PO BOX 1267
375 West Broad Street
Greenville, SC   29601
southernhistoricalpress@gmail.com

Originally published: Philadelphia, PA   1910
ISBN #0-89308-907-9
All rights Reserved.
Printed in the United States of America

Province of Pennsilvania
At the Co^rt at Upland
September 13th 1681

Justices p^rsent

Mr William Clayton   Mr Robert Lucas
Mr William Warner   Mr Lassey Cock
Mr Robert Wade   Mr Swan Swanson
Mr Otto Ern^st Cock   Mr Andreas Bankson
Mr William Byles

Mr John Test Sheriffe
Mr Tho: Revell Clerke

Peter Erickson — Plaint }
Harmon Johnson & } Defend^ts } An Accon of Assault
Margarett his wife }   & Batt'.

Juro^rs

Morgan Drewitt   Richard Pitman
Willm: Woodmanson   Lassey Dalboe
William Hewes   John Akraman
James Browne   Peter Rambo jun^r
Henry Reynolds   Henry Hastings
Robert Scholey   William Oxley

Witnesse Willm Parker

The Jury finde for ye Plaint & give him 6^d dam & his Cost of Suite

Harmon Johnson & } Plaint^s }
Margrett his wife }   } An Accon of Assault
Peter Erickson   Defend^t   } & Batt'.

Juro^rs

Morgan Drewitt   Richard Pitman
Willm: Woodmanson   Lassey Dalboe
William Hewes   John Akraman
James Browne   Peter Rambo jun^r
Henry Reynolds   Henry Hastings
Robert Scholey   William Oxley

Witnesse Anna Coleman, Richd Buffington, Ebenezer Taylor.

The Jury finde for yᵉ Plᵗˢ & give them 40ˢ dam & their Costs of Suite

PETER DALBOE   Plaint ⎫
JOHN EUSTASON   Defᵗ   ⎬ An Accon of Trespasse
                       ⎭

Juroʳs

Richard Noble   Lassey Lawson
Daniell Brenson   John Champion
Richard Ridgeway   Samuell Dart
John Wood   Willm: Clayton Junʳ
ffrancis Stephenson   Thomas Nossiter
Roger Pederick   Albert Hendrickson

Witnesse Lassey Cock

The Jury finde for the Defᵗ & give him 5ˢ dam & his Costs of Suite

PETER ERICKSON   Plaint ⎫
HENRY COLEMAN   Defᵗ   ⎬ An Accon of the Case
                        ⎭

Juroʳs

Morgan Drewitt   Richard Pitman
Willm: Woodmanson   Lassey Dalboe
Willm: Hewes   John Akraman
James Browne   Peter Rambo junʳ
Henry Reynolds   Henry Hastings
Robert Scholey   William Oxley

Witnesse Mʳ John Test

The Jury finde for yᵉ Plaint & give him 10ˢ dam & his Costs of Suite

THOMAS NOSSITER   Plaint ⎫
ANDREAS NEALSON   Defᵗ   ⎬ An Accon of Assault & Batt:
                         ⎭

Juroʳs

Richard Noble   Lassey Lawson
Daniell Brenson   John Champion
Richᵈ Ridgeway   Samuell Dart
John Wood   Willm: Clayton junʳ
ffranc: Stephenson   Walter Pumphrey
Roger Pederick   Albert Hendrickson

Witnesses Mrs Saund'land Mr John Test Peter Cock jun^r Rich^d: Buffington Willm: Cobb John Champion Mary Nealson Carey Nealson.

The Jury finde for ye Plaint & give him 5^lb dam & his Costs of Suite

| PETER ERICKSON | Plaint | An Accon of Trespasse upon the Case |
| MORTIN MORTINSON | Def^t | |

Juro^rs

Morgan Drewitt	Richard Pitman
Willm: Woodmanson	Lassey Dalboe
Willm: Hewes	John Akraman
James Browne	Peter Rambo jun^r
Henry Reynolds	Henry Hastings
Robert Scholey	William Oxley

Witnesse John Cornelius, John Boles

The Jury finde for ye Def^t & give him 5^s dam & his Costs of Suite.

| ANDREAS INKHORNE | Plaint | An Accon of Trespasse |
| LASSEY DALBOE | Def^t | |

Juro^rs

Morgan Drewitt	Richard Pitman
Willm: Woodmanson	Albert Hendrickson
William Hewes	John Akraman
James Browne	Ebenezer Taylor
Henry Reynolds	Henry Hastings
Robert Scholey	William Oxley

Witnesse The Def^t Confest ye Accon

The Jury finde for ye Plaint & give him 6 dam & his Costs of Suite

Andreas Inkhorne on the behalfe of himselfe & others preferred a Bill to the Comission^rs about his Tytle to the Land whereon ye Trespasse was made; But nothing was concluded about ye Tytle.

| JOHN JOHNSON | Plaint | An Accon of Assault & Batt |
| JOHN COCK | Def^t | |

Juro's

Richard Noble	Lassey Lawson
Daniell Brenson	Lassey Dalboe
Richd Ridgeway	Samuell Dart
John Wood	Willm Clayton jur
ffranc: Stephenson	Walter Pumphrey
Roger Pederick	Mons Eustason

Witnesse Otto Ernst Cock, Mons Eustason Israell Helme

The Jury finde for ye Deft & give him 10s dam & his Costs of Suite

LAWRENCE HEADINGS Plaint }
EBENEZER TAYLOR Deft } An Accon of debt

Juro's

Richard Noble	Lassey Lawson
Daniell Brenson	Lassey Dalboe
Richd Ridgeway	Samuell Dart
John Wood	Wm Clayton Junr
ffranc Stephenson	Walter Pumphrey
Roger Pederick	Mons Eustason

Witnesse John Hazell

The Jury finde for ye Plaint & give him his debt being 62 Gildrs & his Costs of Suite

Anne Peirce haveing formerly Sworne ye Peace agst Anne the wife of William Stanford, the said Anne Stanford was by warrant from Wm Byles & Robert Lucas, Justices brought before them, & bound over to this Cort: And was by the Cort then discharged.

Lassey Cock upon Proclamation in this Cort, That if any had anything against him, They should declare it; Whereupon, Daniell Brenson & Charles Brigham upon oath, togeather with Walter Pumphrey upon his Solemne Attestation, declared what they heard certaine Indians speake against him & Capt Edmond Cantwell: The said Lassey Cock upon oath declared his Innocency, And that hee had never spoken those words to the Indians, or any of that nature: Was thereupon Cleared by the Cort.

Thomas Nossiter	Plain^t	
Neales Lawson &		Withdrawne
Annakey his Wife	Defts	
John Hazell	Plain^t	Withdrawne
Ebenezer Taylo^r	Def^t	
Richard Hancock	Plain^t	Withdrawne
John Boles	Def^t	
Henry Reynolds	Plain^t	Withdrawne
Daniell Linzey	Def^t	
Hannah Salter	Plain^t	Withdrawne
John Anderson	Def^t	
Richard Buffington	Plain^t	Withdrawne
Joseph Stubbs	Def^t	
Robert Wade	Plain^t	Withdrawne
Richard Buffington	Def^t	
Mons Eustason to Answer for disobeying the Justices order		Withdrawne
Hance Hopman	Plain^t	Withdrawne
Lassey Dalboe	Def^t	
Henry Reynolds	Plain^t	Withdrawne
William Cobb	Def^t	
Henry Coleman	Plain^t	Withdrawne
Andreas Hoeman	Def^t	
Mons Stockett	Plain^t	Withdrawne
Lassey Dalboe	Def^t	
Lassey Cock	Plain^t	Withdrawne
Ebenezer Taylor	Def^t	
Andreas Bowne	Plain^t	Withdrawne
Mons Stockett	Def^t	
Robert Wade	Plain^t	Withdrawne
John Grubb	Def^t	
Lassey Dalboe to Answer for disobeying ye Justices order		Withdrawne

John Anderson upon the Complaynt of Richard Noble, Peter Rambo jun^r & Lassey Lawson by Warrant from the

Justices was brought before them: And upon Suspition: by Woolley Rawson & Neals Lawson his sureties, was bound to appeare the next Co't And the said Richard Noble, Peter Rambo jun' & Lassey Lawson were bound to appeare against the said John Anderson the next Co't

Casper ffiske had a Letter of Admistracon granted to Administer upon the Goods and Chattells of one Eusta Daniell, who dyed intestate: And thereupon the said Casp ffiske & Peter Rambo Jun' were bound in one Hundred pounds To Robert Wade & William Clayton to give in a True Inventory of the s^d Goods & Chattells at or before the 4th September next & other things Contayned in the said Condicon

---

At the Co't at Upland ⎫ William Markham Esq' Gov'no'
Novemb' 30th 1681   ⎭ & President

  M' William Clayton   M' William Byles
  M' James Saund'lands   M' Lassey Cock
  M' Robert Wade   M' Otto Ern^st Cock
  M' Thomas ffairman   M' Swan Swanson
  M' Robert Lucas   M' Hendrias Bankson

 M' John Test High Sheriffe   M' Thomas Revell Clerke

Mons Hanson Plain^t ⎫
Peter Dalboe Def^t ⎬ An Accon of Debt

Juro^rs

William Hewes   Woolley Rawson
James Browne   Mouns Stockett
Tho: Nossiter   John Greensell
Michael Izard   Mouns Cock
Albert Hendrickson   Willm: Oxley
Lassey Lawson   Erick Cock

Witnesse Peter Yokeham

The Jury finde for the Plaint & give him his Debt being 100 Gild^rs & his Costs of Suite: And order the Def^t to have a Legall discharge

Peter Yokeham   Plaint⎫
Peter Rambo Senr   Def^t ⎬ An Accon of Trespasse
                   Juro^{rs}

William Hewes	Woolley Rawson
James Browne	Mouns Stockett
Tho: Nossiter	John Greensell
Mich: Izard	Mouns Cock
Albert Hendrickson	Willm: Oxley
Willm: Clayton ju^r	Erick Cock

Witnesse Andreas Swanson, John Justason, Neales Lawson, Otto Ernst Cock.

The Jury finde for the Plaint & give him 50^s dam & his Cost of Suite

Otto Ernst Cock Evidenced y^t upon Gov^rno^r of Yorkes order to take Patents for what Land they held ye Def^t gott a Patent & included the Plaints Land therein & after ye pl^t gott a Patent for ye s^d Land in regard hee or P^rdecessor had it in possession.

Andreas Hoeman   Plaint⎫
Israell Helme   Def^t ⎬ An Accon of Trespasse
                   Juro^{rs}

William Hewes	Woolley Rawson
James Browne	Mons Stockett
Tho: Nossiter	John Greensell
Mich: Izard	Mons Cock
Albert Hendrickson	Willm: Oxley
Willm: Clayton ju^r	Erick Cock

Witnesse Robert White, James Saund^rland

The Jury finde for the Plaint^t & give him 15^s dam & for ye losse of his one Horse & his Cost of Suite

Peter Dalboe   Plain^t⎫ An Accon for unjustly takeing
Andreas Inkhorne   Def^t ⎬ & detaining his Land
                   Juro^{rs}

Willm Hewes	Woolley Rawson
James Browne	Mons Stockett

Tho: Nossiter   John Greensell
Mich: Izard   Mons Cock
Albert Hendrickson   Willm Oxley
Willm: Clayton ju^r Erick Cock
  Witnesse Lassey Cock, Peter Rambo Senr

The Jury finde for the Plain^t & give him 6^d dam & his Costs of suite.

HENRY REYNOLDS Plain^t } Withdrawne
DANIELL LINZEY Def^t

CHRISTIAN CLAUSE Plain^t } Action Continued
LASSEY ANDERSON Def^t

John Anderson by his sureties (vizt) Woolley Rawson & Mons Cock bound to appeare ye next Co^{r}t, upon ye Comp^{lt} of Richd Noble, Peter Rambo jun^r, & Lassey Lawson, And alsoe to his good behavio^r till then, And ye Comp^{lts} afores^d bound to ℘secute ye said Anderson the next Co^{r}t

---

At the Co^{r}t at Upland
March 14th 1681

  William Markham Esqr Gov^{r}no^r & President
 Mr William Clayton Mr Otto Ernest Cock
 Mr Robert Wade   Mr Andreas Bankson
 Mr Thomas ffairman Mr Swan Swanson
 Mr James Saunderland Mr Lassey Cock
 Mr William Warner Justices there present
Mr John Test Sheriffe Mr Thomas Revell Clerke

HANCE WOOLSON Plaint } An Accon of Trover &c for a
JOHN JOHNSON Def^t Sowe

    Juro^{r}s
Richard Noble   Mons Peterson alias Stawkitt
John Child   Woolley Rawson
Willm: Clayton ju^r John Cock
Willm: Oxley   Erick Cock
John Akraman   Nathaniell Evans
Albert Hendrickson Nathaniell Allen

Witnesse: Henry Reynolds testifyed yͤ Plᵗ made a demand, but could not averre yᵗ yͤ sowe when she came first into yͤ defᵗˢ possession was bigger then a sucking Pigg

Verdict: The Jury finde for yͤ Defᵗ & give him his Cost of Suite

PETER DALBOE Plainᵗ }
JNᵒ EUSTASEON Defᵗ } an Action of Trespasse

Juroʳs

Richard Noble	Mons Peterson alias Stawkitt
John Child	Woolley Rawson
Wᵐ Clayton juʳ	John Cock
Wᵐ Oxley	Erick Cock
Jnᵒ Akraman	Nathaniell Evans
Albert Hendrickson	Nathaniell Allen

Witnesse: Lassey Cock declared that he made over yͤ Land in Controvʳsie to the Plainᵗ And further that it was ordered by yͤ Coʳt formerly that yͤ Plainᵗ & Defᵗ should have the pʳmisses (in Controversie) betwixt them

Woolly Dalboe declared yᵗ hee saw the Defᵗ Cutt & carry away three stacks of Haye from yͤ Land in Controversie last yeare: Hance Hopman not examined

Lassey Dalboe sent in his Evidence taken before Wᵐ Warner; being yͤ same with Woolley Dalboe

Michaell Baroon an Evidence by Mʳ Molls Testimony taken before him

Andreas Inkhorne sent his Evidence by Wᵐ Warner (vizᵗ) yᵗ hee lived Ten yeares upon yͤ pʳmises in Controvʳsie & in yᵗ tyme none Cut hay there without his Consent

Vʳdict: The Jury find for yͤ Defᵗ & give him 10ˢ dam & Cost Suit & yᵗ John yͤ Defᵗ shall pay yͤ halfe of Quit Rent to yͤ Plᵗ which hee hath pᵈ for yͤ pʳmisses, And alsoe yᵗ hee yͤ Defᵗ shall pay yͤ halfe of quit Rent for yͤ same pʳmisses for yͤ future Alsoe see their agreemᵗ.... other......

At the Coʳt last before menconed, that is to say, the 14ᵗʰ March 1681: It was then Agreed by Peter Dalboe And John

Eustason, To chuse two men indifferently betweene them, who shall make a Division of the meadowe in Controv'sie betweene them; And that the Division thereof shall bee brought in by them the next Co't to bee there Recorded for the prevention of future differences betweene them

MICHAEL IZARD   Plaint   ⎧An Accon of ye case for not
JOHN JOHNSON   Def^t   ⎨bringing in a mare according
                           ⎩to Agreem^t

Juro's

Richard Noble	Mons Peterson alias Stawkit
John Child	Woolley Rawson
Willm: Clayton ju^r	John Cock
Willm: Oxley	Erick Cock
John Akraman	Nathaniell Evans
Albert Hendrickson	Nathaniell Allen

Witnesse John Grubb & John Grice Testifyed ye Agreem^t by the Def^t to fetch in ye mare & y^t ye def^t said hee had seene ye mare after ye Agreem^t. Will: Woodmanson.

Verdict: The Jury finde for the Plain^t & give him 20^s dam & Cost Suite

CHRISTIAN CLAUSE	Plain^t	was Continued to this Co^rt
LASSEY ANDERSON	Def^t	day & now withdrawne
Mr JACOB FFABRUSHES	Plain^t	Continued
DUNCK WILLIAMS	Def^t	
M^r otto ERNEST COOK	Plain^t	Withdrawne
ANDREAS BOWNE	Def^t	
MONS STAWKITT	Plaint	Withdrawne
Mr ABRAHAM MANN	Def^t	
ANDREAS MACKLEWAY	Plain^t	Withdrawne
NEALES MATSON	Def^t	
WILLIAM WARNER SEN^r	Plain^t	Withdrawne
WILLIAM COBB	Def^t	
WILLIAM OREN	Plain^t	Withdrawne
LAWRENCE CAROLUS	Def^t	

| Justa Anderson | Plain^t | Withdrawne |
| Lawrence Carolus | Def^t | |

Henry Reynolds haveing appeared at this Co^rt to Answer for his selling strong Liquors by small measure in his house Contrary, to ye Gov^rno^rs & Councells order: upon his submission to ye Co^rt, was discharged.

John Anderson bound by Recognizance to Appear at this Co^rt to Answer o^r Sov^raigne Lord ye King upon the Accusation of Richard Noble Peter Rambo jun^r & Lawrence Lawrenson, who were bound over to ꝓsecucon this Co^rt

Proceeded upon Indictm^t } To which ye Prison^r Pleaded not Guilty: And Put himselfe upon ye Tryall &c: of this Jury

Juro^rs

George fforeman Gent	Albert Hendrickson
John Child	Mons Peterson
Nathaniell Allen	Woolley Rawson
Nathaniell Evans	John Cock
William Oxley	Erick Cock
John Akraman	Peter Yoakham

Richard Noble Deposed That hee with severall others found diverse peeces of Burnt Porke or Bacon in ye said Andersons house. And alsoe that hee ye said Richard Noble with others found hidden & unfrequented places in an out house belonging to the said John Anderson, where (as an Indian had before then informed them) the said Anderson used to hide Porke: And further Deposed, That the said Anderson gave out Threatning words against ye officers & others who came to search

Peter Rambo jun^r & } Deposed the same as above
Lawrence Lawrenson

Judith Noble Deposed That ye said Anderson gave out Threatning words against ye officers & others who came to search.

ffrancis Walker Deposed that a ꝑson who bought a peece of Porke of ye said Anderson told him ye said Walker y^t the said Porke had a Bullett in it.

ffrancis Stephens Deposed, That the said Anderson being asked concerning a Hoggs head (hee ye said Anderson haveing then a headlesse hogg) where the head then was, hee ye s^d Anderson answered he had left the head downe ye River, And ye said Andersons Boy said noe the Hoggs head is upon the mill att home

John Hollinshead, Gave in his Evidence before Thomas Budd a magistrate at Burlington which was alsoe ⁂duced under ye hand of ye said Thomas Budd, being of ye same import with ye Deposition of ye afores^d ffrancis Stephens.

Tho: Wallis Gave in his Evidence before ye said Thomas Budd, & testifyed under ye hand of ye said Thomas Budd, of ye same import with ye afores^d Judith Nobles Testimony

Another Examinacon of notorious Circumstances, of a stranger who lay at ye s^d And^{r}sons, taken by Mahlon Stacy a magistrate at ye ffalls & signifyed under his hand

Virdict { The Jury bring in ye Prison^r not Guilty and thereupon by Order of Co^{r}t is discharged

Overseers for the High Wayes Nominated & Elected at the Co^{r}t March 14th 1681 ffor one yeare next ensueing; for the Repayring the High wayes within their Respective P^{r}cincts, which is to be done before the last day of Maye next ut sequitr

Woolley Rawson from Marcus Creeke to Namans Creeke
Robert Wade from Namans Creeke to Upland Creeke
William Oxley from Upland Creeke to Ammersland
Mons Stawkett from Ammersland to Karkus Mill
Peter Yokeham from Karkus Mill to Schore Kill ffalls
Andreas Rambo from from Schore Kill ffalls to Taweony Creeke
Erick Mulickay from Taweony Creeke to Poquessink Creeke
Clause Johnson from Poquessinck Creeke to Samuell Cliffs
John Akraman from Sam^{ll} Cliffs to Gilbert Wheelers

Att the Co^{r}t at Upland
June 13th 1682
   Mr William Clayton P^{r}sident

Mr James Saund'land Mr Otto Ernst Cock
Mr Robert Wade Mr Swan Swanson
Mr Thomas ffairman Mr Andreas Bankson
Mr Lassey Cock Justices P^rsent
Mr John Test High Sheriffe Mr Thomas Revell Clerke

JACOBUS FFABRUSHES CLERK Pl^t ⎫
DUNCK WILLIAMS Def^t ⎬ An Accon of the Case
⎭

Juro^rs

Thomas Cobourne William Oxley
William Hewes Peter Yokeham
Mr Geo: fforeman William Shoote
Mr Sylas Crispin Andreas Peterson
Mr Jeremiah Collett Mons Peterson
James Browne Mathias Houlstead:

The Def^t appeares not soe y^t ye Accon is confessed: The Court finding ye debt just, desired ye pl^t to remitt 6 skipps of wheat thereof, which hee freely consented to. The Accon goes by default agst ye Def^t for 9 skips wheat & Costs suite & Judgm^t awarded

CAP^t EDM CANTWELL plaint ⎫
ANDREAS NEALSON Def^t ⎬ An Accon of Debt
⎭

Jurors

Tho: Cobourne William Oxley
Willm: Hewes Peter Yokeham
Mr Geo: fforeman Willm: Shoote
Mr Sylas Crispin Andreas Peterson
Mr Jeremiah Collett Mons Peterson
James Browne Mathias Houlstead

Witnesse

Woolley Rawson proves ye Bill to be signed by ye Def^t: But saith ye Bill was given to the Plain^t upon Consid'acon that hee would und^rtake to cleare ye Def^t from a difference betwixt ye s^d Def^t & others, which appeares ye Plain^t did not Pforme; whereupon the Jury bring in their V^rdict as above

V^rdict—The Jury finde for ye Def^t & give give him Cost of Suite & order ye Bill to be cancelled

J^a Saund'land & Lassey Cock plt^s
Walter fforrest Def^t } An Accon of Debt

Juro^{r}s

Tho: Cobourne	William Oxley
Willm: Hewes	Peter Yokeham
Mr Geo: fforeman	Willm: Shoote
Mr Sylas Crispin	Andreas Peterson
Mr Jeremiah Collett	Mons Peterson
James Browne	Mathias Houlstead

Witnesse Henry Grub

V^{r}dict. The Jury finde for ye Plain^{ts} & give them their Debt in ye s^d Bill & one penny dam

The Def^t acknowledges ye Bill; But saith it was in Consid^{r}acon of Land by ye Plain^{ts} sold to ye Def^t which hee hath not security of, Henry Grub ye Witnesse sayth that ye Plain^{ts} said they would warr^t ye Tytle of ye Land to y^t tyme ye bargaine was made to be good: Whereupon it being made appeare to ye Co^{r}t y^t the Plain^{ts} did make over their Tytle. And thereupon an order was passed & Recorded in ye Records of Co^{r}t formerly held under ye other Gov^{r}nm^t for ye said Land to ye Def^t. The Jury therefore finde for ye Def^t as above:

Mr John Test plaint
Lassey Dalboe Def^t } An Accon of ye case

The Def^t appeares not, soe that ye Accon is confessed: The Plain^t alsoe satisfyed ye Co^{r}t with ye Justnesse of ye Debt in ye declaration, And soe ye Accon goes by default

Judgm^t granted ags^t ye Def^t for 140 Gilders & Costs Suite

Lassey Cock plain^t
Lassey Dalboe Deft } An Accon of ye case

The Def^t appeares not, soe that ye Accon is confessed

Peter Yokeham a witnesse declares y^t the Def^t had a Gelding of the Plain^t for ye Debt declared for, And soe the Accon goes by default

Witnesse Peter Yokeham

Judgm^t granted ags^t ye Def^t for 200 Gild^{r}s & Cost Suite

PETER YOKEHAM   Plain^t } An Accon of ye Case
LASSEY DALBOE   Def^t   }

The Def^t appeares not soe that ye Accon is confessed.

Witnesse Tho: ffairman, John Test

Tho: ffairman & John Test alsoe declared y^t the Def^t acknowledged ye debt in ye declaration, soe y^t the Accon goes by default

Judgm^t granted for 56 Gild^rs & Cost Suit

JAMES SAUND'LAND Plain^t } An Accon of ye Case
LASSEY DALBOE   Def^t   }

The Def^t appeares not soe y^t ye Accon is confessed And ye bill being proved, Hance Hopman declared y^t hee did assigne ye Bill in ye declaration menconed & ye sume therein to ye Plain^t being 70 Gilders: And alsoe the said Pl^t Promised to the Court, That as concerning the Debt due by the Plain^t upon Accompt amounting to 546 Gilders & also memconed in ye declaration, hee the said Plain^t will bee ready at any tyme dureing one yeare & a day next ensueing to answer the said Def^t if within that tyme hee or his Assignes deny ye Justnesse of the said Accompt & be minded to try it: Whereupon ye Accon goes ags^t ye Def^t by default for for the whole sume of 616 Gilders in ye declaracon

Witnesse Hance Hopman

Judgm^t granted for 616 Gild^rs & Cost Suite

MATHEW HOULSTEAD Constable }
Complaynes ags^t PETER DALBOE }

ffor his abuse offered to the said Mathew in the Execution of his office as Constable: The Co^rt ffyne Peter 25^s to be p^d into ye Sheriffes hand to ye order of the Co^rt. Peters ffyne 25^s

CAP^t EDMUND CANTWELL   Plain^t } Declar entered & drawne
JNOH BOULSTON   Def^t   } ye Accon agreed & withdrawne
An Accon of ye Case

CAP^t EDM CANTWELL   Plain^t } declar entered & drawne
JOHN HENDRICKSON   Def^t   } ye Accon agreed & withdrawne
An Accon of Deb^t

Capt Cantwell	Plaint	
Neales Marshall	Deft	Withdrawne
An Accon of Debt		
John Champion	plt	
William Vandiveere	Deft	Withdrawne
An Accon of ye Case		
William Ball	Plaint	
Christian Claus	Deft	Withdrawne
An Accon of ye Case		
John Johnson	plaint	
Mortin Peterson	Deft	Continued
An Accon of ye Case		
Tho: Withers	Plaint	
Henry Reynolds	Deft	Withdrawne
An Accon of ye Case		
ffrancis Stephens	Plaint	
Hance Peterson	Deft	Withdrawne
An Accon of ye Case		
Matthias Vanderhoiden	plt	
Neales Matson	Deft	Withdrawne
An Accon of ye Case		
Gilbert Wheeler	plaint	
Richard Buffington	Deft	Withdrawne
An Accon of ye Case		
Gilbert Wheeler	plaint	
John Grubb	Deft	Withdrawne
An Accon of ye Case		
James Browne	plaint	
Harmon Johnson	Deft	Withdrawne
An Accon of ye Case		
Capt Edmd Cantwell	plt	
Charles Johnson	Deft	Withdrawne
An Accon of ye Case		

Lassey Dalboe   plain^t } a nonsuite
Andreas Inkhorne   Def^t

The Plain^t neglecting to ⍴secute his Accon: Att ye request of ye Def^t the Court grants a nonsute

Marcus Lawrence preferrs a Petition to the Co^{r}t against Cas⍴ ffiske who had Administration formerly granted of Eustas Daniells goods & is deferred till next Co^{r}t day

The Examination of Reneere Peterson, Annakey his Wife & Andreas Peterson upon theire Oathes severally taken [respecing conduct of Lassey Dalboe, for whose apprehension Lassey Cock had granted a warrant and who is not to be found].

The Grant formerly made from Governo^r Markam to ye Inhabittants of Markus Hooke att their Request ffor the calling ye name of ye said Towne Chichester, which said Grant beares date the Twentieth day of Aprill Anno 1682: And was Read & published in ye Co^{r}t held at Upland June ye Thirteenth Anno 1682, according to order, as a Record thereof

---

At the Co^{r}t at Upland } Sep^t 12th 1682

  William Markham Esqr Governo^r & P^{r}sident

William Clayton	otto Ernest Cock
Robert Wade	Swan Swanson
Tho: ffairman	Andreas Bankson
Lassey Cock	Justices p^{r}sent
John Test Sheriffe	Tho: Revell Clerke

Jacobus ffabrushes Cl^{r}us Plain^t } an Accon of defamation
Peter Erickson   Def^t ye Def^t appeares not

      Juro^{r}s

Tho: Coebourne	Henry Hastings
Nath: Allen	Albert Hendrickson
Tho: Crosse	Mons Cock
Jeremiah Collett	John Cock
John Otter	Mons Peterson als Stawkitt
John Harper	James Kennerley

  Witnesse Mr John Test Mr Sylas Crispin

Mr John Test deposeth y^t the Def^t Erickson came to him & said concerning the Plain^t Test, Test, this old Rogue will mee. Mr Sylas Crispin deposeth that hee understands not ye language ye defend^t speakes & therefore can give noe Evidence

V^{r}dict The Jury finde for ye Plain^t & give him his Cost of suite

| NATHANIEL EVANS | Plaint } an Accon of ye Case |
| JOHN HICKMAN | Def^t |

Juro^{r}s

Tho: Coebourne	Henry Hastings
Nath: Allen	Albert Hendrickson
Tho: Crosse	Mons Cock
Jeremiah Collett	John Cock
John Otter	Mons Peterson als Stawkit
John Harper	James Kennerley

Witnesse Nathan: Lamplough, Sam^ll Noyes, Katharin Winchcome, Geo: Andreas

Nathaniel Lamplough & Samuell Noyes proves ye declaration.

Katharine Winchcomes Evidence rejected as a ₱tye.

Geo: Andreas deposeth That hee sawe ye Defd^t come with ye maid to Upland in order to her deliv^{r}y to ye Plain^t ye 4th Aug: last which was within 8 dayes after ye agreem^t; But by the witnesse owne Testimony makes himselfe a ₱tye & invalids his Evidence.

Virdict. The Jury find for ye Plain^t & give him 2^d dam & Cost of suite.

| HARMON ENOCH | Plain^t } an Accon of defamation |
| PETER MATSON als DALBOE | Def^t |

Juro^{r}s

Tho: Coebourne	Henry Hastings
Nathaniell Allen	Joshua Hastings
Tho: Crosse	Richard ffewe
Jeremiah Collett	John Hastings
John Otter	Mons Peterson als Stawkitt
John Harper	James Kennerley

Witnesse Lassey Cock, Britta Rambo, Mich^ll ffredrick, Annakey Lucker

V^rdict The Jury find for ye Plain^t & give him 3^lb dam & Costs of suite

Villamchy Keene by Recognizance bound to answer o^r Lord ye King for ye breach of Peace in Beating &c ye body of Margaretta Clause

Christian Clause ye Husband of ye said Margaretta Clause bound to psecute ye Accon

Villamchy Keene & her bondsmen appeare & Christian Clause & Margarett appeare against ye said Villamchy; But haveing noe Evidence against ye said Villamchy The Court cleare her

Mortin Knewtson bound to appeare to answer at ye Co^rt for his Contempt of Authority in refuseing to aid ye Sheriffe in ye p̶formance of his office

The said Mortin Knewston appeares & upon his acknowledgem^t of his fault & submission to ye Co^rt.

The Court dismisse him

John Martin	Plain^t	an Accon of ye Case
Richd Dymon	Def^t	

The Def^t by Mr Tho: Holmes appeares & desires a reference which ye pl^t yields to And soe ye Accon rests

Jacobus ffabrushes Cl^rus	Pl^t	ye Plain^t Continued it
Peter Erickson	Def^t	
Abraham Mann	Plain^t	The Co^rt cast out ye Accon
Edmond Cantwell	Def^t	
ffrancis Stephens	Plain^t	Withdrawne
Sam^ll Thrumball	Def^t	
Henry Hastings	Plain^t	Withdrawne
Andreas Mackluay	Def^t	
George Oldfield	Plain^t	accon of ye case
Edmond Cantwell	Def^t	

The Plain^t 3 tymes called to ℘secute & appeares not & at ye Def^{t}s request ye Co^{r}t grant a nonsuite

GEORGE OLDFIELD pl^t ⎫
ED^{md} CANTWELL Def^t ⎬

The Plain^t appeares not as afores^d & at ye Def^{t}s request ye Co^{rt} grant a nonsuite.

JOHN MOLL   Plain^t ⎫
JACOBUS FFABRUSHES Def^t ⎬ Withdrawne

JOHN HAZELL   Plain^t ⎫ The Def^t appeares not &
JOHN CHAMPION Def^t ⎬ therefore Confesses ye Accon

JOHN HAZELL   Plain^t ⎫
JOHN CHAMPION Def^t ⎬

The Def^t appeares not & therefore Confesseth ye Accon & Lassey Cock proves ye greatest ℘te of ye Debt The goods Attached called forfeit

Lassey als Lawrence Dalboe by a new Warr^t apprehended & taken & by mittimus from Tho: ffairman Comitted upon his former fact brought in last Co^{r}t, & at this Co^{r}t Indicted—and by

  William Clayton   John Hart
  Tho: Brassey   Nath^{ll} Allen
  John Symcock   Wm Woodmanson
  Tho: Sary   Tho: Cocbourne
  Robert Wade   John Otter
  Lawrence Cock   Joshua Hastings

his Grand Jury the Bill is found

Whereupon ye Prison^r is called to ye Barre & Arraigned, and Pleads not Guilty and referres himselfe to God & ye Country His Petty Jury all accepted by ye prison^r

  Richard ffew   Henry Hastings
  James Kennerley   Nath^{ll} Evans
  John Harper   Mons Peterson
  Albert Hendrickson   Joseph Richards
  Thomas Crosse   Jeremiah Collett
  Richard Worrall   Tho: Nossiter

Evidence, Rencere Peterson & Andreas Peterson can say nothing to yᵉ matter in yᵉ Indictmᵗ

The Jury finde him not Guilty; And yᵉ Coʳt by ℙclamation cleare him.

Cas℞ ffiske appeared at this Coʳt to have his discharge about yᵉ Admistration of yᵉ Goods of Eusta Daniell Deceased: And it was ordered at this Coʳt that yᵉ said Cas℞ shall appeare at yᵉ next Coʳt or yᵉ next Coʳt ensueing after that, And bring into yᵉ Coʳt yᵉ Bills of yᵉ Crediᵗoʳs, or other satisfaccon signifyeing to yᵉ Coʳt yᵉ justnesse of each ℙticular debt & alsoe to ℙduce his receipts for what he hath paid

---

At the Coʳt held at Chester for the County of Chester ffebr: 14ᵗʰ 1682 & adjourned unto yᵉ 27ᵗʰ of yᵉ same moneth

John Simcock Pʳsident

Th: Brasy
William Clayton
Robᵗ Wade
John Bezer
} Justices

Thomas Usher Sheriffe   Tho: Revell Clerke

JOHN MARTIN Plainᵗ
RICHᵈ DYMON Defᵗ
accon Case
} yᵉ accon called & yᵉ Defᵗ appeares not & deferred

JACOBUS FFABRUSHES Plainᵗ
PETER ERICKSON Defᵗ
an Accon Case
} neither Plainᵗ nor Defᵗ appeare. Continued

Jury

William Rawson   Joshua Hastings
James Browne   Willᵐ Woodmanson
Jeremiah Collett   Tho: Colborne
William Hewes   Albert Hendrickson
Walter Martin   Joseph Richards
Nath: Evans   Edward Carter

George Thompson appeared at yᵉ Coʳt & none appeareing against him was Cleared by ℙclamation.

Lawrence Carolus, for marrying yᵉ abovesᵈ Geo: Thompson & one Merriam Short, Contrary to the Lawes of yᵉ Province, according to his warrᵗ appeared this Coʳt, was deferred untill yᵉ next Sitting of yᵉ Coʳt, & yᵉ said Lawrence upon Ja: Saundʳlands Engageing in Coʳt for his appeareance then; yᵉ said Lawrence at that tyme dismissed.

At the same Coʳt by Adjournmᵗ untill yᵉ aforesᵈ 27ᵗʰ ffebr 1682

MICHAEL IZARD against } Izard renewed his Execution
JOHN JOHNSON

John Hazell had Execucon agsᵗ John Champion in 2 Actions brought at yᵉ Coʳt held Sepᵗ 12ᵗʰ 1682

HARMON ENOCH against } Harmon Tooke out his Execucon on yᵉ action tryed Sepᵗ 12ᵗʰ 1682
PETER MATSON ala DALBOE

JACOBUS FFABRUSHES against } Jacobus had Execution granted agsᵗ Erickson, in yᵉ action tryed Sepᵗ 12ᵗʰ 82
PETER ERICKSON

JOHN MARTIN Plainᵗ
RICHᵈ DYMON Defᵗ
Tryed

Jury

William Rawson   Willᵐ Woodmanson
James Browne   Tho: Colbourne
Willᵐ Hewes   Albert Hendrickson
Walter Martin   Joseph Richards
Nath. Evans   Edw: Carter
Joshua Hastings   Tho: Vernon

Witnesse, Joseph Willard, Josh: Hastings

Joseph Willard deposeth that yᵉ Boatswayne belonging to yᵉ said Richard Dymons Ship, did owne they had a Pack of goods & other things of yᵉ said Plainᵗˢ on Board, & yᵗ the said Boatswayne said he would delivʳ yᵉ Plainᵗ (Martin) yᵉ said Pack & goods, & after (this Deponᵗ saith) yᵉ Boatswayne said hee had sent yᵉ said Pack & goods on shore; And yᵉ said Deponᵗ saith yᵗ he believes yᵉ sᵈ Jnᵒ Martin yᵉ Plainᵗ never received yᵉ said Pack & Goods & further sayth yᵗ if yᵉ said Plainᵗ had received them hee should have knowne, being Conversant with him in ye affaire,

Joshua Hastings deposeth, that hee heard ye Boatswayne belonging to ye s^d Richd Dymon say y^t ye s^d Martin ye Plain^t would be undone in his action; for y^t he ye said Plain^t had not a Bill of his goods shipped & further sayth y^t ye Boatswayne after looking into his Booke found ye said goods entered therein, and said hee had sent them on shore but being demanded to whom hee had deliv^red them; hee answered hee knew not,

V^rdict The Jury finde for ye Plain^t & give him in Consid^r of his goods & dam for want thereof 12^lb sterling & Costs of Suite, & Execut taken out

Tho: Usher (Sheriffe) by order of Co^rt, administ^rs on ye goods &c of Canonwell Brittin deceased Intestate, & is to dispose thereof according as ye Co^rt shall appoint

Lawrence Carolus, called & appeares not & by Ja: Saund^r-land Engagem^t to appeare next Co^rt

GEORGE STRODE pl^t
WILL^m CLOUD Def^t } Continued
accon case

HENRY REYNOLDS Plain^t
ROB^T EYRES Deft } Rests
accon case decl & Coppy drawne

Att the Co^rt held at Chester for ye County of Chester 27th of ye 4th Moneth called June 1683. } William Penn Esqr Proprietary & Gov^rno^r p^rsent

Justices P^rsent

Jno Symcock
Willm Clayton
Robt Wade

Tho: Brasey
Otto Erns^t Cock
Ralph Withers

Tho: Usher Sheriffe
Tho. Revell Clerke

The Grand Inquest

James Kennerley	Olle Rawson
James Saund'land	George Wood
George fforeman	Albert Hendrickson
Neales Lawson	Hermon Johnson
Jno Cornelius	Nathaniel Evans
Richd Buffington	Rob^{r}t Robinson
Tho: Minshawe	Willm Woodmanson
Jno Harding	Rich^d ffew
Mons Stawkitt	

The Jury

Jno Blunstone	Tho: Cowbourne
Michael Blunstone	Jno Bartlestawe
Henry Coleman	Jno Mynall
Henry Hastings	Tho: Worth
James Browne	Jn° Chyld
Joshua fferne	Joseph Phipps

Lawrence Carolus by ye Ingagem^t of Ja: Saund'lands was to appeare at this Co^{r}t But was Called three tymes & appeared not;

GEO: STRODE	Plain^t ⎫ Withdrawne
WILL^M CLOUD	Def^t ⎭
JOSEPH RICHARDS	Plain^t ⎫ ye Plain^t 3 tymes called
THO: NOSSITER	Def^t ⎭ but appeared not
JAMES SAUND^{R}LANDS	Pl^t ⎫ ye Def^t appeares not
JN° WARD	Def^t ⎭
ARNOLDG DELA GRANGE	Pl^t ⎫ Referred
OTTO ERNS^T COCK	Def^t ⎭

JNO DAY	Plaint ⎫	Jury
HENRY REYNOLDS	Def^t ⎬	Jn° Blunstone
Tryed	⎭	Mich^{ll} Blunston
		Henry Coleman &c as above

Evidence Richd Buffington

The Decl is for 15ᵇ. 17ˢ: By Bill, which is acknowledged by yᵉ Defᵗ The Plainᵗ acknowledgeth yᵉ receipt of 10£: 14ˢ: 10ᵈ & more 3ˢ. in all 10£. 7ˢ 10ᵈ Rests 4£: 19ˢ: 2ᵈ which to be paid in a Cow & Calfe; but as appeares yᵉ Plainᵗ was to receive yᵉ Cow & calfe yᵉ 20ᵗʰ of yᵉ 2ᵈ mo last & hath not yet received them

Richᵈ Buffington deposeth yᵗ the Defᵗ tendered a young Cow & calfe to yᵉ Plainᵗ And yᵗ the Plainᵗ liked not yᵉ Cowe, whereupon yᵉ Jury bring in yᵉ Vʳdict above, And Judgmᵗ is awarded thereupon.

Vʳdict The Jury find for yᵉ Plainᵗ & give him a Cow & calfe yᵉ same to be delivᵈ within 7 dayes or 4£. 19ˢ 2ᵈ at yᵉ choyce of yᵉ Plainᵗ, or yᵉ value thereof in Porke, Beefe or Corne in yᵉ 8 mo: next & 40ˢ dam & Costs of Suite

Ordered by yᵉ Coʳt that a Tax for defraying Publique Charges be raysed wᵗʰin this County: And in order to yᵉ Effecting yᵉ same with Justice & ₽portion, Three of yᵉ magistrates of yᵉ County are to meet weekly.

Ralph Withers & Henry Reynolds are Admitted to Administer upon yᵉ Goods & Chattells of one John Hazlegrove who deceased Intestate. The Inventory of which Goods &c amounting to 11£: 12ˢ: 6ᵈ

                Appraised by, James Browne &
                            Joseph Phipps
                         Taken by Tho: Usher.

Jnᵒ Ward for Sundry ffelons, Comitted to yᵉ Custody of yᵉ sheriffe; & made his Escape with Irons upon him

James Saundʳlane upon his Complaynt to yᵉ Coʳt against yᵉ sᵈ Jnᵒ Ward, is ordered by the Coʳt to Receive his owne Goods which were found in yᵉ possession of him yᵉ sᵈ Ward

George fforeman alsoe upon his vʳball Complaynt, is alsoe ordered to receive his goods.

Whereas Jeremiah Collett hath Treated with Jnᵒ Barnes late of Bristoll in England for yᵉ service of a Boy named Robᵗ Williams, And declareth that the bargayne was made for six pounds, And ye Boyes M^r was to be at ye charge of Cure of his Legg which appeares to amount to 7£: 12^s: The Co^{r}t thereupon Judg it reasonable y^t the sayd Boy shall serve 4 yeares for satisfying ye same; And ye Boy declareing his willingnesse thereto. The Co^{r}t order him to serve 4 yeares

Constables Chosen

ffor Chichester Liberty	Willm: Hewes
Chester Liberty	Tho: Coubourne
Derby Liberty	Tho: Worth
Ammersland liberty	Willm: Cobb
Concord Liberty	Jno Mendinhall

Ordered That ye Peace makers are to meet ye ffirst fourth day of every moneth.

The next Co^{r}t of Session to be this day Eight weekes.

Att the Co^{r}t held at Chester for ye County of Chester 22th of the 6th moneth called August 1683

{ John Symcock P^{r}sident
William Clayton ⎫
John Bezer   ⎬ Justices
Thomas Brassie ⎪ p^{r}sent
Otto Ernst Cock ⎭ }

Tho: Usher Sheriffe
Tho: Revell Clerke

The Jury Returned & empannelled

John Harding	Tho: Garrett	Tho Vernon
Edward Carter	Tho: Cowbourne	Randolph Vernon
Joshua Hastings	ffrancis Chelsey	Jno Kinsman
Walter Martin	Robert Vernon	Joseph Richardson

ARNOLDUS DELAGRANGE Pl^t ⎫
OTTO ERNEST COCK   Def^t ⎬

The Plain^t sues & declares as Heire to Tynnacu Island & p^{r}misses

It is acknowledged by Jno White (ye Defend^{ts} Attorney) that ye Plain^{ts} ffather was Legally possest of Tynnacu Island & p^{r}mises in ye declaracon menconed, by vertue of his purchase from Armgard Prince; But sayth (in regard ⅌te of ye purchase money was onely paid) that ye sayd Lady Armgard Prince had

Tryall & execucon thereupon & was put into possession of ye same p^{r}misses, and sold ye same p^{r}misses to ye defend^t

The Plain^t (by Abraham Man his Attorney) setts forth that hee ye sayd Plain^t (who was Heire to ye s^d Island) at ye tyme of ye say^d Tryall & Execucon was then und^r Age & in Holland & therefore could make noe defence, & further y^t the said Heire (this Plain^t) was not menconed in ye sayd Tryall; the Accon being Comenced against one Andrew Carre & Prissilla his wife, mistaken in ye Execucon for ye mother of this Plain^t, whose mothers name was Margaretta.

The Testimony of Nicholas More Secretary in writing und^r his hand produced on behalfe of ye Plaint^t:

Shackamackson ye 20th of ye 5th Moneth als July 1683. I doe solemnly declare that about ye moneth of May last past of this p^{r}sent yeare Mr Otto Ernst Cock of Tynnacu Island, came to mee at Shackamackson (haveing before spoken to mee of a Tryall y^t was to bee at Upland, Betweene Mr Lagrange & himselfe, about ye Island of Tynnacu) and told mee among many other things, that hee wished he had never sold mee ye said Island and said hee, Hee wished hee had lost 50^{lb} rather then to have put his hand to eyther my Conveyance, or Mr Lagrange Agreem^t, saying that hee was undone, Why? said I; Because, said hee, I have wronged Lagrange Children from their Rights; Well: said I, M^r otto: If you beleeve in yor Concience that ye Island is his let him have it, I will not take any advantage of it, either against him or yo^u, Yes said hee, it is his, and if yo^u will doe soe & part with it, I shall give yo^u thanks & repay yo^u yor charges: Well: said I you shall have it, and I will endeav^r to make Mr Lagrange & yo^u ffriends without any wrong: This was in ye p^{r}sence of Major ffenwick, Thomas ffairman & Michael Neelson, all which I attest und^r my hand

N: More Secretary

Israell Helmes Deposition: Israell Helme being required to declare what hee knowes, conscerning ye Bargaine betweene ye say^d Armgard Prince, & ye Plaint^s ffather for Tynnacu Island & p'misses, Deposeth That Lagranges ffather was to give ye say^d Armgard for ye same six Thousand Dutch Guilders, & y^t hee knowes there was three Hundred Dutch Guilders thereof p^d but knowes of ye paym^t of noe more; And further sayt^h that ye Three thousand Guild^rs (which is Three Hundred pounds) was to bee paid in this Countrey by agreem^t betweene Jacob Swanson & ye ffather of ye Plain^t & further sayth that when the Plain^ts ffather dyed hee ye say^d Plain^t was a litle Child; and further sayth not.

ffop Johnsons Deposition: ffop Johnson being required to declare what hee knowes in ye p'misses, Deposeth, That hee ye said ffop, & ye above mencioned Israell, was desired by Mrs Armgard Prince als Popinjay to demand ye remaind^r of ye sayd Six Thousand Guild^rs which was Three Hundred pounds of Mrs Delagrange (ye Plain^ts mother) And y^t shee ye said Mrs Delagrange (upon ye same demand) sayd shee could not pay it, & further sayth not.

To which ye sayd Plain^t replyes (by his afores^d Attorney) That if the Def^t can make it appeare ye say^d money is unpayd, and can shew their Right to receive it, hee is ready to discharge what can be made appeare to remayne due of ye s^d Purchace, But denyes y^t ye Def^t hath any legall right to demand ye same.

The Juryes V^rdict: The Jury finde for ye Plain^t and alsoe give him his Costs of Suite, and fforty Shillings damage, the Plain^t paying to ye Def^t Thirty & Seaven pounds & Tenne shillings, according to an agreem^t betweene ye Plain^t & Def^t produced & Read in this Co^rt & alsoe delivering ye Block house & P^rticulers in ye same agreem^t menconed:

Judgm^t is thereupon Awarded

HENRY REYNOLDS Plain^t
MATTHIAS VAND'HOYDEN Def^t

Jury: John Harding Edw: Carter Joshua Hastings &c before returned

The Testimony of Law^r: Headings: Lawrence Headings Deposeth, That ye Plain^t brought certaine skins to him upon his masters accomp^t (ye Def^t) but y^t hee this Depon^t did not accept them for ye sayd Def^t because hee judged they were not m^rchantable.

Sabrant ffolke his Deposition: Sabrant ffoulk Deposeth, That hee was present when ye said skins was brought & laid downe; & after Lassey Cock came in, and say^d they were not Merchantable; the afores^d Lawrence Headings would not accept them, whereupon ye said Reynolds sayd, then lett them lye, till ye s^d Vand^rhoyden come him selfe.

John Cock his Deposition: John Cock deposeth that Reynolds (ye Plain^t) agreed with ye afores^d Headings (serv^t to ye say^d Defend^t, that if ye skins aforemenconed were not M^rchantable hee ye sayd Plain^t would change them.

Vrdict: The Jury Finde for the Defend^t & give him Six pence Damage & his Costs of suite, & Judgm^t is awarded

WILLIAM CLOUD   Plain^t
DANIELL SYMONDS Def^t
an Accon of Case

ye Def^t called three tymes & appeares not, and ye Plain^t produced a Bill of ffive pounds six shillings, which Thomas Usher the sheriffe declares ye Def^t acknowledged, as due to ye Plain^t, whereupon ye Accon goes against ye Def^t by Default & ꝑticulers in ye same agreem^t menconed:

MATTHIAS VAND^rHOYDEN	p^lt	Withdrawne
HENRY REYNOLDS	Def^t	
THO: USHER	Plain^t	The Plain^t suffers a non suite
JEREMIAH COLLETT	Def^t	
accon case		
WOOLLEY RAWSON	p^lt	Withdrawne
DANIELL SYMONDS	Def^t	
accon case		
GEORGE THOMPSON	p^lt	Continued
THO: ELDER	Def^t	
accon case		

Henry Reynolds   pl^t ⎫
Edward Eglinton   Def^t ⎬ Continued
accon case   ⎭

Henry Reynolds   Plain^t ⎫
George Andrewes   Def^t   ⎬ Entred & withdrawne

Lawrence Carolus cleared by Pclamation

John Bezer offered two Deeds to bee Recorded, one from Jn° Harding & another from Willm Hewes, but ye Records of Land being not there it was deferred

The next Co^rt is appointed to be this day Eight weekes.

Att a Cort held att Chester for   John Symcocke Presid^t
the County of Chester y^e   Thomas Brasy   ⎫
17th of ye 8th moneth   Otto Earnest Cocke ⎬ Justices
Called October 1683   Robert Wade   ⎭

                       Thomas Usher: Shreife
                       Robert Eyre: Clerk

The Jury returned

John Blunston   Thomas Worth
Robert Taylor   Wm Cloud June^r
James Browne   Henry Hastings
Thomas Withers   Albertus Henrickson
Nathaniell Evins   Thomas Nositer
Joshua ffirne   Thomas Minkshaw

The Jury being Called the Cort adjourned till the next morning 10 of the Clocke

The next morning the Cort mett according to Adjournm^t

George Tomson: pl^t   ⎫
Thomas Elder: Def^t: ⎬ Withdrawne
action of ye Case   ⎭

Edward Eglinton: pl^t: ⎫
George Stroud: Def^t: ⎬ Continued

Henry Renolds: pl^t: ⎧ the plaintife not appearing at
Edward Eglenton: Def^t: ⎨ the Def^ts: request the action is
                            ⎩ Continued

RICHARD CROSBY: pl^t { Ordered that ye Action be Continued and that ye Def^t give new security or goe to Prison
GEORGE ANDREWS Def^t

JOHN ASHTON: Pl^t { ordered that Satisfaction be made in a fortnight or else the Action to Continew
JAMES SCOTT: Def^t:
upon Attatchment

The Shreife made returne of two Executions one against Henry Renolds att ye Suite of Mathias Vanderhyden which was Satisfied by his Attorney Capt Cocks order to G Andrews the other against Otto Earnest Cocke att ye suite of Arnoldus Delagrange for ye Island of Tenicum

NEALES LAWSON pl^t } Withdrawne
ISRAEL HELME: Def^t:

THOMAS REVELL: pl^t } Withdrawne
JOHN JOHNSON: Def^t:

The Shreife gave an account that he could not take John Johnson by ye Speciall Warrant granted against him by this Cost for his Contempt of a Lawfull Warrant serv^d by ye Shreife Ordered y^t ye Shreife Presente the Warrant.

The Inhabitance of Providence made their Application to this Cort for a highway Leading to ye Towne of Chester. Ordered that the Grand Jury doe meet on ye 22th Instant att Tho: Nositers there to Consider of ye Premises

The names of the Grand Jury Impaneled to looke out a Convenient Highway leading from Providence to Chester

James Kenela	William Oxley	Anthony Nelson
James Saunderlaine	Thomas Minkshaw	Michael Isard
Thomas Nositer	John Harding	John Child
Neales Lawson	Robert Taylor	Richard ffew
John Hastings	Wm Rawson	Thomas Colborne
	George Wood	Robert Robinson

John Henrickson came into Cort and gave Possession to Charles Johnson of a ℔cel of meadow by delivering his deed in open Cort

Albertus Henrickson came into Cort and acknowledged that he had Sold a ℔cell of Marsh ground lying at Harwicke unto John Beasar

The Cort Adjourned till tomorrow eight weekes

Att a Cort held att Chester for the County of Chester ye 14th of the 10th Moth 1683
{ John Symcocke President
Thomas Brasy }
John Beasar } Justices
Robert Wade }

Thomas Withers Shreif
Robert Eyre Clerke

RICHARD CROSBY: Pl^t
GEORGE ANDREWS: Def^t
in an action of ye Case
} The Jury returned & Impanneled

Joseph Richardson   Edw: Beasar
Michael Isard   Wm Loues
Anthony Nelson   Joshua Hastins   } Witnesses
Albertus Henrickson Walter Marten   } Henry Renolds
Jeremy Collett   William Johnson   } Thomas Usher
Henry Hastings   Robert Pile

Before the Jury went forth upon ye Cause it was ordered that ye Plaintife should suffer a nonsuite and so the cause to be referred to ye Peace makers

HENRY RENOLDS   Pl^t } Continued till this Cort and
EDWARD EGLINTON   Def^t } now Withdrawn

GEORGE ASTON   Pl^t }
JAMES SCOTT   Def^t } Withdrawne
upon Attatchm^t }

RICHARD BUFFINGTON: Pl^t }   Jury
JOHN CHILD   Def^t } Joseph Richardson
in an action of Trover and } Michael Isard &c
Convertion   } as above

Witnesses Sumond: Albertus Henrickson William Taylor

the Jury finde for the Plaintife and give him his heifer and thirty Shillings damage with Cost of Suite

       Judgment is hereupon awarded

JAMES SAUNDERLAINE as Attorney to STEPHEN CHAMBERS   Pl^t
WILLIAM OXLEY   Def^t } Continued
in an action of the Case

John Johnson being taken upon a second Warrant and att this Cort Indieted made his appearance and Craved to Come to his Tryall

Witnesses upon Sumons George Stroad Tho: Usher Mary Hickman Wm Hues

Ordered that John Johnsons Tryall be Suspended untill the next Cort

The Cort Adjourne till this day eight Weekes

Att a Cort held att Chester for the County of Chester the 1st day of the 5th moneth, 1684
{ Christopher Taylor President
William Wood
Robert Wade
John Blunstone
George Maris
James Saunderlaine
John Harding } Justices

    Thomas Wither Shreife
    Robert Eyre Clerke

JAMES SAUNDERLAIND as Attorney to STEPHEN CHAMBERS   Pl^t
WILLIAM OXLEY   Def^t } The Defend^{ts} Attorney not Appearing ordered to be Continued

JOSEPH RICHARDSON   Pl^t
MONS STAKETT   Def^t } neither Pl^t nor Defend^t appear

    The Jury Returned

John Minar   Edmond Cartly
Thomas Nositer   Nicholas Newland
Richard Buffington   John Child

James Browne   William Hues
John Kinsman   William Browne
William Cloud Junor   Jeremiah Collett

This Cort Considering the necessity of Defraying the Charge of the Cort House and Prison att Chester by a Publicke levie it was ordered that according to the Law in that Case Provided every man Possessed of Lands should pay towards the Levie after the Rate of one shilling for every hundred Acres within this County And every freeman should pay six pence being above sixteen years of Adge and not Exceeding sixty and every Artificer not Exceeding the afores^d Age of sixty and above sixteen 1/6 by the Pole and every Servant three pence as also non residence having land in this County and not Occupying the same shall pay for every hundred Acres after the rate of one shilling six pence ℔ hundred

The names of the Collectors nominated to gather the Assesment viz

for Darby	
Thomas Worth	⎧ Amos Land and
Joshua fferne	⎨ Calcoone Hooke
	⎪ William Cobb
	⎩ Mons Stakett
Chichester	⎫ Providence
Thomas Usher	⎬ Richard Crosby
Jeremy Collett	⎭ Andrew Nelson

Ridley and in the Woods, James Kenela Randolfe Vernome

Thomas Usher having formerly Administred to the goods of Canowall Britten made his Applycation to this Cort for his discharge who ordered him to pay the Ballance into the hands of Phillip Lemaine being as it appears four pounds fifteen Shillings Sterl money of Old England and so to be Discharged.

George Maris Cattle marks a slitt in the tip of the near year his brand marke G M

William Clayton and James Saunderlaine as Attourneys to George Andrews offered to pass over the Estate of George

Andrews to Henry Renolds butt upon a further debate it was ordered to be referred to another Examination

Ordered att the request of Henry Renolds that John Garrett be Examined by John Harding in the matter relating to the Premisses.

Constaples Chosen for Chichester, James Browne

Supervisars Chosen for the High Wayes

from Namans Creeke to Marcus Hooke alius Chichester, Walter Marten

from Chichester Creeke to Chester Creeke, John Child.

from Chester Creeke to Croome Creeke, Robert Taylor.

The Court Adjourne till the 5th day of the 6th moneth next

Att a Cort held att Chester for the County of Chester the 5th day of the 6th moneth 1684. } John Blunstone, President.
Robert Wade }
George Marris } Justices
John Harding }

Thomas Wither Shreife
Robert Eyre Clerke

STEPHEN CHAMBERS Pl^t }
WILLIAM OXLEY Def^t } an action of the Case

The Jury returned and Impanelled.

William Woodmanson	John Minar
Thomas Worth	John Child
Joshua fferne	Mons Stakett
George Wood	Caleb Pusey
Michaell Blunstone	Richard Crosby
Joseph Richards	Richard Bondson

The Jury returned and cannot by the declaration finde any cause of action Hereupon Judgm^t is Granted

EDWARD PRETCHETT Pl^t }
HENRY RENOLDS Def^t } an action of the Case. Continued

ROBERT WADE Pl^t }
JOHN JOHNSON Def^t } Continued

Richard Crosby made his Complaint for want of his Execution against the Estate of George Andrews upon the award of the Peace makers. ordered that Execution be Granted him.

Henry Renold made his usuall Complaint for not being admitted to ye Estate of George Andrews: ordered that before he be admitted he bring George Andrews in place.

Jeremy Collett Informed that Edward Pretchett Contrary to the Laws of this Province hath abused and made over his Servants

Ordered that Edward Pretchett be sumoned to appear the next Cort to answer the Premisses.

Ordered that upon the Complaint of Thomas Wither Shreife and Robert Eyre Clerke for the non Payment of their fees that Execution be granted to levie the same

Collector nominated and Appointed for Amos Land and Calcoone Hooke: Charles Ashcome

Collectors appointed for the Publicke Aide for Marple: Jonathan Hayes James Stanfield

Constaple and Superviser for the high wayes for Marple: Thomas Person

Constaple appointed for Chester, Richard ffew

Constaples Appointed for Amos Land and Calcoone hooke Henry Toten

Supervisors appointed for ye High Wayes for Amos Land and Calcoone hooke, John Henrickson

Collectors nominated and Appointed for the Publick aide Cort House and Prison: Richard Crosby: Edward Carter for the towne of Chester

Consaple appointed for Darby Samuel Bradshaw

Supervisor appointed for the high way for Darby Michael Blunston

Constaple appointed for Concord Nicholas Neuland

Collectors nominated and Appointed to Levie the Publick Aide and for the Cort house and Prison att Chester, for Concord and Bethell: John Minall Thomas King

Overseers nominated and Appointed to looke after the Estate and Children of William Woborne who dyed Intestate: Edward Beasar Robert Pile

Constaple nominated and Appointed for Providence Thomas Nositer

Appraisers nominated and Appointed for this County: Thomas Usher Jeremy Collett Joshua Hastings

The ear marke of John Blunstone of Darby a Crop in the near ear and a hole in the farr ear his brand marke I B.

The Copy of the Peace makers award on a refferance agreed on at this Cort held the 14th of the 10th moneth 1683 between Richard Crosby Plaintife and George Andrews Defendant: According to the above Order of Cort to us directed wee have Seriously Considered the Premisses Between the Plaintife Richard Crosby and the Defendant.George Andrews Whereupon wee the Peacemakers doe give grant Judge and Allow that the said Defendant George Andrews his heires and Assignes shall pay or Cause to be paid unto the said Plaintife Richard Crosby or his Assignes the full and Just sum of eighteen pounds of Lawfull money of this Province att or upon the 20th day of this Instant December att the now dwelling house of James Saunderlaine att Chester halfe of which said eighteen pounds the said Defendant George Andrews or his Assignes is to pay the said Plaintife Richard Crosby or his Assignes as aforesaid in ready money as aforesaid the other halfe in good and merchantable Wheate or Rye att the Comon markett Price of this River to which Conclusion wee the Peace makers for this County of Chester have sett our hands att the aforesaid Chester the 17th day of the 10th moneth 1683.

John Hastins John Harding

witnes Robert Eyre Clerke Committa°

Richard Crosby had Judgment and Execution granted upon the above award.

The Cort adjourne till this day four weekes

Att a Cort held att Chester for the County of Chester the 2ᵈ day of the 7ᵗʰ moneth 1684

{ Christopher Taylor Presidᵗ
William Wood
James Saunderlaine
Robert Wade
John Blunstone
George Maris
Thomas Usher } Justices

Thomas Wither Shreife
Robert Eyre Clerke

Christopher Taylor Presidᵗ did declare in Open Cort that he would deliver up Arnoldus Delegrange receipt to Robert Turner for one hundred pounds old England money as alsoe the said Christopher Taylor did promise to Save the said Arnoldus Delegrange harmlesse from all Damages that may Accrue thereby

Christopher Taylor Presidᵗ in Open Cort deliver over a Penall Bond of Performance for four hundred pounds unto Arnoldus Delegrange & bearing Date yᵉ 2ᵈ day of September 1684 being for the payment of two hundred pounds att or upon yᵉ 1ˢᵗ day of November 1685

Arnoldus Delegrange Past over a deed in Open Cort unto Christopher Taylor for yᵉ Island Comonly knowne by the name of Mattinnaconcke bearing Date the 2ᵈ of the 12ᵗʰ moneth 1684

Randolfe Vernon was appointed Appraiser for this County in the roome of Thomas Usher

Jeremy Collett in the behalfe of himselfe and the rest of the Appraisers of this County made returne of the Appraisment of William Oborne goods and Lands amounting to the vallue of 108£: 2ˢ: 6ᵈ: bearing date the 20ᵗʰ of the 5ᵗʰ moneth 1864.

Ordered that the Overseeres nominated and Appointed the last Cort doe Administer to the Premisses

Collectors Appointed in the Roome of Charles Ashcome for Amos Land and Calcoone hooke, Mouns Peterson William Cobb

STEPHEN CHAMBERS: Pl^t
WILLIAM OXLY Def^t

The Jury returned

Jeremy Collett   Edward Beasar
William Woodmanson   Albertus Henrickson
Edmond Cartlydge   John Minall
John Bartrum   John Kindsman
John Hollaway   Randolfe Vernon
Robert Pile   Joseph Richards

The Testimony of Henry Hastings:

Who being Attested declareth that he had agreed with Richard ffriend to Build a Cattle house of Clap boards 24: foote long and 16 foote Broad for William Oxly for which he was to receive 6£ 5^s.

William Woodmanson being Attested declareth that James Saunderlanie said he would have bought a house of Neales Lawson to sett up for a Cattle house for Wm Oxly.

A verdict of the Jury on the Case depending between Stephen Chambers and William Oxly William Oxly is to deliver the Plantation with ye Old Stocke and halfe ye Increase that can be made to Appear and whereas there was a Paire of Oxen tooke from ye said William Oxly of the said Old stocke the said Stephen Chambers is to receive them or satisfaction of ye party or partyes that tooke them away the said Stephen Chambers or his Attorney is to bear Wm Oxlys harmless from any ptyes that may or shall lay Claime to the premisses aforesaid

Judgment is hereupon Awarded

THOMAS WITHER Shreife: Pl^t
WILLIAM TAYLOR Def^t } in an acction upon ye Case

Jury as ut supra

The Testimony of Jeremy Collett

Who being Attested declareth that William Taylor did att the house of Henry Renolds declare that Thomas Withers did Abuse his servant and that he meaning Thomas Withers was a

Rogue and Rascall and other Bad Language and said further more that if he went to England he should be kild

Sarah Wilsherie being Attested Declareth, That William Taylor Coming to the house of Thomas Wither Enquired whether the said Sarah had any Letters from England & thereupon told her that if shee humored her master and Mistrise she could not goe of under a great ransome butt that he would carry her to Mary Land and secure her there from her masters service and Custody

Robert Moulder being Attested Declareth, That Thomas Withers maide Servant coming to Wooly Rosens and meeting wth William Taylor the said William Taylor asketh the said Servant what shee did there and Calling her Idle Slutt bid her goe home to her master and mistrisse

The Testimony of James Browne, Who being Attested declareth that Thomas Wither did report in his hearing that his the said Withers maid servant was soe great a lyer that he could not beleeve one word shee said

The Jury find for the Plaintife and give him the Penalty of his Bond being 40£, and alsoe finde that the 29th Law preserving the rights of the magistracy of this Province is Broaken. hereupon Judgment is Granted

John Kinsman was nominated and Appointed Collector in the Roome of Thomas Usher for the Towne of Chichester.

Jeremy Collett Prosecuted his usuall Complaint against Edward Bretchett. Ordered that Edward Pretchett be summoned to ye next Cort.

The Cort Adjourne untill the 1st third day in the 1st weeke of ye next moneth

---

Att a Cort held att Chester for the County of Chester ye 7th day of the 8th month 1684

Robert Wade President
John Blunstone
George Maris
Thomas Usher
James Saunderlaine
} Justices

Thomas Wither Shreife
Robert Eyre Clerke

Justus Anderson   Pl^t ⎫ in an action for unjustly
Lawrentius Carolus   Def^t ⎭ deteining his land. Continued

James Browne had a deede Past unto him by Thomas Usher Attorney to Walter Marten for sixty Acres of land, bearing date the 6th of October 1684.

Woly Rosen Petitioned for his Peacable and quiett Possession and Injoyment of his Land bought of George Andrews.

The Testimony of William Cloud Junior Who saith that Wolly Rosen gave lawfull Possession unto George Andrews of his house and Land att Marcus Hooke alius Chichester.

The Testimony of Robert Eyre Clerke and William Cloud Senior That they being desired somtime about the last fall did meete George Andrews and Woly Rosen att the now Dwelling house of Woly Rosen on Namans Creeke in the Wood and that then George Andrews did deliver full Possession of the said house and Land unto unto Woly Rosen and his heires forever

Whereup it is the Judgm^t of this Co^{rt} that Woly Rosen is Lawfully and Justly Possest of the said Estate of Land and Premisses and that he and his heires shall quietely Possesse and Injoy the same.

Jeremy Collett made Complaint against Edward Pretchard for abusing and selling his servant John Jolife Contrary to Law Whereupon he was Indickted att this Cort

Ordered that Edward Pretchard doe take whome his servant and allow him all things needfull and requisite and soe the matter to rest untill the next Cort

Robert Wade   Pl^t ⎫ Upon Attachment
John Johnson   Def^t ⎭ John Blunstone Presid^t.

Robert Wade being Attested and Proving his debt Judgment is hereupon Granted.

Richard Crosby made his usuall Complaint that he could not gett his Execution served on the Estate of George Andrews

Ordered that the Shreife levie the Execution in the hands of Henry Renolds.

James Kenela Coroner made returne of an Execution granted against John Johnson att this Co't held the 5th day of the 6th moneth 1684, at the Complaint of Thomas Wither Shreife

The Cort adojurne to the 1st 2d day in the 1st weeke of the 10th moneth

Att a Cort held att Chester for the County of Chester the 1st 2d day in y'e 1st weeke of y'e 10th moneth 1684.

William Woode President
John Blunstone
John Harding
Robert Wade
James Saunderlaine
George Maris
Thomas Usher
} Justices

Thomas Wither Shreife
Robert Eyre Clerke

JUSTA ANDERSON	Pl't	in an action for unjustly deteining his Land, a nonsuite
LAWRENTIUS CAROLUS & JAMES SAUNDERLAINE	Def'ts	
JOHN PRUE	Pl't	in an Action of Debt for a mare. Satisfied in Open Cort
ROBERT EYRE	Def't	
JAMES SAUNDERLAINE	Pl't	upon Attachment for 10£: 18s: 0d
GEORGE ANDREWS	Def't	

Suspended untill the after noone and after ward untill a further hearing

The Shreife made returne of Richard Crosbys Execution against the Estate of George Andrews; not to be found

Whereupon the Cor't ordered that it should be suspended untill further Enquiry.

Joseph Cookson was Presented by Robert Wade for taking a Wife Contrary to the good and Wholsome Lawes of this Province

Ordered that he finde Security for tenne pounds.

Robert Taylor Supervisor for the High Wayes Presented Thomas Nositer for tarnning the High way from Providence to Chester.

The names of the Grand Inquest ordered to Inspect the same.

Joseph Richards	Woly Rosen
William Woodmanson	William Hues
John Child	Thomas Vernome
John Sharply	Robert Taylor
Gilbert Williams	Thomas Person
Thomas Powell	Thomas Minkshaw
John Nexen	Randolfe Maline
John Worell	Joseph Steedman
Randolph Vernon	

Margrett Person Complained against her master John Colbert for his ill vsage and beating her Contrary to Law

Ordered that shee be disposed of for seven pounds:

The Cor^t Adjourne untill the 1st 3^d day of the next moneth

Att a Cort held att Chester for the County of Chester the 6th day of the 11th moneth 1684

Justices:
- John Blunstone Presid^t
- Robert Wade
- James Saunderlaine
- George Maris
- John Harding
- Thomas Usher

Jeremy Collett Shreife
Robert Eyre Clerke

JAMES SAUNDERLAINE Pl^t upon Attatchment for 10£:
GEORGE ANDREWS Def^t 18^s: 0^d

Suspended untill the afternoone and afterward untill a farther hearing.

Richard Crosby is further ordered an execution upon the Effects of George Andrews in the hands of Henry Renolds

Thomas Wither formerly High Shreife made returne of an Execution granted against William Oxley att the suite of Stephen Chambers by giving Possession unto his Attorney James Saunderlaine of the said Stephen Chambers Plantation att Chester with the Old Stocke and halfe the Increase that did Appear

Henry Renolds Petitioned that the lands of George Andrews might be Past over unto him by William Clayton and James Saunderlaine whome the said Andrews made Attorneys for that Purpose: ordered that the matter be refered to the Provinciall Councell

Caleb Pusie is ordered Appraiser in the Place of Jeremy Collett.

JUSTA ANDERSON Pl^t In an action upon the case
LAWRENTIUS CAROLUS } Defd^{ts} } for weakning and disparag-
JAMES SAUNDERLAINE } ing his Title of Land

The Jury Returned and Empanelled
  John Kinsman   Walter Marten
  Richard Crosby   John Gibbons
  ffrancis Chads   Robert Pile
  William Browne   Edward Beasar
  Thomas Clifton   John Beales
  Richard Buffington   John Marten

The Testimony of Branty Everts in Writting taken before J Williams.

Brantie Everts Aged five and fifty years of age being Sworne saith that he was present when Here Lasse Carolus sold to Justa Anderson all the said Lasse Carolus right title and Intrest of all his Land and Houses on Upland both Home Lotts and Woodland and that one Evert Aldrets was Present and that Lasse Carolus putt the said Justa Anderson in Possession Imediately of the same in Witness whereof I have hereunto sett my hand att New Castle upon Delaware River this 5th day of September 1684.

                the marke of Branty   ✕   Everts

Sworne before me ye day and year aboves^d John Williams

The Testimony of Evert Alderts taken in writting before Thomas Usher October ye 3^d 1684

Evert Alderts doth Testifie y^t he was Present when Lassey Carolus sold to Justice Andrison all the s^d Lassey Carolus his right Title and Intrest of all his Land and Houses on Upland both Whome lotts and Woodland & y^t Lassey Carolus putt ye said Justice Anderson in Possession Immediately all which ye s^d Evert Alderts doth Promise to Justifie before any of his magisties Justices of the Peace and further the abovs^d Evert Alderts testified y^t the afores^d Justice Anderson was to give eight hundred Guilders for ye aboves^d Land. Attested before me ye 3^d of 8th moth 1684 Tho Usher

the marke of Evert × Alderts

The Testimony of Evert Aldrets taken in writting before Robert Wade one of his majesties Justices of the Peace.

Evert Aldretts Deposses y^t Monday last 6th of this Instant Lasse Carolus the Prist Come to his house In West Jersey There and then the afores^d Carolus Indevoured to perswade the Deponent to falsifie his Evidence and to give him in Writting that he had sold unto Justa Anderson butt his house and Hog Stye with the Erfe belonging to ye same In Upland which s^d Deponent refused to doe saying and declaring to him Carolus he had already deposed and given in Writting before a Justice what he knew Concerning the said Busines and soe went his way In the woods about his worke and further saith not the marke of Evert × Aldrets

Attested before me one of the kings Justices of ye Peace ye 8th of ye 8th moth 1684

The Testimony of Edmond Cantwell taken in writting.

These are to Certifie whome it may concerne that severall years Past when I was Receiver of the Duks quitt rent I was att Upland where I mett with the Prist Lasse Carolus I demanded ye Quitt rent of his land where he lived And of his house and Land in Upland Towne he gave me to answer y^t he would pay the Rent of the Land where he then Lived and as for ye Land att Upland he had sold the same to Justa Anderson and that he should pay the Rent in Witnes whereof I have hereunto sett my hand att New Castle 25th day of 7th ber 1684

E Cantwell

The abous^d Capt Cantwell did attest this in the presence of us 1684 ye 18th of October. James William Henry William

The Testimony of John Grubb taken in writting before Christopher Taylor and afterward att this Cort

John Grubb about thirty two years of Age deposes that about four years agoe he had a minde to buy the Woodland lott that Lasse Carolus had In Upland, being Two hundred Acres and talking with James Saunderlaine about it he told him that Justa Anderson had already bought the s^d two hundred Acres of the afores^d Lasse Carrolus the Sweeds Prist which truth the said John Grubb will att any time afirme before any Justices if thereunto required and further saith not

John Grubb

Test   Peter Jegou   W^m M Green   his marke

Attested before me Christopher Taylor

George Moors Deposition December the 23^d 1684 taken in writting

Doth Solemnly Swear that he heard James Saunderlaine did say coming into ye house of Justa Anderson what thinke you Lasse Carolus would have sold your land to John Grub had it not been for me I knowing that it did belong to Justa Anderson and further saith not.

George Moore

Attested before me James Walliams

The Juries verdickt

Wee give the Plaintife the verdickt against ye Defendants with the Cost and Charge of suite and twelve pounds Damage Whereupon Judgment is Granted against the Defendants. Upon which ye Defendants make their Appeale to the next Cort of Assize held for this County

Richard Buffington is Ordered to Receive the Levies raised for the Cort house and Prison in the Township of Chester

Ordered that Richard Ingeloe Clerke of the Provinciall Councell be Satisfied out of the first levies for the Publicke Aide raised in this County.

Ordered that Peter Taylor and Robert Vernome be received into the Grand Jury in the Roome of John Child and Thomas

Minkshaw and Thomas Colborne in the Roome of John Sharply

Ordered that Randolfe Vernome and Robert Eyre Clerke doe looke out a Convenient master for Margrett Person that will lay downe the seven pounds ordered by the last Cort to free her from her master John Colbert

Ordered that y ᵉ Inhabitance of Concord Bethell and Chichester doe meet on the 3ᵈ day of the next weeke att Henry Renolds to Conferre together how to Provide a maintainance for Miriam Thomson and her Child

Ordered that the Collectors of the Levie for the Cort house and Prison shall be Considered for their time and Paines twelve pence in the pound

Ordered that Joseph Humphry and Thomas Norbry be Appointed Collectors to Collect yᵉ Levie for the Cort house and Prison for yᵉ Township of Newtowne

William Cloud junior and Thomas Garrett was sumoned this Cort to serve in the Jury butt made not their Appearance according to Sumons

The Cort Adjourne untill the 1ˢᵗ 3ᵈ day of the 12ᵗʰ moneth next.

Att a Cort held att Chester for the County of Chester the 3ᵈ day of the 12ᵗʰ moneth 1684

{ Christopher Taylor Presidᵗ
George Maris
John Blunstone
John Harding
Thomas Usher
Robert Wade
James Saunderlaine } Justices

Jeremy Collett Shreife
Robert Eyre Clerke

CHARLES MODY Plᵗ
JOSHUA ELY Defᵗ } in an Action of the Case

The Jury returnd

Phillip Rummine   Albertus Henrickson
Thomas Nositer   William Woodmanson

William Johnson   John Woorell
Walter ffausett   Robert Taylor
Thomas Garrett   John Nickson
William Rosen   Thomas Person

Before the Jury was Impanelled the Action was withdrawne

Joshua Ely   Pl^t ⎫
Mathew Huchison   Def   ⎬ Withdrawne
                             ⎭

Joshua Ely   Pl^t ⎫
Charles Moody   Def^t ⎬ Withdrawne
                             ⎭

Wm Grayborne   Pl^t ⎫
Joshua Ely   Def^t ⎬ Withdrawne
                             ⎭

John Marten being Convickted for Stealing money out of ye House of Wm Browne was Ordered twelve Stripes on his bear Backe well laid on att the Comon Whipping Post att Chichester the 4 Instand between the 10th and 11th houres in the morning

Thomas Nositer made Over a Certaine deed unto Walter ffausett dated the 3^d day of ye 12th moneth 1684 for a Parcell of Land lying and being on the North side of Ridley Creeke.

Ordered that the Grand Jury have Power to Examine all Weights and Measures and that they be sealed according to the Law in that Case Provided

Thomas Nositer was Presented by ye Grand Jury for falling of marked Trees and Blocking up the high Way laid out by them by a former Order of this Cort

Ordered that the Township of Darby pay unto Lasie Dalbo or his Assignes if they see they can soe doe with Safty the sum of seven pounds two shillings six pence or part thereof Out of ye Assesment for the Cort house and Prison

Walter ffausett Tendred seven pounds to lay downe for Margrett Person being ordered her Master Colbert for her freedome from him Ordered by a former Cort

The Cort Adjourne untill ye 1st 3^d day in the 1st weeke of the 1st moneth next

Att a Cort held att Chester for the County of Chester the 1st third day of ye first weeke in ye 1st moneth 1684

John Blunstone President
George Maris ⎫
John Harding ⎬ Justices
Thomas Usher ⎭

Jeremy Collett Shreife
Robert Eyre Clerke

Dennis Rochford   Plt
John Hickman   Deft
} in an Action of ye Case. Continued

John Symcocke   Plt
Henry Renolds   Deft
} Withdrawne

John Gibbons was Sumoned and att this Cort Presented for selling ye Indians Rum: remitted.

John Mendinghall was sumoned and Presented att this Cort for selling rum to the Indians butt upon his Petition remitted.

Mouns Eusta and the Rest Concerned in the Building of the Prison and Cort House are Ordered to receive out of Calcoone Hooke and Amos Land the moneys Assest for that Purpose.

William Dalbo is ordered to receive for his work done on the Court House and Prison so much as he can make Appear to be his Due out of the Levies raised for that Purpose in the Township of Darby

Ordered that all People that shall make use of the Cort house for sellerage of any goods shall for every Tonne Pay after ye rate of three shillings four Pence a Tonne for any time not Exceeding a Weeke And for what time it shall Continew afterwards halfe so much.

The Cort Adjourne untill the 1st third day in the 1st weeke of the 2d moneth next.

Att a Court held att Chest{r} for the County of Chest{r} the 7{th} day of the 2{d} mo{th} 1685

- John Blunstone Presd{t}
- Robert Wade
- James Saunderlaine
- John Harding
- George Maris
- Thomas Usher

Justices

Jeremy Collett Shreife
Robert Eyre Clerke

Dennis Rochford Pl{t}
John Hickman Defd{t} } in an Action of the Case

Jury Return{d} and Impannelled.

  Nathaniell Evins   Walter Marten
  John Beales   Nathaniell Amplue
  Joseph Bushell   W{m} Cloud Junior
  Gilbert William   W{m} Browne
  Thomas Garrett   John Kinsman
  Robert Pile   W{m} Woodmansee

Henry Renolds being Attested declareth that John Sumsion told att his house that he was to pay for his freedome tenne pounds to his M{r} Dennis Rochford and furth{r} saith not.

Robert Moulder being Attested declareth that John Sumtion came to him and desired him to Carry him up to Philadelphia which the said Moulder did delivering him to Dennis Rochfords wife and that the said Jn{o} Sumtion fell mad att Peter rambos house and further saith not.

Henry Hastings being Attested declareth that after he had hired John Sumtion understanding the s{d} Sumtion to be a servant he went up to Philadelphia to treate with Dennis Rochford whom he finding to be the said Sumtions master refused to Imploy him

Prudence Clayton being Attested declareth that Jn{o} Hickman had some goods of Jn{o} Sumtions with the Invoyce of them and that Jn{o} Hickman delivered the said goods to her att her request which she delivered to John Sumtion againe

William Clayton being Attested declareth that Dennis Rochford told him that he had agreed with and was in hopes he should be rid of a troublesome servant after which the said Dennis brought him into Court att Philadelphia where he satisfied the Court that his serv^t John Sumtion could not pay him for his freedome according to Contract whereupon the Court ordered him to returne to his mast^r

Nathaniell Thornton being Attested declareth that John Sumtion came into Henry Renolds house and Complained that he was an hongry an could and dry upon which he was supplyed by the s^d Henry Renolds with those necessarys he then wanted.

The Jury finde for the Plaintife and give him four pounds tenne shillings with Cost of Suite

Whereupon Judgment is granted with Execution

HENRY RENOLDS Pl^t ⎫ in an Action of Scandal and
JUSTA ANDERSON Def^t ⎬ defamation

Jury as on the foregoing Action

James Saunderlaine being Attested declareth that Justa Anderson being in his Company att Chester told him that he did see Henry Renolds beate his serv^t and the next night after shee dyed.

Thomas Persons being Attested declareth that he being in the house of Henry Renolds he the s^d Henry did in his presents lift up the tongs and threatned to stricke his maide for not eating such things as was provided for her

William Haukes being Attested declareth that he being in the house of Henry Renolds he heard Justa Anderson say that he did see Henry Renolds beate and stricke his maide and afterward Carried her into another roome where shee dyed

Wm Cornell being Attested saith that Henry Renolds did Beate his maide with a Broome staffe and afterward kicked her as she was by ye fire and further saith not.

Wooly Rosen being Attested declareth that he coming to Henry Renolds his maide asked him for some milke and afterward Henry Renolds strucke her one Blow with a broome Staffe asking her whether there was not victualls enough in the house

Anneka Saunderlaine being attested declareth that shee did hear Justa Anderson aske Wooly Rosen whether he did not see Henry Renolds stricke his maide his answer was he did and further saith not

Prudence Clayton being Attested declareth that after Henry Renolds maide was dead shee was sent for to lay her out butt doth not remember that shee did see any manner of hurt about her and further saith not

William Haukes being Attested declareth that in the Evening he coming from worke found Henry Renolds maide by his fires side and afterward had her to Bed and Sate by her all the night and further saith not.

Robert Moulder being Attested declareth that that night Henry Renolds maide dyed he see the maide sleeping by ye fires side and some time afterward shee went to bed after which a relation came to him that the maide would dye that night

James Browne being Attested declareth that he and George Stroud mett at Wooly Rosens house where was Justa Anderson and the said Stroud asked Justa Anderson why he had scandalized Henry Renolds who then replyed that he did see Henry Renolds beat and kicke his maide and that he saw her alive no more.

The Jury give the verdicke to the Defend^t with Cost and Charge of suite and six pence Damage

Whereupon Judgment is awarded

Henry Renolds past a mortgage of his houses and Lands att Chichester to James Saunderlaine for 280£ dated 6th of ye 2^d moneth 1685

Morton Cornute Past a Mortgage of his Plantation and Premises to ye s^d James Saunderlaine for pounds dated y^e

The Court Adjourne to ye 1st 3^d day in the 1st weeke of ye 4th moneth next

Att a Court held att Chester for the County of Chester the 1st 3^{d} day in the 1st weeke of the 4th moneth 1685

William Wood President
John Blunstone
Robert Pile
George Maris } Justices
Nicholas Newland
Robert Wade
Thomas Usher

Jeremy Collett Shreife
Robert Eyre Clerke

Samuell Bradshaw Constaple for the last year for Darby made his returne all was well Whereupon Edmond Cartleidge was Elected to serve and Attested for ye Ensuing year

Nicholas Newland Constaple for ye last year for Concord made his returne all was well Whereupon George Stroad was Elected to serve in his Steed for the year Ensuing.

James Browne Constaple the last year for Chichester made his returne by Thomas Usher all was well Whereupon ffrancis Chads was Elected to serve in his roome for the Insuing year.

James Browne was Elected Supervisor of the high Wayes for the Township of Chichester for the Insuing year in the roome of Walter Marten

Albertus Henrickson was Elected Supervisor of the high wayes in the Roome of John Child for the Township of Chester the next Insuing year And Attested

Joseph Powell made over a Deed unto Joseph Steedman for 125 Acres of land lying in ye County of Chester Betweene Darby Creeke and Croome Creeke dated ye 3^d Instant

The Court Accepted John Child att the request of Michaell Isard to be his Attorney for ye Passing a deed the next Court unto John Baldwin

DAVID BRINTNELL   Pl^t } in an Action of Debt upon
JOHN CALBERT   Defend^t } account

The names of the Jury return^d and Impannelled

Jonathan Hayes   John Mendinghall
George Woollard   John Marten

Walter ffaussett	Gilbert Wolam
William Hues	Richard Crosby
George fforeman	John Worrell
Richard Buffington	Nathaniel Lamplue

John Blunstone being Attested declareth that att Chester at ye Court House doore he did aske John Calbert for 51^s due to David Brintnell which he did acknowledge to be due

The Defendant not Appearing according to Sumons And David Brintnell Having by his owne and John Blunstons testimoneys prooved his account hereupon Judgment is Granted. Execution Granted.

Caleb Pusie Came volentarily into open Cort and Confessed Judgment to William fframpton in Behalfe of himselfe Daniell Wherley and Company Owners of Chester Mill upon the said Mill and land thereunto Belonging And other ye Appurtinances Being for Security of Bills of Exchange Drawne by the said Caleb Pusie on the said Daniell Wherly and Company in favour of William fframton payable in London (viz) one sett for 58£ and another sett for 208£

Abraham Effingall Being Lawfully Convickted for abusing and menacing the Majestracy of this County was ordered twenty one lashes att the Publicke Whipping Post on his bear Backe well laid on and 14 dayes Imprisonment at hard labour in ye House of Correction

John Calvert was fined for his Contempt of the Cort 40^s in not Appearing when Lawfully Sumoned And for Abuseing ye oficers of the Court 10^s more.

Caleb Pusie Randall Vernon and Walter ffausett was Elected Peace makers for this County for the Insuing year.

The Court Adjourne to ye 1st 3^d day in ye 1st Weeke of the 7th moneth next

Att a Court held att Chester for ye County of Chester ye 1st 3^d day in the 1st Weeke of ye 7th Moth 1685

{ William Wood Presid^t
John Simcocke
Robert Wade
George Maris
John Blunstone
Nicholas Newland
Robert Pile
Thomas Usher } Justices

Jeremiah Collett Shreife
Robert Eyre Clerke

JOHN FFISHER   Pl^t
JOHN CALVERT   Defend^t } Withdrawn

JOEL BAYLY   Pl^t
THOMAS WITHER Defend^t } in an Action of Debt for wages

Jury returned and Impanelled

Edward Beasar   Michaell Blunstone
William Cloud Junr Thomas Worth
Thomas Minkshaw   George Wood
James Browne   ffrancis Garnall
Thomas Smith   John Smith
Henry Hastings   David Ogden

Thomas Usher being Attested declareth y^t at a monethly meeting att Chichester it was there agreed between Joel Bayly and Thomas Wither that the said Thomas Wither should Pay the Wages due to Joel Bayly and soe discharge him and further saith not

Robert Pile being Attested declareth that he being at a monethly meeting at Chichester he did hear Thomas Wither say that he would willingly allow Joel Bayly his wages and so Discharge him.

Jeremiah Collett being Attested declareth that Joel Bayly desired him to Arbitrate his Cause upon which he the said Collett did aske Thomas Wither whether he did promise the said Joel his wages att a monethly Court held att Chichester who told him he did and further saith not.

Thomas Rawlenson being Attested declareth that Thomas Wither did borrow a Whipe Whipe Cord and Bed Cord of Joel Bayly and did promise to returne or make satisfaction for ye same

The Jury finde for ye Plaintife 4£: 11^s: 8^d and giveth him 6^d damage and Cost of Suite

Hereupon Judgment is granted.

JOEL BAYLY Pl^t } in an Action of Asault and
THOMAS WITHER Defend^t } Battery

Jury as above

The testimony of Thomas Rawlenson who being Attested declareth that Thomas Wither maid speaking Contemptably of Jeremy Collett Joel Bayly undertooke to Correct ye s^d maide in words for Abusing ye reputation of ye s^d Jeremy Collett Whereupon ye said Thomas Wither fell violently with Blowes upon ye said Joel and Beate him soe that he fell to ye ground and Bled all that night and afterward att Certaine seasons for a Weeks time

Richard Rudman being Attested Declareth ye same

Robert Jefferies being Attested declareth the same

Margery Willis being Attested declareth ye same

Richard Rudman and Robert Jefferis did further declare that Joel Bayly did usually Bled before he had any Difference with Thomas Wither and further saith not.

The Jury finde for ye Plaintife and give him 2^d damage and Cost of Suite.

Whereupon Judgment is Awarded

The Shreife made returne of an Execution granted against John Calvert att ye suite of David Brintnell which he levied upon an Oxe vallued by the Appraisers at 4£

Upon ye Petition of James kenela Crowner it was Ordered that forth with Execution be granted against Henry Renolds for ye Crowners fees Charge of Inquest and taking up ye dead Boy of ye said Renolds maide with all other Charges whatsoever thereunto belonging.

Ordered that ye Charges of James Browne (Constaple for Chichester) due upon the abous^d Premisses be alsoe levied on the said Renolds and Included in ye aboues^d Execution

James Saunderlaine as Attorney to Thomas Rudyard made over a Deed in Open Court unto Andrew Robinson for 5000 Acres of land Dated ye 15th day of June 1685

Woola Rosen and Ebritta his Wife made over a Certaine deed for a Plantation lying att Chichester to George fforman and his Heires for ever dated ye 21th day of ye 12th moneth Called ffebruary 1684

George fforeman made over ye Counter p^t of a Deede to Wola Rosen and Ebritta his wife dated ye 21th day of ye 12th moneth Called february 1684

Wolla Rosen made over a pcell of land lying att Chichester to Robert Moulder and his heires for Ever by a deed dated ye 21th of ye 12th Moth 1685

John Child as Attorney to Michael Issard past a deed to Thomas Baldwine for a pcell of land in this County dated ye 2^d day of ye 4th moneth 1684.

Thomas Brasy Passed 4 deeds in Open Court all of one date to these following psons (viz)

To John Smith one for one hundred Acres of land dated ye 30th of ye 6th moth 1685

To Thomas Smith one for 100 Acres dated ye above day

To William Smith one for 100 Acres dated ye above day

To John Bartrome one for 300 Acres dated ye above said day

John Symcocks marke a slitt in ye right ear

His burnt marke I. S.

John ffox Petitioned this Court against his former master Nicholas Nueland for his bad and Cruel usage butt was Rejected for want of Proofe

John Nickson was Presented upon Suspition of killing William Mellings Hogg and Carring of it away from the Sweeds Prists house butt upon his Confession and Submission he is ordered to pay three fould

John Hurst bound by Recognisence to appear at this Court

for Abusing and Beating his master ffrancis Stamfield was upon Petition of ye said Stamfield Brought to a hearing. Witnesses, Thomas Massey, Isacke Brackshaw, who being Attested butt nothing prooved was upon his Submission to ye Court discharged

John Hurst Presents James Stamfield for Abuseing and drawing a knife upon him

Witnesses Attested, Thomas Massy, Isacke Brickshaw, George Gleave. They all declare that James Stamfield did draw a knife upon John Hurst and did run at him

Joseph Clayton being Attested declareth that ye said James Stamfield did draw a Whittle and made a Passe at John Hurst

Upon a Due Examination of the whole matter and upon their Submission each to other and promising ye Court to live peacably and quietely the Court discharge them

Richard ffue Constaple the last year for ye township of Chester made his returne all Well whereupon John Hodskins was nominated Appointed and Attested Consaple in his roome for ye next Ensuing year

Robert Taylor Supervisor for ye High Wayes from Chester Creeke to Croome Creeke made his returne all well Whereupon Bartholomew Coppock was nominated and Appointed Supervisor in his roome for ye next Ensuing year.

John Henrickson Supervisor of the High Wayes for Amosland and Calcoone Hooke made his returne all well Whereupon John Bartlesome was nominated and Appointed Supervisor in his roome for ye next Ensuing year

Walter ffausett was Appointed and Attested Constaple for ye township and liberty of Providence for the next Ensuing year

Henricke Torton Consaple for Amos land and Calcoone Hooke made his returne all well whereup Haunce Vireson was nominated and Appointed Constaple in his roome for ye next Ensuing year

Thomas Pearson Constaple for Marple made his returne all well Whereupon Jonathan Hey was Appointed and Attested

Constaple and Supervisor of ye High Wayes in his roome for the next Ensuing year

The Court Adjourne till the 1st 3^d day of ye 1st Weeke in the 8th Moth next

---

Att a Court held att Chester for ye County of Chester the 1st 3^d day in the 1st Weeke of ye 8th moneth being ye 6th day of ye moneth 1685

John Symcocke Presid^t

John Blunstone
Robert Wade
George Maris
Nicholas Newland
Robert Pile
Thomas Usher
} Justices

Jeremy Collett Shreife
Robert Eyre Clerke

John Barbery being taken up as a runaway was ordered to give in Security not to depart untill Certificate should be brought from his master that he is a free man and untill such time to have lyberty to worke for himselfe

William Johnson made over a deed dated this Instant for fifty Acrees of Land lying on the north side of Chester Creeke to Peter Thomas and his heires for ever he the said Peter Thomas Allowing a Convenient high way through the said land from the house of the said Wm Johnson leading to Chester roade

Jeremy Collett made returne of an Execution granted ye last Court against Henry Renolds for Crowners fees and Constaples Charges &c dated ye 4th 7th moneth 1685 which he levied on an Oxe Appraised at 4£: 10^s

Henry Renolds came into Court and made full Satisfaction for the said Oxe Whereupon the Court Ordered him his Oxe againe

Thomas Usher Presented Henry Renolds for keeping an Ordinary Contrary to Law.

Ordered that William Hues be vewer of Pipe Staves for this County

James Saunderlaine as Attorney to Stephen Chambers offered to Passe over a Plantation to himselfe as being Attorney to Richard ffriend Butt was rejected for want of a new letter of Attorney from ye said Richard ffriend

Ordered that for Defraying the Publicke Charges of this County a levie be raised upon Every hundred Acres of Land taken up and Surveyed after the rate of two shillings and six pence for every hundred Acres within this County And lands taken up by nonresidence and soe not Occupied Shall pay after ye rate of three shillings nine pence for Every hundred Acres And that all the male Inhabitance within this County from sixteen to sixty years of Age doe pay after the Rate of two shillings six pence by the Pole Except men servants who shall pay after the Rate of one shilling and three Pence by the Pole and noe more And that Jeremy Collett High Shreife of this County be Ordered to levie ye same within three monethes whoe is to be allowed after the rate of one Shilling for Every pound soe levied It is alsoe further ordered that the Constaples doe forthwith bring in within fourteen dayes after the date hereof the names and Sir names of all the male Inhabitance residing within their severall presincts unto the Cheife Collector who shall Allow fourteen dayes time after Warning given to every Township to bring in their respective Payments to the Towne of Chester The Collector is further ordered to receive good and merchantable Indian Corne after ye rate of 2^s: 6^d: good and merchantable wheate 4^s: 6^d: good and merchantable rye at 3^s: 6^d, By the Bushell

Ordered that the Township of Chichester Extend its Bounds as formerly laid out by Charles Ashcome untill further order

The Court Adjourne untill ye 3^d day in the 2^d weeke of the 10th moneth next 1685

ffrancis Chads ear marke a Crope . . . on the Inside of the near ear his Brand marke on the near Heipe   FC:

Phillip Rumins ear marke a Swallows forke in the Tipe of the left ear . . . The tope of ye right year Cutt of . . . with a little notch on ye same ear

Robert Cloud had a Passe granted him to depart this Province dated ye 26th day of ye 9th moneth 1685 his Brother Wm Cloud of Concord being his security to safe ye Country Harmlesse

---

Att a Court held att Chester for ye County of Chester the 1st 3^d day in the 2^d Weeke of the 10th moneth 1685

{ John Blunstone Presid^t
John Symcocke ⎫
George Maris ⎪
Robert Wade ⎬ Justices
Robert Pile ⎪
Thomas Usher ⎭ }

Jeremy Collett Shreife
Robert Eyre Clerke

Mouns Peters Pl^t ⎫ in an Action of scandall and
Haunce Urine Defend^t ⎭ Defamation

The Jury returned and Impanelled

John Harding   Thomas Clifton
William Woodmansee William Browne
Edward Beasar   Thomas Smith
John Kinsman   Thomas Garrett
ffrancis Chads   Peter Taylor
James Browne   Randall Vernon

Before the Jury Went out upon the Cause it was Agreed that the Defend^t should pay the Charges and cost of Suite and so ye Action be withdrawn

Thomas Clifton made over a Patent unto James Browne by Assignment Bearing date the 15th day of the 3^d moneth 1685 for a ℔cell of land lying and being In the Township of Chichester

Thomas Garrett Assigned over a Patent bearing Date ye 1st day of ye 2^d moneth 1685 for a parcell of Land lying and being in the Township of Chichester unto James Browne and his heirs for Ever

Ordered that the Collector for the last Publicke Levie doe receive Wheate att 5^s Rye att 4^s and Indian Corne att 3^s pr Bushell

The Court Adjourne to the 1st 3^d day in the 1st weeke of the 1st moneth next.

Att a Court held att Chester for ye County of Chester the 3^d day in the 1st Weeke of ye 1st moneth Called March 1685

Justices:
- John Symcocke Presid^t
- Robert Wade
- John Blunstone
- Thomas Usher
- Robert Pile
- Nicholas Newland
- George Maris

Jeremy Collett Shreife
Robert Eyre Clerke

The Grand Inquest
- Joseph Richards
- John Gibbons
- John Bartram
- Michaell Blunstone
- Thomas Worth
- Thomas Colborne
- Randall Vernon
- Walter Marten
- Edward Beasar
- Joseph Bushell
- Joseph Baker
- William Brainton
- Samuell Levis

George Maris acknowledged the Assignment of one hundred acres of Land to Anne ffincher bearing date ye 9th day of ye 10th: moth 1685.

ffrancis Yarnall acknowledged a Deed to George Maris Ju^r of fifty Acres of Land Bearing date ye 1st day of ye 1st moneth 1685

JOHN BRISTOLL Plaintife
PHILLIP THLEMAINE Defend^t

The Defend^t appearing and saying he had noe declaration given him the Plaintife was nonsuited

Edmond Cartlidge Assigned over in Court unto Phillip Yarnall a Patent for one hundred Acres of Land bearing date ye 2^d day of 12th moneth 1685

ROBERT DYER Pl^t
ROBERT CLOUD and WILLIAM CLOUD Defend^{ts}

in an Action of ye Case

The Jury

George Price	John Child
James Browne	John Woorrell
John Hulbert	Joshua Hastings
Nathaniell Lamplue	John Mendinghall
William Hues	Randall Maline
Nathaniell Parker	Richard Crosby

The Declaration was read and William Taylor attested to the account for his Charges in Recovering y ͤ Servant

The verdicte of y ͤ Jury is that y ͤ Cloathes shall be returned in as good order as it was and to Double what they were sold att here thats y ͤ sum of 21ˢ: 6ᵈ   2£: 13ˢ: 9ᵈ.

And the stockins to be returned with   0: 2: 6

And y ͤ Knife and Sicers and Aules to be returned wth double y ͤ vallue which is   3: 4

The Charges of finding y ͤ servant that the Defend^{ts} pay with Cost of Suite   4: 7: 3

James Browne foreman   7: 6: 10

Hereupon Judgment is Granted

GEORGE FFOREINAN Pl^t
JOHN BRISTOLL
THOMAS POWELL & } Defend^{ts} } in an Action of y ͤ Case
THOMAS JACOBS

Jury as in the foregoing Action where Robert Dyer was Pl^t and Robert and Wm Clouds Defend^{ts}

Anthoney Weaver being Attested declareth that he saw John Bristoll Strugling with Samuell for y ͤ Gunn

Thomas Whitehorne being Attested declareth for y ͤ Pl^t that he heard John Bristoll say that he had nothing to say to Sam^ll Rowland for that he had not done him any harme And y^t he saw Samuell Rowland Bloody that Sam^ll Rowland was an abettor

Lydia Wade being Attested for y ͤ Pl^t declars y ͤ same

Mary Marten being Attested for y ͤ Defend^t declareth y^t shee heard Wm Taylor say that he would meete with John

Bristoll an other time and that he had seen Better men then he come shorter by ye Pocketts and Called him Stoginge

William Clayton being Attested Declars that he heard John Bristoll say that after he had sett up three Posts John Bristoll and his men went towards Alberts mett Taylor who Bid John Bristoll Stand or he would fire att him and snapped the gunn twice att him John Bristoll went towards taylor and then Sam^{ll} Rowland had ye Gunn in his hand and John Bristoll forced ye Gunn by ye Assistance of a Carpenter from him the Carpenter wringing the said Samuell Rowland by the nose

John Symes being Attested declareth that he did see Sam^{ll} Rowland Come into Robert Wads with his haire torne and face Bloody and there Samuell Rowland asked John Bristoll why he did stop him and head him

The Jury finde for the Defend^t with Cost of Suite and one penny Damage James Browne foreman

hereupon Judgment is granted

Joseph Steedman made over a Bill of Sale to ffrancis Yarnall for twenty five Acres dated ye 1st day of ye 1st moneth 1685

Walter Marten delivered to Nathaniell Thornton a Bill of Sale for fifty Acres of Land bearing date ye 7th day of ffebruary 1684

John Hastings as Attorney to John Marsh of Hay ford past over a Deed to Thomas Marten dated ye 1st day of ye 1st moneth 1685 for 73 Acres of Land lying in the County of Chester near Chester Creeke

Nathaniel Evins Past a Deed unto Edward Collier for fifty Acres of Land dated ye 18th day of ye 12th moneth 1685

Nathaniel Evins Past a deed unto Andrew Moore for fifty Acres of Land dated ye 18th day of ye 12th moneth 1685

Nathaniell Parker Past over a deed to William Clayton Junr for 200 Acres of land lying in Concord dated ye 10th day of ye 12th moneth 1685

Ordered that the Shreife take into his Custody the Body of David Lewis upon Suspition of Treason as alsoe ye Body of Robert Cloud for Conceeling ye same for that he the said

Robert Cloud being Attested before this Court declared that upon y⁰ 3ᵈ day of the Weeke before Christmas last att the house of George ffloreman the said David Lewis did declare in his hearing that he was accused for Being Concernd with the Duke of Monmouth in yᵉ West Country

Robert Dyer Became Security that his Servant David Lewis shall Appear att the next Provinciall Court held att Philadelphia yᵉ 10ᵗʰ day of yᵉ 2ᵈ moneth 1686 to answer yᵉ Premisses

William Cloud Senior became Security for his sonne Robert Cloud that he should appear att the said Court to answer his Concealing the same

The Court Adjourne untill yᵉ next morning and mett againe according to Adojurnment

SAMUELL ROWLAND Plᵗ
JOHN BRISTOLL
THOMAS POWELL } Defendᵗˢ in an Action of Assault and
THOMAS JACOBS Battery

The Jury Impanelled

Joseph Richards   Randall Vernon
John Gibbons   Walter Marten
John Bartram   Edward Beaser
Michael Blunstone   Joseph Bushell
Thomas Worth   Joseph Baker
Thomas Colborne   Wᵐ Brainton

Witnesses as in the Case of George ffloreman Plᵗ
John Bristoll Thomas Powell and Tho: Jacobs Defendᵗˢ

The Juryes verdickt Wee finde for yᵉ Defendᵗˢ with Cost of Suite and six pence damage

Whereupon Judgment is granted

THOMAS REVILL by his
Attorney THOMAS USHER } Plᵗ
ROBERT EYRE Clerke   Defendᵗ } in an Action of yᵉ Case

The Jurys names

George Pirce   Jnᵒ Child
James Browne   Jnᵒ Worrell

John Hulbert   Joshua Hastins
Nathaniell Lamplue   Jnº Mendinghall
William Hues   Randˡᵉ Malin
Nathaniell Parker   Rich: Crosby

The Jury finde for yᵉ Plaintife yᵉ sum of 1£: 15ˢ: 4ᵈ: with Cost of Suite and 3ᵈ Damage and that yᵉ 16ˢ due from Lacy Cocke to remaine Due to the Plaintife: James Browne foreman

ffrancis Smith Junior being Convicted before Thomas Usher by Richard Renolds for breaking Open the Trunke and Box of yᵉ said Richard Renolds and taking thence three Gold Rings and one paire of Silver Buttons sett with Bristoll Stones was by yᵉ said Thomas Usher Bound by Recognisance to answer yᵉ said Complaint att this Court.

ffrancis Smith making his Appearance according to Recognisance and Rich Renolds being Called to Prosecute his Complaint according to law butt not appearing the Prisoner was Cleared by Proclamation.

James Saunderlaine was Presented by yᵉ Grand Jury for keeping an Ordinary att Chester without Lysence as alsoe for keeping disorders in his house upon yᵉ 1ˢᵗ dayes of yᵉ weeke Witnes Randall Vernon

To which he made his appearance

The Court Dispencis wᵗʰ his keeping an Ordinary untill yᵉ Provinciall Councell shall sitt and in respect of his disorders upon his Promise it shall be soe noe more it is Remitted

Phillip Lemaine Past a receipt to Thomas Usher bearing Date yᵉ 11ᵗʰ day of yᵉ 3ᵈ moneth 1685 for yᵉ account of Cananawell Britton for 4£ 15ˢ old England money

The Grand Jury Presented a Bill against William Taylor Samuell Rowland and Thomas Butterfield for maliciously and tumultuously Assaulting and Presenting a Gunn against the Body of John Bristoll

George fforeman Became Security that his man Samuell Rowland shall Appear att the next Provinciall Court held att Philadelphia there to answer yᵉ Premises

Ordered that upon ye Complaint of George fforeman an Expresse be forthwith sent to Robert Moulder that he fall noe more timber upon ye Estate of George Andrews nor to Carry any timber of ye said Plantation that is already fallen

Jeremy Collett Past a deed dated ye 1st day of ye 1st moneth 1685 for a parcell of Land lying on Chichester Creeke Conteining 63 Acres to John Hulbert his heires and Assignes for ever he ye said Hulbert paying ye usuall quit rent due to ye Govern^r on said Land

Ordered that John Symcocke Robert Wade Thomas Usher James Saunderlaine John Blunstone and Susannah Wood doe receive out of their respective Townships they live in soe much of ye Levies granted for ye Publicke use as shall appear to be due to them on that account

Ordered that upon ye returne of ye Grand Jury Albertus Henrickson supervisor of ye High wayes belonging to Chester doe forthwith Erect a Horse Bridge in such place as ye Grand Jury have already layd it out

Ordered y^t upon ye same returne Bartholomew Coppocke Supervisor of ye High wayes for Croome Creeke doe forthwith Erect a Bridge in ye Kings Road over said Croome Creeke

The Court Adjourne untill ye 1st 3^d day in ye weeke of ye 4th moneth next

---

Att a Court held att Chester for the County of Chester the 3^d day in ye 1st Weeke of ye 4th moneth 1686 and soe held by Adjournment untill ye next day

John Symcock Presid^t
John Blunstone
Robert Pile
ffrancis Harrison } Justices
George Maris
Bartholomew Coppocke
Samuell Levis

Thomas Usher Shreife
Robert Eyre Clerke

Mouns Peterson	Pl^t	
Hauns Urine	Defend^t	Witnesses Sumoned

George Wood
Jno Bartlesome
Mort Mortenson
John Bartrum
} nonsuite

Dennis Rochford	Pl^t	The Plaintifs Petition was
John Hickman	Defend^t	read against ye Defendant

Continued untill the after noone & then withdrawn.

Phillip Roman was Presented and Attested Constaple for ye Township of Chichester

William Cloud was Presented and Attested Constaple for ye Township of Concord

Richard Bondsall was Presented and Attested Constaple for ye Township of Darby

        The names of the Grand Inquest

Joseph Richards	Randall Vernon
John Gibbons	Walter Marten
John Bartrome	Edward Beasar
Michaell Blunstone	Joseph Bushell
Thomas Woorth	Joseph Baker
Thomas Colborne	ffrancis Chadsy

Robert Moulder made over a Deed unto Peter Baynton dated ye 1st of ye 4th moneth 1686

Thomas Whithorne	Pl^t	
Thomas Cooper	Defend^t	agreed

John Blunstone Past a Deed bearing date the 1st day of the 4th moneth 1686 to John Hood

Robert Cloud made over a Deed dated the 1st day of the 4th moneth 1686 unto his Brother William Cloud for a parcell of Land lying and being in ye Township of Chichester

William Taylor upon his Submission and acknowledgment of his faults for which ye grand Inquest Presented him the last Court and upon his Promise to doe soe noe more he is Remitted

The Grand Inquest made returne of a High way from Bethell to Chichester of sixty foote broad as followes (viz) Beginning at the Side of Concord towards the River on the street or High way of Concord first through the land of John Gibbons his House on the Right Side then through the land of Robert Southry late Disceased his house on the left Side thence through Robert Piles Land his house on the right hand then through Joseph Bushells land his House on the Left hand thence through ffrancis Smithes Land thence through Thomas Garretts Land his house on ye Right hand thence through ffrancis Harison and Jacob Chandlers Land downe the Point to a small branch of Namans Creek thence up ye Hill to ye first Inclosed of ffrancis Harrisons the field on ye left hand Then through James Brownes land thence downe to another Branch of Namans Creeke though Walter Martens land up the Point his House on ye right hand thence through Jeremy Colletts land Bearing toward the left hand his house standing on ye left hand from thence to the lands of Chichester beginning att the head of a Small Swamp on the left hand thence downe Crosse the Kings road or High way towards ye foote of ye Hill to a lyne tree marked with 5 notches thence downe to ye Rivers Side the lyne between James Browne and William Clayton Junior Whereunto wee the Present grand Jury of ye County of Chester have sett our Hands

    Joseph Richards foreman

Tho: Worth	Joseph Baker
Joseph Bushell	John Bartrome
Jno Gibbons	Edward Beasar
Michaell Blunstone	Wm Brainton
Tho Coleborne	Walter Marten
Randall Vernon	Sam^{ll} Levis

Richard Crosby mooved the Court for a new Execution agst ye Estate of George Andrews which was granted him

John Jones Past over a deed by his Attorney James Saunderlaine to Jno Jennins by his Atto George fforeman dated ye 4th day of May 1686

John Hannum and Jn° Palmer Convickted before Robert Pile for Stealing of a Hogg from Nicholas Newland of Concord was bound by Recognisance to answer the Complaint att this Court and by their grand Jury whose names are recorded on the other side of ye Leafe are found guilty of their Bill of Indickm^t

Whereupon the Prisoners are Called to ye Barr and Arreigned and Pleads not guilty and referrs themselves to God and ye Country

The names of their Petty Jury all Accepted by the Prisoners

Richard Crosby	William Cloud
John Mendinghall	Thomas Crosse
Anthony Weaver	Edward Walker
John Child	Peter Baynton
Edward Prichard	Moses Mendinghall
Caleb Pusie	Joseph Lownes

Witnesses George Stroud Thomas Moore John Saunger Richard ffarr

who being Attested declareth ye same thing that they had formerly done before Robert Pile whose testimony remaines upon ye file

The Jury finde them Guilty

Whereupon Judgment is granted that they pay unto Nicholas Newland 40^s: as also to receive 12 Strips a peece well laid on upon their bear Backs

The Appraisers Continued

ROBERT EYRE and ANNE his wife Pl^{ts}
FFRANCIS SMITH Senior Defend^t

in an Action of ye Case they Joyne Issue by Concent without arrest or sumons

The names of ye Jury

Richard Crosby	William Cloud
John Mendinghall	Edward Walker
Edward Pritchard	Peter Baynton
Anthoney Weaver	Joseph Baker
John Child	Joseph Richards
Caleb Pusey	Thomas Colborne

The declaration was Read wherein the Plaintifes declareth for 239¹: 12ˢ: 2½ᵈ due by account for settling the Defendants Plantation att Chichester & the Stocke thereon

A letter was read from ffrancis Smith Defend^t to his Daughter Anne Smith Plaintife bearing date Lammas day 84: directing her to John Buckly for Advice

John Buckley being legally Attested declareth that ffrancis Smith said to him that he had sent men servants by his sonne ffrancis & desired the deponent that when he came over he should Incourage his Sonne Eyre and his sonne ffrancis to goe on with ye Plantation lovingly together And that when he came over he would Indevour to Settle them to their Content and ye first that made the Difference should fare the worse for it when he Came.

A Letter was read from the Defend^t ffrancis Smith to ye other Pl^t Robert Eyre dated July 24th 84, Importing his good liking of ye Plaintifs Building on his land as also directing him for Advice to the said Bucklin.

The Plaintifs account was read over in Court Article after Article amounting to ye aforesaid sum of 239¹: 12ˢ: 2½ᵈ. another letter was read Directed to John Beasar from ye Defend^t dated 1st day of May 84.

The Defend^t by his answer utterly denyeth and disowneth all.

the 1st of ye 4th moneth 86.

The verdickt of ye Jury in the Cause depending between Robert Eyre and Anne his wife Plt^s and ffrancis Smith Defend^t after due Examination of each of their accounts And Papers wee finde for ye Plaintifs one Hundred and fifty pounds and Cost of Suite.

All goods Cattle and utensells of Houshold stuffe of ye Plaintifs now in the Defend^{ts} Custody is to be Properly and Intirely the Defend^{ts} owne

The Judgment of ye Court is they doe approve of ye verdickt of ye Jury and Esteeme it resonable

Vewers of fence for Amos Land Charles Ashcome Henry Toten

Vewers of fence for Chester David Ogden Wm Colborne

Vewers of fence for Chichester James Browne Thomas Vither

Vewers of fence for Springfield Joseph Steedman Jno Steedman

Vewers of fence for Providence Edward Pritchard Thomas Vernome

Vewers of fence for Concord Nathaniell Newland Benj Mendinghall

Vewers of fence for Darby Richard Tucker John Bartrome

Peter Lester was presented Constaple for ye Township of Springfield

John Mendinghall assigned over unto his Brother Benjamine Mendinghall a Patent for a parcell of Land lying and being in the Township of Concord Bearing date ye 6th day of ye 12th moneth 1682

James Kennerlay Corner made Returne of an Execution Levied upon John Johnsons Oxen Apraised att nine Pounds and delivered Into the Possession of Thomas Wither the then Shreife

John Hannums Ear marke a Crop under Slitt of both eares his Brand marke I H on the near Buttocke

The Court Adjourne the 3^d day in the 1st weeke of ye 7th moneth next

---

| Att a Court held att Chester for ye County of Chester ye 3^d day in the 1st weeke of ye 7th moneth 1686 | John Blunstone Presid^t
 George Maris
 Bartholomew Coppocke
 Robert Pile
 Samuell Levis } Justices |

Thomas Usher Shreife
Robert Eyre Clerke

CHARLES ASHCOME Pl^t
JOHN VANCULINE Defend^t } in an Action of Trespasse

The names of the Petty Jury

Thomas Worth	Nathaⁿ Parker
William Hues	Jnº Bartrum
John Bristow	Tho: King
John Sanger	Jnº Edge
Richard ffarr	Jnº Child
Michall Blunstone	Moses Mendinghall

A paper was Read Importing an Agreement to be made up between the Plaintife and Defendᵗ by order from yᵉ Governour to John Symcocke & John Blunstone.

Charles Whitacre being Attested declareth that he being Desired by the Plᵗ to speake to yᵉ Defendᵗ not to cutt downe the Plaintifs tymer his answer was that he would Cutt the Tymber downe in dispite of yᵉ Plaintifes nose and further saith not

The Jury finde for yᵉ Plaintife with five pounds Damage and Cost of Suite

Hereup Judgment is Granted.

The Shreife made returne of an Execution granted yᵉ last Court against the Estate of George Andrews att the Suite of Richard Crosby for Eighteen pounds and Appraised by yᵉ County Appraisers the 8ᵗʰ day of yᵉ 4ᵗʰ moneth last att sixty Pounds

The Grand Jury Whose names are under Written Presented Richard Crosby for Keeping an unlawful fence to the great damage of John Marten in his swine

The names of yᵉ Grand Inquest

George fforeman	Richard Barnet
James Browne	Wᵐ Coborne
Nathaniell Lamplue	Robert Pennill
Thomas Powell	John Marten
Joseph Cookson	Thomas Marten
Thomas Vernon	George Woodier
Robert Burrows	Peter Dickes
George Wellard	George Stroad
Thomas Moore	William Collett

Albertus Henrickson Supervisor for ye High Wayes between Chester Creeke and Chichester Creeke presented John Bristow to serve in his roome for ye Ensuing year

Haunse Urine former Constaple for Calcoone Hooke and Amos Land Presented all Well Whereupon Mort Mortenson was appointed Constap in his roome for ye ensuing year

Walter ffansett Constaple for Chester Presented all Well Whereup Edward Pritchard was Elected Constaple in his room for the Ensuing year

Peter Lester was Attested Constable for the Township of Springfield for ye Ensuing year

ffrancis Chadsey was Ordered Supervisor for the High Wayes for ye Township of Chichester for the Ensuing year

Thomas Usher Shreife made Complaint against William Collett in the Behalfe of Thomas Cooper for holding him in his service by an unlawfull Contract; upon which it was Ordered that Wm Collett doe forthwith sett the said Thomas Cooper att Lyberty and allow him the Custome and Law of the Country in that case Provided for Servants

John Hodskins Constaple for Chester made returne all well Where upon Neales Lawson was ordered Constaple in his roome for the Ensuing year

Ordered that Nathaniel Parke be Supervisor for the High Wayes of Concord for the Ensuing year

Robert Eyre Clerke signed and Sealed a Bond of Performance unto ffrancis Smith Senior for the said Smithes Peacable Injoyment of the House and Plantation of ye said Robert Eyre for two year Comencing from the day of June last upon Condition that he the said ffrancis Smith should not cutt or fall five trees more otherwise the Bond to be voyd and of none Efect

Thomas Smith of Darby made over a Deed Dated the 7th day of ye seventh moneth 1686 for fifty Acres of Land in the Township of Darby unto Thomas Coates his heires and Assignes for ever

John Palmer and John Hannum by and with the Consent

of their Wives Mary Palmer and Margery Hannum made over a deed for one hundred Acres of Land lying and being in the Township of Concord to Edward Bennett his heires and Assignes for Ever.

The Inhabitance of Bethell and Concord presented a Paper to this Court signifieing their good liking of the Road lately laid out by the Grand Jury to Chichester

John Holsone Past Over a Deed unto William Mailen dated the 9th day of ye 10th moneth 1685 for one hundred Acres of land

John Hardings ear marke a Crop in the Inside of ye farr eare his Brand marke I H on the farr Buttocke

---

Att a Court held att Chester for the County of Chester the 3d day in the 1st Weeke of the 10th moneth 1686 and soe held by Adjournment the next day

John Blunstone Presidt
John Smycocke
George Maris
Bartholomew Coppocke
Samuell Levis
Robert Wade
Robert Pile
}Justices

Thomas Usher Shreife
Robert Eyre Clerke

The Shreife made returne of an Execution granted unto Charles Ashcome against John Vanculine which was Levied upon two Steers appraised at eight pound Butt was Countermanded by a warrant from the Councell

Edward Hulbert Taylor being Comitted by John Symcocke att the Complaint of William Rawlence for stealing severall goods and merchandize out of the house of Jeremy Collett was bound by Recognisence to Prosecute his Complaint at this Court

The names of ye Grand Inquest

George fforeman
James Browne
Nathaniell Lamplue

Richard Barnard
Robert Pennill
John Marten

Thomas Powell
Joseph Cookson
Thomas Vernon
Robert Burrows
Thomas Moore

Thomas Marten
George Woodier
Peter Dicks
George Stroad
William Collett

The Grand Inquest finde the Bill against the Prisoner upon which he was Arreigned and Pleads nott Guilty and refers himselfe to God and ye Country

The names of ye Petty Jury all accepted by ye Prisoner

Robert Vernon
Edmond Cartleidge
Edward Carter
John Taylor
Nathaniell Evins
John Child

Randall Mailen
John Edge
Walter ffaussett
Thomas Minshall
Caleb Puzy
John Mendinghall

William Rawlence being Attested declareth that he brought in his goods Into the logg house of Jeremy Collett att ye 11th hour att night And y^t ye Prisoner was up att about the second hour that morning next and that ye Prisoner went out of Doore and after ward said he went to ease himselfe

John Collett being Attested declareth that ye Prisoner told him that William Rawlence goods was Come and that his Cousen John Hulbert came before day to receive part of the said goods of this Deponent to ye vallue of three pounds.

Samuel Phillips being Attested declareth y^t he carried ye goods into ye house and further saith not

Robert Way being Attested declareth that he knew ye goods to be brought into the said house and further saith not.

Charles Pickering Pleads as Attorney to ye King

The Petty Jury returne their Verdickte and finds the Prisoner not guilty of the Indicktment butt guilty of Suspicious circumstances in relation to the Indicktment upon which by his Securitys Haunce Peters of y^e County of New Castle and Andrew ffriend of this County he is bound to appear att the next Court

JEREMY COLLETT Pl^{t} \
HENRY RENOLDS Defend^{t} } in an Action of y^{e} Case

Jury as in the Case of Edward Hulbert

The Declaration was read The answer was read

Robert Moulder being Attested declareth that he went downe to Namans Creeke with Henry Renolds in the said Renolds Shallope Where they found a Canow and loaded the Shallope with stones with the same Canow and further saith not

James Browne being Attested declareth that he doe Remember he did see Jeremy Colletts Canow att his Landing and afterward he did see the same Canow hald up att Henry Renolds Landing

John Hickman being Attested Declareth that he did hear Jeremy Collett and Richard Buffington lend the said Canow to Henry Renolds and that he the Deponent did Hale up the Canow at the said Renolds landing

Robert Moulder being Attested again in behalfe of ye Defend^{t} declareth that he did see John Hickman hale up the Canow to ye said Renolds landing

Isacke Warner being Attested declareth that Henry Renolds Wife did offer to returne the same Canow to Jeremy Collett

Edward Hulbert being Attested declareth that he being att worke att Henry Renolds House the Plaintife desired the Defend^{t} Henry Renolds to lett him have some Skinns and that there they came to an account and as this Deponent can best remember there was about one hundred and twenty Guilders due upon ye Defend^{ts} account butt he doe certainly aferme there was not more then one hundred and fourty due

The Jury find for the Defend^{t} two pence Damage upon ye account of ye Canow and that he shall pay to ye Plaintife Eighteen Shillings and four Pence upon Ballancing ye accounts and that ye Plaintife shall pay ye Cost of Suite Hereupon Judgment is granted Upon which the Pl^{t} makes his Appeale to ye next Court of Equity held for this County

JEREMY COLLETT Pl^t } in an Action of Scandall and
GEORGE STROAD Defend^t } Defamation withdrawn

John Bristow made over a Deed unto William Lewis bearing date ye 15th day of ye 7th moneth 1686 for four hundred and ninty acres of land

MOUNS PETERSON Pl^t } In an Action of ye Case
HAUNS URINE Defend^t } They Joyne Issue by Concent

The names of the Jury

James Browne	Thomas Wither
Thomas Powell	Jeremy Collett
Jacob Symcocke	Richard Crosby
John Bristow	ffrancis Chadsey
Benja: Mendinghall	Caleb Puzic
Moses Mendinghall	John Hallwell

The Declaration was Read

Thomas Bowles being Attested for ye Plaintife declareth that Haunce Urine came among his Carpenters and stole his nayles and afterward the said Haunce gave the Carpenters a Pott of Rum not to call him Theife butt coming some time afterward to Tenicome he the Defend^t did there report that the pl^t Mouns Peterson had gotten all his Estate by Privatearing and murdering of men and that he the Deponent should have a care of him

Robert Brothers being Attested declareth ye same

Samuell Weight being Attested declareth as aforesaid and further declares that ye Defend^t offered him two Piggs to stop his Evidence

The Jury finde for ye Plaintife twenty shillings Damage and Cost of Suite

Hereupon Judgment is Granted

JOSHUA HASTINGS Pl^t } in an Action of trespasse
FFRANCIS YARNALL Defend^t }

The names of ye Petty Jury

| Robert Vernon | Joseph Richards |
| Edmond Cartleidge | John Edge |

Edward Carter   Walter ffaussett
John Taylor   Thomas Minshall
Nathaniell Evins   Caleb Pusie
John Child   John Mendinghall

The Declaration was read   The answer was read

Allen Robenett being Attested declareth that he knew the boore of ye Pl^t Joshua Hastings and that to ye best of his knowledge it was ye same boore and further saith not

ffrancis Baldwin being Attested declareth that ye boore in possession of ffrancis Yarnall was ye Pl^{ts} boore & that he saw the said Boore att Allen Robenetts

Randall Mailen being Attested declareth that he being att ye House of Allen Robenett he did there as he was told see ye Pl^{ts} boore and that the boore as he was alsoe told by said Robenett was Bitten in the stones by David Ogdens dog he was alsoe told ye same by John Holstone

John Hastins being Attested declareth that he did with his owne knife marke ye Pl^{ts} Boore and that s^d boore was att home all one Sumer and all the Winter following and that he saw him noe more Butt heard of him and that he never saw him att all untill he saw him att ffra Yarnalls and doe further more declare y^t he knew it to be ye Pl^{ts} Boore

William Mailen being Attested declareth that he did see a sandy Collowrd Boore butt he knew not whose it was and further saith not

Judith Colvert being Attested declareth there was a Boore y^t kept Company with their Swine Butt afterward shee did hear y^t ye Boore was ye Pl^{ts} Boore and that he went from thence and was away some time and when he came againe he had been Bitten on ye right side of ye stones as shee thinks Butt when ffrancis Yarnall came to their House to see ye Boore he said he did thinke this Boores marke was very much like his and that ye Boore was of a lighter Collour then his and further saith not.

George Maris the Elder being Attested for ye Defend^t Declareth that he knew ffrancis Yarnall did Brid a Boore of a

Sandy Collour And that he have often Served him with meat and that his marke was ye Defendt^s marke and after ye Defend^t fetching home ye said Boore Called upon this deponent to vew ye said Boore And according to ye best of his Judgment both by ye marke and by ye Stones and in every respect both of grouth and shap it was the Defend^ts Boore

John Calvert being Attested for ye Defend^t declareth that ye Boore which ffrancis Yarnall tooke away was about three months att times att his House and afterward about ye 1st moneth ffran Yarnall ye Defend^t tooke him away and that ye Boore was Bitten behind on ye right side of ye stones.

John ffox being Attested for ye Defend^t declareth y^t he Knew ye Boore and y^t he had one stone hanging downe lower then ye other and that he was Bitten by the dogs on ye right side of ye Stones.

Jane Calvert being Attested declareth that ffrancis Yarnall came to John Calverts and did there drive a Boore into ye Hog yard and did there say that he thought his Boore was of a lighter Collour and that ye marke was not altogether like his marke and further saith not

Margrett Hollingsworth being Attested declareth that ye Boore was a Right Boore Before he was Bitten and that he was supposed to be Joshua Hastings Boore by ye neighborhood and that ye Boore was there most part of ye Winter

Caleb Puzie being Attested declareth that ffrancis Yarnall did enquire of him whether there was not a Boore about his House with one stone Who told him he had seen a strange Boore there

Thomas Bristow being Attested declareth for ye Defend^t that he did certainly know ye said Boore and y^t it was ye very Boore of ye Defend^ts ffrancis Yarnall

John Maris being Attested for ye Defend^t declareth that he had knowledge of ye Defend^t ffrancis Yarnalls Boore and when the said Boore was Brought againe by ye Defend^t he knew it Certainly to be ye same Boore and further saith not

George Maris ye Younger being Attested for ye Defend^t

declareth that he had certain knowledge of ffrancis Yarnalls Boore and that it was ye same Boore which ffrancis Yarnall brought to them to vew when he fetcht him home.

John Hallawell being Attested for ye Defend^t declareth ye Boore was att his House & that it was ye same Boore which he saw att ye latter end of ye Sumer and y^t ye Boore was att Jacob Symcocks and he Believes it was ye Defend^t ffra: Yarnalls Boore

The Jury finde for ye Plaintife twenty five shillings with Cost of Suite   Hereupon Judgment is granted Upon which ye Defend^t makes his Appeale to ye next Court of Equity held for this County

Mouns Peterson Pl^t } In an action of Scandall and Defamation Withdrawne upon Condition that ye Defend^t Mort Mortenson pay the Cost of Suite
Mort Mortenson Defend^t

John Symcocke made over a Deed dated the 7th day of ye 10th moneth 1686 to John Hallawell for a Parcell of Land to the use of ye said Hallewell his heires and Assignes for ever

Nathaniell Evins made over a Deed for fifty Acres of Land bearing Date ye 1st day of ye 4th moneth 1686 to John Baldwin his heires and Assignes for ever

Robert Pile made over a Deed unto his Brother Nicholas Pile for one hundred Acres of Land lying in Concord dated ye 27th day of ye 9th moneth 1686

Benjamine Mendinghall made over a Deed dated ye 27th day of ye 9th moneth 1686 to Moses Mendinghall for a parcell of land lying and being in Concord

John Mendinghall made over a Deed dated ye 27th day of ye 9th moneth 1686 to Thomas Marten his heires and Assignes for Ever for a parcell of Land lying and being in Concord

Robert Wade made over a Deed unto John Bristow his heires and Assignes for ever dated ye 8th day of ye 10th moneth 1686 for a parcell of Land lying and being in the Township of Chester

John Blunstone made over a Deed bearing Date ye 26th day of ye 9th moneth 1686 to Robert Smith his heires and Assignes for ever

George Wood made over a Deed dated ye 27th day of ye 9th moneth 1686 for two parcells of Land unto John Blunstone his heires and Assignes for Ever

John Blunstone made over a Deed Bearing Date ye 8th day of ye 10th moneth 1686 for a parcell of Land in Darby to George Wood his Heires and Assignes for ever by his Attorney Samuell Levis

Thomas Powell made over a Deed unto Charles Whitacre dated ye 27th day of ye 9th moneth 1686 for a parcell of Land Conteining two hundred acres lying upon Ridley Creeke

Thomas Persons Samuell Baker and William Haukes being presented by ye Grand Jury for being Drunke and Sam^ll Baker and Tho Persons for Swearing the two latter (viz) Samuell Baker and William Haukes was Apprehended and brought to ye Barr

Nicholas Pile being Attested declareth that Samuell Baker did Swear Severall Oathes that John Symcocke was Drunke for which he was fined thirty shillings, Benjamine Mendinghall Attesting ye same

William Haukes was fined five shillings for being Drunke and Appearing soe att ye Barr

Urine Keene made Complaint against John Vanculine for Deteining his servant Renear Vanculine sonne of ye said John Vanculine from his service upon which it was ordered that John Vanculine doe forthwith send backe the said Renear Vanculine to his service and that he serve the time he have been wanting

John Collett Petitioned against ye Shreife for not Executing a Warrant granted against ffrancis Smith ye younger on his behalfe. William Collett being Attested declareth y^t he heard ffrancis Smith say he mett with ye Shreife and asked for ye Warrant he had against him

Richard Crosby being Presented by y*e* grand Inquest y*e* last Court for keeping an unlawful fence made his appearance and was att this Court fined thirty shillings

Edward Hulbert Petitioned against y*e* Shreife for his hard usage in the Comon Prison

This Court in y*e* Behalfe of y*e* County have bargained and sold unto Robert Wade his Heirs and Assignes y*e* Court house and Prison att Chester upon Consideration Whereof y*e* said Wade doe Obleidge himselfe his heires Executors and Assignes to Defray all Charges which are already Due from y*e* first Erecting said Houses Provided that from y*e* day of y*e* Date hereof to y*e* full End and terme of two years and a halfe the said Robert Wade shall have liberty to reimburst what moneyes he have already received of y*e* Levie raised in this County toward y*e* Purchasing and Building of said Houses. Upon all Which this Court doth Engage to make y*e* said Wade a firme and sure Title to said Houses and to give him lawfull and quiete Possession thereof

James Saunderlaine for himselfe his heires and Assignes doe Promise this Court a Convenient Peece of Land in y*e* Towne of Chester where they may Erect a Court house and Prison and to make a firme title of y*e* same to y*e* Proper use and Behoofe of this County

Andrew ffriend was Attested Constaple for y*e* Township of Chester in the Roome of his ffather Neales Lawson

James Saunderlaines ear marke both ears Cropt and slitt his brand marke   I. S.

George fforemans ear marke a Crop and Slit in y*e* farr ear his brand marke   G F

Samuell Levis his ear marke a Swallow fork taken out of y*e* middle of y*e* near ear his brand marke   S. L

Haunce Urine was fined five shillings for being Drunke upon Tenicum Island

George Strod made over a Deed dated y*e* 27th day of y*e* 9th month 1686 for a parcell of Land lying and being in Concord to Goddin Walter his heires and Assignes for ever.

George Strod made over a Deed Dated ye above day for a parcell of Land in the s^d Township of Concord unto Thomas Hale his Heires and Assignes for ever

Constaples Chossen

ffor Bethell Lyberty   Edward Beasar
Burmingham   John Bennett
Chester   Andrew ffriend in ye roome of his father Neales Lawson
Northley   Edward Carter
Gilead   Joseph Baker
Providence   John Nickson in ye roome of Edward Pritchard
Marple   ffrancis Stamfield
Newtowne   Thomas Norbury
Upper Providence   Thomas Powell

Ordered that all Constaples y^t are not Attested doe forthwith repaire to their next Justice to be Attested according to law

Ordered that all Constaples have forthwith Warrants directed unto them under ye Clerks hand and County Seale that they forthwith Call a Towne meeting in their severall Precincks in order to make a true returne of all ye male Inhabitance therein as well Servants as free men from sixteen years of age to sixty as alsoe of what Lands they are seized of; as alsoe what Lands are surveyed to non residence and soe remaining unoccupied unto ye Commissioners Sitting att Walter ffausetts att Ridley Creeke ye 1st day of ye next moneth 1686

The Court adjourne unto ye 3^d day in ye 1st Weeke of ye 1st moneth next and ye next day Sate in Equity

---

Att a Court of Equity held att Chester ye 5th day in the 1st Weeke of ye 10th moneth 1686.

Commissioners Present
John Blunstone
John Simcocke
George Maris
Bartholomew Coppocke
Samuell Levis
Robert Wade
Robert Pile

Robert Eyre Clerke

ffrancis Yarnall of this County Preferred a Bill to this Court Wherein he required a Remedy against yᵉ Verdickt of Jury and Judgment of Court Obteined against him by Joshua Hastings of yᵉ same County att the last Court of Comon Pleas held for this County of Chester the 3ᵈ and 4ᵗʰ days of this Present Weeke

Upon which it was Decreed that ffrancis Yarnall should pay 10ˢ and bear butt halfe the Charges of that Court.

Jeremy Collett of this County Preferred a Bill to this Court requiring a Remedy against yᵉ Verdickt of Jury and Judgment of Court in a Case Depending between himselfe & Henry Renolds of yᵉ same County att the last Court of Comon Ples held for this County of Chester the 3ᵈ and 4ᵗʰ dayes of this Present Weeke. Upon which it was Decreed that Henry Renolds should pay one halfe of the Charges of Court and Cost of Suite.

The Court Adjourne

Att a Court held att Chester for yᵉ County of Chester yᵉ 3ᵈ day in the 1ˢᵗ Weeke of yᵉ 1ˢᵗ moneth 1686

{ George Maris President
John Symcocke
John Blunstone
ffrancis Harrison
Bartholomew Coppocke
Robert Pile } Justices

Thomas Usher Shreife
Robert Eyre Clerke

JAMES BROWNE   Plᵗ
TIMOTHY CLEMENT   Defendᵗ
In an action of Debt upon
Attatchment in yᵉ hands of
Thomas Coborne.
} Continued

The Shreife made returne of a Warrant Issued out against Timothy Clement in behalfe of yᵉ King:
not to be found.

The names of such of yᵉ Grand Inquest that absented themselves this Court

George floreman, Richard Barnard, Peter Dicks, William Collett

The Presentiments of ye Grand Inquest viz

Andrew Nealson Als friend for unlawfully Ranging ye Woods and for Driving Peoples Cattle as Horses and Mares backe into the Woods to ye great Detryment of many of ye Inhabitance. Who being Indickted upon ye same the cause was att his request traversed untill the next Court

Thomas Brasy was Presented for Hanging gates upon ye Kings High Way by reason Whereof Cattle Cannot Passe and when a gate lyes open and ye neighbourhoods Cattle Gett into ye said Brasyes Pasture they are many times stopt att night to their Detryment for Want of ye milke of their udder Beasts

The Township of Chester was Presented for not finding and making a foote Bridge over ye mill Creeke in ye Kings High way hard by Wm Woodmansees

John Symcocke made over a Deed for one hundred acres of land unto Charles Whitacre dated this Instant

Haunce Peters of New Castle County came into ye Court and delivered up Edw: Hulbert into ye Custody of ye Shreife upon which it was ordered that ye said Haunce Peters bond given ye last Court should be Cancelled.

Thomas King made over a Deed to Wm Branton for fifty acres of land lying in Concord dated this Instant.

Thomas Duckett made over a Patent by Assignment unto Barnabas Wilcox for three hundred acres of land lying in ye County of Chester dated the 9th day of the 10th moneth 1686

William Morgan made over a Patent by Assignment to William Brainton for two hundred acres of land in Burmingham dated ye 5th day of ye 8th mo^{th} 1686

Jeremy Collett made over a Deed to John Hannum for 200 acres of land lying in ye 3^d lott in Concord dated this Instant

Jeremy Collett of this County and John White Clerke of ye County of new Castle was Attested to a Bond signed and sealed by Richard Bridgman unto Charles Pickering dated ye 10th day of December 1686.

Charles Ashcome Pl^t } in an action of ye Case
Thomas Usher Defend^t

Ordered that ye Shreife have a new Execution against John Vanculine and soe ye matter to be ended

Edward Hulbert Appearing according to Recognisence and noe body appearing to Prosecute ye Prisoner is acquitted by Proclamation

Samuell Baker upon his acknowledgment and submission to John Symcocke is remitted his fine which was laid on him for abusing ye said Symcocke ye last Court

Ordered that Thomas Usher Shreife and Richard Crosby have Power to sell and Dispose of ye Plantation of George Andrews lying att Chichester

Caleb Puzie Petitioned against Thomas Coborne for setting a Water mill above him upon Upland Creeke The Court Considering the Premisses and finding it to bee for ye Comon good Dispenceth therewith

Nathaniell Thornton being found upon his Confession before ffrancis Harrison and Robert Pile to be Justly Indebted unto Thomas Hale in ye Sum of Seventeen shillings and tenne pence halfe Penny it was ordered to be entred as ye Judgm^t of this Court and upon non payment Execution to follow

The names of ye Grand Inquest Attested at this Court

Walter ffausett	Joshua fferne
John Edge	Thomas Person
Jonathan Hayes	Anthony Weaver
Randall Maylen	George Wood
Joshua Hastings	Jacob Symcocke
Peter Taylor	Joseph Edge
Caleb Puzie	Bartholomew Coppocke
	George Churchman

John Nickson Petitioned against a former order of this Court butt was Rejected

Richard Crosby Preferred a Bill to ye late Grand Inquest against David Ogden which was found to be cronious ffrancis Harrison and Jacob Chandler acknowledged ye Exchange of one moity of two hundred and fifty acres of land in the Township of Chichester from ye said ffrancis to ye said Jacob for ye one moity of two hundred and fifty Acres lying on Chester Creeke from ye s^d Jacob to ye said ffrancis

The Court Adjourne untill ye 3^d day in ye 2^d Weeke of ye 2^d moth next.

Att a Court held att Chester for ye County of Chester ye 3^d day in the 2^d Weeke of ye 2^d moth 1687

John Blunstone President
George Maris
John Bristow
Sam^{ll} Levis } Justices
Bartho Coppocke
ffrancis Harrison

Thomas Usher Shreife
Robert Eyre Clerke

The Shreife made returne of an Execution granted against John Vanculine att the suite of Charles Ashcome which was Levied upon two Cowes appraised by Joshua Hastings and Caleb Pusic att 9^{lb}

Ordered that ye appraisers doe Discharge the Shreife of said Cowes and doe take them into their Custody and keeping untill further order.

JEREMY COLLETT by his wife Jane his Attorney   Pl^t } in an action of ye Case
EDWARD HULBERT   Defend^t The Defend^t Confesses Judgment.

William Cloud Junior made Complaint in behalfe of his ffather Wm Cloud that ye officers of new Castle have Demanded ye Publick levies of his said ffather for that County Whereupon it was ordered that ye Clerke doe forthwith send downe a request under his owne hand desiring them to forbear to Levie any thing upon ye said Cloud till a desision be made of ye Premisses by ye Governour

Urine Keine made over a Deed for a ℔cell of land lying and being in Chester with all ye Appurtinances and lotts dated ye 18th day of ye 11th moneth 1686 to James Saunderlaine and his heires for ever

Anne ffinch made over a Deed for a ꝑcell of land Conteining one hundred acres lying between Ridly Creeke and Chester Creeke unto William ffindlow dated ye 11th day of ye 2^d Month 1687

William ffindlow past over a mortgage for said Land to ye said Anne ffince for twenty pounds to be paid ye 2^d day of ye 5th Moneth 1690 dated ye 12th day of ye 2^d moneth 1687

John Nickson made over a Deed to Bartholomew Coppocke dated ye 12th day of ye 2^d moneth in ye 7th year of ye Proprietarys Government for a ꝑcell of Land lying on ye West side of Darby Creeke

Wilham Cloud Constaple for Concord returned all well Whereupon Nathaniell Newland was ordered Constaple in his roome for ye ensuing year

Phillip Roman Constaple of Chichester returned all well whereupon Nathaniell Lamplue was ordered Constaple in his roome for the ensuing year

ffrancis Chadsey Supervisor of ye High wayes between Chichester Creeke and Namans Creeke returnd all well whereupon Phillip Roman was ordered in his roome for ye ensuing year

Ordered that Nathaniell Evins be Supervisor of ye High wayes for ye Township of Chester in ye roome of John Bristow

Richard Crosby being Convickted for being Drunke and abusing ye majestracy of this Court and County was fined seven pounds

The Court Adjourne untill ye 3^d day in ye 1st Weeke of ye 4th moneth next

---

Att a Court held att Chester for ye County of Chester ye 7th day of ye 4th moneth 1687

John Bristow Presid^t
John Symcocke
John Blunstone
Bartholomew Coppocke } Justices
George Maris
ffrancis Harrison

Joshua ffirene Shreife
Robert Eyre Clerke

FFRANCIS STAMFIELD	Pl^t	withdrawne
JOHANES FFRIEND	Defen^t	
JAMES SAUNDERLAINE	Pl^t	the Shreife returnd y^e
RICHARD RUDMAN	Defend^t	Defend^t not to be found
THOMAS HOLMES	Pl^t	returned as above
CHARLES ASHCOME	Defend^t	
ROBERT EYRE	Pl^t	returned as above
HENRY WOOD	Defend^t	
FFRANCIS STAMFIELD	Pl^t	withdrawne
JAMES STAMFIELD	Defend^t	
JAMES STAMFIELD	Pl^t	in an action of Trover
JOHN ORION	Defend^t	and Conversion

The names of the Jury

Thomas Vernon	John Hallawell
Thomas Worth	Adam Roads
Samuell Bradshaw	John Mendinghall
Richard Tucker	John Kinsman
Joseph Richards	Edmond Cartleidge
John Gibbons	Thomas Brodshaw

The Declaration was read and Haunce Urine being attested declareth y^t ye mare he sold to ye Plaintife was a Brown Bay mare and was markt in both ears with a Swallow fforke and had a small starr in her fforehead and a long tayle

Peter Peterson being Attested declareth That he was with ye Defend^t John Orion when he took up a Chestnut mare and a Blacke Colt near Harford markt with a Swallow forke on both eares and a long tayle with a small starr in her forehead

John Smith being Attested declareth that ye mares marks was as before Attested and that shee had a black fillow Colt and that when he saw them the Colt was branded with F S on ye near Buttocke

Thomas Massie being Attested declareth that the mare was marke as before Attested by Per Peterson and that Orion did confesse he had a black Colt markt F S about 2 years old and y^t he knew not how he came to be markt with that marke

Mouns Usta being attested for yᵉ Defendᵗ declareth yᵗ yᵉ mare and Colt which yᵉ Defendᵗ carried over yᵉ River was yᵉ Defendᵗˢ owne mare and Colt and that he knew for a great While since yᵉ mare did use yᵉ woods near Harford and that he tamed her and saith alsoe that about yᵉ time that James Stamfield tooke up this mare and Colt that mare and Colt was wanting

Usta Usta being attested declareth for yᵉ Defendᵗ yᵗ he in Company with Peter Peters & Jnᵒ Orion tooke up yᵉ mare near Harford and yᵗ to his knowledge it was Orions owne mare

Joseph Wood being attested for yᵉ Defendᵗ declareth yᵗ he knew yᵉ mare to be Orions mare and that about 3 years since Mouns Peters did take her up and that this deponent did ofer to by her

Before yᵉ Jury went out upon yᵉ Cause it was agreed that the Plᵗ and defendᵗ should pay their equal shares of yᵉ Charge and Cost of Suite and soe yᵉ matter to Rest.

Andrew Neales alius ffriend was Called to yᵉ Barr upon a former Bill of Indicktment Exhibitted against him att a Court held for this County yᵉ 3ᵈ day in yᵉ 1ˢᵗ Weeke of yᵉ 1ˢᵗ moneth last

The Petty Jury as in yᵉ Case of Stamfield & Orion

Charles Whitacres being atteste declareth that Andrew Neales alius ffriend told him yᵗ John Symcocke should never have any good of a mare which yᵉ said Andrew Pretended to have tooke up att Concord Before yᵉ said Jnᵒ Symcocke had her and that he have often sworne yᵉ same in this deponents hearing who further declareth that yᵉ sweeds Prists sonne did offer to sale in yᵉ name of yᵉ said Andrew ffriend 2 Colts of 3 years old and 2 of 2 years old a peece which he said was Blacke mare Colts

James Lownes being attested declareth that yᵉ said Andrew Neales alius ffriend did Pretend he had Driven or brought downe yᵉ mare from Concord and that upon John Symcockes taking her up he did both threaten and Swear that yᵉ said mare should doe yᵉ said Symcocke noe good.

Uppon his request the Cause is Suspended untill the next Court

Andrew ffriend was ffined five shillings for Swearing.

Thomas Mercer made over a Deed for tenne Acres of Land lying in Astone dated ye 9th day of ye 2^d moneth 1687 unto Peter Tremaine his heires and Assignes for ever

Thomas Brasie made over a Deed dated ye 5th day of ffebruary 1686 to Joseph Needs for a parcell of Land Conteining one hundred acrees lying in Darby

George Maris made over a Deed dated ye 7th day of ye 4th moneth 1687 to Phillip Yarnall for a parcell of Land Conteining two hundred Acrees Between Chester Creeke and Ridly Creeke

Jane Jones Servant to George fforeman for Confessing Incontinency was ordered ye next morning att ye 9th hour to receive nine lashes upon her bear Backe well laid on att ye Comon Whipping Post

The grand Inquest Presented the want of three Convenient horse Bridges on ye Kings Road one over Chester Creeke one over Ridley Creeke and one over Croome Creeke

Ordered that forthwith Bridges be Erected over Ridley Creeke and Croome Creeke an a horse Bridge over Chester Creeke near Chester Mill upon ye lower side of ye Dam

They alsoe Present Thomas Colborne of this Township of Chester for selling rum to ye Indians Contrary to the lawes of this Province Upon which he was bound by recognisence to answer it the next Court:

The names of ye grand Inquest wanting:

Anthony Weaver dead—George Churchman absent.

John Symcocke by Powers from Elizabeth fframton wife of the late Disceaced William fframton acknowledged and Confessed in Oppen Court ye receipt of two hundred and Eight pounds Currant English money which said sum he Confessed to be Satisfied by the payment of the said Calebs Bills for security of which att a Court held for this County ye 3^d day in ye 1st Weeke of ye 4th moneth 1685, Judgment was then Confessed by ye said Caleb upon Chester mill and Premisses

John Gibbons Jacob Symcocke and Charles Whitacre was ordered and Attested Appraisers for this County for ye next Ensuing year

Ordered that Thomas Hood be Attested Constaple of ye Township of Darby for ye next ensuing year

Ordered that Charles Whitacre be supervisor of the highwayes for ye Township of Ridley for ye next ensuing year

Ordered that John Bartrome be supervisor of High wayes for Darby for ye next Ensuing year.

Ordered that John Mendinghall be supervisor of the high wayes for Concord for ye next Ensuing year.

Thomas King made over a deed for 100 acres of Land in Concord unto Robert Chamberlaine & his heires for ever dated ye 27th of ye 9th moth 1686.

Joseph Bushell made over a Deed for one hundred acres of Land lying in Thornbury to Wm Brainton and his heires for ever dated ye 7th of ye 4th moneth 1687.

Samuell Bradshaw made over a Deed for one hundred & eleven acrees of land lying upon Mill Creeke to Thomas Bradshaw and his heires and Assignes for ever dated ye 7th day of ye 4th moth 1687.

John Blunstone made over a Deed for one acre of Land in the Township of Darby to build a meeting house thereon to ye use of ye said Township for ever to Exercise the true worship of God therein.

George fforeman Complaining to this Court that his Servant maide Jane Jones by her often running away taking up and other charges Depending with loss of time stands Damnified to ye vallue of nine pounds six pence upon his and Samuel Rowlands Proofe thereof shee is ordered for satisfaction to serve her said master or his assignes from ye Termination of her Indenture dated ye 22^d of Aprill 1686 untill ye full end and terme of four years next ensuing.

Allen Robinett made over a Deed for fifty acres of Land with all the houses and Appurtinances knowne by y° name of Nethercutt unto Phillip Denning his heires and Assignes for ever dated y° 7th day of y° 4th moneth 1687

Phillip Denning made over a Deed for y° above[d] land and premisses unto William Buckingham his heires Executo[rs] and assignes for ever dated y° above day.

William Buckingham past over a Penall Bond of eighty pounds for y° payment of fourty pounds unto Phillip Denning att severall payments att or before y° Expiration of seven years from y° date hereof being dated y° above day

Robert Barber was Attested Constaple for Chester in the roome of Andrew ffriend for y° time said ffriend had to serve.

The Court Adjourne untill y° 3d day in y° 1st Weeke of y° 7th mo[th] next

---

Att a Court held att Chester for y° County of Chester y° 3d day in y° 1st Weeke of the 7th Moneth 1687 and soe held by Adjournment untill y° next day

John Bristow Presid[t]
John Blunstone
John Harding
George Maris
Bartholomew Coppocke
Edward Beasar
} Justices

Joshua ffirne Shreife
Robert Eyre Clerke

Thomas Colborne Bound over y° last Court for Selling y° Indians Rum made his appearance according to recognisence and was att this Court Indickted To which he Pleads not Guilty

The names of y° Petty Jury

Thomas Worth	Thomas Coates
James Browne	Nathaniell Evins
Thomas Rawlenson	Geo Churchman
Thomas Smith	Randall Vernon
Sam[ll] Bradshaw	John Howell
Adam Roades	Edward Waters

Isacke few being Attested declareth that a drunken Indian Coming by him wth an Emtie Bottle he asked him whether he was going the Indian made answer to Thomas Colbornes for rum and the same Indian Coming backe had two Bottles which he saw was full of rum

Thomas Lasie being attested declareth ye same as Isacke few.

The verdickt of ye jury

They finde Thomas Colborne not Guilty according to evidence. Upon which he is acquitted by ye Court paying his fees.

Samuell Rowland by his Surtie George ffroeman became bound to ffrancis Harrison to make his appearance att this Court to answer his Beating and abusing Samuell Baker and accordingly made his appearance and was Indickted

Thomas Usher was Constituted by the Court attorney to ye king and Cheife Proprietary in this case.

The names of the Grand Inquest

Richard Parker	William Garrett
Edmond Cartleige	Thomas ffox
Thomas Bradshaw	Albertus Henrickson
John Kinsman	William Colborne
John Mendinghall	Edward Pritchard
William Cloud Junr	Walter Marten
Richard Thatcher	George Willard
John Beales	

the Bill is found

Whereupon he is called to ye Barr and Pleads not Guilty and refers himselfe to God and the Country.

The Petty Jury the same as in the Case of Thomas Colborne (all accepted by the Prisoner) onely William Branton in steed of Thomas Rawlenson.

Samuel Noys being Attested Declareth that he being about his Business in ye kings High way near George fforemans Where Samuel Baker meeting him on their Occations ye Prisoner Samuell Rowland came forth of George fforemans with halfe a Boule of Punch in his hand and spying them did Swear by God these be ye Rogues y^t did abuse me att new

Castle and thereupon did strick this deponent several Blowes butt he making his Escape ye Prisoner fell upon Samuell Baker and tooke a Paddle out of his hand and did beate him upon ye head Backe and Shoulders and severall other parts of his Body therewith which Caused him to Bleed att ye mouth and nose for twelve or fourteen hours after

Richard Buffington being Attested declareth that Samuell Baker lived with him more then two years and in that time he never knew that he did Bleed.

Isacke Warner being Attested declareth that he being sitting upon some Pipe Staves near George fforemans Barne Samuell Baker and Samuell Noyes came together and stood near this deponent and Samuell Rowland spying them asked them what they did there att that time of night Butt he doe not remember that he did hear any Blowes.

Edward Jonnings being Attested declareth that he coming out of George fforemans house with Samuell Rowland ye said Samuell spying Samuell Noyes and Samuell Baker near George fforemans House asked them what they did there at that time of night and told them he would sett them further butt this deponent going his way he did think Samuell Baker Cryed out to Samuell Rowland not to stricke him any more telling him he had broake his head already

William White being Attested Declareth that he did see Samuell Baker in ye night near James Brownes and asked him what he did there att that time of night who told him he stayed for ye tyde then he asked ye said Sam^ll where he lay all night he told him in his Canow And Invighting him ye said Sam^ll to lye att his house he answered he would first call his mate this deponent asked him where he was he answered that Samuell Rowland had beat them both and almost killed him.

Lidea Wade being Attested declareth that Samuell Noyes Borrowed a Canow of her Husband to Carry a Calfe to Thomas Wither and Sam^ll Baker going with him, When he came back againe Complained that Samuell Rowland had knockt him downe with ye flatt side of ye Paddle and beate him Uppon y^e

Stomacke Butt ye said Sam^{ll} Baker told this deponent he knew not what he did to him when he was downe and further this deponent saith that ye said Samuell Baker did often say in her hearing that if he did dye the Blowes he received from Samuell Rowland would be ye Cause of his Death.

Robert Stephens being Attested declareth that Samuell Rowland and Samuell Baker did drink together att John Hodskins where they shooke hands together in way of friendship as he doe suppose And after he did see ye said Samuell Baker Drunke att Philadelphia.

William Goforth being Attested declareth y^t Samuell Rowland came into John Hodskins where meeting with Samuell Baker he was desired to drink to Samuell Rowland and be friends which ye said Baker did some time after

The Petty Juries Verdickt

Wee finde Samuell Rowland Guilty of ye Indicktment charged against him likewise y^t Samuell Rowland be kept safe untill Samuell Baker be throughly recovered againe likewise y^t Samuell Rowland shall pay all ye Damage y^t Samuell Baker shall suffer through his abuse with Cost of Suite

Hereupon Judgment is granted and that the Defend^t finde Security for his good behaviour and appearance att next County Court or goe to Prison

George fforeman and James Browne became bound for the Prisoners good behaviour & appearance at ye next Court

James Stamfield	Pl^t	upon a former action of Trover and Conversion Comenced ye last Court
John Orion	Defend^t	

Jury as in ye foregoing Case of Samuell Rowland & Samuell Baker

Thomas Vernone being Attested declareth that ye mare which James Stamfield had was about six years old and that shee was a brown bay mare

Mouns Peters being Attested declareth that he did marke a mare for Haunce Urine when shee was about two years old which was about four years since

The Testimony of Andrew Swanson taken att Philadelphia:

Andrew Swanson of ye County aforesaid being legally Attested before me Humphry Murry one of ye Justices of ye said County deposeth and saith as follows that is to say

That he this Deponent hath formerly Sold unto John Orion two mares one being Chestnutt browne and ye other a blacke one with a White Streak down her forehead of this deponents owne & his fathers Ear marke to witt ye Browne mare has a swallow Tayle in both her ears and ye Blacke mare onely one Swallow Tayle in ye near ear And further deposeth not

the marke of Andrew   A   Swanson

Attested by and before me ye 26th day of ye 5th moneth 1687

The Testimoney of Andrew Swanson taken by John Goodson att Philadelphia

The Deposition of Andrew Swanson sayth that he marketh with a Swallow fforke in ye left ear and noe other ear marke And ye two mares that I sold to John Orion was marked with no other marke no my Posecion butt a Swallow forke in ye left ear which hath been my marke all along and my fathers marke before me.   Attested ye third day of ye 7th moneth 1687.

John Goodson

The Juryes verdickt

Wee finde it for ye Defend^t with six pence damage & Cost of Suite

Hereupon Judgment is Granted

Robert Stephens was Presented by ye Grand Inquest for being Drunke att Chester since ye last Court for which he was fined by ye Court 5^s.

John Chard was Presened by ye Grand Inquest for being Drunke about ye beginning of July last for which he was fined by ye Court 5^s.

John Bradshaw Presented a Bill to ye Grand Inquest against Nathaniell Lamplue Constaple of Chichester for not Prosecuting his hue and cry. The Bill is found

Upon which Nathaniell Lamplue Petitioned the Court. Continued untill ye morning & afterward referd to arbitration

John Edge being Convickted before John Blunstone and George Maris for being Drunke was fine by ye Court 5^s.

Edward Pritchard was Presented by the Grand Inquest for absenting himselfe from them. Whereupon his is fined by ye Court 10^s

Haunce Urine and Mort Mortenson being Convickted before John Blunstone for Beating and abusing Mouns Peters was bound by recognisence to answer ye same att this Court. Upon which they were Indickted.

The Bill is found by the Grand Inquest:

Upon which they are called to the Barr and Pleads not Guilty and referrs themselves to God and the Country

The names of ye Petty Jury all accepted by the Prisoners

Joshua Hastings	Jacob Simcocke
Peter Lester	Thomas Norbury
Nathaniel Newland	Thomas Powell
Joseph Baker	William Gregory
Thomas Coates	Thomas Vernon
George Gleaves	Joseph Richards

Peter Peters being Attested declareth he did see Mort Mortson beat and strike his ffather Mouns Peters with a Paddle att Calcoone Hooke

Adam Roads being Attested declareth that he being att the house of Mouns Peters he did see that his head was Broaken wounded and Bloody

The Jurys verdick^t

Wee finde Mort Mortenson guilty according to fact as he stands Indickted with 3£ 3^s Damage with Cost of Suite and Haunce Urine an abettor. Hereupon Judgment is granted

James Saunderlaine was fined 5^s for Suffering Robert Stephens to be Drunke in his House.

Neales Quist paid 5^s for Being Drunke att Chester.

Andrew ffriend was Called to ye Barr upon his former Indicktmen^t butt noe Prosecutor appearing he is Discharged paying his fees.

Thomas Boules being summoned to appear att this Court

to answer y̆ᵉ Complaint of our Sovereign lord y̆ᵉ King and Cheife Proprietary for Suffering the Kings Leidge People to be Drunke att his house was upon the same Indickted.

The Grand Inquest find the Bill

Whereupon he is called to y̆ᵉ Barr and Pleads not Guilty and referrs himselfe to God & y̆ᵉ Country.

The names of y̆ᵉ Petty Jury y̆ᵉ same as in y̆ᵉ foregoing Case of Mort Mortenson and Haunce Urine Except James Swaford in y̆ᵉ roome of William Gregory and accepted by y̆ᵉ Defendant.

John Taylor being attested declareth that Thomas Boules told him that he lett Lasie Coleman have soe much rum till he was soe drunke that he was forct to be Carried to his Canow

Albertus Henrickson being Attested declareth that he did see Harmon Johnson soe drunke att Thomas Boules house that he lay and * himselfe

Thomas Usher being Attested declareth that Samuell Weight did call for tife att Thomas Boules house and he heard Thomas Boules say why might he not have it since he doe pay for it.

Andrew ffriend being Attested declareth that Thomas Boules sold him and Wᵐ Cob two boules of Punch and att another time he sold y̆ᵉ Trumpeters sonne a Cann of Tife

The Jurys Verdickt: know this that we doe finde Thomas Boules Guilty according to y̆ᵉ Indicktment

Hereupon Judgmᵗ is granted & that he pay 10ˢ with cost of Suite.

Thomas Boules was also Presented by y̆ᵉ Grand Inquest for selling rum by small measure without lysence.

Witnes upon Sumons: Robert Brothers Andrew ffriend John Taylor: remitted upon Condition that he doe soe noe more and that he pay his fees

| Robert Eyre Clerke | Plᵗ | In an action of y̆ᵉ Case for Clerks fees and other |
| William Tally | Defendᵗ | Charges due from his Predicessor John Johnson |

The Plaintife Prooving his account Judgment is thereupon granted for y̆ᵉ sum of 3£ 00ˢ 10½ᵈ

WILLIAM TALLY	Pl^t	in an action of Trover and Conversion. Continued
ANDREW FFRIEND	Defend^t	

ROBERT EYRE Clerke	Pl^t	in an action of ye Case for Clerks fees
EDWARD PRITCHARD	Defend^t	

Upon Prooving ye account Judgment is granted for 13^s 4½^d

THOMAS BROWN JOHN	Pl^t	withdrawne
WILLIAM WHITE	Defend^t	

PETER BAYNTON	Pl^t	withdrawne
EDWARD JONNINS	Defend^t	

JONATHAN HAYES	Pl^t	withdrawne
ANDREW FFRIEND & ROBERT STEPHENS	Defend^{ts}	

Richard Crosby being Sumoned to appear att this Court to answer the Complaint of our Sovereigne Lord the king and the Cheife Proprietary for being Drunke and Comitting other misdemeanours was for ye same Indickted.

   The Grand Inquest finde the Bill.

 The names of ye psons bound over to Prosecute:

William Goford John Clue and Johannes ffriend.

 The Testimony of Anne Saunderlaine taken att Chester v^e 4th day of ye 5th moneth last before John Simcocke John Bristow ffrancis Harrison and Edward Beasar: Who being Attested declareth that upon ye 29th day of ye 4th moneth last Richard Crosby was in Drinke att Chester and very unruly.

 Phillip Denning being attested as afores^d declareth that ye same day Richard Crosby was very much disordered by drinke and that he was very abusive. Phillip Denning.

 William Goford being Attested declareth that Richard Crosby being much in Drinke Challenged ye Sweads or English or any other man att Cudgells Wrasling or any other such violent exercise and further more did Strike him upon ye head and did trip up his heeles twice and y^t he heard him say ye Sweades were rogues and did take part with ye Indians.

 John Clue being Attested as a foresaid declareth ye same.

Johannes ffriend being Attested as aforesaid declareth that he heard Richard Crosby call ye Sweads Rogues and that they did take part with ye Indians against ye English.

Before ye Petty Jury went out upon ye Cause he submitting himselfe unto ye Court was fined 5^s and ordered to pay Court Charges and soe to be Acquitted.

Ordered that Hugh Derby be Attested Constaple for ye Township of Thornbury and John Marten for Middle Towne

Anne the reliqut and Executrix of Neales Lawson late of Chester and Andrew ffriend her sonne Past a deed to Robert Wade for two ℔cells of Land in ye Towne of Chester dated ye 7th day of ye 7th moneth 1687.

ffrancis Harrison was fined by ye Court 30^s for absenting himselfe this Sesion.

The grand Inquest Presented a bill against Elius Keach for Spreading falce news Contrary to Law: remitted he doing soe noe more

ffrancis Smith Senior for and in ye Behalfe of himselfe and his wife Anne Past over a Deed unto Robert Eyre and Anne his wife &c dated ye seventh day of ye seventh moneth one thousand six hundred eighty six for a Plantation Conteining one hundred and fifty acres of land and premisses lying in Bethell alsoe ye Stocke of Horses Cattle & Hoggs thereupon to the same uses.

The names of those persons fined in ye Township of Chester for not appearing to mend ye High wayes

    Jonas Holmes absent 3 days, 6^s
    Richard ffew absent 2 days, 4^s
    Wm Coborne absent 3 days, 6^s
    George Churchman absent 2 days, 4^s
    Robert Barber 3 days, 6^s

The Court adjourne to ye 3^d day in ye 1st Weeke of ye 8th moneth next.

Att a Court held att Chester for y⁶ County of Chester y⁶ 3ᵈ day in y⁶ 1ˢᵗ Weeke of y⁶ 8ᵗʰ moneth 1687

{ John Bristow President
John Symcocke
John Blunstone
George Maris
Bartholomew Coppocke
Edward Beasar } Justices Present

Joshua ffirne Shreife
Robert Eyre Clerke

WILLIAM TALLY Plᵗ } in an action of Trover
ANDREW FFRIEND Defendᵗ

The names of y⁶ Petty Jury Sumoned

Hugh Durbury	ffrancis Chadsey	James Swaford
George Pearce	Jacob Chandler	William Swaford
Wᵐ Browne	Richard Buffington	Jacob Symcocke
Andrew Moore	Joseph Richards	Joshua Hastings

The Jury Called butt before they were Attested it was ordered to be referred

The Grand Inquest Presented Robert Moulder for suffering Thomas Clifton & Samuell Baker to be Drunke att his house where were present John Bradshaw William Haukes Isacke Warner

Witnes Attested William Tally

Ordered that they be all Summoned unto the next Court.

SAMUELL BAKER Plᵗ } in an action of Assault and
SAMUELL ROWLAND Defendᵗ Battery

Witnesses upon Sumons, Samuell Noyes, Thomas Green: ordered to be referred unto Caleb Pusie George fforeman & Joshua Hastings.

The arbitrators award that Samuell Rowland shall pay y⁶ lawfull Charges of this Court and give the said Samuell Baker a Hatt & so to Discharge each other of all manner of Differences from y⁶ Begining of the world to this Present day.

Hereupon Judgment is Granted.

James Browne required his Bayle Bond to be delivered up Samuell Rowland Appearing according to recognisence

Ordered that John Bradshaw doe pay the Shreife & Clerkes fees in his case against Nathaniell Lamplue ye last Court and that he bring it them to their Houses.

Albertus Henrickson was Attested vewer of Pipe Staves for this County

Ordered that ye Grand Inquest doe lay out a Sufficient Cart Road from Burmingham to Concord and from thence to ye Bridge near Chester Mill and from thence to Chester and that John Mendinghall and Nicholas Newland be assisting in ye matter

Thomas Wither was Sumoned to this Court att the Complaint of William Tally Successor to John Johnson for not making returne of a paire of Oxen formerly taken by James Kenerly Coroner upon Execution att ye Suite of ye said Withers and others vallued by ye appraisers att nine pounds & delivered by ye said Coroner into ye hands of the said Wither the then Shreife—who made returne as followeth, viz. Due to himselfe and Thomas Usher 4£ 8^s. Expence & Charge driving ye Oxen to Chester 13^s: 2 dayes spent weighting on ye Crowner 6^s: appraisers fees 2^s: 3^d: Robert Wads attachm^t 1£ 12^s: Shreifes fees 5^s 6^d: Coroners fees 4^s 6^d: Clerkes fees in Robert Wads Suite 8^s 10^d: amounting in all to ye sum of 8£ 00^s 01^d

Due to John Johnson 0 19 11

Ordered that ye Grand Inquest doe lay out a Sufficient Cart Road from Edgmond to Chester

Ordered that Thomas Wither pay for ye Sumons Issued out against him att ye Complaint of William Tally.

Nathaniell Evins Past over a Deed unto Richard Mason dated ye 4th day of ye 8th moneth 1687 for a parcell of Land Conteining 150 acres lying in ye Township of Ashtone.

John Harding one of the Commissioners was Called three times butt answer being made that he was sicke his fine was Excused by ye Court.

Jeremy Collett for his Insolency and abuse to ye Court and asserting lawes which he could not Produce being thereunto required by the Court was upon ye same ordered to finde Surties for his good behaviour & Appearance att ye next Court Butt upon Refusall was Comitted to ye Shreifes Custody.

ffrancis Harrison was Called three times but appearing not was fined thirty shillings

George fforeman for Confessing to ye Court that he kept ordinary Without Lysence was fined five pounds he submitting himselfe to ye Court.

Samuel Noyes paid 5^s for being drunk

John Shard was fined 10^s for being drunke this being ye second time.

The Court adjourne untill ye 3^d day in ye 1st Weeke of ye 10th mo^th next and began the Orphans Court

Att an Orphans Court held att Chester ye 3^d day in ye 1st Weeke of ye 8th moneth 1678. [1687]
{
John Bristow Presid^t
John Symcocke
John Blunstone
George Maris
Bartholomew Coppock
Edward Beasar
}

Joshua ffirne Shreife
Robert Eyre Clerke

Richard ffew Appearing was ordered to bring an account to ye next Orphans Court held ye 3^d day in ye 1st Weeke of ye 1st moneth next of the Estate usage and Imployment of his Grand Daughter Susanah ffew.

Margrett Smith Petitioned ye Court against Richard ffew for his Breach of Promise made to her relations in England.

Ordered that Richard ffew bring in his account of Charges against Margrett Smith ye next Court of Sesion.

The Court adjourne untill ye 3^d day in ye 1st Weeke of the 1st moneth next.

Att a Court held att Chester for y{e} County of Chester y{e} 3{d} day in y{e} 1{st} Weeke of the 10{th} moneth 1687

{ John Bristow Presid{t}
John Symcocke
John Blunstone
John Harding   } Justices
George Maris   present
Bartholomew Coppocke
Edward Beasar
ffrancis Harrison }

Joshua ffirne Shreife
Robert Eyre Clerke

THOMAS USHER Pl{t}   } in an action of y{e} Case.
THOMAS BOULES Defend{t} } withdrawne.

Jeremy Collett being Presented by y{e} Grand Inquest for his Assault and Breach of Peace Comitted against ffrancis Little under Shreife, and uppon his misbehaviour to y{e} last Court was for y{e} same Called to y{e} Barr & fined five pounds.

MORTEN CURNUTE Pl{t}   } in an action of y{e} Case
WILLIAM TALLY Defend{t} }

witnes upon Sum{ns}: Joel Bayly, Thomas Cooper.

The Declaration was read. The Defd{t} ownes taking y{e} Canow

The names of y{e} Jury

George Greaves	Thomas Vernon
Robert Vernon	Jacob Chandler
John Woorrell	John Child
Joseph Edge	George Churchman
William Maillon	John Edge
Peter Taylor	Richard ffew

Albertus Henrickson being Attested declareth that he knew Morton Cornutes Canow and that a man might make such a Canow for 15{s}.

John Harding being attested declareth that he did hale a small Canow out of y{e} Woods belonging to Morten Cornute and that it seemed to be a thicke bottom Strong Canow and very shorte.

The verdickt of y{e} Jury is the finde for y{e} Plaintife six

Pence Damage and to have ye Canow restored or 10^s for it with what the law allowes and Cost of Suite 6th 10th moneth 1687

Judgment is hereupon awarded

DANIELL LINSEY Pl^t
THOMAS BOULES Defend^t } in an action of ye Case

The names of ye Jury

Joshua Hastings	Randal Mailen
Caleb Pusey	Jacob Simcoeke
Joseph Bushell	David Ogden
Edward Carter	John Marten
Richard Mason	Joseph Richardson
Joseph Wood	James Swaford

The Declaration was read The Defend^t Pleads Nihill Habitt.

Witnesses upon Sumons.

Robert Brothers, James Hayes, William West.

Robert Brothers being Attested declareth that ye Defend^t told him that he had bought a Canow of ye Plaintife and that Samuel Weight told this Deponent that ye Defend^t was to pay 30^s for it and y^t ye Defend^t received ye Canow from this Deponent.

James Hayes being attested Declareth that he did see the Defend^ts negros make fast ye Canow and that they did it by ye Defend^ts ord^r and that ye Plaintife brought five shillings in Barley to ballance accounts with ye Defend^t which he refused to receive Saying twas noe Corne.

William West being attested declareth that ye Plaintife did offer Barley to ye Defend^t for pay which ye Defend^t refused Saying twas noe Corne

The Jurys Verdickt

Wee of ye Petty Jury doe finde for ye Plaintife thirty shillings being ye Price of ye Canow & Cost of Suite.

Judgment is hereupon granted.

George Wood Past over a Deed of Settlement to John Beaven and Joshua ffirne in Trust for a tract of land therein mentioned to y⁰ use and Behoofe of John Wood and Jane his wife dated y⁰ last day of y⁰ 9ᵗʰ moneth 1687.

John Simcocke Past over a Deed to John Steedman for sixty acres of Land lying and being in y⁰ Township of Ridley Dated y⁰ 6ᵗʰ day of y⁰ 7ᵗʰ moneth 1687.

Thomas Worth and Samuell Bradshaw Past over a deed to Joshua ffirne for fifty acres of Land lying in Darby dated y⁰ 4ᵗʰ day of y⁰ 8ᵗʰ moneth 1687

Joshua ffirne Past over a Deed to Thomas Bradshaw for a Parcell of Land Conteining sixty five acres lying in y⁰ Township of Darby dated y⁰ 6ᵗʰ day of y⁰ 7ᵗʰ moneth 1687

Thomas Powell Past over a Deed dated y⁰ 27ᵗʰ day of y⁰ 9ᵗʰ moneth 1686 unto Charles Whitacres for 200 acres of land lying upon Ridley Creeke

GEORGE ANDREWS Plᵗ ⎱ in an action of Debt
HENRY RENOLDS   Defendᵗ ⎰ Jury as in the Case of Morten Cornute and William Tally.

The Declaration was read

Robert Moulder being Attested declareth that he knoweth nothing of y⁰ matter touching y⁰ Plaintifes Attorniship to James Wroth

Nathaniell Thornton being Attested declareth y⁰ same as above

The Defendᵗ Pleads to have y⁰ Plaintifes letter of Attorney to James Wroth Prooved to be y⁰ Plaintifes act and deed which Thomas Usher Attorney to said Wroth not doing y⁰ Plaintife upon y⁰ same Suffered a non Suite

Richard ffew Petitioned against his former servant Margrett Smith

upon which John Buckley was Attested Who declareth that he brought noe Cloth out of England for y⁰ said Margrett

ROBERT MOULDER Plᵗ ⎱ in an action of y⁰ Case
WILLIAM TALLY   Defendᵗ ⎰ Jury as in y⁰ Case of Morton Cornute and William Tally.

The Declaration was read

James Browne being attested declareth that Margrett Johnsons mother enquiring of ye Pl^t where her daughter was he told her he knew not he thought shee knew Best Butt ye next day this deponent saith that he saw ye said Margarett making Hay in Company of ye Defend^t

And Mary Best being attested Declareth that after Mary Johnson had run away the Plaintife and his wife did often offer her time and oppertunity to vissitt her Perents and that shee have often run away since without any occation given her.

Morton Canute being legally Attested Declareth that Margrett Johnson told him that shee did looke after her Parrents Cattle and that shee could not live with ye Plaintife by reason of her hard usage by ye Plaintifes wife and Mary Bisse and that shee further told him her father knew nothing of her being att home butt her mother did And ye next day after shee came againe with her Parence Cattle to this Deponents where he shewed her a Paper threatning her that if shee came any more he would send her to her master Moulder.

William Hamby being attested Declareth that the Defend^t and his wife came to the Plaintifes upon a first day of ye weeke ye Defend^{ts} wife Pretending shee came to looke her Daughter Margretts head upon which ye Plaintifes wife answered shee would make her doe it her selfe the Defend^{ts} wife replyed she was Better be Damned then meddle with her.

William Haukes being Attested for ye Defend^t Declareth that he heard ye Plaintife say att his owne House that he would be troubled himselfe noe more with her as a servant since George Stroad had given his Judgment that ye Indenture was not good

The verdickt of ye Jury is they allow ye Plaintife twenty seven shillings with Cost of Suite and ye Girle to remaine with her mother. Hereupon, Judgment is Granted.

The Court adjourne untill ye next morning eighth Houre and mett againe according to adjournment

JOHN MAYOW   Pl^t   ⎫
ANNE JOHNSON   Defend^t ⎬ nonsuite
                                     ⎭
   Witnesses upon Sumons John Neales John Marten.

WILLIAM TALLY   Pl^t   ⎫
ROBERT EYRE   Defend^t ⎬ in an action of ye Case
                                     ⎭
               The names of ye Jury

Joshua Hasstings	Joseph Richards
Walter ffausett	James Swaford
Joseph Wood	Joseph Baker
Randall Maylen	Wm Cloud Junior
David Ogden	Thomas Cartwrite
John Marten	Edward Carter

Before ye Jury went out upon ye Cause ye Pl^t suffered a nonsuite

ffrancis Harrison Past over a Deed unto Jacob Chandler dated ye 6th day of ye 7th moneth 1687, for three tracts of land laid out by lott in ye Township of Chichester Conteining one hundred twenty six acres

James Saunderlaine was Attested Consaple for ye Township and liberty of Chester or that he see ye office Duely Executed untill another be attested in his Roome which service is upon ye account of his father in Law Urine Keens farme which ye s^d James Purchased.

William Chambers Past over an Indenture unto Jeremy Collett for four years service from ye date of ye s^d Indenture.

ELIUS KEACH   Pl^t   ⎫
WILLIAM WHITE   Defend^t ⎬ in an action of ye Case.
                                     ⎭

Witnes upon Sumons, John Child William Tally and his wife: nonsuite

JOHN MAYOW   Pl^t   ⎫
THOMAS CARTWRIGHT   Defend^t ⎬
                                           ⎭

Jury called as in ye Case of Robert Eyre and William Tally Except Jacob Chandler for Thomas Cartwright: nonsuite

A negro man and a White Woman servant being taken up

by John Bradshaw Nathaniel Lukins Isacke Warner and Samuell Rowland and brought before John Simcocke, Justice in Commission for runaways, Who upon Examination finding they had noe lawfull Passe Comitted them to Prison and this day was delivered by order of Court into ye Custody of Thomas Smith and John Henson with a Black nagg

The Shreife made returne of an Execution Levied upon a Horse belonging to William Tally as successor to John Johnson att ye suite of Robert Eyre Clerke which Horse was appraised att 4£ 15^s (viz)

ffor Shreifes fees serving Execution	00£	01^s	06^d
for Serving ye Sumons	00	02	00
for a Warrant	00	01	06
for Clerks fees	00	08	04½
for Expencis	00	02	06
for keeping ye Horse	00	05	03
for Appraisers fees	00	00	06
for ye Prime Debt	3	00	10½
	4	2	06

Jeremy Collett Petitioned to have his fine remitted which was ordered this Court to be levied upon him

The Court Considering his Petition and that he putts himselfe upon ye mercy of ye King and Govern^r mittigates his former fine and admitts him to a fine of 10/ to be levied upon his goods &c with all manner of Court Charge to Shreife & Clerks &c

John Worell Petitioned against ye road laid out by ye Grand Inquest from Edgmond to ye Kings High way in Chester ordered that ye road be made by the Petitioners fence

ffrancis Little was fined 5/ and Suspended selling drinke and keeping ordinary for suffering George Stroad to be drunk in his House.

George Stroad was finned 5/ for his being Drunke att the s^d ffrancis Littles.

Ordered that all Warrants for Publicke uses to be levied by

the Constaples this Court be paid in by the Inhabitance living on yᵉ upper side of Ridley Creeke to John Simcocke and on yᵉ lower Side to John Bristow, Tresurars appointed for yᵉ same.

Ordered that Warrants be Directed to yᵉ respective Constaples of each Township in this County for raising of a Levie to be used toward yᵉ destroying Woolves and other Hurtfull Vermin as followes (viz)

for all Lands taken up and Inhabited one shilling for every hundred Acres

for all Lands taken up by non residence and soe remaining unoccupied eighteen pence for every hundred acres

all free men from sixteen years of adge to sixty one shilling —all Servants soe qualified six Pence

Joseph Baker returned John Hoolistone Supervisor of yᵉ High wayes for yᵉ Township of Edgmond for yᵉ next ensuing year

Richard Crosby was presented Supervisor of yᵉ High wayes for Middletowne (by John Marten Constaple of yᵉ same) for the next ensuing year

Ordered that yᵉ Township of Darby finde out a Convenient High way from thence to yᵉ Township of Hartford.

Ordered also that High wayes be laid out by yᵉ Grand Inquest or any five of them from Newtowne Marple and Springfield to yᵉ landing att Amos Land.

Andrew Carolus was attested Constaple for yᵉ Township of Ridley for yᵉ next ensuing year

The Grand Inquest Presented Thomas Boules of yᵉ Island of Tenecum for killing and Converting to his owne use divers Hoggs and Piggs of Thomas Smith with others belonging to yᵉ Leidge People; Thomas Smith prosecutor.

Witnesses Nathaniel Dawson, Mouns Peterson, John Henrickson, James Hayes.

The Grand Inquested Presented George ffloreman for rescuing one Cox from Robert Barber, then Constaple of Chester. Butt Before Conviction the said ffloreman Protesting inoncency and not willing to Plead with yᵉ King and Govenour putts himselfe upon their mercy and craves to be admitted to a fine upon which he is fined 5/ to ye Governours use to be levied by ye Shreife of this County and that ye said George pay all Court Charges and Shreife and Clerks fees.

The Grand Inquest doe also Present Annie Neales Widdow for keeping and Harbouring Doggs that woories and kills her neighbours Hoggs as alsoe for Deteining in her Service one Indian Boy named Chato who with ye said Dogg have been found to woory and kill ye neighbours Hoggs as aforesd. Walter ffausett Prosecutor

Witnesses Walter ffausett John Symcocke Junr

The said Anne Neales came into Court and before her arreignm^t declared that ye said Dogg Belonged to one Peter Cox butt because shee is not willing to Pleade to the said Indicktment Putts herselfe upon ye mercy of ye King & Governour and Craves to be admitted to a fine upon which shee is fined tenne shillings and to pay all Court Charges with Shreifes and Clerks fees &c.

Andrew ffriend became bound to ye King and Governour in twenty pounds for ye Indian Boyes Catos good abareing towards all ye Kings Leidge People

Robert Moulder being ye last Court Indickted for Suffering Thomas Clifton and Samuell Baker to be Drunke att his house was upon ye same called to ye Barr Butt nothing being Prooved against him he is acquitted paying his fees & ordered to keep an ordinary provided he keep Horse meate and mans meate.

Andrew Moore made over a Deed Dated ye 6th day of ye 10th moneth 1687 unto John Moore for fifty acres of land lying in Ashtone

October ye 25 day 1687

Laid out a High way from Burmingham to Concord being a thirty foote way by vertue of an order of Court bearing date ye 4th of October 1687 laid out by us Walter Marten John Mendenhall John Kingsman William Cloud Rich Thatcher being one third part of ye present grand Jury of ye County of Chester as followes (viz)

Beginning att a White Oake Standing on a Small Branch att William Brantons marked with five knotches thence along a lyne of marked trees between Alice Brunson and land lat Edward Turner to Concord Corner tree thence downe Concord lyne Between ye said Alice Brunson and Phillip Roman to a White Oake marked with five knotches then Crosse ye Corner of said Phillip Romans land then Crosse William Hitchcocks land then Crosse land that was William Biases thence Crosse John Mendenhalls land thence Crosse land that was Peter Lounders then Crosse part of John Symcockes land to ye foote Bridge of Thomas Moore then crosse part of ye said Thomas Moores land to a White Oake marked with five knotches.

Laid out by vertue of ye aforesaid Order a fourty foote Road from Concord to ye Kings High way in Chester as followeth by us whose hands are under Written ye 25th of October 1687.

Beginning at a White Oake with five knotches standing att ye Corner of Nathaniell Parks land next Thomas Moors land thence through ye land of ye said Nathaniell thence cross John Hannums land thence Crosse George Stroads land thence crosse John Palmers land thence crosse land late William Oburnes thence Crosse land late John Beasars thence Crosse Dennis Rochfords Land thence Crosse William Clayton Juni^r land to ye Hamlett of Bethell.

Thence Crosse Edward Beasars land thence Crosse ffrancis Smiths land thence Crosse Robert Eyres land to Chichester, Thence Crosse Walter Martens land thence Crosse land late John Beasars thence Crosse John Kingsmans land thence Crosse Henry Hastings and Richard Buffingtons land thence Crosse James Browns land thence Thomas Withers land to Chester.

Then Crosse part of Robert Wads land to a small blacke Oake marked with 5 knotches standing att the kings High Way. Walter Marten, John Mendenhall, Richard Thatcher, John Kingsman, William Cloud. Likwise by vertue of ye abous^d Order of Court being dated ye 4th of October 1687 new altered the Kings high Way by us whose hands are under written ye 25th of Octob^r 1687 as followeth in Chester (viz)

Beginning att a small blacke marked with five knotches in Robert Wads land thence through part of ye said Robert Wads land thence Crosse John Mathorks land thence downe to ye Creeke in ye mill land to ye Bridge from thence over by ye mill head round ye side of ye Hill in ye mill land thence streight through Caleb Puesyes land to ye Old Kings High way

Walter Marten, John Mendenhall, Rich Thatcher, John Kingsman William Cloud.

December ye 11th 1687

Laid out a High way from Edgmond to ye Kings High way in Chester being a sixty foote road by vertue of an order of Court bearing date ye 4th of October 1687 laid out by us whose hands are under Written as followeth (viz)

Beginning att Joseph Bakers fence of his Cleared land thence through ye land of ye said Joseph Baker thence crosse William Lewis land thence Crosse Howel James land thence Crosse Jacob Simcocks land thence Crosse James Kenerly thence Crosse a parcell of vacant Land then Crosse Roger Jackson thence Crosse vacant land thence Crosse John Boweter land thence Crosse David Ogdens land thence Crosse John Hodgkins land thence Crosse George Smedleys land thence Crosse Wm Edwards land thence Widdow Misgroves land thence Crosse Robert Burrowes land thence Crosse John Maylens land thence Crosse John Bowetters land thence Crosse Joseph Cooksons land thence Crosse Jeremy Carters land thence Crosse Richard Barnards land thence Crosse John Worells land thence Crosse Thomas Taylors land then Crosse Richard Crosbyes land then Crosse John Martens land then Crosse John Hastens land. Walter Marten, John Beales Edward Pritchard, George Willard, Wm Coborne.

Att a Court held at Chester for ye County of Chester ye sixth day of ye 1st moneth 1687

{ John Bristow Presidt
Bartholomew Coppocke
ffrancis Harrison
George Maris
Edward Beasar } Justices

Joshua ffirne Shreife
Robert Eyre Clerke

John ffriend Mounse Locke and Andrew ffriend was called three times to save their recognisence butt made noe appearance.

William Tally being presented the last Court by ye grand Inquest for keeping and deteining a Strayed Calfe was upon ye same Called to ye Barr and upon his submission ordered to pay all Charges of Court

Richard Buffington was called to ye Barr to answer his Contempt of an order of Petty Sessions held ye 27th day of ye 10th moneth last att George fforemans:

remitted paying his fees

Thomas Boules was Called three times to Safe his recognisence butt appeared not.

Upon which Joseph Wood being attested declareth that he seemed to him to be sick upon which his tryall is suspended untill ye next Court

Nathaniel Evins Supervisor of ye High wayes for Chester Presented Caleb Pusie and John Hodskins for not laying ye Plankes on ye bridge over Chester Creeke.

Thomas Marten made over a deed (by assignment) dated ye 1st day of ye 1st moneth 1685 unto Caleb Pusie and Thomas Crosse for seventy three acres of land & Premisses lying and being in Middletowne

Walter Marten made over a Deed dated ye 22th day of ye 7th moneth 1687 for fifty acres of land in ye Township of Chichester unto William Thomas

The names of ye Constaples Chosen to serve ye next ensuing year

ffor Burmingham	Richard Thatcher	
Concord	William Collett	
Chichester	Richard Buffington	attested in Court
Ashtone	John Neales	
Marple	George Williard	attested as above
Springfield	Joseph Lounes	attested as above
Darby	Samuell Sellars	
Middletowne	Robert Pennell	
Upper Providence	John Calvert	
Newtowne	Joseph Humphryes	

The names of y'e' Grand Inquest attested att this Court (viz)

William Branton	Peter Lester
Thomas Crosse	George Gleaves
George fforeman	John Edge
Woola Rosen	Jonathan Hayes
Edward Carter	Peter Peterson
John Sharple	Samuell Bradshaw
James Staznfield	Richard Bondsall
Thomas Marten	William Woodmanson
	John Baldwin

Robert Pennell was finned 5^s for not appearing to be attested upon y'e' grand Inquest

John Blunstone Thomas Worth and Samuel Bradshaw past over a deed unto Henry Gibbons for 10 acres of land lying in y'e' Township of Darby

Robert Stephens past over a Deed unto Nathaniel Lokins dated y'e' 5th day of y'e' 1st moneth 1687 for 250 acres of land lying in Burmingham

John Mendenhall and Benjamine Mendenhall made over a Deed for 100 acres of land lying in Concord dated y'e' 5th day of february 1687 unto George Pearce of Thornbury

George Pearce made over a Deed of y'e' same land dated this Instant unto y'e' said Benjamine Mendenhall

George Maris made over a Deed dated this Instant for a Parcell of land Conteining 280 acres unto Phillip Yarnall for severall Considerations therein mentioned

George Willard made over a deed dated this Instant unto Roger Jackson for a parcell of land lying and being in this County Conteining 220 acres

Urine Keen made over a Deed dated ye 1st day of ye 1st moneth 1687 unto John Simcocke Thomas Brassy John Bristow Caleb Pussey Randall Vernon Thomas Vernon Joshua Hastings Mordecay Maddock Thomas Marten Richard ffew Walter ffausett & Edward Carter for a peece of land Conteing as therein mentioned lying and being in Chester Towne to ye uses therein mentioned

The Inhabitance of ye Township of Astone Petitioned for one Road Way to ye Towne of Chester and another to ye Towne of Chichester

Upon the 9th of ye 12th moneth 1687

By vertue of an order from ye last County Court given to us whose names are hereunto subscribed being of ye Grand Jury for to lay out a road way that should serve for Newtowne Marple and Springfield and ye Inhabitance that way to ye landing Place att Amos land did upon ye day above written Begin att a Road way in ye land of George Maris which road goeth from Chester through Marple to Newtowne soe from that road through Bartholomew Coppocks land near to his house his House being on ye left hand soe on through Robert Taylors land streight on through more of George Maris his land leaving his Plantation on ye right hand soe bearing on a little on ye right hand through George Simcocks land soe on through Jacob Simcocks land leaving his Plantation on ye left hand soe on streight forward through Land joyning to Amos land soe into ye Kings road that comes from Darby marking the trees as wee came soe on to ye landing Place by the maine creeks Side beyond Morten Mortensons House William Garrett Richard Parker Edmond Cartleidge Thomas Bradshaw Thomas ffox

A High way laid out by ye grand Jury and other neighbours betwixt Hartfoot and Darby upon ye 7th day of the twelfe moneth 1687 Beginning at Widow Panthirs and from thence on ye head lyne betwixt ye said Widdows land and ye land of John Lewis from thence Crosse ye land of William Howell from thence Crosse ye land of Arthur Bruce from thence crosse ye land of Henry Lewis thence Entring the Township of Darby from thence Crosse ye land of Adam Roads thence crosse ye land of John Kirk then Crosse ye land of Matthew Gratton then Crosse ye land of Joshua ffirne then Crosse ye land of William Garrett then Crosse ye land of Michael Blunstone then Crosse ye land of George Wood then Crosse ye land of Robert Smith then Crosse ye land of Thomas Worth thence Coming upon the land of Joshua ffirne soe downe ye Towne Street of Darby to ye Kings road and soe to ye Landing this High way to be sixty foote as need requires

William Garrett, Richard Parker, Edmond Cartledge, Thomas Bradshaw, Thomas ffox.

The Court adjourne unto ye 10th day of ye 1st mo 1687

Att an Orphans Court held att Chester ye 6th day of ye 1st moneth 1687

Where was Present
John Bristow President
Bartholomew Coppocke
ffrancis Harrison
George Maris
Edward Beasar
} Justices

Joshua ffirne Shreife
Robert Eyre Clerke

Ordered that Phillip Roman doe forthwith gett out letters of Administration from ye Registry of this County in the behalfe of his Predisesor William Beasar Diseaced and that he give in Security according to law faithfully to performe his trust according to Enventory

Ordered that Jane Sharples give in Security to this Court faithfully and Truely to discharge her trust as Administratrix to her Diseaced Husband John Sharples

Ordered that William Tally give in Security to this Court faithfully and Truely to Discharge his trust as Administrator in the right of his wife to his Predisesor John Johnson

Ordered that Joseph Wood sonne and heire to William Wood Disceased doe forthwith gett letters of Administration from ye Registry of this County and that he give Security to this Court faithfully to discharge his trust

Ordered that ffrancis Little give in Security to this court to pay unto John Simcocke and Thomas Brasie as trustees to William and Elin Baines for ye sum of twenty Eight shillings

The Court adjourne unt ye 3^d day in ye 1st Weeke of ye 8th mo next

---

Att a Court held att Chester for ye County of Chester ye 10th day of ye 1st moneth 1687

John Bristow President
John Blunstone
George Maris
ffrancis Harrison
Bartholomew Coppock

} Justices

Joshua ffirne Shreife
Robert Eyre Clerke

Thomas Boules was Called three times to save his Traverse butt not appearing his surety John Hodskins was ordered to bring the Body of ye said Thomas into this Court by the afternoone of this day

This Court being Informed that Richard Crosby was Drunk on this 6th Instant last he was upon ye same Called to ye Barr And upon his submission was amerced tenne shillings to the Governours use to be levied upon his goods and Chattles this being the second time.

John ffriend Mounse locke and Andrew ffriend was called to the Barr the two former John and Mounse onely appearing was demanded why Judgment should not Passe against them upon ye forfiture of their recognisence the last Court.

John Grubb Petitioned for Payment of Boards which he formerly Delivered to ye use of the Court House—granted

The Court adjourne till 3 in ye afternoone and mett according to adjournment

Thomas Boules making his Appearance was Called to ye Barr upon a former Traverse att a Court held y 3^d day in the 1st

Weeke of the 10th moneth 1687, To which he Pleads not Guilty and referrs himselfe to God and the Country.

Witnesses whose Testimoneys being taken before in Writing remaines upon yᵉ ffile.

Mounse Peterson
Emanuell Dauson
John Henrickson
James Hayes

The names of yᵉ Petty Jury all accepted by yᵉ Prisoner:

Caleb Pusie
John Mendenhall
John Wood
Joseph Baker
Jeremy Carter
Robert Barber
Thomas Rawlenson
Joseph Edge
Richard ffew
Edward Peerson
John Marten
Benjamine Mendenhall.

John Henrickson being againe attested in Oppen Court saith yᵗ yᵉ last fall he was up mill or Darby Creeke where he heard two gunns goe of and when he came to yᵉ place he heard dogs barque & Thomas Boules with his Gunn Presented and did Shoote att his Neighbours Hogs and that James Hayes was with him yᵉ said Boules and further saith that he yᵉ said James sᵈ that Boules was an Old ffoole for shooting twice and missing.

Peter Peterson being Attested in Oppen Court declareth that Thomas Boules did say that Tho: Smith might fetch away his sow butt not yᵉ Piggs and yᵗ yᵉ saw was bought of his ffathʳ Mounse Peterson and delivered at sᵈ Mouns plantation and furthʳ he saith yᵗ he did see Tho Boules catch a small shoate from John Henricksons sow & give his negro to carry home

Mounse Peterson being againe attested in Oppen Court saith yᵗ he heard Tho: Boules say that Tho: Smith might fetch yᵉ sow butt yᵗ he would kill yᵉ Piggs markt or unmarkt.

Wee of yᵉ Petty Jury doe finde Thomas Boules Guilty of yᵉ Indicktment wherein he stands Indickted.

Judgment is hereupon granted and that he pay Thomas Smith 32ˢ and all Court Charges.

Richard Mason was Attested Supervisor of the High wayes for the Township of Astone

John ffriend and Mouns locke Petitioned y[e] Court to have their neglect of appearance to their Recognisence taken of

Ordered that it be remitted paying all Court Charges

The Township of Astone Petitioned to have two High Roads laid out one leading from thence to Chester y[e] other to Chichester.

Ordered that George fforeman with any other six of y[e] Grand Inquest doe lay out a Sufficient Cart Road from Astone to Chester as alsoe another Sufficient Cart Road from s[d] Astone to Chichester Ord[r]ed alsoe that neither Edward Carter nor William Woodmansee be of y[e] number of y[e] six

John Edge was Attested Supervisor of the High wayes for y[e] Township of Lower Providence.

The Testimony of Harmon Johnson in the aforegoing Case of Thomas Boules and Ought there to be Entred

Who being lawfully Attested Declareth that he did see a graw Sow the last fall upon Tenicome Island with a White face and four Piggs by her side and that he knew y[e] sow had been Mouns Petersons.

The Court adjourne unto y[e] 3[d] day of y[e] 2[d] Weeke of y[e] 7th moneth next

---

Att a Court held att Chester for y[e] County of Chester the 3[d] day in y[e] 1st Weeke of y[e] 4th mo[th] 1688

John Symcocke Presid[t]
John Bristow
George Maris
Bartholomew Coppocke
} Justices Present

Joshua ffirne Shreife
Robert Eyre Clerke

NATHANIEL THORNTON	Pl[t]	} in an action of y[e] Case Withdrawne
JOHN PREW	Defend[t]	
WILLIAM HAUKES	Pl[t]	} in an action of Debt
HENRY RENOLDS	Defend[t]	

The names of yᵉ Petty Jury

Nathaniel Thornton	John Child
James Swaford	Richard ffarr
Joseph Richards	Caleb Pusie
John Worrell	Thomas Robinson
Randall Vernon	Richard Woodworth
John Beales	William Browne

James Saunderlaine being Attested declareth that about yᵉ latter end of March last the Plaintife meeting with this Deponent yᵉ Plᵗ told him he had a Bill given by one vines to yᵉ Defendᵗ and assigned by yᵉ Defendᵗ to yᵉ Plᵗ Who att yᵉ Same time made over said Bill to this Deponent Who carring yᵉ same downe into this Bay Demanded payment for yᵉ same of yᵉ said Vines Who denyed payment Saying he had paid yᵉ greatest part to one Plumer by a former assignment (by one Streatcher) Upon which for further Information this deponent went to said Streatcher Butt meeting with his Book-keeper he afirmed that his master Streatcher had paid yᵉ greatest part of said Bill, already to said Plumer and that he was ready to attest yᵉ same.

Edward Jonnins Being attested Saith When yᵉ Plᵗ came to an account with yᵉ Defendᵗ yᵉ Defendᵗ was Indebted unto yᵉ Plᵗ in yᵉ sum of two shillings and three pence which with 58ˢ yᵉ Defendᵗ received of James Browne made up 3£ 00ˢ 3ᵈ for wᶜʰ odd 3ᵈ yᵉ Plᵗ had of yᵉ Defendᵗ one Pott of Peach Drinke upon which Henry Renolds Produced Vines bill for 3£ with a former assignment in favour of Thomas Plumer which yᵉ Plᵗ denyed to take untill yᵉ Defendᵗ affirmed that said Bill was never sent downe for paymᵗ nor received by said Plumer uppon which yᵉ Plᵗ tooke yᵉ Bill

Joseph Richards Horeman yᵉ 5ᵗʰ of yᵉ 4ᵗʰ moneth 1688

The verdickt is They ffinde for yᵉ Plaintife that yᵉ Defendᵗ doe pay yᵉ Plaintife the Sum of three pounds with Cost of Suite and 2ᵈ Damage. Hereupon judgment is granted

Henry Jones   Plᵗ   ⎫ in an action of yᵉ Case and
James Browne Defendᵗ ⎭ declares for 152£ 1ˢ 4ᵈ

Jury as in yᵉ aforegoing Case of Wᵐ Haukes and Henry Renolds Except Phillip Roman and ffrancis Chadsey for John Beales and Wᵐ Browne.

The Defendᵗ in his answer Setts forth yᵉ Declaration to be falce untrue and vexatious

The names of those Witnesses taken in Writting which remains upon the file

Cornelius Emson, Isacke Warner, Thomas Green, for yᵉ Defendᵗ.

Joseph Jones being attested declareth yᵉ account to be true and Just and that James Browne did acknowledge yᵉ same.

Zacary Patricke being attested in Oppen Court for yᵉ Defendᵗ declareth that Henry Jones did order James Browne to give him one gallon of Rum to make hast with yᵉ Pipe Staves and did aske him when he Came over yᵉ River whether he could hew Tymber as even as a Dye

Katherne Davis being attested in Oppen Court declareth for yᵉ Defendᵗ that shee did hear Henry Jones give order to James Browne to give Zacary Patricke one gallon of rum to make hast with yᵉ Pipe Staves and yᵉ Tymber att Rackcoone Creeke.

Joseph Jones being againe attested in Oppen Court for yᵉ Plᵗ declareth that his father Henry Jones ordered him to make Bills for yᵉ Ballance of yᵉ Defendᵗˢ account upon which yᵉ Defendᵗ desired the Plᵗ to know in what Produce who answered in Indian Corne and Wheate upon which yᵉ Defendᵗ replyed he would goe downe and sell two Plantations and in 14 dayes would come againe and pay it in money.

The 5ᵗʰ of yᵉ 4ᵗʰ moneth Joseph Richards fforeman 1688

The verdickte of yᵉ Jury is yᵗ yᵉ Defendᵗ doe pay to yᵉ Plᵗ thirty pounds in Tymber at 4¼ᵈ ℔ foote and fifty pounds in Pipe Staves att 2£ 10ˢ ℔ thousand and yᵉ remainder is to be paid in other Lawfull produce of yᵉ Country alsoe with Cost of Suite and 2ᵈ Damage.

Hereupon Judgment is Granted.

Richard Crosby Pl^t } referred
Robert Moulder Defend^t

Jonathan Hey Pl^t } not sumoned
John Calvert Defend^t

Joseph Baker as Attorney to William Lewis made over a Deed by assignment dated ye 10th day of ye 1st moneth 1688 for 400 acres of land and premisses unto Worrylaw which was formerly made over by deed from John Bristow to ye s^d Lewis dated ye 15th day of ye 7th moneth 1686

Elizabeth Steedman made over a deed dated ye 5th day of ye 4th moneth 1687 unto Peter Thomas for fifty acres of land in Springtowne.

George Strode made over a lease and release for 200 acres of Land unto Henry Renolds to be taken up the lease dated ye 1st day of March 1686/7 and ye release dated ye 2^d day of ye Same Instant

John Hannum made over a deed dated ye 5th day of ye 4th moth 1688 unto John Wickham for 105 acres of land lying in Concord.

John Blunstone Past over a Deed for 2 parcells of land Conteining 250 acres (viz) 100 acres in Newtowne and 150 acres in Darby dated ye 6th day of ye 4th moneth 1688

Ordered that the Townships of Upper and Neither Providence and Ridley doe for this time repaire ye Bridge in ye Kings road near Walter ffaussetts and uppon Croome Creeke

Thomas Brasie for himselfe and as Attorney to Edward Gibbs made over a Deed dated ye 6th day of ye 4th moneth 1688 for a parcell of Land lying on ye West Syde of Darby Creeke unto Edward Person which s^d land Conteines 200 acres.

James Saunderlaine past over all his right and title to ye above mentioned land and ꝑmisses ye same time by assignm^t upon ye above deed to ye aforesaid Thomas Person

The Grand Inquest ꝑsented Thomas Eveson and Elizabeth Woodward for ye Sin of fornication

The said Thomas Eveson acknowledging ye fact and not

willing to plead thereunto putts himselfe upon ye mercy of ye King and Govern^r upon which ye said Thomas Eveson with Richard Woodward become bound unto ye King and Governour in ye Penalty of 40£ that ye said Thomas Eveson shall Contract marriage with ye above named Elizabeth Woodward att or before ye 6th day of ye 5th moneth next.

The names of ye Justices who was absent

John Blunstone Edward Beasar ffrancis Harrison.

The names of ye Grand Inquest absent

Thomas Crosse Jonathan Hayes Richard Bondsall.

Thomas Garretts ear marke a Swallow forke in both ears

The Court adjourne untill ye 3^d day in ye 1st Weeke of ye 8th month next

---

Att a Court held att Chester for ye County of Chester ye 3^d day in ye 2^d Weeke of ye 7th moth 1688

John Bristow Presid^t
John Simcocke
Bartholomew Coppocke
George Maris
John Blunstone

} Justices ℙsent

Joshua ffirne Shreife
Robert Eyre Clerke

The names of ye grand Inquest attested

Thomas Person   Walter ffausett
John Smith   Thomas Minshaw
John Hallawell   Randall Vernon
John Whood   Peter Taylor
Joseph Need   Robert Pennel
Robert Taylor   George Pearce
Bartho Coppock Senr Nathaniel Newland
Daniel Williamson   Jacob Chandler
Joseph Humpry

Hannah Taylor   Pl^t
Thomas Boules   Defend^t
} in an action of ye Case

Ordered that ye Defend^t give a Penall Bond for ye Debt and Court Charges and soe the action to be Withdrawne.

Joseph Wood	Pl^t	in an action of Debt
Robert Eyre	Defend^t	Withdrawne
John Clerke	Pl^t	in an action of ye Case
Michael Isard	Defend^t	Withdrawne
Joseph Richards	Pl^t	in an action of Debt
William Buckenham	Defend^t	

The names of ye Petty Jury

  John Worrell   Richard Woodworth
  Robert Barber   Robert Woodworth
  Thomas Vernon   Benj Mendenhall
  James Browne   Caleb Pusie
  Robert Chamberlaine   John Mendenhall
  Thomas Rawlenson   Jonathan Hayes

The Jury was Attested butt before they went out uppon ye Case ye Defend^t Confessed Judgm^t for 6£ 5^s

Roger Waldron	Pl^t	in an action of ye Case
Thomas Colborne	Defend^t	

The names of ye Petty Jury

  Jno Worrell   Richard Woodworth
  Robt Barber   Robert Woodworth
  Thomas Vernon   Benj Mendenhall
  James Browne   Richard Buffington
  Robt Chamberlaine   John Child
  Thomas Rawlenson   Jonathan Hayes

Caleb Pusie Being attested for ye Pl^t declareth as before Thomas Brasy have attested ye Same and further saith that he & ye said Brasie did desire ye Defend^t to pay 49^s for ye 3^s which ye Defend^t received of Richard Ridgway ye Pl^t Concenting to ye Same

Thomas Brasie being attested for ye Pl^t declareth that being desired by ye Pl^t to goe to Thomas Colbornes house he ye Pl^t did there offer to take 20^s lesse then ye meeting ordered him to receive of ye Defend^t.

William Woodmansee being attested for ye Defend^t Declareth that ye Pl^t Importuned him to Speake to his master y^e

Defend^t to Dispose of his time to one Richard Rudgway which he doing the Defend^t Seemed to be unwilling telling this Deponent that he would teach him his trade butt att last prevailling with ye Defend^t for his Concent the Pl^t for ye Same thanked him for his Kindness.

The verdickt of the Jury is they finde for ye Defend^t with cost of Suite and 2^d Damage

Lassy Coleman of West Jersey being Convicted for being Drunke att this towne of Chester was for ye same called to ye Barr Butt submitting to ye Court was fined 5^s to ye Govern^{rs} use

Thomas Robins and Thomas Woodmans being Convickted before John Bristow for Drunkennes breach of Peace breaking ye great Cabin doore and ye head of Samuel Harison mate on board of ye Ship Tryall was for ye Same Called to ye Barr Butt upon their submission to ye Court was ordered to pay 5^s/ with all Court Charges

Caleb Pusie came volentarily into Oppen Court and Confessed Judgment to Robert Turner upon ye twenty two thirty two parts of Chester Mill and Premisses being for Security of Bills of Exchange drawne by ye said Caleb Pusie on Daniel Wherely and Company Owners of s^d mill for ye vallue of one hundred Eighty Seven pounds English money bearing date ye 21th day of ye 4th moneth to be paid att 40 dayes sight

Ordered that ye grand Inquest doe vew all ye High wayes that have been lately laid out and doe as they see fitt alter or change ye same and that noe lesse then twelve doe make report thereof to ye next County Court

The grand Inquests presentments

We of the grand Inquest doe p̄sent Samuel Rowland for [offering abuse to Woley Rosen's wife and] his abuse to Woley Rosen in laying violent hands upon him and Stricking him throughing him on ye ground and taking him by the throat near to strangling him.

George fforeman and Jeremy Collett came Into Court and acknowledged themselves Joyntly and Severally bound in y^e

Penalty of fourty pounds to be levied upon their goods & Chattles of ye Shreife of this County to ye Proprietary and Governours use that ye aboves^d Samuel Rowland shall appear att ye next County Court held for this County there to answer ye Premisses and that ye s^d Samuel shall not depart ye Court without leave

Wee likewise p^rsent George fforeman for hauing knowledge of ye same Disorder afores^d and not p^rsenting itt being one of the Grand Inquest.

George fforeman came Into Court and acknowledged himselfe bound in ye Penalty of fourty pounds to be levied upon his goods and Chattles by ye shreife of this County to ye use of ye Proprietary and Governour that he doe personally appear att ye next County Court held for this County there to answer ye Pmisses and not to depart ye said Court without leave.

Wee likewise p^rsent Jacob Johnson Rignea Johnson and Gurstow Johnson for their abuse to Edward Pritchard upon Edward Pritchards Complaint

Ordered that their ffather John Vanculine doe pay the just Charges Edward Pritchard have Contracted in and about ye Pmisses in ye space of one Weeke from this time (they first submitting themselves to ye Court)

Wee likewise Psent Edward Pritchard for his abuse to ye said Boyes upon his owne Confession.

Butt upon his submission to ye Court it was ordered that he live quietely without giving Occation of Disturbance or if any doe arise to Complaine to ye majestrates.

Wee likewise Psent Joseph Colborne for his abuse to Thomas Lassey both by tongue and hands upon ye s^d Thomas Lasseys Complaint. Upon which he was Called three times butt making noe appearance he was ordered to be Sumoned to ye next Court

George fforeman Petitioned for this pay that is Due unto him upon ye account of ye Court house and Prison

Ordered that a Corce be taken there about att ye next County Court.

George Strode Nathaniel Parker John Palmer John Hannum Thomas Moore John Sanger Robert Pile Petitioneg against ye Road lately laid out through the towne of Concord:

Ordered that ye Grand Inquest doe Inspect ye Road and make report to ye next Court under ye hands of noe lesse then twelve.

John Bristow and George Maris made report to this Court that upon hearing of a Difference Between Thomas Brasie Complainant and Richard Crosby they found the said Crosby to be in ye Complainants debt ye Sum of 20^s and that ye s^d money has been Due 6 years: Ordered that ye s^d Report be entred as ye Judgment of this Court and that ye said Crosby pay the 6 years Intrest Due.

Anne Johnson made over a Deed dated ye 16th day of ye 11th moneth 1687/8 unto John Mayo for 50 acres of land and ꝑmisses lying and being in Middletowne

ffrancis Little as Attorney to Michael Issard made over a Deed dated ye 11th day of ye 7th moneth 1688 unto James Saunderlaine as Attorney to John Nicholson for 300 acres of land and ꝑmisses lying in ye Township of Chester

Anne Johnson made over a Deed dated ye 11th day of ye 7th moneth 1688 unto Thomas Rawlenson for fifty acres of land and ꝑmisses lying and being in Middle Towne

John Hodskins as Attorney to Justa Anderson past over a Patent by assignment unto Charles Pickering for a parcell of land and ꝑmisses in the Township of Chester Conteining 197 acres ye Patent bearing date ye 2^d day of ye 2^d moth called April 1688 the assignment bearing Date ye 25th day of ye 4th moneth 1688

The Testimony of William Colborne in ye foregoing Case of Thomas Colborne and Roger Waldron & ought there to be Inserted Who being attested for ye Defend^t Saith that he paid 10 English money upon ye acc^e of his father ye Defend^t for which he had a gunn in paune which was delivered him againe uppon the payment of the money by this Deponent or his father the Defend^t.

The High Shreife made returne of an Execution granted against James Browne att the suite of Henry Jones which was levied as followeth (viz)

on twenty thousand of Pipe Staves Vallue.	50£	00ˢ
on Tymber att 4½ᵈ ℔ foote vallue......	30	00
on a little Parcell of Land lying in the towne of Chichester fronting yᵉ River Deleware with one Dwelling House and one Out House Appraised att........	50	00
on one hundred acres of land lying by Chichester meeting House with one little House there upon appraised att......	10	00
on 59ˡ of Cotten wooll and one gunn appraised att	3	11
	143£	11ˢ

The Court Adjourne untill yᵉ 3ᵈ day in yᵉ 1ˢᵗ Weeke of yᵉ 8ᵗʰ moneth next

---

Att a Court held att Chester for yᵉ County of Chester yᵉ 3ᵈ day in yᵉ 1ˢᵗ Weeke of yᵉ 8ᵗʰ moneth 1688.

John Bristow Presidᵗ
John Blunstone } Justices
George Maris
        Joshua ffirne Shreife
        Robert Eyre Clerke

Joseph Colbone was called to yᵉ Barr to answer the grand Inquest ℔sentment against him yᵉ last Court which was this Court drawne Into forme and preferred against him:

Butt upon his Submission to the Court he was fined 2/ 6ᵈ to yᵉ Governʳˢ use to be levied by yᵉ High Shreife of this County.

Roger Waldron made his appearance att this Court and before Judgment granted craved an appeale in Equity upon a verdickte given in an action between him and Thomas Colborne the last Court

Upon which Joseph Colborne making appearance in the behalfe of his father Thomas Colborne the matter was by Concent of both ℔tyes Continued untill yᵉ next Court.

Charles Pickering made over a Deed dated ye 1st day of October 1688 unto David Loyd for a parcell of land and ℘misses Conteining 197 acres lying in the Township of Chester

Joseph Richards made over a lease and release for 200 acres of land an ℘misses lying in Astone unto Thomas Marten the lease dated the 30th of ye 7th moneth ye release dated ye 1st of ye 8th moneth 1688.

Samuell Rowland was Called to ye Barr upon a former Traverse on a presentment found ye last Court which att this Court was drawne into ye forme of three Bills and preferred against him (viz)

Chester 1 The Jurors for ye King and Governour doe p'sent that Samuel Rowland of Marcus Hooke in ye said County of Chester and Andrew ffriend yeoman the 27th day of ye 4th moneth last past 1688 were Drunke agst the Publicke peace and against ye law in that Case ℘vided.

Wolle Rawson ℘secutor and Witnes :—a true bill.

2 The said Jurors also ℘sent that ye said Samuel Rowland the day year and place afores^d [did abuse Wolle Rosens Wife] against ye Publicke peace and agst ye law in that case made & provided.—a true bill.

3 The s^d Jurors also p'sent that ye s^d Samuel Rowland the day time and place afores^d and with force assault beate an evill Intreat ye s^d Wolle Rawson soe that of his life he much dispaired against ye Publick Peace and ye law in that case made and Provided &c, a true bill—Upon which he was Called to ye Barr and Pleads not guilty and refers himselfe to God and the Country

The names of ye Petty Jury all accepted by the Prisoner

Robert Woodward	John Woorrell
William Haukes	John Chandler
Benjamin Mendenhall	Henry Swift
Richard Clues	Thomas Marten
John Smith	Joshua Hastins
James Stamfield	George Stroad

William Browne was called three tymes to give in his Evidence butt made noe appearance

The Petty Jurys Verdickt

To ye first and second p^{r}sentments against him wee finde him not guilty

To ye third by his owne Confession wee finde him guilty of taking Wolle Rosen by the Throate

Whereupon Judgment is granted that Samuel Rowland pay 50 shillings for a fine to ye Governours use and fifty shillings to Wolle Rosen y^e ℞ty wronged and to remaine in the Shreifes Custody without baile till paym^t be made and y^t Wolle Rosen pay all Court Charges

The s^d Jurors also ℞sent that Breetah the Wife of Wolle Rawson the day year and Place afores^d [did act improperly with Samuel Rowland]

Ordered that Breetah Rawson be sumoned to appear before some Justice of ye Peace of this County in order to give in Security to appear att the next County Court att Chester to answer ye Premisses.

The s^d Jurors alsoe p^{r}sent that Peter Steward of ye said County of Chester yeoman the 22th day of ye 7th moneth last past floniously did steal and carry away from John Wickham of ye said County to witt out of his ye said John Wickhams Chest then being att William Claytons house the sum of tenne pounds spanish money fourty shillings Boston money two gold rings price 40^s one Silver Watch price about 6£ and one Silver Spoone price about 12^s/ and hath not restored the same agst the Publicke Peace and agst ye law in that case made and provided &c:—a true Bill Robert Taylor foreman.

Uppon which he is called to ye Barr and Pleads not guilty and referrs himselfe to good and the Country

The names of ye Petty Jury all accepted by ye Prisoner

 Jacob Simcocke   Peter Peterson
 Jeremy Carter   John Parker
 Robert Naylor   Wolle Rawson

Henry Hames	George fforeman
Robert Barber	John Calvert
Thomas Vernon	John Hodskins

Witnesses whose testimoneys was taken in Writting before Jn° Bristow one of y° Kings Justices att Severall times,— John Wickham, William Clayton, Jeremy Collett, Richard Buffington.

John Wickham being againe attested in Oppen Court Declareth y^t out of his Chest att William Claytons he did loose 40^s Boston money 10£ Spanish money two gold Rings and 1 Brasse Ring 1 Watch and one Silver Spoone he doe alsoe declare that he knew a certaine ps of $\frac{8}{8}$ taken out of y° Prisoners Pockett which he saith was in y° till of his Chest.

William Clayton being attested in Oppen Court declareth that John Wickham having putt a Chest into his house and upon y° mooving him out of one roome into another he found y° Chest to be loose and Broaken which he Informed John Wickham of Who told him that he had in y° Chest 10£ Spanish money two pounds Boston money 2 gold rings 1 Brasse ring one Silver Watch and one silver Spoone which when y° said Wickham came to Examine he found Wanting and this Deponent Saith he doe beleeve noe other ꝑson had y° Oppertunity to breake it oppen butt this prisoner

Jeremy Collett being againe attested in Oppen Court declareth that coming downe to Chichester with John Wickham he the s^d John Imediately putt his hand into y° Chest and said he was undone for he had left those things which before William Clayton had attested y° same and while they sent for y° Constaple he did Conceive that y° Prisoner was Surprised with fear and troubled

Richard Buffington being againe attested in Oppen Court Declareth that when he tooke the money out of y° Prisoners Pockett the Prisoner told him that he brought y° ps $\frac{8}{8}$ out of Jamaica which afterward y° told John Bristow he had from Thomas Budds sonne and further y° Prisoner said he would proove y° same

The Court adjourne untill y^e next morning the 7th hour and mett according to adjournment

Wee of y^e Petty Jury doe finde Peter Steward to be Guilty of y^e Presentment and wee doe vallue the whole sum to be Eighteen pounds

Upon which Judgment is granted that if ye said Peter Steward doe not pay unto John Wickham within two moneths next ensuing ye sum of 25£ and 12^s to ye Attorney generall that then he the said Steward shall remaine a Servant unto ye said Wickham or his assignes for ye full terme of 9 years ensuing from this Instant.

Wee the Grand jury for ye County of Chester this 2^d day of ye 8th moneth 1688

Doe lay out a Street and a landing in ye Towne of Chester Beginning att ye River Deleware Bounding upon ye Creeke to ye Corner soe farr as over against the North West Corner of ye Court House fifty foote in breadth and from thence up ye s^d Chester Towne for a Street thirty foote in Breadth. Robert Taylor fforeman

Wee ye Inhabitance of upper and neither Providence doe present ye Inhabitance of Ridley for not Cutting and mending the Road from Chester to upper and neither Providence.

Albertus Henrickson made over a Deed for a Peece of land known by ye name of Cripples dated ye 2^d day of ye 8th moneth 1688 lying in ye Township of Chester Conteining what therein is mentioned.

Ordered that William Brown be sumoned to ye next County Court to answer his Contempt for not appearing att this Court when lawfully sumoned.

John Calvert was attested Constaple of upper Providence for next ensuing year

Bartholomew Coppock was fined 30^s for absenting himselfe from this Court.

Att an Orphans Court held ye 3^d day in ye 1st Weeke of ye 8th moneth 1688 } John Bristow Presid^t John Blunstone George Maris } Justices

Joshua ffirne Shreife
Robert Eyre Clerke

Jane Sharples being called came into Court and made appear by Thomas Brasie and Jacob Simcocke Register that shee had given in Security to ye Registry of this County according to law in the behalfe of ye Children of her late Husband John Sharples Disceased

Joseph Wood was called three times butt made noe appearance.—Contempt.

ffrancis Little was Called in the Case of William and Elin Baines Butt satisfying the Court that he had paid part he was ordered to pay ye rest before ye next Court.

Phillip Roman was called three times butt made noe appearance.—Contempt

William Haukes being called and making his Appearance was ordered that both himselfe and his Wife Jane doe repaire to ye Register of this County and there give in Security according to law faithfully to discharge the office of gaurdian to ye Children of his Predisesor George Chandler Diceased

William Tally gave in Security according to ye last Corts order

---

Att a Court held att Chester for ye County of Chester ye 3^d day in ye 1st Weeke of ye 10th moth 1688 } John Simcocke Presid^t John Blunstone George Maris Bartholomew Coppocke } Justices ℔sent

Joshua ffirne Shreife
Robert Eyre Clerke

FFRANCIS SMITH Junr Pl^t
JONATHAN COMTON   Defend^t } In an action of ye Case

Witnesses William Vanderver Thomas Browne
The Plaintife Declares for 2£ 12^s by account

The names of yᵉ Petty Jury

Thomas Vernon	Richard Thatcher
John Neald	Richard Parker
George Churchman	John Woorrell
Thomas Crosse	Thomas ffox
Nathaniel Thornton	Randall Maylen
James Browne	John Person

The Defendᵗ in his answer saith he have not his evidence ready &c.

The Verdict of yᵉ Jury is Wee finde yᵉ Defendᵗ Indebted 2£ 6ˢ on Ballance of yᵉ account whereupon wee finde for yᵉ Plᵗ with Cost of Suite & 2ᵈ Damage.

Hereupon Judgment is granted

JEREMY COLLETT   Plᵗ   } In an action of Trespasse and
GEORGE FFOREMAN   Defendᵗ } Ejectment.—Continued.

The Court Adjourne untill yᵉ next morning 7 a Clocke and mett againe according to Adjournment

James Browne past over a Deed dated yᵉ 4ᵗʰ day of yᵉ 10ᵗʰ moneth 1688 unto William Clayton Seniᵒʳ Phillip Roman Robert Pile Jacob Chandler Joseph Bushell and John Kinsman for two acres of land in the Township of Chichester to yᵉ uses therein mentioned.

Joseph Wood of Darby made over five deeds all dated the 4ᵗʰ day of yᵉ 10ᵗʰ moneth 1688 (viz)

One to Thomas Collier for 100 acres of land more or lesse lying in the same Township

One to Thomas ffox for 50 acres of Land more or less lying in the same Township.

One to Richard Parker for 148 acres of Land more or lesse lying in yᵉ Same Township

One to John Kirke for 100 acres of Land in yᵉ Same Township

One to Samuell Levis for 100 acres of Land in yᵉ Same Township

John Symcocke made over a Deed dated yᵉ 6ᵗʰ day of yᵉ 1ˢᵗ

moneth 1687 for 120 acres of Land lying in Thornbury unto Thomas Eveson by his Attorney John Hodskins

John Symcocke made over a Deed dated ye 6th day of ye 1st moneth 1687 for 230 acres of Land lying in Thornbury unto Richard Woodward by his Attorney John Hodskins

John Bound by his Attorney John Blunstone made over a deede dated ye 28th day of ye 9th moneth called november 1688 unto John Roads for 250 acres of land lying in Darby.

ffrancis Harrison past over a Patent by assignment unto Thomas Usher bearing date ye 17th day of ye 9th moth 1688 for 200 acres of Land Joyning to Concord and Bethell lynes

Thomas Marten made over a Conveyance dated ye 1st day of ye 8th moth 1688 by assignment backe againe unto Joseph Richards Senior for a parcell of land and Plantation &c Conteining 200 acres lying in Asstone

The s^d Joseph Richards Senior made over ye s^d Land and Plantation by a deed dated ye 5th day of ye 10th moneth 1688 unto Joseph Richards Junior.

Joshua ffirnes Eare marke a little of ye top of Both ears Cutt and a Slitt in ye farr ear his brand marke I F

Darbys Towne marke D

Ordered att ye request of Thomas Usher y^t ye receipt following be recorded: Philadelphia ye 11th 3^d mo 1685

Received y^n of Thomas Usher on account of Thomas Willis out of ye Estate of Cannawell Brittaine deceased according to ye order of Court (by ye Authority and appointment of wch he did administer) ye full sum of four pounds fifteen shillings old England money for which this is his acquittance I say received by me Phillip Th. Lehmaine.

James Browne made over a Patent by assignment dated ye 9th day of ye 1st moneth 1687/8 unto John and Jane Chandler for a Plantation and Land Conteining 100 acres lying in Chichester.

William Haukes in ye behalfe of his wife Jane Chandler past over her part of ye aforementioned land unto her Brother in

Law John Chandler by assignment of s^d Patent dated ye 10th day of ye 7th moneth 1688

The Inhabitance of the Township of Thornbury Petitioned for a High Way to ye River Deleware.

Ordered that ye Grand Inquest doe lay out a Convenient High way and y^t George Pearce be assisting.

The Grand Inquest presentments.

We of ye Grand Inquest for ye County of Chester this 4th day of ye 10th moneth in ye year 1688 doe present as followeth.

Imp^rs Wee present William Collett of Concord for travelling upon ye road on ye first day of ye Weeke being ye 21th of ye 8th moneth in ye year 1688 with a yoake of Oxen and a wayne and a Horse or mare before them

Wee likewise p^rsent Susannah Willard of Marple for being found with Child and having noe Husband

Wee likewise p^rsent the Road betwixt George Wollads fence and Jonathan Hayeses for being not Passable likewise the Mill way to Darby Creeke to be Cutt both being in ye Township of Marple

Wee likewise p^rsent the way laid Out Betwixt Over and Neather Providence for being not Cutt and Cleared in Ridley Township toward Chester having been formerly p^rsented and not yett Cleared

Wee likewise present the Township of Chester for want of a foote Bridge over Chester Creeke By William Woodmansees —Continued to ye next Court.

Wee likewise p^rsent John Wickham of Chichester for Having Clippings of money which he Owned to be his.

Wee alsoe present James Stanfield of Marple for selling a mare and Colt that was none of his owne.

Robert Taylor foreman in ye behalfe of ye rest.

The Grand Inquests returnes of ye High wayes.

Wee of ye Grand Inquest according to ord^r received from ye Court have vewed and doe p^rsent as followes (viz)

Imp^rs ffrom Burmingham to Chester landing Beginning att a marked white Oake over ye Runn near William Brintons and soe along ye road ye Other Jury laid Out on ye Runn near Thomas Moores to a marked Stake fourty foote Wide towards his Plantation and soe right unto a marked Hickery from thence to a marked White Oake att ye Corner of Thomas Moores ffence then over Nathaniel Parks land Where ye other Jury went then heading the Spring going againe to ye Same Road thence along ye s^d Road which ye other Jury Went to a Spannish Oake standing by ye Kings road and soe along to Chester Mill soe going on ye North West Side of ye Mill and Plantation to a marked blacke Oake on ye Side of ye Hill from thence by a Streight lyne to a marked Blacke Oake by ye old Road.

from Bethell to Chichester:

Beginning at Concord Street end and so along ye Road formerly laid out to a marked White Oake below Walter Martens by a lyne of marked trees on ye South West Side of ye Old Road to a marked great White Oake from thence along ye road formerly laid out to Deleware by or near James Browns House

from Chichester to Astone { ffrom Delleware by James Brownes along ye old Road Betwixt Jeremy Colletts and John Hulberts soe along ye same Road to a marked White Oake thence along on ye West Side of a marked Poplar tree near ye meeting House from thence by a lyne of marked trees to ye West Corner of Joseph Richardsons fence from thence by a lyne of marked trees to a marked Blacke Oake standing by Astone Road.

ffrom Astone to Edgmond Road { Beginning att a Spannish Oake above Edward Carters and soe along ye Cutt Road and downe ye vallie which Joseph Richards had fenced in from thence through John Beales Pasture along by William Woodmansees along ye Old Road over Chester Creeke soe along ye Old Road.

ffrom Chester to Edgmond	Beginning att a Pear tree above John Symcocks Orchard soe by a streight lyne through ye Old ffield to a marked Hickery att the North East Corner of ye Old ffields soe along by a lyne of marked trees to a marked Spannish Oake in Edgmond Road soe along Edgmond Road to a White Oake on ye East Side of ye Road from thence by a lyne of marked trees to a marked Black Oake on ye East Side of ye Road soe along ye Road by John Worrells fence then along by John Boeter and soe to Joseph Bakers as it lay before.
The Road betwixt Darby Road and Chester	Beginning att a marked Burnt Oake standing by ye Road from Darby to George Maris on ye land of Joseph Potter acrosse ye sd Joseph Potters land to Thomas Whittbyes Land thence Crossing ye said Thomas Whittbyes Land by a lyne of marked trees to ye Runn to a marked Saxifrax thence to ye lyne Betwixt Thomas Whittbyes and Edmond Cartleidge and up ye sd lyne to a marked Chestnutt being ye Corner markt tree betwixt Edmond Cartleidge and Thomas Whittby from thence Over John Hallawells land to a Crooked Blacke Oake near Jacob Simcocks Barne thence over Jacob Simcocks Land on ye north side of his Barne by a lyne of marked trees on ye north Side of Charles Whittacres then along Henry Mattocks Land by a lyne of marked trees to ye Road betwixt Henry Mattocks and Chester and along ye sd Road up ye Hill over Ridley Creeke to a

marked Spanish Oake on y⁰ West Side of y⁰ Old Road then by a lyne of marked trees to a Blacke Oake standing by Edgmond Road and thence to Chester.

The Court adjourne untill y⁰ next morning 7 a Clocke and then mett againe according to adjournm^t and afterward adjourned again unto y⁰ next morning being y⁰ 6th day of y⁰ Weeke of y⁰ 10th moneth and mett againe according to adjournm^t

Ordered that Roger Jacksons 150 acres of Land formerly Included in Middletowne be from Henceforth taken into y⁰ Township of Edgmond and be therein Included

Ordered that Joshua ffirne have Power to Levie y⁰ assestments layd upon unseated Land and non residence for which he is to have 2^d in y⁰ pound.

The Grand Inquest having inquired into and found y⁰ Publicke Charges of this County for y⁰ service of y⁰ Provinciall Councellmen and Assembly the Cost of y⁰ Court House and Prison &c presented y⁰ Same to this Court in a Schedulle by them drawne up and Concluded

Upon which the Court for defraying y⁰ same ordered a Levie to be raised (viz)

On every hundred acres of Land taken up and
  Inhabited ....3^s 0^d
On Every hundred acres of Land taken up by
  nonresidence and unoccupied 4 6
Every ffreeman from 16 years of age to 60 by
  the Pole............................3 0
Every male Servant soe quallified..........1 6

Ordered that Warrants be forthwith Issued out to y⁰ Respective Constaples of this County for levying y⁰ same halfe of which is to be levyed att or before y⁰ 25th day of y⁰ 1st moneth next the other halfe att or before y⁰ 29th day of y⁰ 7th moneth following

The Grand Inquest doe alsoe allow of y⁰ Tax for y⁰ Woolves heads and that Power be forthwith Issued forth to Compell those to pay that are behinde in their arrears And that receipts and disbursments thereof be made to y⁰ grand Inquest att y⁰ next County Court

Att an Orphans Court held att Chester for y⁰ County of Chester y⁰ 3ᵈ day in y⁰ 1ˢᵗ Weeke of y⁰ 1ˢᵗ moᵗʰ 1688

John Bristow Presidᵗ
John Simcocke
John Blunstone
Bartho. Coppocke
George Maris
ffra: Harrison

Justices ⅌sent

Joshua ffirne Shreife
Robert Eyre Clerke

Joseph Wood was Called to answer his Contempt the last Court butt upon his submission to y⁰ Court and promising to make applycation to y⁰ Governour and to give in Such Security as he should appoint in behalfe of his Brothers and Sisters he is hereupon Dismist.

ffrancis Little was Called in y⁰ Case of William and Elinor Baines.

Ordered that he make them satisfaction of what remaines behind in one Weeke

Phillip Roman was Called to answer his Contempt the last Court.

Ordered that y⁰ matter be Continued untill a Report of y⁰ ⅌misses be given in by y⁰ next monethly meeting

William Haukes was Called who making his appearance was ordered to make his application to y⁰ Governʳ: in persuance of a former order of Court for his taking out letters of Administration in the Behalfe of his ⅌diceasors Children George Chandler disceasᵗ

The Court adjourne untill y⁰ 3ᵈ day in y⁰ 1ˢᵗ weeke of y⁰ 8ᵗʰ moᵗʰ next

Att a Court held att Chester for y͏ᵉ County of Chester y͏ᵉ 3ᵈ day in y͏ᵉ 1ˢᵗ Weeke of y͏ᵉ 1ˢᵗ mo͏ᵗʰ 1688
{ John Bristow Presid͏ᵗ
John Simcocke
John Blunstone
Bartho: Coppocke
George Maris
ffrancis Harrison } Justices ℔sent

Joshua ffirne Shreife
Rob͏ᵗ Eyre Clerke

The Grand Inquest ℔sentments and returnes y͏ᵉ 5͏ᵗʰ of y͏ᵉ 1ˢᵗ mo͏ᵗʰ 168⅜

We of y͏ᵉ grand Inquest for y͏ᵉ County of Chester have laid out y͏ᵉ Road from Thornbury to Middletowne Beginning att a Spanish Oake upon Thomas Bradfords land near Thomas Evinsons along y͏ᵉ lyne of marked trees through Edward Béasars Land thence along y͏ᵉ lyne of mark͏ᵗ trees through John Simcocks Land to a marked blacke Walenutt standing by Chester Creeke thence Crossing y͏ᵉ Creeke along Edward Blackes land along y͏ᵉ lyne of marked trees through Joshua Hastings land along Crossing y͏ᵉ head of Caleb Pusies land thence through David Ogdens land to Middletownes road ending att a marked white Oake Standing by y͏ᵉ Roads Side.

Wee likewise ℔sent John Servant of James Stamfield in Marple in this County of Chester for taking away from y͏ᵉ House of William Buckenham of upper Providence Several wearing Cloathes ffeloniously Contrary to y͏ᵉ law in that Case made and Provided

Wee likewise psent William Buckingham for receiving y͏ᵉ s͏ᵈ goods otherwise then y͏ᵉ law alloweth of

Wee likewise ℔sent Anne Weaver of Astone in this County of Chester for being with Child and having noe Husband

The names of y͏ᵉ Grand Inquest attested for y͏ᵉ time ensuing

William Gabitter	John Hulbert
Thomas Hood	Benjamine Mendenhall
Thomas King	Peter Worrell
Robert Burrowes	ffrancis Yarnall

ffrances Chadsey
Thomas Rawlenson
John Gibbons
Joseph Richards Junr
Thomas Worrelo
Edward Walter
Richard Mason
Thomas Baldwine
Nathaniel Lamplue

John Wickham was Called to ye Barr to answer ye Presentm^t of ye Grand Inquest ye last Court

The testimoneys of ye Evidences (viz)

ffrancis Little being attested declareth that upon ye taking of Peter Stewart they found about him Clippings which he saith was Clippings of Spannish money which he ye s^d Peter Stewart s^d was John Wickhams

James Saunderlaine being attested saith y^t Nathanial Lukin having taken Peter Stewart John Wickhams Servant and brought him to George Foremans House Where this deponent looking over the goods which ye s^d Peter tooke away with him amongst ye rest found a ⅌sell of Clippings of Coined money about the thicknes of peeces of eight which John Wickham owned to be his and tooke ye same into his Possession

Nathanial Lukin being attested declareth that when Peter Stewart was taken and Examined before a Justice of ye Peace on ye other Side ye River he found upon him some Clippings of Spanish money which after he ye said Peter told this Deponent did belong to John Wickham and that ye s^d Wickham did att Chichester owne ye same to be his

Randall Vernon being attested declareth that he meeting with John Wickham att Walter ffausetts he asked him how he came by Clippings of money Who told him that when he was att Yorke there was a man Clipping a Cand lide or saucer which after he tooke up and further saith not

John Eldridge was attested butt his Evidence being insignifiecant he was Sett by

Jeremy Collett being attested declareth that he did see a ⅌cell of Clippings which he beleeves was Spanish money delivered att George fforemans to John Wickham which sd Wickham Owned to be his the Court adjourne

Richard Buffington Constaple of Chichester being attested declareth that when he went downe to Chichester about ye levies John Wickham did Swear if any one should levie any thing upon him he would have a tyme of him

Who being upon ye Same Called to ye Barr againe: upon his submission to ye Court and his Petition for Pardon he is remitted ye Contempt } Ordered he pay 5^s for Swearing for a fine

Jeremy Collett Pl^t
George fforeman Defend^t

William Rawlence Pl^t
Zacariah Patricke Defend^t

upon an action of Trespasse and ejectment Commenced ye last Court } Continued

In an action of ye Case Withdrawne

Susannah Willard was Called to ye Barr to answer her p'sentment ye last Court Shee having been delivered and ye Child Dead

The midwife Grace Stamfield with Margrett Coppocke Ellen Coppocke and Margery Pearson being all streightly Examined did testifie that ye child received noe harme

The Prisoner Confesseth one John Bradshaw to be ye father of her Child and that she was beguiled by him under a Promise of marriage and that shee was sorry for ye same and putts her selfe upon ye mercy of ye King & Gover^e

Whereupon ye Court ordered her to pay to ye Governour 50^s for a fine with Court Charges and soe to be Discharged

William Collett was Called to answer his p^rsentment ye last Court

Butt upon his Submission to ye Court he is ordered to pay Court Charges & soe to be Dismist

Neales Marshall Pl^t
Ralfe Dracott Defend^t } withdrawne

George fforeman Pl^t
James Browne Defend^t
withdrawne

John Sanger petitioned to have his pay for keeping Edward Kinison 26 weekes in his sicknes amounting to 5£ 18^s 6^d } Ordered that Nicholas Newland doe take care to pay the S^d Sum out of ye Publick levies

John Chandler past over a Deed dated ye 11th day of ye 7th moneth 1688 to William Haukes for a parcell of land Conteining 60 acres lying in Chichester.

William Clayton past over a Deed dated ye 5th day of ye 1st moneth 1688/9 unto Francis Chadsey for a parcell of land in Chichester Conteining 3 acres more or lesse Called ye Comon as alsoe for another parcell of land Conteining seven acres and a halfe more or lesse as alsoe for another parcell of land Conteining 6 acres and a halfe lying above Phillip Romans House

Joseph Phips by his Attorney ffrancis Little past over a Patent by assignment dated ye 7th day of ye 12th moneth 1688 for 200 acres of land unto William Collett lying in Concord

Thomas Budd past over a Deed dated ye last day of ye 10th moneth 1688 unto John Simcocke for a Plantation and ℔misses lying in Chester Conteining ye number of acres according to ye Schedull thereunto afixed

John Blunstone as Attorney to Luke Hanke past over a Patent by assignment dated ye 5th day of ye 1st moneth 1688 unto William Garrett and Thomas Bradshaw for a parcell of land near Muckaraton Creeke viz one hundred acres thereof to s^d Thomas Bradshaw ye remainder to ye sd William Garrett

Thomas Collier Past over a Deed dated ye 4th day of ye 1st moneth 1689 unto William Trotter for a parcell of land lying in Darby Conteining 50 acres

David Ogden past over a Deed for 50 acres of land unto John Boiter dated ye 24th day of ye 9th moneth 1685

James Saunderlaine and Caleb Pusie as Attorneys to John Nicholson past over a Deed dated ye 26th day of ye 12th moneth called February 1688 unto Lawrence Routh for a Plantation and ℙmisses Conteining 300 cares lying upon Chester Creeke

John Bowiter and David Ogden past over a Deed dated ye 5th day of ye 1st moneth 1688 unto   for 100 acres of land lying in Middle towne

ffrancis Chadsey made over a Deed for 300 acres of land in Chichester dated ye 5th day of ye 1st moneth 1688 unto Thomas Usher

Thomas Usher past over ye same land by assignment dated ye same day unto Francis Harrison

The s^d Thomas Usher past over a Deed for a Plantation and ℙmisses by assignm^t dated ye above day unto ye s^d ffrancis Harrison it being the remainder of a parcell of land^s Conteining by Estimation 60 acres lying in ye afores^d Chichester

John Hannum with Margery his wife and John Palmer with Mary his wife past over a Deed by assignment bearing date ye 1st day of ye 1st moneth 1688 unto Nicholas Pile for a Parcell of land therein Conteined

The above partyes made over a Deed of Conveyance unto ye s^d Nicholas Pile for a Plantation and Premisses Conteining 150 acres being part of ye above mentioned land dated ye same with ye above assignm^t.

John Simcocke as Attorney to Arthur Cooke past a Deed to Francis Gamble for 1500 acres of land dated ye 2^d day of ye 1st moneth 1688

Nathaniell Thornton being Convickted before John Bristow for receiving stolne money of John Marten Servant to James Browne was for ye Same att this Court Indickted

The Grand Inquest finde ye Bill

Whereupon he is Called to ye Barr and Pleads not guilty and referrs himselfe to God and ye Country

The names of ye Petty Jury all accepted by ye Prisoner

John Bartrum	Robert Barber
Michaell Blunstone	Edward Beasar
Thomas Worth	Caleb Pusie
Richard Tucker	Albert Henrickson
John Child	Thomas Bowlter
John Beales	Randall Maylen

Witness and Prosecutrix Elizabeth Locke

Jeremy Collett being attested declareth y^t he did hear Nath. Thornton say when he was Examined before John Bristow y^t he did receive 8^s of John Marten and that Marten told him he came honestly by the money

Elizabeth Locke being attested saith that Nathaniell Thornton being Examined denyed that he received 25^s of John Marten but confessed to 8^s & further said he knew not where Marten had it

James Browne being attested declareth that upon Examination Nathaniel Thornton did Confesse that he had of John Marten 6^s afterwards he Confest to 9^s then againe to 12^s then to 6^s againe and further saith not

The Juryes Verdicte ye 6th of ye 1st mo^{th} 168⅔

Wee of ye Petty Jury doe finde Nathaniel Thornton to be guilty of ye Indicktment he stands Indickted of

John Bartrum foreman

Judgment is hereupon granted that he pay unto Elizabeth Locke y^e ₱ty wronged 24^s/ with all Court Charges

John Marten Servant to James Browne of Chichester being Convickted before John Bristow for felloniously Breaking open the Box of Elizabeth Locke and taking thence 44^s in money or thereabout was for ye Same att this Court Indickted

The grand Inquest finde ye Bill

Whereupon he is Called to ye Barr and arrained he Confesseth the fact Thereupon Judgment is awarded that he receive twenty one laishes on his bear Backe at ye Comon Whipping Post att Chester and that his master James Browne pay unto Elizabeth locke yᵉ party wronged yᵉ sum of 5£ 8ˢ with all Court Charges and that he have Power to Dispose of him for such time as may be thought fitt and resonable for his satisfaction

John Wickham being againe Called to yᵉ Barr and yᵉ Court Seriously taking his Cause into Consideration and not finding matter sufficient in yᵉ ℔sentment Whereon to ground an Indicktment according to law Therefore yᵉ Court discharge him and his Baile from further attendance he paying Court Charges

The names of yᵉ Constaples Chosen

Chester	Jeremy Carter	Lower Providence	Jnᵒ. Edge
Chichester	Henry Renolds	Burmingham	Hugh Harry
Bethel	Edward Beasar	Edgmond	James Swaford
Middletowne	Jnᵒ Worrell	Upper Providence	Geo Woodward
Concord	Thomas Moore	Springfield	Robert Taylor
Newton	Jenkin Griffith	Marple	James Stamfield
Darby	John Hallawell		

Ordered that yᵉ former Constaples of each respective Township doe deliver up their Warrants for yᵉ Levies unto their respective Successors above named in order to have yᵉ same assest according to yᵉ Tenour Thereof

John Holstone Past over a Deed dated yᵉ 13ᵗʰ day of yᵉ 6ᵗʰ moᵗʰ 1688 unto William Mayling for a parcell of land and ℔mises Conteining 50 acres more or lesse lying in upper Providence.

John Blunstone as Attorney to Joseph Potter past a deed dated yᵉ 5ᵗʰ day of yᵉ 1ˢᵗ moneth 1688 unto John Hallowell for a ℔cell of land in Darby Conteining 50 acres

George Simcocke made over a Deed dated yᵉ 4ᵗʰ day of yᵉ 1ˢᵗ moneth 1689 unto Robert Smith for a parcell of land Conteining 106 acres lyin in the Township of   In Chester County

. Henry Renolds Past over 2 Deeds one Dated yᵉ 10ᵗʰ day of yᵉ 11ᵗʰ moneth 1688 for 15 acres of land in Chichester the other dated ye 14th day of ye same moneth for 11 acres in ye Same Township: both unto Phillip Roman his heires &c

William Tally was Chossen Supervisor of ye High wayes for ye Township of Chichester for ye next insuing year in ye Rome of Phillip Roman

The grand Inquest P̄sentments

Wee of ye Grand Inquest doe P̄sent ye Townships of Bethell and Chichester for neglecting ye Clearing of a Road in ye respective Libertyes between Concord and Chester

Alsoe wee P̄sent ye Kings Road between namans Creeke and Chichester Creeke for not being Cleared from Loggs

Wee also P̄sent ye Township of Chester for want of a Sufficient ffoot Bridge over Chester Creeke near to William Woodmansees

Wee alsoe P̄sent ye want of a foote Bridge over ye Mill Creeke between this County and Philadelphia it being in ye Kings Road

Wee also P̄sent ye Road lying between ye Townships of Bethell and Chichester for not being Cleared and made passable

John Chandler past over a mortgage of a Plantation and Premisses lying in Chichester unto James Browne dated ye 1st day of ye 1st moneth Called March 1688

Att a Court Held Att Chester for the County of Chester the nineth day of ye first moneth 169⅔ John Hoskings and Peter Taylor Acknowledged A Deed to William Beckingham for one hundred Acres of land lying in upper Province the deed beareing date the Twenty first Day of the Tenth moneth 1696

ffrancis Baldwin Acknowledged A Deed To Joseph Coebourn for his Plantation lying in Chester Township The Deed Beareing Date the Eight day of March 169⅔ Att the S^d Co^rt

John Jarman Attorney for David Powell Acknowledged a Deed to Hugh Samuell for one hundred Acres of land lying in Radnor Township ye Deed bearing Date ye 17th Day of ye 11th moneth 1696

Nicholes Pyle Acknowledged A Deed To his Brother Robert Pyle for his Plantation lying in Beathell one hundred and fifty Acres of land the Deed beareing Date the 2^d day first moth 1696/7

John Childe Attorney for John Gibbons Past A Deed to Edward Bennett for one hundred Acres of land lying in Thornbury the Deed beareing Date the 9th of March 1696/7

John Golding Acknowledged A Deed To Abraham Beakes for one hundred Acres of land lying in Edgmond the Deed beareing Date the ninth day of ye first moneth 1696/7

John Buckley Acknowledged A Deed to Nicholas Newlin for Two hundred and fifty Acres of land lying in Concord the Deed Beareing Date the 9th day of March 1696/7

Abraham Beakes Past A Deed to Jonathan Heyes for A plantation in Edgmond the Deed beareing Date the 10th day of March 1696/7

Robert Woodyard Acknowledged A Deed To John Powell ffor a plantation being seventy seven Acres of land lying in Neither Providence bereing Date the 3 day 10th month 1696

All these Above mentioned Deeds were Acknowledged Att the S^d Court held ye 9th & 10th dayes of March 1696/7

Att a Court Called att Chester ye 19th day of ye 1st moneth 1688/9 { Where after Proclamation made and Silence Comanded in ye name of ye King and Proprietary a Comission for ye Peace to ye Respective persons under written was read Signed by ye Governour John Blackwell Esqr under. ye Seale of ye Province dated ye 25th day of ye 11th moneth 1688

William Collett Complained against his servant William Ratewe for running from his service as alsoe for ye Cost and Charge in persuing & taking him up which ye Complainant delivered to ye Court in a Schedull amounting to ye sum of 3£ 11^s 7^d½ besides this present Court Charge

William Markham Esqr
John Simcocke ....present
John Bristow ....present
Bartholomew Coppocke Junr..present
John Blunstone
George Maris ....present
ffrancis Harrison ....present
Nicholas Newland

As alsoe a Commission for High Shreife of this County to Joshua ffirne was att ye same time read and Published

Whereupon ye Court ordered ye said Servant to Serve his s^d Master William Collett or his assignes ye full terme of one whole year after ye Expiration of his Indenturs

Att a Court held att Chester for ye County of Chester ye 3^d day in ye 1st Weeke of ye 4th mo 1689

John Simcocke Presid^t
John Bristow
John Blunstone
George Maris   } Justices
ffrancis Harison
Nicholas Newland
William Howell

Joshua ffirne Shreife
Robt Eyre Clerke

Edward Bennett was attested Constaple of Thornbury for ye next ensuing year

John Radley was ordered Constaple of West Towne for ye next ensuing year

William Howells Comission for ye Peace was read and Published dated ye 29th day of ye 2^d moneth 168⅜ and did afterward Subscribe to ye solemne Declaration prepared by ye 57 Chapter of ye great law of this Province

The Divission lyne between this County and Philadelphia County was read dated ye 1st of ye 2^d mo^th 1685

John Test Pl^t
Gideon Gamble Defend^t
in an action of ye Case upon attachment in ye hands of Richard Buffington
{ Richard Buffington Confesseth that he have fourty shillings of Gideon Gambles in his hand Whereupon Judgment is granted unto ye Pl^t for ye same and for what more shall appear in his hand

Lawrence Hadings Pl^t
Lawrence Homan Defend^t
with-drawne
{ John Fox Pl^t
James Stamfield Defend^t
withdrawne

Robert Barber Pl^t
Anne Ffriend Defend^t
with-drawne
{ Robert Smith acknowledged a deed dated ye 3^d day of ye 4th moneth 1689 unto Nicholas Ireland for a parcell of land in Darby

Josiah Elfrith Pl^t
Joseph Clayton Defend^t
in an action of ye Case
{ the Pl^t declares for 2£ 5^s 8^d due by account
{ The names of ye witnesses taken in New Castle County before Jno Cann and Edward Blacke product in writting

The names of ye Petty Jury
William Jenkin   John Wood
Robert Barber   Adam Roades
John Child   Nathaniel Parkes
Albertus Henrickson John Mendenhall
Walter Marten   Joseph Steedman
Thomas Smith   James Swaford

{ under ye Clerks hand and County Scale
Elizabeth Priestner
Edward Bolton
Wm Stanyard
Richard Renolds
Mary Evans

The Defend.^{t} saith in his answer that he hath satisfied ye debt and produced an account for ye same

January ye 4th 89 The Jury give ye verdickt for ye Plaintife with Cost & Charge of Suite & Six pence damage } Hereupon Judgment is granted

Anne ye Wife of Richard Buffington being by Warrant apprehended and Convicted before John Bristow for defiling her marriage Bed was by her Suirtyes Richard Buffington and ffrancis Little bound over to this Court and accordingly made her appearance and was Indickted

Witnes and Prosecutor James Chivers

The grand Inquest finde ye Bill Whereupon shee is Called to ye Barr and Pleads not guilty and referrs her Selfe to God and ye Country

The names of ye Petty Jury

William Jenkin	Adam Roads	The testimony of James Chivers taken in writting before John Bristow remaines on ye file The said James Chivers being againe attested in Open Court saith that as he was coming from Concord downe
Robert Barber	Nathaniel Parkes	
Albertus Henrickson	John Mendenhall	
Walter Marten	James Swaford	
Thomas Smith	Caleb Pusie	
John Whood	Randall Vernon	

to Chichester He did see a man and a Woman lying upon ye Ground and ye man lying Upon ye Top of ye woman and ye woman looking up he saw it was Anne Buffington

John Eldridge being attested declareth as aboves^d

James Chivers upon his Attest further saith that Anne Buffington was very earnest to know who this man and woman was for said shee there is never a Woman hereabouts that hath a Black Hatt butt I and then it must needs be me
June 5th 89

Wee yᵉ Jury unanimously agree that Anne yᵉ wife of Richard Buffington is guilty of this Indicktment

    Walter Marten
     foreman

Whereupon Judgment is granted that shee receive 10 strips upon her bear backe well laid on and 12 months Imprisonment att hard labour in yᵉ house of Correction and to pay all Court Charges.

Anne Weaver of Astone Widdow being on yᵉ 29ᵗʰ day of yᵉ 2ᵈ moneth Convickted before John Simcocke and John Bristow Justices Sitting att Chester for having two Bastard Children shee there Confessed yᵉ fact & that William Weaver of Boston in New-England was the true father of them upon which by her surtyes Joseph Richards and Nathaniel Richards shee was bound over to this Court and accordingly made her appearance and was Indickted

The grand Inquest finde yᵉ bill

Shee being attested in Open Court declared as before & that yᵉ abousᵈ William Weaver was yᵉ true father of her two Children

Her midwife and mother Jone Richards being attested declareth that att yᵉ time of her labour shee Confessed yᵉ Same to her

Whereupon Judgment is granted that shee receive tenne strips upon her bear Backe well laid on and halfe yᵉ Charge of her owne and Wᵐ Weavers tryall

William Weaver of Boston in New England upon yᵉ attestation of Anne Weaver that he was yᵉ true father of her two Bastard Children was for yᵉ same apprehended and brought before John Bristow Where upon Examination he denyed the fact and was by his Surtyes Albertus Henrickson and John Child bound over to this Court and accordingly made his appearance and was Indickted

The grand Inquest { Whereupon he is Called to the Barr and
finde ye bill   Pleads not Guilty and by Petition putts
                    himselfe upon y° mercy of y° King and
                    Governour.

Whereupon Judgment is awarded that he should give in Security that y° Children should be brought up till they can Shift for themselves and to pay 20ˢ for a fine to y° Governour

JOHN BRISTOW   Plᵗ   { in an action of y° case
JOHN ANDERSON and }   upon Attachment in y°
his mother Anderson } Defendᵗˢ   hands of John Gibbons

The Plaintife declares for 2£ 12ˢ 6ᵈ due by account and Craves Judgment for y° same with reasonable damages and Cost of Suite

Upon which Judgment is awarded for 15 bushells of Wheate in y° hands of sᵈ John Gibbons

The Inhabitance of Concord Bethell and
Chichester Petitioned against y° High-
way lately laid out from Concord and   ordered that the
Bethell to y° River for that between   former way be
Walter Martens and Jeremy Colletts the there Continued
way is not soe good and Passable as the
former Road

Walter Marten ffrancis Chadsey and Jonathan Hayes was ordered to be appraisers of this County for y° next ensuing year the two first attested to their office in Open Court

James Saunderlaine made his appearance att this Court according to recognisence to answer y° Complaint of Henry Reynolds and thereby Saved his Baile and was discharged from any further attendance

John Sanger Petitioned y° Court for y° } The Court promise
remaining part of his pay for keeping   to take y° matter
Edward kinison   into Consideration

Isacke ffew Past over a deed dated y° 4ᵗʰ day of y° 1ˢᵗ moneth 1688 unto George Churchman for a parcell of land in Chester

George fforeman Pl^t
Anne ffriend Defend^t
in an action of ye Case
} referred by Concent {
Jeremy Collett Pl^t
George fforeman Defend^t
in an action of Trespasse
and ejectment Continued

Henry Renolds acknowledged a deed for all his Houses and lands therein Conteined and premisses lying att Chichester near ye River Deleware unto James Saunderlaine dated ye 3^d day of ye 4th moneth 1689

Ordered that William Woodmansee have an order sent him to make up a Bridge near his house

Anne ffriend Widdow with Andrew ffriend and Johanes ffriend her Sonns acknowledged a deed unto Robert Barber dated ye 21th day of ye 3^d moneth 1689 for a House and ground therein mentioned lying in Chester Towne

The Grand Inquest ℙsentments (viz)

Wee of ye grand Inquest for ye County of Chester ye 5th of ye 4th moneth 1689 doe lay out a Publicke landing place and Open Street for ye Service of this County Beginning att ye north westerly Corner of ye Court House to low water marke by Chester Creeke and soe of ye same Breadth by ye said Creeke downe to Deleware River to low water marke thence and alsoe from ye first mentioned Corner of ye Court House A Publicke Street 30 foote Wide through Chester towne

Wee also present John Hodskins for a Hogsty upon ye Same land.

James Saunderlaine Pl^t
Henry Reynolds Defend^t
in an action of ye Case
} withdrawne

Richard Crosby Pl^t
James Stamfield defend^t
in an action of ye Case withdrawne

Idem Pl^t
Idem Defend^t
in an action of ye Case
} withdrawne

John Bristow Pl^t
Andrew ffriend Defend^t
in an action of ye Case withdrawne

William Haukes Pl^t
John Hickman Defend^t
in an action of ye Case
} withdrawne

John Maddocke of the Township of Ridley being Convickted before John Simcocke and John Bristow for speaking and uttering Scandelous and Dishonourable words against ye life ⅌son and government of ye Cheife Proprietary Wm Penn Esqr as alsoe against ye life and ⅌son of this present Governour John Blackwell Esqr was for ye Same by them Comitted and att this Court Indickted

The Grand Inquest finde the Bill Whereupon he is Called to ye Barr and putts himselfe upon ye mercy of ye King and Govern^r	upon which he is fined 5£ to ye use of ye Cheife Proprietary & to pay all Court Charges

Att a Court held att Chester for ye County of Chester ye 3^d day in ye last weeke of ye 6th moneth 1689	John Bristow Presid^t John Simcocke George Marris Nicholas Newland ffrancis Harrison	Justices ⅌sent

George fforeman Shreife
Robert Eyre Clerke

HENRY CADMAN Pl^t
JOSEPH CLAYTON Defend^t
in an action of Debt upon
Bond
   Chester

Declaration   Henry Cadman of Chester County Complaines of Joseph Clayton of ye County of New Castle in ye Territoryes of Pensilvania of a Plea that he renders him six pounds twelve shillings lawfulle money of this Province which to him he oweth & unjustly deteineth &c And thereupon ye said Pl^t saith that whereas ye said Defend^t by his written Obligation under his hand and Seale here in Court Produced dated ye 27 day of Aprill 1687 did acknowledge himselfe to owe and stand Justly Indebted unto ye s^d Pl^t in ye sum of six pounds twelve shillings to be paid to ye said Pl^t when he ye s^d Defend^t should be thereunto required neverthelesse ye s^d Defend^t though often required the s^d 6£ 12^s to ye Pl^t hath not rendred butt ye same to him hitherto to render hath denyed and still doth deny to ye Plt^s damage of fourty shillings and thereof brings suite &c

The Defend^t Confesseth Judgment upon ye Bond being six pounds twelve shillings with Cost of Suite.

Abraham Hooper Pl^t
Henry Barnes Defend^t by his Attorney William Clerke
In an action of Debt by Bill
} Continued untill ye next Court Ordered also that ye Pl^t pay Court Charge with halfe fees to ye Jury

William Collett Pl^t
Richard Green Defend^t
in an action of ye Case
} Continued untill ye after noone } and afterward withdrawne

Robert Brothers Pl^t
Mary Boules Defend^t
in an action of ye Case
} The Plaintife appears by his Attorney Jeremy Collett } Continued untill ye next Court

Robert and Anne Eyre Pl^t
Mary Best Defend^t
In an action of Scandall and Defamation

The Plaintife Declares for one hundred pounds Damage
The 27th of ye 6th moneth

The names of ye Petty Jury Impanelled
Thomas Vernon   Wm Haukes
John Child   Jno Chandler
James Browne   Nich: Pile
Albertus Henrickson Rich: Thatcher
Randall Maylen   James Swarford
Jacob Chandler   Robt Vernon

The verdit is that wee finde noe Cause of action and Therefore finde for ye Defend^t Cost of Suite and 2^s Damage
Jacob Chandler f o r e m a n
Judgment is granted according to ye verdict of ye Jury

ROBERT EYRE and ANNE his wife Plt^s
JAMES BAYLIES Defend^t
In an action of Scandall and
Defamation

} The Pl^{ts} suffered a nonsuite

Thomas Cartwright was Appointed Supervisor of ye Highwayes for ye Township of Astone for ye next ensuing year.

The Grand Inquest Presentments

Wee ye Grand Jury for ye County of Chester doe present the Township of Thornbury and Middletowne not Clearing ye Roads between ye s^d Thornbury and Edgmond Road

Wee alsoe present ye Township of Chester Middle Towne and Edgmond for not Clearing ye Roads through the said Townships

Chester—The Jurors for ye Proprietary and Governour by ye Kings Authority doe p^{r}sent That ffrancis Smith ye younger of ye s^d County of Chester yeoman on ye 6th day of ye fourth moneth last past in ye County afores^d with force did Comitt an assault upon Mary ye wife of James Bayless of ye s^d County and her ye s^d Mary then and there did violently force to ye Bed Side in her s^d Husbands House with an intent to have Comitted fornication with her And ye s^d Jurors further present that ye s^d ffrancis Smith did then and there swear two severall Oathes (by God) against ye Publick Peace and against ye forme of ye Seve^{r}all lawes in such Cases made and Provided

The names of ye Grand Inquest that appeared not amongst their fellows this Court

William Gabiter
Thomas King
Edward Walter

for which they was fined 10^s a Peece

ffrancis Smith Pl^t
James Bayless Defend^t
{ The Pl^t not appearing non Suite is granted
{ ffrancis Smith was Called three times to answer ye above psentment butt made noe appearance

The names of ye Grand Inquest attested att this Court

Caleb Pusie
David Lawrence
Walter ffausett
John Sharples
Woolla Rosen
William Clayton
Lawrence Raugh
John Bennett
William Cloud
William Collett

Walter Marten
John Kinsman
Joseph Richards Sen^{er}
Edward Carter
John Beales
Peter Peterson
Richard Parker
Thomas Bradshaw
Thomas Worth

George Phillips Pl^t
James Stamfield Defend^t
In an action of ye Case
} Jury the same in ye Case of Robert Eyre and Mary Best.

County Court of Chester

Declaration — Whereupon ye Pl^t Saith that he having formerly wrought att ye Defend^{ts} House for severall of his workmen and of them att his Taylors Trad did earne Severall sums of money according to a Schedull hear ready to be delivered in Court may more att large appear as alsoe money lent amounting in all to ye Sum of 4£ 3^s 5^d which upon Some Considerations the Defend^t did take upon Himselfe to Satisfie and did assume to pay ye same unto ye Pl^t notwithstanding which assumtion and Promise the Defend^t have not made satisfaction unto ye Plaintife Butt Sill withholdeth ye Same although he have long Since had ye Same in Possession Whereupon ye Pl^t

brings his action for ye s^d Sum of four pounds three shillings and five pence and Craves Judgment of this Court for ye Same with reasonable Damage and Cost of Suite

Witnesses   Henry Hames being Attested declareth that about 2 years since William Winter did Sell a Sadle to George Phillips upon James Stamfields account

John Smith being attested declareth that about 2 years Since George Phillips told him that he and James Stanfield was att that time Clear in accounts

Richard Clues being attested Declareth that George Phillips did make him Cloathes twice butt att what time he Cannot be Certaine

Robert Barber being attested Saith about ye time he bought leather of James Stamfield he did see George Phillips att worke att s^d Stamfields which was about ye 11th moneth 87

Andrew Job being attested Saith that he doe know that in ye Spring George Phillips was att worke att James Stamfields but what Spring he is uncertaine he further Saith that he did draw out an account for George Phillips last spring was two years.

Randall Vernon being attested Declareth that about ye last Spring faire was a twelve moneth he received money of Robert Barber for account of James Stamfield

Mary Stamfield being attested Saith that before ye arbitration her Brother and George Phillips made up accounts and her brother James Stamfield owed George Phillips a paire of Shooes which aferward he had

the 27th of ye 6th moneth 1689
The Verdickt of ye Jury is they finde
for ye Plaintife to have due to him } Hereupon Judgment
on Ballance of accounts the sum of   is granted
ninteen Shillings and eleven pence
with Cost of Suite and 1d Damage

The grand Inquest   The 27th of ye 6th moneth 1689
p'sentment of Mary   Wee of ye Grand Jury p'sent Mary
Turberfield &   Turberfield Servant to Nathaniel Evans
John Eldridge   for that about the begenning of ye 3d
moneth last Shee Comitted fornication
with John Eldridge in a Boate upon ye
River and Confesseth her Selfe by ye
said Act with Child And in Confirmation
of ye truth hereof the said John Eldridge
Confesseth ye same whome for that
Cause wee likewise psent

Upon which they are both Called to ye Barr where they made their appearance and upon her farther confession & submission a Jury of Women whose names are under written ordered to Inspect the said Mary Turberfields Condition

The names of ye Jury Impanelled

Lidea Wade   Elizabeth Musgrove
Sarah Usher   Mary Bayliss   They make returne that
Hester Rawlence   Elizabeth Hastings   they Cannot finde shee
Mary Carter   Mary Little   is with Child neither be
Jane Haukes   Jane Moulder   they Sure Shee is not
Mary Hodskinns   Anne Saunderlaine

Whereupon her master was ordered to Defray this p'sent Court Charge and to see her forth Coming att ye next County Court.

John Eldridge Confesseth the fact in Open Court and Humbly Craves (by his Petition) the favour and Mercy of ye Court

Judgment is hereupon awarded that he Pay three pounds to ye Governour for a fine and to remaine in ye Shreifes Custody till paid and to give Security that if shee proove with Child according to time to defray all Cost and Charge that may accrue to her master Thereby as alsoe to discharge the Township of ye Child.

Nathaniel Evans Petitioned for a Remedy against all his great Charge and Expence which his Servant Mary Turberfield had Contracted (by her often running away) according to his Schedull delivered into this Court as alsoe for his Charge and Expence this p^{r}sent Court

Whereupon Judgment is awarded that shee serve one year and a halfe with her s^d master to make good his Damage and Charge and absence by running away after ye Expiration of her Indenture

Ordered that Richard Woodward be supervisor of ye High Wayes for ye Township of Thornbury for ye next ensuing year.

Ordered that John Jerman be Constaple for Radnor and John Lewis for Harfort for ye next ensuing year

William Hudson acknowledged a Deed unto Olife Roberts for a tract of land Conteining 300 acres lying in Newtowne dated ye 24th day of ye 6th moneth Called Aug^o 1689

ffrancis Chadsey as Attorney to Dennis Rotchford acknowledged a Deed for a parcell of land in Concord Conteining two hundred acres unto Thomas Green dated ye 4th day of ye 4th moneth 1689

Thomas Brasy acknowledged a Deed for a parcell of land lying in ye forke of Chester Creeke unto Thomas Marten Conteing by Estimation 119 acres Dated ye 27th day of ye 6th Mo 1689

George Simcocke acknowledged a Deed unto John Wood for a parcell of land Conteining one hundred acres lying in Darby dated ye 24 day of ye 6th moneth 1689

James Browne Petitioned that an order of Court may be allowed him what time his boy John Marten should Serve him or his assignes for his Cost and Charge Contracted att a Court held att Chester ye 3ᵈ day in yᵉ 1ˢᵗ weeke of yᵉ 1ˢᵗ moneth last

Ordered that yᵉ sᵈ John Marten doe serve him yᵉ sᵈ James Browne or his assignes two full years and a Halfe after yᵉ Expiration of his Indenture

A Declaration from yᵉ Governour and Councell was read dated yᵉ 20ᵗʰ of yᵉ 3ᵈ moᵗʰ 1689

ffrancis Smith Senior was Comitted to yᵉ Shreifes Custody for Breach of Peace Comitted against Richard Buffington

Sarah Usher as Attorney to her Husband Thomas Usher acknowledged an assignment of a Patent for two hundred acres of Land beginning att Concord thence north West of Bethell Township unto William Haukes dated yᵉ 2ᵈ day of yᵉ 2ᵈ moneth 1689

The Court adjourne untill yᵉ 3ᵈ day in yᵉ 1ˢᵗ weeke of yᵉ 8ᵗʰ mo 1689

Att an Orphans Court held att Chester yᵉ 3ᵈ day in yᵉ 1ˢᵗ weeke of yᵉ 8ᵗʰ moneth 1689

John Bristow Presidᵗ
John Simcocke
ffrancis Harison
Bartholomew Coppocke
James Saunderlaine
Nicholas Newland
George Maris
William Howell
} Justices

George fforeman Shreife
Robert Eyre Clerke

Joseph Wood was called 3 times butt making noe appearance it was ordered that a speciall Warrant be Issued out to the Shreife to apprehend him and to Carry him before Some Justice of yᵉ Peace for this County in order to give an account what application he have made unto yᵉ Governour in persuance of an order made yᵉ last Orphans Court

ffrancis Little was Called in yᵉ Case of William and Ellin Baines which att his request was Continued untill yᵉ next morning att what time he made his appearance and produced a receipt in full Satisfaction

Phillip Roman was Called 3 times butt making noe appearance it was ordered that a Warrant be Issued out to ye Shreife to apprehend him and to Carry him before ye next Justice of ye Peace for this County in order to give an account why he doe not per forme ye Order of ye last Orphans Court

William Haukes being Called made his appearance and was ordered forthwith to accomplish ye last Courts order which he promised to doe and to make a true returne thereof to ye next Orphans Court.

Ordered att ye request of Robert Pile that Nicholas Newland doe Succead Edward Beasar Disceast in ye gaurdionship of William Oborns Children and that ye said Nicholas and Jacob Chandler Doe vew and make up an account of ye Estate of ye afores^d Diceast Wm Oborne in order to Render unto the Disceaseds Daughter Mary Oborne (who is now arrived to age) the Just proportion of her s^d Disceast ffathers Estate And that ye s^d Jacob Chandler and Nicholas Newland in persuance Hereof have Power to call Anne ye Reliqut of ye Disceast Edward Beasar to an account in order to take ye efects of ye Disceast Wm Oborns out of her hand

The Court adjourne untill ye next morning & mett according to adjournment

Phillip Roman was Called who made his appearance and was ordered to bring in a Copy of ye Enventory of ye Estate of his Prediceasor Wm Beasar to Satisfie this Court what is Become of ye Estate of ye Disceased

Joshua ffirne and Samuell Levis appointed by this Court Trustees to ye Estate of Joseph Humphryes Disceast brought forth a Copy of ye Enventory thereof amounting to ye Sum of thirty nine pounds and Seven Pence whose Copy followes

An Enventory of ye Goods and Chattles of Joseph Humphry of Newtowne Disceast appraised by us whose names are hereunto Subscribed

	£	s	d
5 augers		4	6
1 frow		1	0
1 falling axe		1	0
2 old howes		0	6
6 Chessells 1 goudge		2	6
2 Plaines 1 Shave		2	0
1 Drawing knife		1	0
3 hamers		1	0
2 Iron Wedges		3	0
1 Tosting Iron		0	6
2 Carving tooles		0	2
1 p^r nipers		0	3
some old Iron		0	6
1 trouell		0	9
3 gimbletts 1 aule		0	6
1 fire Shovle		0	9
1 Cupp		0	6
1 p^r of old Pott hookes		0	6
1 broaken Sqare		0	4
1 broad Axe		5	0
1 hand Saw		1	0
1 old Plaine		0	6
1 whip Saw		10	0
1 Crosse cutt Saw		3	0
1 Brasse kettle		7	0
2 Posnetts		4	0
1 frying Pann		4	0
1 old Brasse Pott		8	0
1 Churne		2	0
feathers		1	0
1 old Pack Cloth		1	0
1 Spade		0	6
4 Skimers		2	6
2 Bowles		1	0
2 little Piggins		0	9

	£	s	d
1 doz Trenchers		1	0
2 tinne Panns		1	6
1 Little Sumer	00	00	6
2 candle Stickes	0	4	0
2 little Brushes	0	0	6
1 Brush	0	0	4
8 Spoones	0	1	0
1 Dram Cupp 1 Sisar	0	0	6
1 tinne Tankard	0	0	6
1 Pepper Box	0	0	6
2 files	0	0	6
2 Smoothing Irons	0	1	6
1 Grater	0	0	4
1 Spice Box	0	1	0
1 paire Hindges	0	0	6
2 old Hatts	0	5	0
1 Baskett 1 Pinn coochin	0	2	0
2 pr of old Stockins	0	1	6
3 whiskes	0	2	3
1 little Skarfe	0	2	0
2 blacke hoods	0	1	6
2 pr Gloves	0	1	6
Some yarne	0	5	0
1 Ink horne	0	0	4
6 Pinners	0	2	0
4 quaifs	0	2	0
6 old quaifs	0	2	0
1 linnen Capp	0	0	6
3 handkercheifes	0	2	6
2 pr Sleeves	0	1	6
3 neck cloathes	0	1	0
3 pr little sleeves	0	1	0
10 Pinners	0	1	8
1 Cravatt	0	0	4
1 Pillow Coates	0	4	0

	£	s	d
5 Napkinns	0	5	0
10 towells	0	3	0
1 napkin 2 Pillow Coates	0	3	0
1 p^r sheets	0	7	0
1 haire Ceive		1	6
1 girdle		1	0
3 Spotted Plates		1	6
1 Pewter Dish		4	0
1 Pewter Dish		2	6
7 Porringers		7	0
1 Possett Cupp		2	6
1 Chamber Pott		2	6
1 Cullender		0	6
Some old Pewter		0	6
1 Plate		1	4
1 Rasor	0	1	0
1 Ads 1 Chessle	0	4	0
1 looking glasse 1 Pillow	0	6	0
1 Cow and Calfe	3	10	0
1 Bullocke	2	5	0
1 mare and Colt	4	0	0
8 hoggs and Sowes	6	0	0
1 p^r sheets	0	6	0
1 Sheete	0	2	0
1 Sett of Curtaines and vallens	1	0	00
2 Shirts	0	6	00
1 p^r Bodyes	0	1	00
1 Stomager	0	0	6
1 p^r Searge Sleeves	0	2	0
1 p^r Compasses	0	0	6
some old linnen	0	3	0
1 Chest	0	6	0
1 Chest	0	4	0
1 Saddle	0	10	0
1 Gunn	0	12	0

	£	s	d
1 Bed 4 Pillowes: 1 Bolster	1	3	0
4 Cover lide: 2 Blanketts	1	3	0
7 Petty Coatess	3	0	0
mens apparell	2	0	0
2 gowne Bodyes	0	16	0
1 mento: 2 hoods 1 loose gowne 2 green aprons 1 p^r stayes	2	10	0
ye sum is	39	0	7

John Blunstone
John Bartram
Jacob Simcocke

Andrew ffriend and Woolla Rosen became Bound unto this Court under ye Penalty of
that Andrew Locke shall faithfully performe ye office of guardian to his Orphan Brothers and Sisters

---

Att a Court held att Chester for ye County of Chester ye 3^d day in ye 1st Weeke of ye 8th Moth 1689

{ John Bristow President
John Simcocke
ffrancis Harrison
Bartholomew Coppocke
James Saunderlaine
Nicholas Newland
George Maris
William Howell } Justices p^{r}sent

George fforeman Shreife
Robert Eyre Clerke

Mary Tuberfield being called to to ye Barr and being further Examined Concerning her Indicktm^t the last Court declared that notwithstanding her Testimony to ye last Court that shee was with Child by John Eldridge shee doe now freely declare to ye Contrary and Submitts to ye mercy of ye King and Governour

Ordered that Albertus Henrickson and John Child see her forth Coming in ye afternoone

The Court adjourne untill y̨ᵉ afternoone and mett againe according to adjournment

Ordered that William Colborne Supervisor of yᵉ High wayes for yᵉ Towne of Chester have Power to Sumon yᵉ Inhabitance of Sᵈ Township to erect a foote Bridge over Chester Creeke att or near William Woodmansees And that John Baldwin have another order to Sumon the Inhabitance of yᵉ Township of Astone to assist yᵉ Inhabitance of Chester in yᵉ matter

Robert Taylor past over 2 deeds to his 2 Sonns Isacke and Josiah Taylor both dated yᵉ 20ᵗʰ day of yᵉ 6ᵗʰ moneth 1689, viz.

one to Isacke for a Plantation and premisses Conteining 300 acres of land lying in Springtowne

another to Josiah for a Plantation and pʳmisses lying in Marple

James Bayless Petitioned against ffrancis Smith Junior and Robert Eyre for Putting him to unnessessary Charge

Ordered that Warrants be forthwith Issued out to yᵉ Shreife to apprehend yᵉ sᵈ ffrancis Smith and that yᵉ Constaples of Burmingham and Thornbury be assisting in yᵉ matter.

Ordered that Warrants of Contemp be Derected to yᵉ Shreife to apprehend yᵉ Bodyes of John Lewis and John Jerman for their Contempt of not entring into their respective offices of Constaple (viz) John Lewis for Harfort and John Jerman for Radnor when thereunto required by this Court

Ordered that Morris Lewellin be Suppervisor of yᵉ High wayes for yᵉ Township of Harfort and Richard Armes for yᵉ Township of Radnor for yᵉ next ensuing yeare

Andrew Locke and Mouns Locke acknowledged a deed to Anne ffriend Widdow and her two Sonns Andrew and John ffriend for a Plantation and pʳmisses Conteining 300 acres lying by yᵉ River Deleware in Ridley Township

John Hodskinns Past over a deed for a message or Tenement lying in yᵉ Towne of Chester now in Possession of ffrancis Little with yᵉ pʳmisses therein mentioned unto yᵉ sᵈ ffrancis Little dated yᵉ 19ᵗʰ day of yᵉ 4ᵗʰ moneth 1689

The above s^d ffrancis Little Past over a mortgage of ye above said message and p'misses unto Robert Wade dated ye 2^d day of ye 8th moneth 1689

Declaration

BARTHOLOMEW COPPOCKE Pl^t } The plea declares y^t ye Defend^t
JOHN BUTLER Defend^t became Indebted to him in y^e
in an action of Debt upon Sum of twenty two pounds
Attatchment in ye hands of tenne shillings for severall
James Stamfield goods and merchandizes sold him as by bill under ye Defendt^s hand and Seale hear in Court to be produced and ye Pl^t finding effects in ye hands of James Stamfield of ye s^d Defend^{ts} for ye s^d Sum of 22£ 10^s: soe ye Pl^t craves Judgment of this Court for ye s^d Sum with cost of Suite

Whereupon James Stamfield acknowledged that he had in Passession Efects of John Butlers to ye same vallue and Confessed Judgment upon ye same

Andrew Locke and Mouns Locke acknowledged a Deed unto Samuell Rowland for 30 acres of Land lying upon Ridley Creeke Dated y^e of ye moneth

ABRAHAM HOOPER Pl^t } Continued since ye last
HENRY BARNES Defend^t Court and now withdrawn

ffrancis Smith Senio^r was called but his wife Anne making it appear that he was sicke therefore he is suspended till ye next Court

ROBERT BROTHERS Pl^t } Continued } RICHARD CLUES Pl^t
MARY BOULES Defend^t since ye ANDREW LOCKE Defend^t
in an action of ye Case last Court Withdrawne

William Collett Complained against his servant man William Rateway for his Charges and Expense and lost of time in taking him up when he last ran away being absent from ye 10th of ye 4th moneth last to ye 27th of ye Same Instant amounting according to yᵉ Colletts Schedull delivered to this Court to yᵉ Sum of one pound five shillings and three pence

Ordered that yᵉ said William Rateway for defraying yᵉ said Charges and lost of time doe Serve his sᵈ master or his assignes the full terme of 5 monethes from yᵉ Expiration and Termination of a late Court order on yᵉ like behalfe

John Sanger of Concord Petitioned againe for his Pay for keeping Edward Kinison amounting according to his Petition to yᵉ sum of 8£ 11ˢ which yᵉ Court did allow and tooke yᵉ matter into Consideration.

Thomas Lasy his Indicktment { The Jurors for yᵉ Proprietary and Governour by yᵉ Kings Authority doe present Thomas lasy Sometime Servant to Richard ffew of this County Disceast for Stamping and making Base and counterfeite peeces of Eight and Bartering and Exposing yᵉ same for goods and other merchandize within this Province to yᵉ great Hurt and damage of yᵉ Kings leidge People and Contrary to yᵉ Peace of our Sovereigne Lord yᵉ King &c   Joseph Richards foreman.

Whereupon Thomas Lasy is Called to yᵉ Barr and by Petition Confesseth his fact and putts himselfe upon yᵉ mercy of yᵉ King and Governour

Judgment is granted that he stand att yᵉ Publicke Place of Correction att yᵉ Towne of Chester two Severall Court Dayes 3 hours each day with a Paper of his Crimes written in Capitall letters afixed upon his Brest and that he remaine in yᵉ Shreifes Custody untill he give good Security to performe this Judgment and pay his fees

Allen Robinett his Indicktment { The Jurors for yᵉ Proprietary and Governour by the Kings Authority doe present Allen Robinett Senior of this County for writting Scandelous and abusive Papers against John Bristow one of ye Kings Justices and representative in Councell of ye People of this County Contrary to ye 29th law of this Province and against ye Peace of our Sovereigne lord ye King

Joseph Richards foreman

Whereupon he is Called to ye Barr and putts himselfe upon ye mercy of ye King and Governour { Judgment is awarded that he shall here in Publicke acknowledge in perticular his fault and Crimes for which he stands Indickted and pay all Court Charge

The Grand Inquest Presentments

Wee ye Jurors &c p^{r}sent Haunce Urine for doing his servill labour the Lords day or first day of ye Weeke Contrary to ye lawes of ye Province

upon which he was Called to ye Barr butt making noe appearance he was ordered to be sumoned to ye next Court

Wee p^{r}sent Richard Clues for being Drunke on ye 27th day of Aug^o att Chester 1689

Joseph Richards foreman

upon which he was Called to ye Barr where he made his appearance and putts himselfe upon ye mercy of ye King and Governour { Whereupon he is fined 5^s to ye Govern^{r}s use which he promised to pay

Wee the Grand Jury p^{r}sent David Lawrence of Harfort being of ye members of ye grand Jury for not giving his Attendance att ye Court October 2: 89

Joseph Richard fforeman

Ordered that he pay for his Default 10^s for a fine to ye Governours use

George Stroad was fined 5^s to ye use of ye Governour for being Drunke ye last Court he first putting himselfe upon ye mercy of ye King and Governour

The Grand Inquest of p^{r}sentments

Wee ye Grand Inquest by ye Kings Authority for ye County of Chester doe p^{r}sent ye want of ye Inhabitance of ye Township of Radnor and Harfort and y̆ᵉ Inhabitance adjacent they not being brought in to Joyne with us in yᵉ Levies and other Publicke Services of this County

Joseph Richards foreman

Ordered that Sumons be Issued out to bring them in

The Jurors pʳsent Isacke Brealy for being Drunke att Chester on yᵉ 27ᵗʰ of Augº last

Whereupon he is Called to yᵉ Barr where he makes his appearance and putts himselfe upon yᵉ mercy of yᵉ King and Governour } Judgment is Granted yᵗ he pay 5/ to yᵉ Governᵣ for a fine

They likewise pʳsent John ffox and Henry Barnes for being Drunke betweene yᵉ last Court and this Court

Whereup they are Called to yᵉ Barr and making their appearance are Comitted to yᵉ Shreifes Custody for refusing to pay their fines   They afterward appear & submitt whereupon Judgmᵗ is awarded yᵗ they pay 5ˢ apeece for a fine to yᵉ Governours use

Wee pʳsent George Stroad for being drunke and Swearing an Oath yᵉ 27ᵗʰ day of August 1689

    Witnesses   Joseph Richards foreman
Walter Marten
Joseph Richards

James Stamfield Petitioned yᵉ Court against his three servants Richard Bestrasor Owen Mackdaniell and John Turner for his great Charge and Expence their lost time &c when they last run away   Whereupon it was ordered that 3 Comessioners of yᵉ Peace should Inspect yᵉ matter and make report to yᵉ Court whose returne is yᵉ Same as followes
1689 Oct 2ᵈ

Wee whose hands are under written doe order by concent of yᵉ bench that Richard Bestrasor Servant to James Stamfield shall serve att yᵉ Expiration of his time three years for his running away and other Charges that he hath putt his master to in taking him up

Wee likewise order James Stamfields other two men Owen

Mack-Daniell and John Turner for their running away and other Charges to serve him nine monethes a peece after ye Expiration of their Indentures as alsoe wee order the said James Stamfield to finde and allow his said Servants with Sufficient meate drinke Lodging and apparrell dureing their times of Servitude And if their s^d m^r James Stamfield doe not performe this order then they are to make their Complaint to ye next Justice of ye Peace and they shall have Care taken for them according to law

Hereupon ye Court grants Judgment

James Saunderlaine
George Maris
Bartho: Coppocke

Ordered that for a further Explanation of ye late Grand Inquest returne (att a Court held att Chester ye 3^d day in ye 1st weeke of ye 10th moneth moneth 1688 last) the Publicke Charges of this County for ye Payment of ye Court House and Prison the Service of ye Councell and assemblymen and releife of ye Poore &c by and with ye Concent of this present grand Inquest be made up in a faire Schedull and accordingly recorded by an account of Debt^{or} and Creditor in ye Booke of Record which is as followes (viz)

County of Chester Debitor

	£	s	d
To John Simcocke	45	00	00
To George fforeman	19	8	3
To Capt Wm Markham	5	1	8
To John Bristow	10	19	6
To Wm Clayton	16	00	
To Thomas Brasy	00	12	
To Joshua Hastings			
To George Wood			
To John Blunstone			
To Thomas Brasy			
To Dennis Rochford	08	00	00
To John Beasar			
To John Harding			
To Joseph Phips			
To John Hastings			

County of Chester Debitor

	£	s	d
To Thomas Brasy To John Beasar To George Wood To Joseph Phips To John Blunstone To Dennis Rochford	02	8	00
To Joshua Hastins To George Maris To John Harding To John Blunstone	04	16	00
To what brought from ye other Side..	111	8	5
To John Blunstone To George Maris To John Harding To Thomas Usher To Joshua ffirne To ffra: Stamfield	06	06	00
To John Blunstone To George Maris To Bartho: Coppocke To Sam^{ll} Levis To Caleb Pewsie	06	15	00
To John Blunstone To George Maris To Bartho: Coppocke To Caleb Pewsey To Edward Beasar To Randall Vernome	02	14	00

County of Chester Debitor

	£	s	d
To John Blunstone			
To James Saunderlaine			
To George Maris	08	2	00
To Robert Pile			
To Edward Carter			
To Thomas Colborne			

135 5 5

County of Chester Debitor

	£	s	d
To what brought from ye other side	135	05	5
To Travelling Charges for the assembly amounting to	8	08	00
To John Hodskinns	3	9	10
To ye Charges of ye grand Inquest 17 in numb^r	2	3	3
To Caleb Pusie	1	10	0
To Expence for Justices Shreife and Clerke	1	10	0
To James Saunderlaine	30	13	9
To William Clayton	5	01	6
To Robert Wade	103	10	11
To ye Widdow ffriend	11	8	3
To Edward Kinistone	9	15	00
To Nicholas Newland	9	18	00
To John Grubb and Rich Buffington			

Contra is Cre

	£	s	d
By severall paid George fforeman	8	16	10
By Severall paid James Saunderlaine	13	01	3
By abatement by ye grand Inquest out of James Saund'lain^s acc^o	4	6	0
By severall paid Robert Wade	89	17	
By Edward Kinison	1	4	

117 5 1

Ordered that Warrants be Issued out to ye Respective Collecto^{r}s hereafter mentioned to Collect ye aforegoing Levie and that ye Same be raised according to a former order of Court (viz) one every hundred acres of land taken up and Inhabited 3^s: and on every hundred acres of land taken up by nonresidence and not Inhabited 4^s/ 6^d and on all freemen from 16 years of age to 60: 3^s:/ by ye Pole and all male Servants soe quallified 1^s 6^d and for soe doing ye Collect^{rs} are to receive 6^d in ye pound

for Chester Township } to be paid to James
   Caleb Pusie   } Saunderlaine &
   Thomas Brasie } Robert Wade

for Ridley Township } to be paid to
   Walter ffausett   } John Simcocke
   Andrew ffriend

for Springtowne
   ffrancis Yarnall   } Idem
   Bartho: Coppocke seni^r

for Marple Township
   James Stamfield } Idem
   Thomas Person

for Newtowne
   Thomas Norbury— Idem

for Darby Township   to be paid to
   Joshua ffirne   } John Blunstone
   John Wood Seni^r } Geo: Maris Sam^{ll} Levis

for Chichester   { to be paid to
   Nathaniel Lamplue { George fforeman
   Walter Marten   { William Clayton
                       ffrancis Harison

for Bethell
   Robert Pile   } Idem
   Joseph Bushell

for yᵉ Township of Harfort
  William Jenkin } to John Blunstone
  David Lawrence } Geo: Maris Samˡˡ Levis

for Radnor Township
  Richard Armes } Idem
  Howell James }

for Upper Providence
  Thomas Powell } to be paid to
  Peter Taylor } John Simcocke

for neither Providence
  Randall Vernone } Idem
  Joshua Hastings }

for Middletowne   to be paid to
  John Marten } Thomas Colborne
  Thomas Marten }

for Astone   to be paid to
  Robert Carter } James Saundʳlane
  Joseph Richards Junʳ } Robert Wade

for Burmingham
  Richard Thatcher } to be paid to
  John Bennett } Nicholas Newland

for Westtowne
  John Radley   Idem

for Concord
  John Mendenhall } to be paid to
  Nathaniell Newland } Nicholas Newland

for Thornbury
  George Pearce } Idem
  Hugh Durberow }

for Edgmond
  Joseph Baker } Idem
  Thomas Worrell }

Ordered that John Bristow take his pay out of ye non-residents land as farr as the same will satisfie him and ye remainder if any out of ye other Levies

Ordered that George Churchman pay Court Charges and Constaples fees for his Cause this day in Court

William Clayton was Chosen Constaple for ye Township of Chichester in ye Roome of Henry Renolds for ye next ensuing year.

Mary Turberfield was Called to ye Barr and Judgment awarded to receive 10 Strips upon her bear backe well laid on att ye Comon Whipping Post att Chester

The aforesaid John Eldridge was called to ye bar and pleaded Gilty whereupon Judgment was awarded that hee should pay a fine of Three pounds and all the Court Charges and bee discharged

---

Att a Court held att Chester for ye County of Chester ye 3^d day in ye 1st weeke of ye 10th Mo 1689

{ John Simcocke Presid^t
John Bristow
John Blunstone
ffrancis Harrison
Bartholomew Coppocke
Nicholas Newland
William Howell } Justices psent

Nicholas White and William Thomas was Called to ye Barr upon their fact of speaking words tending to Sedition and breach of Peace and perswading people (Contrary to an order of Court) not to pay ye Publicke Levies of this County when thereunto lawfully required Butt upon their Submission and acknowledgment of ye fact and putting themselves upon ye mercy of ye King and Governour they are acquitted paying their fees

Haunce Urine was Called to answer ye presentment of ye Grand Inquest ye last Court Who making his appearance and Putting himselfe upon ye mercy of ye King and Govern^r was acquitted paying ye Court Charge

Thomas Rawlence Pl[t] Thomas Persons Defend[t] In an action of Debt	withdrawne	Robert Moulder Pl[t] Peter Erickson Defend[t] In an action of Assault & Battery — withdrawne

ffrancis Smith Senior was Called to answer a former assault Comitted upon Richard Buffington butt y[e] said Buffington not appearing he was acquitted paying his fees

John Jerman was Attested Constaple for y[e] Township of Radnor for y[e] next Ensuing year

George Strod was Called butt y[e] Court being Satisfied y[t] he was gone over y[e] River to West Jersey Therefore his presentm[t] is Continued to y[e] next Court

David Lawrence was remitted his former fine

John Simcocke Informed y[e] Court that Robert Wade passing by Thomas Lasy who was suffering y[e] last Courts sentance reflectingly s[d] what Law hath he broaken or what Kings law hath he Broaken

John Nickson	Pl[t]	Continued & afterward withdrawne
Andrew Locke	Defend[t]	
In an action of debt		

Robert Barber	Pl[t]	Continued and afterward with ward
James Stamfield	Defend[t]	
In an action of Scandall and Defamation		

Anne ffriend Widdow and Andrew ffriend her Sonne Petitioned for their pay which they had been out upon y[e] Court house and prison

The Petition was read and Considered

Att a Court held att Chester for the County of Chester the 1st 3[d] day of the 1st Weeke in the 1st moneth 168$\frac{9}{90}$

John Bristow Presid[t]
Job Blunston
Nicholas Newland
ffrancesHarrison
Samuell Levis
James Sandilands
Joshua ffearne

Justices There pres[t]

John Simcocke Junr in Open Court declared that he was overtaken wth Drinke soe was Ordered to pay his ffine wch was Three Shillings

Samuell Levis past A deed in Oppen Court bearing deat the 2^d of the 11th month 1688 To Thomas Marle

John Blonston Attorney to Thomas Holemes past A deed in Oppen Court bearing deat the 1st day of the of the 5 mo 1688 To Joseph Wood

Charles Pickering and Patrick Robinson } Attornies for Thomas Holmes Pl^{t}f against Charles Ashcomb Df^t

In action of Tresspass on the Case
Continued until next Court

Charles Pickering and Patrick Robinson } Attornies for Thomas Holmes pl^{t}f Charles Ashcomb Defdt

In an action of Tresspass on the Case
Continewed untill next Court

Thomas Cross in Oppen Court past A deed bearing deat the 4th day of the 1st Mont 1689 to Thomas Martine

Josias Jones being Convicted for Swaring was finde five Shillings

William Buckinham in oppen Court past a deed bearing deat the 8th day of ye 5 mo 1689 To ffrances Baldwin.

RICHARD BUFFINTON	pl^t	Peter Taylor	
SAMUELL BAKER	Dfd^t	Thomas Powell	
In an action on the Case		Joshu Hastings	
		Thomas Cartwright	
		John Baldwin	
		Philip Roman	
		William Tally	Juro^{rs}
		James Browne	
		Thomas Cross	
		Thomas Moore	
		George Woodard	
		Randel Varnam	

County Court of Chester
Declaretion

The plaintife Declareth that the Def^d hath Long time ben indepted unto the plaintife in the full and Just Sum of three pounds Ten Shillings Corrant Money of this Province as by a bill Apeareth Bearing date the 25th of the 9th month 1686 and likewise the Def^{dt} is indepted unto the plaintife in the Sume of One pound four Shillings and nine pence for diat money lent and goods and the pltf: hath often tymes required the Def^{dt} to pay him but the Def^d taking noe Corse to doe it Although he hath a long time and often promised him payment yett still neglecting it the plaintife brings his Action against the Def^d Craives Judgement of the Court with Reasonable Damage

Richard Boffinton being Attested Decleares that his acco^t is Trew

Joseph Hickman being Attested Decleares the Def^{dt} worked wth him 5 dayes and halfe att att Grubing and Clearing the Land

Zachary Patrick being Attested Decleares that he did worke att Nathaniell Lamplues att Sawing wth Df^{dt}

John Eldrige being Attested Decleares the best of his knowledg saith that about three yeares agoe that ffrances Harrison p^d Richard Boffinton 10 shillings for Sam^{ll} Beake

Jeremy Collett being Attested Decleares that he and Thomas Withers was to end a Diferance that was Betwixt the pl^{t}f and Defd^t wch they did and found the said Samuell Beker to be Indebted to the Richard Boffinton the Sume of £3 : 10^s or wch accordingly the said Samuell Beker gaive his Bill the 5 of the 1st Month 16$\frac{89}{90}$

The virdit of the Jury doe find for the p^lt^f: with Cost of Sut and Six pence Damage: And upon Ball^a of accounts the Defendent to be indebted to the plantife One pounds four Shillings and six pence } Heare upon Judgment was granted according to verd^t

George Willarde in Oppen Court past a Deed bearing deat the 2 day 10 mo 1689 To Ralph Dracott

ROBERT TURNER   Pl^tf
CALEB PUSEY   Def^dt
Decleration
} In an action of Tresspass on the Case &c

Robert Torner of the town and County of Philadelphia in the s^d province in America Merch^t Complains against Caleb Pusey of Chester County in said province yeoman in an action of Tresspass on the Casse for that Whereas upon the Twentieth and first day of the fourth mo^th 1688 the said Defend^t did draw three Bills of Exch^a all of the same date tener and Contents upon Daniell Whearley and Comp. Merch^ts in London for the Sume of One hundred Eighty Seven pounds Sterling Money of England peyable to the p^ltf or his Ord^r att Fourtye dayes Sight and that for the value received of the sd p^ltf here And wch Three bills of Exch^a the p^ltf did Indorse thus vizt pay the Contents of the within Bill to George Watt or ord^r jts myne Robert Torner: As two of the said Originall Bills of Exch^a here wth in Court to be produced and duly indorsed as a above will Testifie As also for that wheras William Scorey Notary and Tabellion Publick by Royall Authority admitted and Sworn Dwelling in London wth in the Kingdom of England did on the 15th day of Octob^r anno 1688 att the Request of m^r John Watt of London Merch^t Exhibit the s^d Originall Bill of Exch^a indorsed as is aforesaid unto the said Mr Daniell Whearley to whom and Comp. the Same was Directed Requesting him to accept the same where upon he Answered that he would not accept the said bill for that the others Concerned in the Same wold not allow their proportionable

Shares, and wch Answere he the said Notary publick having heard, did (att the request of the said Mr John Watt) Solemnly protest as well against the said Caleb Pusey defd^t drawer of the said bills as against all others whom it should or might Concern of Exch^a and Rexch^a and of all Costs dammages and interests Suffered and to be Suffered for want of acceptance of the Said Bills of Exch^a And on the Twentieth and Eight day of Novemb^r 1688 the s^d Notary Publick did att the request aforesaid Exhibit the said Originall Bill of Exch^a to to the said Daniell Whearley demanding of him payment of its Contents Whereupon hee Answered that hee would not pay the same for that the other Concerned would not allow their proportionable Shares And which answer hee the said Notary publick having heard did (att the request afore said) Solemnly protest as we^all against the said Caleb Pusey defd^t drawer of the said Bills of Exchange as also against all others whom it should or might Concern, of Exchange and reExchange and of all Costs damages and Interests Suffered and to be Suffered for want of payment of the said Bills as the said Two protests, the one for non-acceptance, and the other for Non. payment, under the signe and Subscription Manual of the said William Scarey herew^th also in Court to be produced will Testify. And the said pl^tf hath often requested and desired the said Caleb Pusey to have made paym^t to him not only of the said sum of One hundred eighty seven pounds Lawfull Money of England Being in Current Sillver Mony of Pensilvania Two hundred thirty three pounds fifteen Shillings as the Contents of the said bills of Exchange, but also the sum of thirty Seven pounds eight Shillings Lawfull money of England being in Current Silver Money of the said Province ffourty six pounds Six Shillings and Six pence as the proportionable part of Twenty ⅌ Cent Advance for the said protest Together with Twelve Shillings Lawfull Money of England being being in Current Money of Pensilvania ffifteen Shillings, Together wth the Lawfull interest of the said Sume of Two hundred thirty three pounds ffifteen Shillings Lawfull money of the said province from the eighteenth day of June 1689, att wch tyme the protested Bills arryved here to the eighteenth day of february 16$\frac{8}{9}$ being eight Months att eight ₱ Cent is Twelve pounds Thirteen Shillings and Ten pence, Amounting in the whole the said four sumes to the Sum of Two hundred Ninty three pounds ten Shillings and fouer pence in Courront Sillver Money of the Said Province of Pennsilvania Saving Just accompt rekonin of of all the said Sums Never the Less the said Def^{dt} Still Refuses and Delayes to doe the same, Whereupon the said Pl^tf brings this Suit and Craves Judgment of this Court for the said sum of Two hundred Ninty three pounds Ten Shillings and fouer pence Lawfull Curront Silver Money of the said province The plaintiffe allowing that the Def^{dt} hath paid thereof the Sume of Three pounds thirteen Shillings and nine pence And so the Judgment Craved is for the Remaining Two hundred Eighty nyne pounds Sixteen Shillings and Seven pence Lawfull Money of the Said province wth Costs of Suite

Calibe Pusey the Def^{dt} Appeared in Oppen Court and Confesed Judgem^t to the Same } And accordingly Judgem^t was Granted

JOHN NEELD pl^tf
JOHN MADOX Defd^t } in an action of the Case for Breach of Articles

Decleration

John Neelde of the Town of Aston in the said County yeaman Complains against John Madox of Ridly Joyner in an action on the Case for that whereas the said Def^{dt} was to Build for the said pl^tf Severall Buildings as by Two Articles of agreem^t under the hand and Seale of Boath partyes will make it appeare In the first agreem^t the said Def^{dt} was to Build for the pl^tf Two peeses of Building one to be fifteen foote Long and Twelve foot wide wth in and Ten foote and half high of the Wall and the other to be Eighteen foot Long and fifteen foot Wide wth in Ten foot and a half of the Wall and to make One Doore and a Doore plase in Each of them

Windowes att the End to hich in att and to Lay barens over One End for a threshing place and to Lay a flore of plankes but the s^d pl^{t}f was to Cleave the plankes and to Sett on Two Locks, And all the Worke was to be Compleated and Don by the 24th day of the 4th month And the pl^{t}f was to pay Said Def^{dt} Two Steares and fouer bushalls Indian Corne when the Worke was ffinished. And in the Second agreem^t the said Def^{dt} was to build for the Said pl^{tt} A Dwelling house Twenty four foot in Lengh and Eighteen foot in Width and Ten foot in hight Betwen Sell and Wale plate Two pertictons below and a Closett and One pertion above and a Closett And to face the Roof wth Clapboards in the Inside and to make the Botom fflore wth Sufecient plank and the first Loft wth sufecient inch board and to Cover the house Sufeciently wth Shingles and to doe all the Timber Worke about the making of one Chimley, and to make ffouer Windowes two below and two above and a porch to the ffront of the house and little windowes to the afore Said Closetts, and one peare of Staires and to face all the whole house in the Inside and the said Def^{dt} doth promise to make the house Suffeeient to live in att or before the 25th of the Tenth Month next ensuing the Date of the said agreem^t and in Nine months after to ffinish the whole worke belonging to the house. And the said pl^{t}f is to pay unto the said Def^{dt} Sixteen pounds Ten Shillings as ffol. in Three Cattle that is Two Cowes and a bullock Twelve pounds in Bacon Twenty Shillings att Six pence the pound a paire of Boots and spurs att Twenty Shillings and some other Goods to the value of ffifty Shillings. Now the said Def^{dt} hath not ꝑformed his part in Eith of the Two Articles of agreem^t And Delayes soe to doe although the pl^{t}f. on his part hath allways Supplyed the Def^{dt} wth pay and is Redy to make him paym^t wth the Remainder Soe that the said Def^{dt} had finished the said Buildings But he Neglects soe to doe soe that the pl^{t}f is Damnifyed In the full sume of five pounds Lawfull money of this Province whereupon the pl^{t}f brings this sute and Craves Judgment of this Court against the said def^{dt} wth Cost of Sute

Jury

Peter Taylor	James Browne
Joshua Hestings	Thomas Cross
Thomas Cartwrite	Thomas Moore
John Baldwin	ffrances Baldwin
Philip Roman	George Wooder
William Talley	Randell Varnam

Wittnesse Thomas Cartwrit Jeane Cartwrit Thomas Browne Margeret Carter Peter Tremaine

The virdit of the Jury

wee of the petty Jury find for the pl^{tt} wth Cost of Sute and Two pence Damage & allso the defendant shall finish the Barens which was the first Bargen and to be Clear of the Dweling house the Df^{dt} losing what he have don att it and retorning all the pay he have rec^d att the Rates he Tooke them att

heareupon Judgm^t was granted according to Virdit

The Grand Inquest Presentments

The Jurors present Isaac Brickshaw for Defaming John Simcockes one of the Propte^{rs} Representatives in Counsell in these words that he was Drunk att Last Court att Chester the 5th of Decemb

Whereupon he is Called to the Barr where he makes his appearance and putts himself upon the mercy of the King and Govern^r

Judgem^t is granted that he is to be bound to his good Behaver and to Sett up a paper of what is Crime was And Likewise Henry Barnes was Ordred to find Surityes for his good behavor and to putt up his paper

Caleb Pusey Attorney To ffrances Cooke Delivred a patten wth a Deed upon it bearing deat the 19th day of the 9 mo 1687 To Thomas Cross

Robert Woodward being Called to the Barre for Speaking abusifely against the Majestretes espetialy against John Simcockes Soe he Submitted himselfe Ordred that he should finde Two Surityes for his Good behavor

William Hawekes in Oppen Court passt bearing deat the 5th day of the first Month 1689 to Nicolas Piles

The Grand Inquest presentm^{ts}
Pensilvania

Wee The Jurors for the Governor and County of Chester by the King and Queens Authority Upon the Genarall Complaint of the people of this County about the Sevall taxes that have bin paid formerly to the building of the Court house and prison which yet the County ar not Satisfyed because there hath not as yet bin given any parfect Acco^t. and Likwise the Last Composir of Taxes together wherin your Warrents you Charge the County to be 312£: 15^s: 4^d Indebted for the Court house and prison the Counsell Men and the Asembly mens wages the poore and other publick uses according as you Charge it in yor Warrants And Likewise the tax for the Woules heads no account as yet have bin given for it

We the Grand Inquest for the County of Chester doe desire an account in the behalfe of the County wch way our Debts arise in Gennarall and perticular and Likwise what moneys that have bin raised by way of publick taxes for to defray publick charge of the County and have bin paid by the County already we desire the account in every perticular as fol.

1.st The Charge of the Cort house and prison what the charge of the building of them com to wth the matteralls by the Severall receipts of the Workmen that built them or make it apeare by the perticulers receipts upon the Records

2. Likwise we desire an account of the Tax that was formarly gathered for the paiment of Charg of building the Co^{r}thouse and prison which was 2^s 6^d ⅌ hundred Accars and 2^s: 6^d ⅌ head for freemen and 1^s: 3^d ⅌ head for Bond Servants and for Land non resident not settled on half more then resident we desire the perticular Duplicats or Returns of every Township wth their Severall rats or make the perticular recepts of every Township plainly apear by the Records.

3. Likewise the Severall Consell men and Assembly mens wages what is allowed to each person.

4. Likewise what money is paid to the releefe of the poor and what persons that receives Releefe.

5. Likwise what is the other publicke Charge the County is Charged wth as it is in y^r Warrants.

6. Likwise we desire an account of this Last Composier of taxes together vizt. for the Court house and prison Counsell men and Assembly mens wages and the Releefe of the poor and other publick uses as it is in your Warrents.

7. Likwise an account of the Tax for the Woules heads wch was 1^s: ℔ hundred Accars & 1^s: ℔ head for freem and 6^d. ℔ head for Servants and Land nonresident on halfe more then resident.

Likewise what Woules heads have bin paid for or to pay for that they may be paid if any be out of purse or wether any Money remaine in hand.

Wee the Grand Inquest present this in the behalf of the County whereunto we have Subscribed our hands the 4th of the first Month 1689/90

Joseph Richards fforeman	Tho Bradshaw
Lau: Routh	Richard Parker
Tho: Worth	William Cloud
John Sharples	John Bennett
Petter Peterson	Wm Collett
W^a: Marten	David Lawrance
Wa: faccit	Edward Carter
John Kinsman	John Beals

The Jurors present Robert Eyre for Exstortion on his ffees on his bill to Nathaniell Evins in Casse of his Maid Servant Mary Turberfield.

They Likewise present Robert Eyre for Exstortion on his bill of ffees to Henry Barnes.

They Likewise present Robert Eyre for Exstortion on his bill of ffees to John ffox.

Wee Likewise present as a Generall Grevance of this County for want of a Standerd to try both dry mesure and Liquid

Mesur for ther is great Diversity in Mesures Som are to bige and others are Somthing to Little we desire that all Mesurs be Made by the Winchester Measure.

Wee Likewise present William Coborin being Surveior of the Highways for not Ordring the Inhabitants of Chester to Mend the way by the River Syde between Chichester & Chester.

Wee Likwise present the s^d William Coborin for want of a bridge over the Creek att William Woodmanseys

Wee the Grand Jury do desire that a Table of ffees may be hung up in the Court house according to the Law in that Case provided, We the Grand Jury present it as a Generall Greavance of the County

Joseph Richards foreman.

James Hayes Petitioned to have Right done against His Master Jeremy Collett. Reade And Considred

Ordred that the Article in the Acco^t Charge to Grand Jurey being 17 men in N^o: amo to £2 : 03 : 3^d be raised out of the acco^t.

The Names of the Constaples Chosen to Searve the Next ensuing yeare

ffor Springfield	Bartholomew Coppick Senr.
Chester	John Child
Aston	Thomas Cartwright
Burmingham	John Bennett in behalf of John Jones
Middel Towne	Joseph Cookson
Edgment	William Gregory
Thornbury	George Pearss
Concord	John Hannam
Darby	John Wood
Upper Providence	Peter Taylor
Marple	John Howell
Lower Providence	John Sharples

JAMES SANDILANDS pl^{tt}
WILLIAM WHITE Defd^t } wthdrawne
in an Action of Debt

James Browne pl^{tt} ⎫
William White Def^{dt} ⎬ wthdrawne
in an action of Debt ⎭

James Standfield Pl^{tt} ⎫
George Philips Def^{dt} ⎬ wthdrawne
in an Action of Scandel ⎪
and Defamation ⎭

Whereas upon the Complaint of Thomas Rawlins against George Chandler of a Debt of $34^s\ 8\frac{1}{2}^d$ wch appred att this Court

Ordered that the Said George Chandler by his Owne Consent doe Sell him self a servant ffor Two yeares and five Months wth Edward Beazer he the said Edward Beazer paying to the said Rawlins the said Sume of $34^s\ 8\frac{1}{2}^d$ and the Remainder wch would make up the Sume of Ten pounds wch was $£8:5^s:3\frac{1}{2}^d$ to be paid to his ffather in Law William Hawkes.

Att an Orphans Court Held att Chester the first Third Day of the 1st Week in the 1st Month 16$\frac{82}{90}$

⎧ John Bristow presid^t
⎪ John Blonston ⎫
⎨ Nicolas Newland ⎪
⎪ ffrances Harrison ⎬ Justices
⎪ Samuell Levis ⎪
⎪ James Sandilands ⎪
⎩ Joshua fferne ⎭

George fforman Sheriff

Joseph Wood being Called gaive Satisfaction to this Court

Philip Roman Being Called meade his Apperance and gaive Satisfaction to this Court Relating to the former

William Hawkes being Called Meade his Apperance Was Ordred to give in Security to this Court wch accordingly he did.

Mary Obarin One of the Orphans of William Obarin being Called gaive Satisfaction to this Court that She was off Eage and that she had received her full part of the Said William Obarin Estate of the Trustes thereunto appointed by this Court.

Anne Beazer Widdow to Edward Beazer Deceased being Called she appered not. Soe it was Ordred that her Sonne

Edward Should Bring in a Trew Inventory to Morrow Morning and to give in Security to this Court to performe Trust according to Law.

Thomas Powell and } Calibe Pewsey Trustes of Joseph Powell being Called to make good their Complaint against Hester Gleves the Widdow of y⁰ Said Joseph Powell the Said Widdow was Ordred to bring in a Trew Enventory of the Estate of George Gleves wth an acco^t: of his Debts how paid and if She Should alter her Condition that She Should apply her Selfe to John Bristow James Sandilands and Samuell Levis to Take farther Care and Order in the matter and Soe She was Desmist this Court

Edward Beazer Brought in the Enventory of the Estate of his Decesed ffather Edward Beazer and it was Ordred that Two Sufficient Securityes to be given the next Court.

The True appraisment of the Goods and Lands of Edward Bezer of Bethell Late Decesed the 28th of the 12 month 1688

4 Cows and Calfs .... £ 15:	00:	00
3 hafers .... £ 8:	00:	00
3 2 yearlins Steers .... £ 6:	00:	00
2 youak of Oxen .... £ 18:	00:	00
2 yearlin Calves .... £ 2:	05:	
1 Gray Gelding .... £ 5:	10:	
1 Black Mare & Colt if they are found .... £ 8:	00:	
1 Cart and pear of Wheels one pear and Irons .... £ 4:	10:	
1 set of hors harnes .... £ 1:	00:	00
1 Old Cart Line .... £ 0:	03:	
90^{lb} of Irone plow geare att 7^d y^e £..£ 2:	12:	6
40^{lb} of puwt att 14^d ℔ £. .... £ 2:	13:	8
24^{lb} of bel bras att 11^d y^e £...... £ 1:	02:	
74:	16:	2

Brought from below ....£	74:	16:	2
128ᵇ of Bras att 2ˢ yᵉ £. ....£	12:	16	
1 warming pann ... .£	:	10:	
1 fouling peese ....£	1:	04:	
The best bed and beding with Cortins ....£	6:		
4 old bedes and beding ....£	15:		
Edward Wareing Clothes ....£	5:		
6 Table napkins 2 Old Table Cloaths £	:	12:	6
132ᵇ of Irone att 6ᵈ a pound......£	3:	6:	
3 Thume Laches and One pʳ of Stereps ....£		07:	
5 old Reep hookes .. ..£	:	04:	
Mason and Carpenters Tooles.....£	6:		
Carrie To yᵉ Other Syde.........	125:	15:	8
Sev'all brought from yᵉ Other Syde being yᵉ Inventory of Edward Beazer £125:		15:	8
3 Cow Bells ....£	:	08:	
2 fforks 2 Old Irone Speeads 2 Old Sweif [?] ....£	:	08:	
1 Beame and Skeals ....£	:	10:	
Waits and Musterd Boull ....£	:	09:	
1 Bible ....£	:	15:	
1 ffriing pan and Chest Locke.....£	:	05:	
1 Steel box Clancq and Other things £	:	05:	
1 Old Sadle One Old pade Old Saks.£	:	09:	
2 Speening Wheels ....£	:	10:	
1 ffan and Household Lomber goods £	3:	00:	00
19 Sowes and hogs ....£	12:	00:	00
Gees and ffoulls ....£	:	12:	
200 Ackers Land Lying in Concord.£	13:	00:	
The Housing and Plantation Containing 500 ackers £150:		00:	
debts dew ....£	4:	00:	

1 Grind Stone	£ :	10:
2 Thousand of pipe Staves........	£ 1:	05:
	£314: 10:	8

Nichlas Nulen
Robert Piles

Att a Court Held att Chester for the County of Chester the 1st 3d day in the 1st Weeke of the 4th Month 1690
{ John Bristow president
Nicº. Newland
ffrancis Harrison
Samuell Levis
James Sandilands
Joshua ffearne } Justices there presant

George fforman High Sherif

The King and Queens Justices Being Called John Blonston and John Bevins appered Not. The Grand Inquest Being Called Wollo Rawson not appered.

The Names of the Grand Inquest Attested att this Court.

John Worrell	Robert Nailer	John Mendenall
Randel Mallin	Adam Roades	Jacob Chandler
Thomas Worrollo	Thomas Martin	Nicº. Piles
Joseph Beaker	Robert Borros	James Standfeild
Nathaniell Evence	Albert Hendrickson	Thomas Moore
Thomas Smith	Josiah Taylor	Randel Varnam

Joshua Heastings being Sumonsed to Scarve upon the Grand Inquest being Called appered not. But afterwards Apered And Gaive Satisfaction to this Court.

John Baldwin being Sumonsed to Searve upon the Grand Inquest bein Called appered not.

Robert Woodward Being Called to Seave his Recognience wᶜʰ accordingly he appered Ordered he Should be Discharged paying his Charges

Henry Barnes Being Called to Seave his Recognience wᶜʰ accordingly he Appered Ordered he Should be Discharged paying his Charges.

Isaac Brickshaw Being Called to Seave his Recognience wᶜʰ

accordingly he Appered. Ordered he Should be Discharged paying his Charges.

John White being Appointed the Kings Attorney By the Court Accordingly he accepted of it.

Charles Pickerin and Patrick Robinson attorneys for
Thomas Holmes Pltf } In an Action of Trespass on the Case } Continewed till next Court
against
Charles Ashcomb Defdt

Charles Pickerin and Patrick Robinson Attorneys for
Thomas Holmes Pltf } In an Action of Trespass on the Case } Continewed till next Court
against
Charles Ashcomb Defdt

John Martin Attorney
To Richard Crosbe Pltf } In an Action on ye Case wth drawne
against
James Standfeild Defdt

Nathaniell Loakince pltf } In an Action on the Case
against
Ralph Dracott Defdt

The petty Jury being Inpannieled Boath partyes Left it to the Bench

Thomas Hollinsworth pltf } wth drawne
against
John Calvert Defdt

We ye Grand Jurey present Ralp Dracot for Swaring in the house of Walter ffausett

          Joseph Richards forman

Ordred to pay 2s 6d into the hands of George fforman

Davide LLoyde Petitioned to have a Roade or Street Layde Out from His plantation to Chester Creek to the publik Landing place

Ordred that the Grand Inquest make inquirey into the Conveniency and Accordingly make Report thereof to this Court

And allsoe to Inspect into a Conveniant way or Roade through the March of Robert Wads Down to Chichester

Chester this 4th of the 4th m^o 1690

Wee of the grand Inquest doe Lay out a Street 30 foot Wide the One halfe of this publike Street to be on One Syde the line deviding betwixt David Loyds Land and the Green L. C. one halfe on David Loyds Land the other halfe on the Greens Side: Note that this Street begins att the publike Landing place att Chester Creek and ending att the further Side of Joseph Richards his Lott neere David Loyds House note also that if any part of the 15 foot on David Loyd his side wch is Laid out for the Street it must so remaine

Andros Bone Appered in Oppen Court and Delivered a Deed for 36 Ackers Land to Monce Peterson

Monce Peterson Appered in Oppen Court and Delivred a Deed for 36 Acker Land to Andros Bone

Roger Jackson Delivred a Deed for 70 Ackers of Land to William Swafford

John Kingsman Delivred a Deed for 50 Ackers of Land to Humphry Scarlett

Joshua fferne Attorney to Joseph Wood Delivred a Deed for 500 Ackes of Land to John Wood

George Simcakes appred in Open Court and Delivred a Deed for 43 Ackers of Land to John Wood being Appointed Attorney for Robert Scothorne to receive Said Deed.

Robert Smith Delivred a Deed for 16 Ackers ½ Land to John Wood being appointed Attorney Robert Scotherine

Robert Smith Delivred A Deed for 90 Ackers Land to Joseph Need.

Robert Smith Attorney to Philip England Delivred a deed in Oppen Court for 100 Ackers of Land to Jenkin Griffen

George Simcock Delivred A Deed for 100 ackers Land to John Wood

John Hoskince Attorney to Robert Robinson Delivred A Deed for 150 Ackers to Mary Jones and now ye wife of David Maridieth

Ralph Dracot being Presented and Indited By the Grand Inquest for Wickedly lustfully unlawfully and incestuously Defile the Body of Susannah Willard his Daughter in Law and wth her had Carnall Copulation and Did Comit Adultry whereby the Said Susannah Did conceive and was Delivred of a Bastard man Child

Upon wch he is Called to the Barre and pleades not Gilty and putt himselfe upon God And the Country

And being Called the Second Tyme he pleaded Gilty to the Inditment

Judgem^t past that the said Ralph Dracot Shall forfit One halfe of his Estate and Suffer Imprisonment One whole yeare And that he Take Care in brining up of the Child And pay all Charges Boath for his Daughter in Law as well as his Owne

Ordred that a Warret be granted to the County praisers to Praise the Estate and make Retorne thereof To James Sandilands and John Bristow

The Court Appoints   Thomas Varnam ⎫
                               Joshua Hestings ⎬ Appraisers
                               Robert Borrows ⎭

And for the Said Ralph Dracot Breaking of Prison Ordred that he Appeares att the next Court and to finde Two Surityes

Chester County SS

The Grand Inquest of the Body of the County of Chester by the King and Queens Authority for the Honble Wm Penn Propriatary and Governer of the Province of Pennsilvania and Territorys att a Session held for the County of Chester this 3^d of the Fourth Month 1690 doe present and Indict Susannah Willard of the County aforesaid that she not haveing the ffeare of God before her Eyes did Wickedly Lustfully and unlawfully and incestuously Commit ffornication wth Ralph Dracot her ffather in Law whereby she the said Susannah did Conceive and was delivered of a Bastard man Childe on or about the 6th day of the 1st month Last past in the Township of Marple in the County aforesaid to the High dishoner of

God and Great Scandall of the Goverment against ye peace of our Soveraign Lord and Lady the King and Queen and to the Dishonour of our Propriatary and his Dominion and Goverm^t and Expresly against the Statute in that Case Expresly made and Provided.

Upon which ye Said Susannah Willard is Called to the Barre and pleades Gilty to this Indictm^t

Judgem^t Past that the s^d Susannah Willard One halfe of her estate to the Governer and if none found she be Inprisined One whole yeare and Kept att hard Labar to be for the use of the Publick.

John Martin being presented by the Grand Inquest That the Said John Martin of Chichester Weavor for that he the said John Martin having not the feare of God Before his Eyes did on the One and Twentieth day of the first Month Last past felonishly take Steal and Carry Away out of the Dweling house of Thomas Browne John in Chichester fourteen Drest Deer skins att the vallew of Thirty Shillings in Contempt of the King and Queen and their Lawes and the Propriatary and Governer William Penn his Dominion and Goverm^t

Upon wch the said John Martin was Called to the Barre and pleaded not Gilty and putt himself upon God and the Country

Names of ye Jurey Inpanueled

Thomas Rawlins	Joshua Heastings
Nathaniel Lamplugh	Thomas Varnam
Caleb Pewsey	Philip Roman
John Thomas	Joseph Richards Senr
John Neelde	George Pearce
William Hawkes	Thomas Cross

Thomas Browne John being attested Declearcath { That John Martin himself tould him that he Stole the Skines and that he did Intend to goe in 3 dayes Tyme And the print of his foot nailes and Clamps was like the print that

	was upon the earth and that Two Nailes was towards the end of his Shoue
ffrances Chades being attested } Decleareth	That he Mended John Martins Shoues with two nailes and Two pleates Towards ye Toues of his shoues.
James Browne Being Attested } Decleareth	That Morning the Skins was Stolen the Corrier was Roning by our house and Martin Seamed to have a great Coller in his face and he prest Sev^{r}all tymes upon him to tell him wether he had stoled them and S^d Browne to Martin thou art Gilty of Stealing ye s^d Skines then he Seamed to have gilt in his face and then Said Martin if I should Confess then I should bring my Self to publick Shame
Willia Clayton being Attested } Decleareth	that when Tho: Brow Jno and he was dicoring s^d I will not Confess befor 2 Evidece Soe we went to Thomas Browne John's house and there we saw the print a shoue and we ffollowed it and we perceived it to be print wth nailes and a pleat wth nailes and we ffollowed it to the Swamp and There in a hollow Tree we found the Skins and afterwards we took the Mesure and

George fforman being Attested Decleareth

went to James Brownes and Compeared it wth John Martins and it Seemed to be the very Same.

That ye same Morning that the Skines was missing Thomas Browne John Came to my house and made his Complaint and said that he had Lost Sixteen drest Skines and that his house was Broken oppen and wth all desired me to writte him a Warran to Make Search through the naughboroughood wch accordingly I did but afterward he made a Search but could find none Soe I bid him goe to his house and wether ther was no Tracking of any body soe he imediatly went and retorned to my house that there was a print of a foot then I went to his house my Selfe and there I saw the Window oppen and upon the Ground there was a print of a Shoue wth nailes and Clampes of Iron soe we ffollowed the Trecking down the syde of the ffence and then along the Swamp untill we Came upon Wm Clayto new Cleared feild and there in the Swamp in a hollow Tree we found fourteen drest Skines then we went to James Brownes house and toke along wth us The Mesure of the print of the shoue and mesured John Martins and it Seemed to us to be the very Same and s^d Martin seemed to be startled att my taking his shoue of

Andros ffreind ⎫
Being attested ⎪ The Jurey ffind him Gilty of the Inditm^t.
Charles Jestice ⎬ John Martin being Called to the Barr and
Being attested ⎭ Judgment Awarded That he be Sould into a nother province to make good all Damages of the parson agreevied and his Masters Charge wth all Lawfull Charges and Three fould according to Law and Receive 39 Lashes well Laide One on his Bare back att ye Carts Tayl

Ordred that John Martin be Sould for Eight yeares Service to Make Satisfaction Three ffould To Thomas Browne John for Stealing 14 deare Skines and the Charges of Court being 6^lb 12^s 2½^d due ye Sheriff Clarkes Wittness and Kings Attorny and 17^lb 07 : 9¼^d due before to his Master James Browne for service due on Indenture and Moneys paid to Ellizabeth Looke to make Satisfaction for Goods Stollen by John Martin from her

James Hayes petitioned this Court to have his Toles from Jeremy Collett wch according was Ordred that the Said Toles was to be delivred Imediatly into the hands of James Sandilands for the Use of the Said Hayes The said Hayes paying to Jeremy Collett what he Justly Owes him The said James Hayes Promised Here in Open Court to searve James Sandilands his Heirs Ex^rs Adm^rs or Assignes the Residue of the Tyme of his Indenture Excepting Two Monthes and fifteen day wch James Sandilands gaive him.

James Standfeild Petitioned this Court for Tyme allowed for his servant Richard Bestrazer Runing away accordingly Reade. Ordred one years Service.

Isaac Warner pl^{tt} against Henry Reynolds Def^{dt} in an action on the Case } Declaration

Isaac Warner of the County of Chester Complains against Henry Reynolds of the said County Taylor in an Action on the Case ffor that whereas the said Def^{dt} for Worke and Severall Delivered him became Indebted unto the said Pl^{t}f in the full and Just Sume of ffifteen pounds Eighteen Shillings and five pence Current Money of this Province as by acco^t in Court to be prodused will make it appeare And the said Def^{dt} hath neglected to make paym^t unto the said Pl^{tt}: the sume of ffifteen pounds Eighteen Shillings and five pence although offten requested thereunto Whereby action Doth Accrew to the said Pl^{tt} notwthstanding whereof the said Def^{dt} delayes to make payment of the aforesaid sume wth Resonable Damage Therefor the Pl^{tt} brings this Sute and Craves Judgment of this Court against the Said Def^{dt} for the said Sume of ffifteen pounds Eighteen Shillings and ffive pence wth Cost of Sute

Thomas Rawlins		Joshua Hestings	
Nathaniel Lamplugh		Thomas Varnam	
Jonathan Hayes	Jurors	Philip Roman	Jurors
John Thomas		ffrances Chades	
John Neeld		George Pearce	
William Hawkes		James Browne	

Walter Martin being Attested { Decleareth that he was upon an Arbitration Saith that Henry Reynolds acknowledge that he Owed Isaac Wardner 8£ and Isaac Warner to give him 6 dayes Worke ye s^d Reynolds giveing him 14 dayes warning and tocke hands upon it and Isaac Warner Gaive him Tyme upon the paym^t of the money till the first month and s^d Henry Reynolds to discharge ye s^d Warner from all Dewes Debts and Demands

John Hulbert   } Decleareth y⁰ Same
being Attested }

Edward Beaser { Decleareth that Henry Reynolds was to pay
being Attested { Isaac Warner 8£ in the first month and to
Cleare S^d Isaac Wardner of all Charges wth the Sheriff and Clarkes wth George fforman and s^d Warner give him 6 day's worke att 14 days Warning

The Names of the Wittness Taken in New Castell County befor William Stockdone prodused in writting

John Grubb   { The Verdit of the Jurey
John Buckley { the 4 day of the 4 Month 1690

Wee the Jurey find for the Plaintife that the Defend^t pay to the plantif Eight pounds the first of March next Insuing and Cost of Court wth Two pence Damage and the plantife pay to the Def^dt Six dayes Woorke att fourteen dayes Warning } upon wh^ch Judgm^t is awarded according to Virdit

Joshua Hestings foreman

County Chester SS

The Grand Inquest for ye Body of the County of Chester in the Province of Pennsilvania att a Court of Quarter Sessions held by the Justices of S^d County by the Kings and Queens Authority and in the name of William Penn Propriatary and Governer of the Province of Pennsilvania & Territorys on the 4th day of the 4th month 1690 att the Towne of Chester in the County afores^d doe present and Indict Phillip Conway late of the County of Bucks in the Province afores^d Labourer that he the said Phillip Conway not having the ffear of God befor his eyes nor any regard to his duty notwithstanding he the Said Phillip Conway was att a Court Lately held in the County of Buckes in the Province afores^d indicted arrained and Convicted of ffelonious Stealing a mare upon wch conviction it being a Third offence commited by the Said Phillip Conway he the

S^d Phillip Received Judgment of Corporall punishment & Judgment allso of Banishment wch Should have Obliged the Said Phillip dureing his Stay in this Governm^t to have Comported himself peacably and honestly but he the Said Phillip being a person of ill ffame and life did on or near the 25th of the 3^d month Last past Aid abett and Counsell one Patrick Conway Suspected of ffelonious Stealing a Certain bay horse upon the Suspicon whereof the said Patrick was Committed to the County Goale and hath Since made his escap and thereby Confest the ffelony and he the S^d Phillip att the Tyme and place aforesaid did produce a Certain Key belonging to the ffetters wth wch the Said Stolen horse was ffettered and he is guilty of Remaining in this Governm^t contrary to the Late Order of banishment, and of being an abettor of ffelons in their ffelony.

        Billa Vera   Jacob Chandler foreman

        The Jurey Impanneled

Jurors	Jur^{rs}
Thomas Rawlins	Joshua Hestings
Nathaniel Lamplugh	Thomas Varnam
Calibe Pewsey	ffrances Chades
John Thomas	Joseph Richards
William Hawkes	George Pearce
John Neelde	Thomas Cross

William Beakes High Sheriff his Evidence Taken in Writting befor Justice James Sandilands.

Joseph Richards Being attested

        Declareth that when John Child the Constaple went to inquire for the ffetters he Serched up and downe the house att the Last William Woodmasell put his hand in a Caske and Said heare is the ffetters and ye s^d Partrick Conway being asked where the Key was he s^d he knew not where it was but att the Last his wife s^d her husband had it and accordingly it was found in his pockett

| John Buckenham being Attested | Decleareth that ye Prisoner Owned Partrick Conway to be his Brother and S^d Patrick asked him what Shall I say about the Horse Say it was Thomas Kerseyes but what sh I say about the ffetters Say you Bought them |

| John Childe being Attested | Decleareth that he being att Mortons house asked Morton wether ther was not a horse but the man that was by would not redyly answere but afterward Partrick Conway seamed to be faint-harted and asked Phillip Conway what he Should doe ye S^d Phillip Said thou art the faint harted man that lives (and in discorse said that Partrick had bin Cheated of a boat and they Intend to Cheat him of a horse). And ye Deponent asked where was the Key of the ffetters they was very loath to bring him out, but afterwards Patrick brought forth the Key but Partrick Could not open the Locke but Philip tooke the Key and oppened the Locke redely And Owened the S^d Partrick Conway to be his Brother and S^d it was Thomas Kerseyes horse and s^d Phillip Conway polled the Key out of his pockett |

| Mordecay Maddock being Attested | Decleareth that Partrick Conway came to him when he was att plow S^d he was a minde to Exch^a the Horse if he Could gett a Mare and Money to Boote and did Say the Horse was is Three yeares and that he was a Tanner by Trade and he Ground Barke wth the Horse |

Robert Moulder | Decleareth that he Coming to Mortons being Attested along wth John Childe and That Partrick Conway tooke the Key out of his pockett and S^d that Philip and partrick said that the Horse was had from Kersey and if Philip and Partrick could have Liberty that they would bring Kersey the Owner of the Horse

ffrances Littell | Decleareth S^d that Philip Stode much in being attested the behalfe of his Brother and Said he would goe and fetch the man that would Cleare his Brother And that the Lock was Phillips

Randall Varnam | Decleareth that Phillip Conway Vindibeing attested cated Partrack Conway to be an honest man and put in prison unlawfully

The Jurey finde him Gilty | Phillip Conway Being Called to of the Inditment the Barre and Judgement Awarded
That thou Phillip Conaway shall goe wth all Convaniet Speed wth all that is thy Owen and to Depart this Province and not to Retorne againe and to pay all Lawfull Charges and to have Liberty for 14 dayes to settel his Concernes and to make sale sale of his Goods to make Satisfaction.

Thomas Person and Peter Worrall appointed to be fence vewers for the Towneship of Marple

John Chambers presented his pettion for his Liberty from Jeremy Collett Ex^e to Joseph Shaw Decesed reade and accordingly Considered

And Jeremy Collett meade it Appeare that he had a Lawfull Titell or Claime to ye Said John Chambers.

Ordred that the Said John Chambers Shall Searve Jeremy Collett or his Order from the Tyme of his Deceseed Mr Joseph Shaw wch is 9 weeke and after untill his Tyme be Expired and s^d Collett shall pay ye Lawfull Charges.

Samuell Adams Pl^tt
 against
Henry Reynolds Def^dt } wth Drawne
in an action on ye Case

James Sandilands Pltf
 against
John Smith Def^dt } wth Drawne
in an action on ye Case

James Sandilands Pl^tt
Jonathan Hayes Def^dt } wth Drawne
in an Action On ye Case

Jeremy Collete Petitioned this Court for a Convaniant Roade to Brandy Wyne Reade and Considered.

Chester the 4th of the 4th Month 1690

Wee of the Grand Inquest doe Lay out A foot way of six foot Wid att the Lest begining att Chester Creek over against the Comon Landing place from thence upon a Strait Line over the Swamp of Robert Wades to the Corner of Robert Wades pales and So a long by the Said pales and fence to a popeler and White Wallnot Standing by the Said Robert Wades fence and so to Remaine a Longe the Syde way accordingly as it is already Marked and Cutt out unto Chichester Creeke.

The 3^d 4th Mo 1690 Wee of the Grand Inquest present Bethell Hamlett for not repaireing the Bridge in the said hamlett

All so we present Chichester Towneship for not repaireing a Mirey place betwixt John Kinsmans and ye Kings Roade

Also we present Chester Towneship for not repareing a Miry Place in the Same Road from Concord to Calebs Mill

Also we present Chester for not repareing the foot Road betwixt Robert Wades and Chichester through there respective Towne Ships

Also we present John Thomas of Marple for Keeping of unlawfull fences and Disturbeing his Neighbours Catle.

Upon wch s^d Presentm^t John Thomas was Called and Promised a mendm^t

Ordred that notice be given to the Supervisors of the Respective Towne Ships for the mendm^t of the High wayes.

Ordred that George fforman High Sheriff be appointed Resciver Generall for all the Remainder of those Three Levies that was the 2^s 6^d ℔ hundred and 12^d ℔ hundred and 3^s ℔ hundred that is unpaid and that a full power be Granted to s^d George fforman for to Compell them to Make paym^t And Likewise that a Warrant be Sent to the Respective Constaples of Each Towne Ship to be Ayding and assisting unto the Said George fforman in Collecting the Same

---

Att a Court held at Chester for the County of Chester ye 1th 3^d day in ye first weeke in ye 7th month 1690	John Bristow president Nicolas Newland ⎫ James Sandilanes ⎬ Justices Samuell Levis ⎭ present George forman Sherif Joshua ffearne Clerk

The Grand Inquest being Called James Stanfield appeared not

DAVID LOYD   Plaintiff
JAMES SANDILANES deft

refered untill ye after noon & soe also untill ye next morning this action being Called againe ye plaint appeared by his attorney John White and aledged that ye Jury was not Lawfully Sumoned soe would not Com to tryall whereupon ye def^d Craved a none sute and being refered to ye Court ye Court granted ye same

Charles Pickring & } attornys to Tho: holmes plaint
Patrick Robinson

John White & } attornys to Charles ash Com Defd[t]
Caleb Pusey in an action of trespas on y[e] Case

    y[e] Jury Impanelled

 Richard Bonsall   William Hawkes
 John Smith   Walter Martin
 John Bartram   philip rumon
 John Bailes   Edward Cartter
 Robert penall   Tho: powell
 Nathaniell Ampley   petter Taylor

Jurior somoned & not appeared

Edward peerson ⎤ y[e] sheriff was attested wheather he Law-
Johnathan hayes ⎢ fully somoned these men who declared that
franses Yarnall ⎢ he somoned them a month before y[e] Court
david Morris ⎦

the plaint declareth for tow hundred & five pounds Eleven shillings & one penny and acknowledged the recept of foure pounds of y[e] same

The def[dt] play is we owe nothing to ye plaint

the plaint Comission was read

A list of lands & Survay mony was read

A paper under Governor penns hand Concerning Charles Ash Com making Returns & Giving part of ye Survay mony to Tho: holmes was read

    Evidences

Charles Ash Coms Comission was read

A warrant from Tho: holmes to Charles Ashcom Survayor was read

A recept produced for foure pounds English mony Borrowed of Charles Ashcom under y[e] hand of tryall holmes sonn to y[e] s[d] Tho: holmes was read

An order to resurvay Land of y[e] old in habittants on this side ye skulkiln in Chester County & make returnes into y[e] Secretarys offices under Governor penns hand to Charles Ashcom was read

ye Verdite

we ye Jurors are unanimusly agreed and Gives ye verdite for ye defd^t wth the Cost & Charge of Sute & tenn shillings damage

Walter Martin foreman

Judgment is Awarded according to the verdite

Whereupon ye plaint Craved an appeale to ye next provinctiall Court in Law And it was Granted paying all Cost & Charges due according to Law and Giving Security to prosecute: who accordingly did ye same

The plaint by his attorneys Charles peickering & Robert Long Shore Recognize them selves there executors Administerators in ye sum of one hundred pounds Corent money of this province that if we ye above s^d Charles pickering & Robert Longshore Attorneys to ye s^d thomas holmes shall prosecute ye appeale now Granted to ye next provinciall Court in Law against a Judgment now obtained & to pay all Cost and damage if ye appealant be againe Cast

Charles pickering
Robert Longshore

	Jury	
JAMES STANFIELD plaint	Rich Bonsall	phillip ruman
RICHARD CLUSE defd^t	John Smith	Walter Martin
in an Action of ye Case	John Bartram	Joseph Wood
ye plaint declares for	John Bailes	Mordikai Madock
tenn pounds	Robert pennall	Caleb pusey
	Will Haukes	James Swafer

Witneses John Smith Andrew Jobe George Willard

We ye Juriors Give ye verdite for ye defendant wth ye Cost and Charge of Sute and six shillings damage being all unanimusly agreed thereto Walter Martin foreman Judgm^t awarded according to verdite

This 3^d of ye 7th month 1690 we of ye Grand Inquest doe present Andrew ffriend Alias Neales and John ffriend Alias Neales for Killing and taking away on ye 26th day of ye 6th month 1690 a hogg or hoggs from of ye red banke Island of

petter dalbos or wlloe dalboe Contrary to yᵉ Law in that Case made and provided   Jacob Chandler forman
    the presentmᵗ being red unto wᶜʰ yᵉ pleaded not Gilty
Thomas Gardner pleaded as attorney for ye King
            yᵉ Jury impanielled
                    Jury

Rich Bousall	phillip rumon	the Juriors finds Andrew
John Smith	Walter Martin	freind alies Neals and
John Bartram	Joseph Wood	John freind alias Neals
John Bayles	Mordikai Madock	Gilty in maner and forme
Robert Pennall	Robert Barber	according to yᵉ presentmᵗ
William Haukes	James Swaffer	Walter Martin foreman
Witnesses		
Mounce Lock	John ramboe	Judgmᵗ was awarded
James Whiticor	henrick hendrickson	that the shall pay four pounds tenn shillings and Cost of Sute &c.

    Edward pritchitt entered a Caviu Concerning a parcell of Land Lying att Crum Creeke.

    Chester yᵉ 3ᵈ of yᵉ 7ᵗʰ mo 1690 Wee of yᵉ Grand Inquest doe present William Collit of Concord and Edward Beazer of Bethell for Breaking yᵉ peace in fighting to yᵉ wounding and sheding of Blood Contrary to yᵉ Law in that Case mad and provided;   Jacob Chandler foreman

    Chester yᵉ 3ᵈ of yᵉ 7ᵗʰ mo 1690 we of yᵉ Grand inquest present James Stanfield for absenting himself from yᵉ Grand Jury he Being on of them Contrary to yᵉ law on that Case provided: Jacob Chandler foreman

    Chester yᵉ 3ᵈ of yᵉ 7ᵗʰ mo 1690 wee of yᵉ Grand Jury present William Cobern supervizer for yᵉ township of Chester for not mending yᵉ miery place from Calebs mill up Concord road
                Jacob Chandler foreman

    Chester ye 3ᵈ of yᵉ 7ᵗʰ mo 1690 wee of yᵉ Grand Jury doe present Joseph Coborne for e legall fettering yᵉ horse of Thomas Marttin alsoe wee present thomas Coborn for sufering his man servant Richard Woodward to ride ye horse of ye sd Thomas Martin Contrary to ye Law in that Case provided:

Jacob Chandler foreman

Patrick Robinson
Charles pickering } Attorneys to thomas
in action of trespas holmes plaintiff
on ye Case

John White } attorneys to Charles Ashcom
Caleb pusey defendant with drawne

Ordered that Robert penall be supervizer for Midle towne ye yeare in suing

Ordered that david Morris be supervizer for Marple ye yeare insuing

Ordered that henry hastings be supervizer for Chichester ye year insuing

Ordered that Tho peerson & petter worrell be ye vewers of fences ye yeare insuing for Marple

Anne vanculin was Called & examoned Concerning her Giving out evell words against some magistrats but upon her submission was discharged paying ye fees.

Jacobus hendrickson was Called upon ye susspition of hogg stealing but none prosecuting he was discharged paying his fees

A deed of Effeofment delivered in Open Court by George foreman attorney to petter Banton for a parcell of Land Lying in Chichester to Samuell Rowlland dated ye 5th day of ye 4th month 1690

A deed of Efeofment delivered in Oppen Court by Robert Pile attorney to James Browne unto John Kingsman attorney to Amey harding & for ye use of ye s^d Amy harding for A certaine parcell of Land Lying in Chichester towneship with all ye building upon ye same bearing date ye 5th day of ye 4th month 1690

A deed of Efeafment delivered in Oppen Court by John Kingsman attorny to Amy harding unto Robert pile in ye behalf and for ye use of Amy James for A Certaine parcell of land Lying in Chichester towneship wth all ye building upon y^e

same bearing date the twenty forth of yᵉ fourth month 1690

A deed of Efeofment delivered in Oppen Court by thomas powell unto petter Taylor and Randle Malin in yᵉ behalf of severall others for A parcell of Land Lying in uper providence for yᵉ use of A burying place bearing date the second day of the seventh month 1690

Charles Whitticor delivered a deed of Efeofment in Oppen Court unto Randle vernon for A parcell of Land Containing tow hundred acers bearing date the third day of the seventh month 1690

The Court Adjournes untill yᵉ 1ᵗʰ 3ᵈ day in yᵉ 1ᵗʰ weeke in yᵉ 8ᵗʰ Mo 1690

Att A Orphans Courtt held at Chester yᵉ 1ᵗʰ 3ᵈ day in yᵉ 1ᵗʰ weeke in yᵉ 8ᵗʰ Mo 1690

{ John Blunston Presidᵗ
John Simcocke
John Bristow
Nicolas NewLine
Samuell Levis
James Sandilanes } Justices Present

Geo. foreman Sheriff
Joshua ffearne Clerke

hester Gleaves being Called appeared & brought in an Inventory of yᵉ Goods and Cattles of George GLeave Late of Springfield deceased taken by us whose names are here under written the 12ᵗʰ of yᵉ 11ᵗʰ month 1688;   l   s   d

for 3 Cowes one heafer one bull...... 18 00 00
for 4 shotes & 2 Sowes............. 03 05 00
for plowing & seed for eleven acers Corn 07 03 00
for 3 mares 2 Colts one horse at home 14 00 00
fore one mare & a 2 years old Colt & one
  horse hassartable in ye woods....... 07 00 00
for one whip saw one Cross Cut Saw 2
  hand sawes 01 02 00
for Corne in yᵉ Stack 00 12 00
for Corne in yᵉ house 00 04 06
for 2 Sucks (?) & 2 Coulters....... 01 00 00

for 4 paire of hames & 4 paire of Cheains & 2 horse Collers............	01	10	00
for Sithes & Sickles	00	14	00
for nailes	01	10	00
for 2 Casments & 2 other panes of Glass	00	14	00
for flax undresed	00	15	00
for one bed & beding & bed stids in ye uper rome	04	00	00
for one bed & beding Curtains & bed-stead in the parlor	05	10	00
for table Linnin	01	00	00
for 5 paire of Sheets	03	00	00
for 2 warming panes	01	00	00
for black silke	00	10	00
for 5 speckled hand Cherifs	00	10	00
for 2 paire of Linin stockins & 1 paire shoes	00	09	00
for 5 yards of broad Cloath and foure yards of Collered fustion..........	02	16	08
for a pound of whalbone & 1 piece of Uper Leathers	00	04	00
for one Looking Glass	00	05	00
for one Match Coate	00	08	00
for Edge tooles	01	06	00
	l	s	d
2 Chests one trunke & boxes in ye parllor	01	05	00
for 8 augers 3 wedges 1 square 1 dung forke with some other Loose Iron...	01	04	00
for one mathack one Iron Crow......	00	10	00
for 5 pound of steele	00	03	08
for a peece of Leather	00	02	06
for ye Loume & Metterials to it......	01	00	00
for Linin yarne in ye Loume.........	00	14	00
for Sadle & pillion	01	04	00
for 44 pound of wooll	02	07	04
for 2 pound of Comed Jarsey	00	05	00
for 2 pound of Spun Jersey	00	10	00

for a gun barrell and Lock 00 05 00
for a Cuberd & table & 4 Cheirs and
dishboard 02 00 00
for 2 plowes 00 05 00
for 2 brass pots one brass pann one
cettle & one skellitt 02 15 00
for 3 Iron pots 01 10 00
for pewtter & alkemy Spoons 01 10 00
for foure pound of tallow 00 02 00
for 6 flitches of bacon & braken meat.. 02 05 00
for treane ware 00 15 00
for tow Cushons 00 02 00
for 3 frying pans one baking pan a
paire of Iron Goberts 2 paire of tongs
wth other Irons in ye Chimney...... 01 00 00
for 2 Spining wheils 00 08 00
for 2 Shovels & other ode Lumber... 00 08 00
for George wearing apparrel 05 00 00

   Apraysed by   Bartholomew Coppock
           Robert Taylor

ye Sum is 105 18 8

An account of what was owing Geo^e GLeaves when he dyed
              l   s   d

petter Leaster depter 03 15 00
James Stanfield depter 00 15 00
Barthollomew Coppock ye elder depter. 01 00 00
John ffox depter 00 19 00
Thomas Cross depter 05 11 00
The sum of all is 12 00 00

An account of ye depts of Geo^e GLeaves deceased that are already paid by ye widdow   £   s   d

To James Stanfield 03 17 00
To Joseph Lownes & George 00 07 08
To William dillion 01 04 00
To Griffith Owin 00 06 00
To Philip England 00 06 00

To Edward Peerson	00	04	06
To John Madocks	00	12	06
To Mordicai Madocks	02	14	09
To Robert Woodward	00	15	00
To John Edge	00	01	05
To Walter ffossitt	01	01	06
To Richard Cross	00	07	00
To John Cross	00	08	00
To Petter Leaster	00	11	00
To Henry Barnes	02	12	00
To John Simcock	02	17	00
To Thomas Brasey	01	10	00
To Henry Cadman	00	01	00
To John Hodkinson	00	01	02
To hendrick Totten	00	13	00
To Matthew Mortton	00	02	06
To James SandiLanes	04	04	08
To Jacob Simcock	00	05	10½
To John Peerson	00	07	00
To Eliz: Penall	01	15	02
To Robert Taylor	05	16	08
To Bartholomew Coppock eld^r	00	03	00
To Thomas Peerson	00	02	00
To A Coffin	00	05	00
To A Levey	00	04	06
ye sum of all is	35	13	08½

An Inventory of ye Goos belonging to Wm Taylor deceased taken ye 9th day of ye 1th Mo 1683

	lb	s	d
Imp^s 10 doz & 10 Knives Cost	00	10	00
2 doz: & 2 Combs Cost	00	01	03
2 doz: & eight paire of Sisers Cost	00	02	00
1 doz: & 3 paire of Shoe buckles Cost	00	01	03
16 grosse & ½ of buttons Cost	00	13	00
8 paire of Shooes Cost	01	03	04
for a parcell of old Iron	00	13	00
for 100 waight of nails	01	12	09

for Edge tooles & frying pan pitch forks one square one paire of Compases	02	05	00
A mare & Colt	04	12	00
for part of tow Cowes	04	00	00
for houshold Linin beding & Cloathes.	08	09	00
for brass & peutter	03	12	00
A sadle bridle & wearing apparrell	05	00	00
for Lumber	00	10	00
ye sum of all is	33	11	05

Apraysers Randle Mallin Robertt Vernon Thomas Menshaw was Caled & appeared & brought in ye inventory above mentioned with ye will of ye s^d William Taylor & an account of dep^{tr} & Crdt^r as followeth

	l	s	d
To funerall Expences & taking up mare And proving the will & taking up a mare	01	12	00
To Petter Taylor for bringing up tow of ye Children &c	21	06	03
To my selfe for bringing up ye other child	10	13	1½
To one of ye s^d Children as by recept Appeareth	05	00	00
To Mary Taylor one of ye s^d Children	04	04	06
To 6 days & a halfe to gett a letter of Attorney with other expences	00	16	03
To taking up ye mare & Colt & 2 days About dissposing of ye Estate	00	07	06
The sum of all is	43	19	7½

Errors & omissions excepted ye 6th of ye 7th mo 1690

Contra   Cr^{e}dt

	l	s	d
To recived being ye whole Esstate of William Taylor deceased ye sum of	33	11	05
To received more for a Citty Lott	09	17	00
To Ballance due to Thomas Menshaw 00^l 11^s 02½^d 43 19 07½	43	08	05

Memorandom there is 1¹ & 5ᵈ due to me wᶜʰ I paid Mary Taylor more than her wages wⁿ shee Lived wᵗʰ mee wᶜʰ by agreement yᵉ sᵈ Mary was to pay mee againe and to give mee a Discharg

The Pittisson of Mary Taylor exhibited to yᵉ Court shee being one of yᵉ orphans of William Taylor deceased Concerning her Cloaths being detained & Kept from her by Tho: Menshaw whereupon Thomas Menshaw was ordered by yᵉ Court to pay 12ˢ 6ᵈ & to deliver yᵉ Cloaths to yᵉ sᵈ Mary and to deliver as many planks as was taken of yᵉ Childrens house upon which yᵉ said Thomas Menshaw is fully discharged by this Court; yᵉ Court adjourns untill yᵉ 4ᵗʰ hour in yᵉ afternoon And mett again according to adjournment.

The Court ordered that yᵉ widdow Gleaves Give Security to yᵉ next orphans Court to make Good yᵉ Estate of Joseph Powell deceased unto yᵉ Children

Joseph Wood exhibited a pittission to yᵉ Court & upon yᵉ reading thereof an Inventory was produced of yᵉ Goods and Cattles of William Wood deceased yᵉ Court finding things not well amongst yᵉ orphans of yᵉ deceased ordered John Blunston Samuell Leuis And Joshua ffearne to Inspectt into them and indeavor to Composs matters amongst the orphans of yᵉ deceased and alsoe orders John Bartram to Appeare for him that Cannot speake for him selfe and make return to yᵉ next orphans Court.

The Court orders Robert pile Jacob Chandler and Joseph Bushell bee trustees for yᵉ orphans of Edward Beazer deceased according to inventory and make return to the next orphans Court

The Court Adjourns untill yᵉ 1ᵗʰ 3ᵈ day in ye 1ᵗʰ weeke in yᵉ 1ᵗʰ month next

This orphans Court Adjorns untill ye 23ᵗʰ day in ye 2ᵗʰ weeke in yᵉ 1 mo next

Att A Court held at Chester the 1th 3^{d} day in ye 1th weeke in the 8th month 1690

{ John Blunston Presid^t
John Simcocke
John Bristow
nic^o newline
Samuell Levis
James Sandilands } Justices present

Geo: foreman Sheriff
Joshua ffearne Clerke

JOHN ANDERSON   pl^t
ANDREW BOONE   dft
in an action of ye case } withdrawne

JAMES SANDILANDS Pl^t
DAVID LOYD   Df^t
in an action of ye Case } Continued

MATHEW HOMAN
LARRONS HOMAN   Pl^t
WILLIAM HOMAN
HANCE URIN   Df^t
in an action of ye Case } withdrawne

Edward Beazer and William Collitt was Caled to answer to a presentment of ye Grand inquest and upon examination ye s^d Edward Beazar was Cleared And William Collitt was ordered to find surtys to appoint at ye next County Court and the Court ordered that ye s^d Beazer and Collitt doo pay this Court Charges equally between them.

the Jury Impaneled

monce Petterson Pl^t
Petter Petterson
Anne ffriend Deff^{dt}
John ffriend
Sarah ffriend
in an action of
Scandall and
defamation

Jury
walter fossitt
Joseph Richards elder
Edward Cartter
William Browne
Joseph Richards yonger
thomas minshaw

Sam: Sellers
Robert Vernon
John Kingsman
John Marttin
Thomas powell
James swafford

Witneses Edward pritchitt Ringneare petterson and his wife Andrew hendrickson Jacob Johnson Tatton hendrickson

CHESTER COUNTY, PENNSYLVANIA 225

The Jury finds for ye Def^t wth two pence damage and Cost of Sute

Judgment awarded according to verdite

The Court Adjourns until ye 2^d 3^d day in ye 2^d weeke in ye 10th month.

Joseph Wood acknowledged and Pased over a deed unto George Simcocke and Susanah his wife for 500 acers of Land in tow parcels Lying in new towne: bearing date ye 1st day of the 7th month September 1690

Hendrick Jacobson Pased over a deed unto Ringneare Petterson for fifty Acers of Land Lying upon Crum Creek bearing date the third day of the first month 1690

Att A Court att Chester
The 9th day of ye 10th
Mo 1690
the Kings Justices
being Caled John
Beavon Appeared not

John Bristow President
John Simcock
John Blunston
NicoLas NewLine
Samuell Levis
James SandiLands
} Justices p^{r}sentt

George fforman Sheriff
Joshua ffearne Clerke

The Grand Inquest was Caled over and John Mendinghall appeared not but upon good reasons given he was excused for this Courtt

Thomas Cowborn was Called and gave satisfacttion to the Court and was discharged

James Standfield was Called and gave satisfaction to the Court and was discharged

William Cowborn superveisser of the towneship of Chester made his Complaint to the Court that the inhabittants thereof would not Come to mend the highways upon which Complaint the Court ordered that those That have made neglectt of the same shall make satisffaction either in worke or pay tow shillings p^r day for every Days Neglectt

JEREMIAH COLLITT Pl^{tt}
FFRANCIS LITTLE D^{tdt}
in an action of ye Case
} ye Jury Impanieled

Walter ffositt William Talley
Robertt Cartter Caleb pusey
James Swaford John Wood
Richard Buffington Mordica Madock
William hauks Joseph Richards yonger
ffrancis Cadscy Thomas Rollinson

The Jury finds for the plaintiff with tow pounds thirttene shillings six pence with tow pence damage and Cost of Sute

Judgment Awarded according to ye verdite

Micah Thomas Pl^{tt}
Thomas Kirck Def^{dt}
in an action of ye Case } The same Jury Attested as before

The Jury finds for ye plaintiff Six pound ye Cost of Sute and damage being therein included. Judgm^t awarded according to verdite

Ralph Dracott Pl^{tt}
James Standfield Df^{dt} } in an action of ye Case The Jury attested as before

The Jury finds for the plaint fourteene shillings with Cost of Sute and tow pence Damage Judgment Awarded according to ye verdite

James Sandilands Plaint
David Loyd Def^{dt}
in like action ye Court before Continued } now withdrawne

Joseph Knight Plaint
Evan Prodera Def^{dt}
in an action of ye Case } withdrawne

Jeremiah Collitt Plaint
Nathaniell Thornton Def^{dt}
in an action of ye Case } Continued

John Wickham Plaint
John Holston Def^{dt}
in an action of dept } withdrawne

The Court AdJorned for an hour and a halfe and mett againe according to adjornm^t. Alexsander Deverix exhibited a pitishon but ye Court gave noe answer to it

Jsack few superviser for Chester for ye yeare insuing

ye Grand Inquest p^{r}sentment

Wee the Jurors doe p^{r}sent Johanas ffriend for Killing a horse of John Simcocks by shooting of him

Wee alsoe p^{r}sent Susannah freind for takeing a false Test to the p^{r}vertting of Justice In the Case Above Said

Wee alsoe pr^{e}sent Johanas ffreind for felloniously cilling and bearing away a sow of John vanculines Contrary to the Law in that Cas made and provided Jacob Chandler foreman

We of the Grand Inquest p^{r}sent John hoskins for Encroching upon the Countys Land Belonging to the prison house in Chester, Jacob Chandler foreman

James Sanderlands being Called and Examined aboute the abovesaid Land Declareth that he did give all that Land on which the Prison now standeth btweene the streett and the Creek att the first begining of this Government for to build A Prison upon

Johannas ffreind being Caled to answer to tow p^{r}sentments the Court Granted him Liberty untill the next Court and then to make his appearance

Susannah ffreind being Called to answer to A p^{r}sentment the Court Granted her Liberty untill the next Court and then to make her appearance.

John Vanculin Called to Prosecute his Complaint Against Johanas freind and save his Recognances who appeared not: upon which the Court ordered that a proses be Issued out to bring in the s^d vanculin to the next Court

ye Court adjornes to John hoskins Chamber

William Collitt being Called appeared not, Joseph Cowborn was Called & appeared not

William Woodmeson Delivered a Deed in oppen Court unto Jeremy Cartter for twenty Acers of Land be the same more or Less bearing date the 9th day of the Tenth month 1690

Nicolass Piles Delivered a Deed in Oppen Court unto Thomas Hope for one Hundred Acers of Land Lying in Thornbery bearing date the bearing date the Thirthtyeth day of the ninth month one Thousand six hundred and ninty

George Willerd Delivered a Deed of Efeofment in open Court unto Ralph Dracott for tow hundred acers of Land Lying in Marple bearing date the 5th of ye 10th month 1690

Ralph Dracott Delivered a Deed of Morgage in open Court unto George Willerd for one Hundred acers and Premises Lying in Marple bearing date the fifth of ye 10th month 1690

John Blunston Delivered a Deed of Efeofment in open Court being the attorney of Edward Peerson, unto William Gregory for one hundred acers of Land or there aboutes Lying in Darby bearing date the twenty Second of ye ninth month 1690

John Blunston Delivered a Deed of Conveance unto Joshua ffearne for ye use of Henry Gibins in open Court for nine acers of Land Lying in Darby ye s^d Joshua being attorney for ye s^d Gibins bearing date ye 4th day of ye 10th month 1690

Adam Roads being attorney to Thomas Worth Delivered a Deed in open Court unto Joshua ffearne for ye use of Henry Gibins for three acers of Land Lying in Darby ye s^d Joshua being attorney to ye s^d Gibins it bearing date ye fourth of ye 10th month 1690

John Wood DeLivered A Deed of Efeofment in open Court unto Joshua ffearne for ye use of John Ellott for one Hundred Acers of Land Lying in Darby ye s^d Joshua being attorney to ye s^d Ellott bearing date ye 1th of December 1690

Ordered that John Neeles be supervisor for Aston the yeare insuing

The Court Adjornes untill the second Third day in ye 2th month next

---

Att an Orphans Courtt held att Chester for the County of Chester the the first third day in the first month 1690/1

John Simcock president
John Bristow
John Blunston   Justices
Nicolas NewLine   present
Samuell Levis

Geo: fforman sheriff
Joshua ffearne Clerke

Joseph Taylor Exhibited a petition to the Court and the Court Considered the same but the trusstee having given in his accounts the Last Courtt and the Co᷉t being satisied therewith will not medle any further. Except any new matter shall appeare before them; and then hee shall bee heard

Robert pile and Jacob Chandler appeared according to the Last Co᷉ts order and brought an account of the sum of the inventory and of debts and an accountt of the devistion of the Estate belonging to the Orphans and alsoe a bond for the payment of forty pounds nine shillings and two pence under the hand and seale of Edward Beazer

	lb	s	d
The inventory amounts to the sum of..	314	10	8
William Clayton debtor to the Esstate.	017	8	0
The Steel mill	003	5	0
Edward Browne debtor to the esstate..	004	2	9
	339	5	9
The debts amounts to	096	7	1
remaines	242	8	8
The widdows thirds amounts to	080	16	2
remains due among the orphans	162	12	5
To be divided in eight parts each part amounting to	020	4	1

Edward Beazer exhibited a petition to the Co᷉t and the Co᷉t Considered the same and upon a full hearing of the matter it was ordered that the said Edward Beazer be fully Discharged and he is hereby discharged of the Estate of Edward Beazer deceased belonging to his Brothers and Sisters as may appeare by a bond brought in by Robert pile and Jacob Chandler amounting to ye sum of forty pounds nine shillings and two pence

John Blunston Samuell Lewis and Joshua ffearne made return to this Co᷉t according to the Last Co᷉ts order Concerning the Orphans of William Wood Deceased (vizt) that the have Indevored to Compose the matter Amongst the said Orphans and hath brought them to an agreement which said agreement was produced in Co't under the hands of the said Orphans; the being Contented therewith; whose shares and parts of the said William Woods Estate amounteth to one hundred and Twenty nine pounds five shillings a peece being three of them (vit) John Johnathan and Susanah

---

Att a Court held att Chester for ye County of Chester ye second third day in ye first month 1691 and held by adJornment tow days aftter

John Blunston President
John Simcock
John Bristow
Nicolas Newlin } Justices present
James Sandelands
Samuell Levis

Geo: fforman sheriff
Joshua ffearne Clerke

The Court being Called did AJorne untill the afternoone and mett againe according to AdJornment

The Grand Inquest Called and Impaniled

William Smith	Caleb Pusey	Joseph Cuckson
Joseph Wood	Evan prodera	Edward Cartter
Samuell Sellers	Samuell Miles	Thomas Peerson
William Woodmansee	Humphrey Ellis	Joshua Hastins
John Bayles	Walter ffossitt	Charles Whitecor
John Neild	John Gibins	
Philip rumon		

ye Courtt AdJorned untill the eight hour the next morning The Orphans Co't was Called and noe business appearing was AdJorned untill the first Third day in the eight month next

WILLIAM CLAYTON   Pl^{tt}
JEREMIAH COLLITT   Def^{dt} } defered
in an accon of trespas
and Ejecment

NATHANIELL THORNTON   Pl^{tt}
THOMAS BROWNE JOHN   Def^{dt} } withdrawne
in an accon of debt

JAMES SANDILANDS   Pl^{tt}
JOHN SMITH   Def^{dt} } withdrawne
in an accon of debt

JAMES SANDILANDS   Pltf
THOMAS SIDBOTTOM   Defd^t } withdrawne
in an accon of Debt

JOHN NIXON   Pl^{ttt}
JOHN MADOCK   Def^{dt} } withdrawne

JAMES SANDILANDS   Pltff
EDWARD and ANN BEAZER   Def^{dt} } withdrawne
in an accon of debt

GEORGE FORMAN   Pl^{tt}
GEORGE ANDROS   Defd^t } Continued
upon attachment

GEO: FFORMAN   Pl^{tt}
RALPH DRACOTT   Def^{dt} } withdrawne
in an accon of Debt

THOMAS ROLLINSON   Pl^{tt}
NATHANIELL LUKINS   Def^{dt} } Continued
in an accon of Debt

JOHN HENDRICKSON   Pltf
JAMES STANDFIELD   Def^{dt} } withdrawne
in an accon of Debt

JOHN WORRELL   Pl^{ttt}
THOMAS ROLLINSON   Deff^{dt} } withdrawne

THOMAS BROWNE JOHN   Pltf
FFRANCIS SMITH   Defd^t } wthdrawne
in an action of ye Case

The Sheriff made Return of an Execution against Thomas kirke: not to be found.

Johanas ffriend was Called and did not appeare Susanah ffriend Called did not apear

Jeremiah Collitt   Pl'tt   ⎧ the Pl'ff and Def'dt both ap-
Nathaniell Thornton Def'dt ⎨ peared and the Pl'ff produced
in an accon of Debt   ⎩ a bond under y'e Def'dts owne
                              hand and seale and a bill of
                              Three pounds; all which the
                              Def'dt owned.

The Declaration was read and y'e Def'dt put in his plea in writing

ye Jury Impaneled

John hood		Robert vernan
Thomas Bradshaw		John Balwin
William Garett	Juryos	Thomas vernan
John Holston		Robert Barber
William Hauks		James Browne
Thomas Rollinson		James Standfield

we the Juriors finds for y'e Pltff the sum of five pounds tenn shillings nine pence due from Interest for the same and tow pence damage with Cost of suite

Judgment according to verdite   John hood foreman

The Court adJorned for two hours and mett againe according to adJornment

Caleb pusey attorney to ⎫ the same Jury as as above Except-
Charles ashcom   Pl'tt ⎬ ing Tho: Cross instead of William
John vanculin   Def'dt ⎭ hauks
in an accon of trespass   the declaration was read but y'e
on y'e Case   Def'dt denyeth the declaration and
                          saith that the Land is his owne

Thomas Powell attested to y'e declaration An order from the Proprietary and Governour under the hand of Philip Leihmaine was read

A paper under the hand of Otto Ernescock and Isarell helme was read

Otter ernesteock being attested declareth that before this Government Vanculin had a grant of one hundred acres of Land and Ephrim harman was spoaken to for to record it

The Jury finds for the Def'dt with Cost of Suite and two

pence Damage whereupon the Pl'ff Craved an Apeale to the next Provintiall Court in Law to be held att Chester and it was Granted

presentment

We present Andrew freind Mordecai Madock & Joseph Wood for taking and bearing away the Indians goods out of there traps to the indangering of the peace and wellfare of ye King and Queons subjects in this province, Jacob Chandler foreman

Joseph Wood Mordecai Madock and Andrew ffreind was Called to answer to a presentment of the Grand inquest and was put to there Choice whether ye would Come to tryall or travis it; whereupon the submited themselves to the Court and upon there submission having made satisfaction to the Indians was discharged

The names of the constables for the yeare insuing

George Churchman	for Chester
Micaell Blunston	for Darby
Tho: Jones	for Uper providence
Richard Bernard	for Midle towne
ffrancis Yarnall	for Springfield
Tho: Menshaw	for Neither providence
Daniell Willimson	for Marple
Tho: Boweter	for Edgment
Tho: King	for Concord
Nicolas pile	for Beathell
John Baldwin	for Aston
John Jerman	for Radnor
Daniell Humphrey	for haverford

the Court adJorned untill ye seventh houre ye next morning and meet againe

A presentment of ye Grand inquest wee of ye Grand inquest doe present the supervisor of ye Towneship of Chester for not mending that mirey place that is next to ye Kings road in ye way that Leads to Concord this being ye 3^d time, we alsoe present ye Towneship of Ridley for not Clearing trees and

Loggs that Lyes in y̆ᵉ Kings roade betwixt amors Land and Crum Creeke   Jacob Chandler forman

ffrancis Balding Acknowledged a Deed in oppen Court unto John Madock for fifty aceres of Land with all the housing and Improvements upon y̆ᵉ same and all its appurtenancis Lying in uper providence bearing date y̆ᵉ Tenth day of y̆ᵉ first month 1690

John Kingsman acknowledged a deed in oppen Court unto Ayre for one hundred aceres of Land and appurtenances Lying in Chichester bearing date y̆ᵉ 10ᵗʰ Day of ye 1ˢᵗ month 1691

George fforman attorney to John Wickham acknowledged a deed unto Thomas King for one hundred aceres of Land Lying in Concord bearing date y̆ᵉ 1ˢᵗ Day of y̆ᵉ 10ᵗʰ mo 1691

Thomas Vernan Randle vernan and Walter fositt acknowledged a deed in oppen Court unto Caleb Pusey for two hundred and fifty aceres of Land Lying in Chester County beareing date The Tenth day of the first month 1691.

John Simcock John Bristow and Randle Vernon executors to Thomas Brasie acknowledged a deed in open Court unto Charles Brooks for three parcels of Land Containing Three hundred and Thirty aceres in aston bearing date y̆ᵉ 10ᵗʰ day of y̆ᵉ first month 1691

John Simcock John Bristow and Randle vernan Executors to Thomas Brasie acknowledged a deed in open Court unto Thomas England for one hundred aceres of Land Lying in yᵉ fork of Chester Creek bearing date the 10ᵗʰ day of y̆ᵉ first month 1691

William Clayton assigned over a deed in open Court unto William Rowe for one hundred and fifty aceres of Land Lying in Concord bearing date y̆ᵉ 10ᵗʰ Day of y̆ᵉ 12ᵗʰ mo 1684

Joseph Richards y̆ᵉ elder acknowledged a deed in open Court unto Nathaniell Richards for one hundred aceres of Land Lying in Chester County bearing date y̆ᵉ 10ᵗʰ day of y̆ᵉ 1ˢᵗ mo 1691

John Wood Acknowledged A deed in open Court unto Howell James for five hundred aceres of Land Lying att the uper end of newtowne bearing date y̆ᵉ 10ᵗʰ day of the first month one Thousand six hundred ninety and one.

Howell James Acknowledged a deed in open Court unto John Wood for two hundred and fifty acres of Land Lying in Edgment bearing date ye 10th day of ye first month 1691

Caleb pusey acknowledged a deed in open Court unto Elizabeth Redmeale for Thirty acres of Land Lying in Midletowne bearing date ye 10th day of ye first mo 1691

Whereas Complaint hath been made by severall persons of This County for want of an account of the Levies what hath been paid and who hath paid and who hath received and what the have received upon which the Court hath Called for an account to all the receivers and the was produced and the Countys Charges made up in open Courtt and the severall papers presented to the Grand Inquest to perruse that if possible the may give satisfaction to there neighbors.

The Court ordered that the Grand inquest have on Order to Lay out a Convenient Road from Radnor to Chester

The Court ordered that the sheriff have an Order for the Gathering of the County Levies that are yet unpaid and that destress bee made of those that refuse to pay after notice given

The Court AdJornes until the second Third day in the fourth Month next.

A p^{r}sentment of ye Grand Inquest

We of the Grand Jury present the want of the mending the bridge on the kings Road over ye trench near the mill alsoe we present the want of mending the bridge over the mill trench by William Woodmanseys.

We also p^{r}sent the want of a Convenient Road between the Towne of Radnor and Chester, we alsoe present the want of the road over and on both sides ye run between William Woodmanseys and Larrons roothes to be made Convenientt for a Cartt to pass. we present the want of LeLather searchers in this County according to Law we present the want of fence vewers in the Towne of Aston we present Edward Cartter for absenting himselfe from the service of this Grand Jury; wee present George Stoude of Concord for swearing by the name of God on the Third day of this Instant Contrary to the Law of this

Province we present the want of the booke of Laws in this County for the publick service thereof

    Caleb pusey foreman

ye Court AdJorns untill ye second Third day in ye fourth month next

---

Att a Co^{r}t held at Chester for ye County of Chester the 9th day of ye 4th mo 1691 After silence was comanded The Comission of ye yeare was read

John Simcocke p^{r}sident
John Brisstow
Samuell Levis
James Sandilande
} Justices present

    George fforman Sheriff
    Joshua ffearne Clerke

The Grand Inquest was Called and apeared except Joseph Wood who was Excused.

WILLIAM CLAYTON Pl^{t}ff
JEREMIA COLLITT Def^{dt}
in an accon of a Trespas and Ejectment defered the Last Co^{r}t now Called againe

was this Co^{r}t offered by John Bristow and John Simcocke to come to Tryall by ye Country but Robt Ewre did aledge that There was not A Corrum of Justices to which John Bristow reployed that care should be Taken that Justices should be provided by the Afternoon but Robert Ewre said he was unprovided and desired that the cause might bee bee defered untill ye next Co^{r}t to which the parttys concerned did Agree then to come to Tryall.

JOHN WORALL pl^{t}ff
EDWARD PRITHITT Def^{dt}
in an accon of Debt

The Declaration was read and the bill under the Def^{dts} hand for four pounds was read and owned but Defd^ts play was that ye pl'ff gave him further time than ye bill mentioned

Jury

John Jerman	William Tally
Joseph Need	Tho: vernon
John Hallowell	Robt Barber
Joseph Richards elder	Tho Baldwin
Albertt Hendrickson	Robt Carter
Jacob Hendrickson	Jeremiah Collitt

ye Jury finds for ye pl'ff five pounds wth Cost of Sute & one peny Damage Judgment according to verditt

CORNELIOUS EMPSON pl'ff   ⎧ The Pl'ff and Def^dt hath Apeared
JEREMIAH COLLITT Def^dt   ⎨ and the Def^dt made it Apeare
In an accon of Debt   ⎩ that The prossess was not exhibited in time according to Law

Therefore the Co't granted ye Def^dt A none suite

GEORGE FFORMAN pl'ff   ⎫
GEORGE ANDROSS Def^dt ⎬ now Called and
upon attachment   ⎪ Continued again
Continued ye Last Co^rt ⎭ This Co^rt

Joseph Richards ye Elder Entered A Cavett against his sonn Concerning a parcell of Land The Co't AdJorned for one houre and a halfe and mett againe according to AdJornment

THO ROLLINSON pl'ff   ⎧ Andrew Lock and Isarell Holme
NATHANIEL LUKINS Def^dt ⎨ was called and apeared The
Continued ye Last Cortt ⎪ Charge Against them was killing
and now withdrawne   ⎩ of geese to which Isarell Holme did confess that hee did kill one Goose but upon his submission promising never to doe such acts any more was discharged paying there fees

Mortton Morttonson exhibited A pittion to ye Co't and ye Co't Considered ye same and ordered that it might be returned to ye Grand Inquest that the matter may be accomodated.

Afterwards Isarell Holme was ordered to give securyty to the Sheriff for his apearance the next Coʳt to Answer to a Complaint made against him Concerning hogg stailing into whose Custody he was Committed

yᵉ return of Radnor Road to Chester

The Grand inquest made return of A Roade Laid out from Radnor to Chester Towne the 20ᵗʰ of yᵉ 2ᵈ mo 1691 wee of the grand inquest for yᵉ County of Chester in persuance of an order of Coʳt bearing date the third of the first mo 1691 having Laid out a Road for yᵉ Township of Radnor begining at a marked black oak standing by the great road from Chester to Marple yᵉ sᵈ oak standing in yᵉ sᵈ Marple Township near John Howells house thence north Easterly Through yᵉ sᵈ Howels Land to Daniell Williamsons Land then Through the sᵈ Williamsons Land near his house to a run near Josias Taylors house then through the sᵈ Taylors Land to William Howells Land then Through the sᵈ Howells Land to the widdow Elis Land, then Through the sᵈ Elis Land to David Morris Land Then Through the sᵈ Morris Land to a black oak with Ten knoches standing thereon then downe the sᵈ Land through a valley Called the dry holew to Darby Creeke then over the sᵈ Creek and through morris lewelins hollow to Evan proderos Land then along yᵉ said Evans land to Thomas Joanes Land then thorrow yᵉ sᵈ Joanes Land to James James Land to a white oak marked with Ten knoches in yᵉ sᵈ James Land then through the said James Land to Richard Miles Land then Through the sᵈ Miles Land to Elis Joans Land then through yᵉ sᵈ Joans to James Moors Land then Through the sᵈ Moors Land to Evan Ollivers Land then through the sᵈ Ollivers Land to William Davis Land in Radnor township then through the sᵈ Davis Land to the high road it being the Corner Stake of the sᵈ Davis and Richard Cooks Land from thence Along the sᵈ road northerly to a black oak marked on foure sides with five knoches a peece standing in the Center of ye s^d Radnor township the s^d road having trees marked from one End to the other   Calleb pusey foreman

David Lloyd offered in the behalfe of the Welsh that the was willing to pay according to there proporcons from the time the have been Leagally of this County And after some debate it was agreed and acknowledged by David Lloyd that the Welsh who are reputed to bee within the bounds of Chester County shall Contribute towards paying of the tax, the same being assesed and Levied upon them as upon the upon the Inhabittants of Chester County according to due proporcon and priority of residence and settlement. The Inhabitants of the County of Chester Indemnifying them ye said Welsh from paying in Philadelphia County and be at the Charge of altering the pattents and Deeds which mencon philadelphia Instead of Chester County provided that such thoro Contrebuton to the said tax shall not bee prejediciall or made use of to debar them of any priveledges that the proprietor is or shall be willing and Capable to grant or Confirme unto them.

According to the order of the Governor the Co^rt ordered walter fositt and philip Rumon for Leather Searchers for this County and Sealers of the Same with the Seale C for Chester

The Grand Jury presented the want of a supervisor in Ridley whereupon the Co^rt ordered John Sharples to bee supervisor for the year insuing

Thomas Coeborne Acknowledged a deed in open Co^rt unto ffrancis Balding for one hundred acres of Land Lying in Chester township with ye mesnage and appurtenances, bearing date the ninth day of ye 4th month 1691

Thomas Coeborne acknowledged a deed in open Co^rt unto his son William Coeborne for one hundred and five acres more or Less with ye housing and plantacon and appurtenances bearing date ye 9th day of ye 4th month 1691

Thomas Coeborne acknowledged a Deed in open Co^rt unto Joseph Coeborne for one hundred acres of Land more or less with the mill and hous and appurtenances Lying in Chester towneship bearing date ye ninth day of the fourth month 1691

Thomas Worilaw acknowledged a Deed of setlement in open Co͏ʳt unto John Worilaw and Ann his wife for two hundred and fifty Acres of Land with halfe the housing and Improvments upon the same Lying in Edgmont bearing date the first day of the seventh month 1691

Joshua Hastings acknowledged a deed in open Co͏ʳt unto John Sharples for fourty acres of Land Lying in neither providence bearing date the 10th day of yᵉ 4th mo 1691

George Simcock by his Attorney John hallawell acknowledged a Deed in open Court unto John Clewes for fifty acres of Land Lying in Darby bearing date the Eight day of the fourth month 1691

The Sheriff made return of an Execution against Andros ffreind and Johanas ffreind att the suite of Petter Dalboe This Execution is satisfied onely nineteen shillings and two pence which was made up by John Bristow and James Sandilands which was ordered to be paid by Andros friend

The Sheriff made return of an executon against nathaniell Thornton at the suite of Jeremiah Collitt That the third day of the six month 1691 did Levie the same upon the house and plantacon of the said Thornton which was apraysed by Twelve men of the neibourhood to the sum of Eighteen pounds, the said Thornton having the Corn now growing upon the ground.

yᵉ Co͏ʳt AdJorned untill yᵉ second Third day in yᵉ seventh month next

HANCE PETTERS	pl͏ᵗff	
EDWARD EGLINTON	Def͏ᵈᵗ	Withdrawne
in an accon of debt		
EDWARD EGLINTON	pl͏ᵗff	
HANCE PETTERSON	Def͏ᵈᵗ	withdrawne
in an accon on ye Case		
ALBERT HENDRICKSON	pl͏ᵗff	
ANN FFRIEND	Def͏ᵈᵗ	withdrawne
In an accon of Debt		

Att A Co^rt held att Chester for ye County of Chester ye 6th day of ye 8th mo 1691

{ John Simcocke p^rsident
John Blunston
John Bristow
Wm Jenkins
Geo: Maris
James Sandilands
Samuell Levis } Justices p^rsent

George fforman Sheriff
Joshua ffearne Clerke

The Co^rt was called and Silence was Commanded and ye Grand Jury was called Over. The accon of George fforman pl^tff and George Andross Def^dt which have been depending these Three Co^rts was now called and ye Declaracon was read wherein ye pl^tff declareth for Eleven pounds Ten Shillings and Three pence upon balance of accts as by accots in Co^rt produced doth appear And ye pl^tff was attested to his accots and then Craved Judgment against ye Def^dt And ye Co^rt Granted ye same

JOHN NIXSON pl^tff
JOHN MADOCK Def^dt
the accon was called ye pl^tff and Def^dt Appeared and Def^dt Aledged that he had noe declaracon and Therefore Craved a none Suite, and ye Court Granted the Same

JOSEPH RICHARDS pl^tff
RICHARD CROSSBEY Def^dt
The accon was called ye pl^tff and Def^dt Appeared and the Def^dt aledged that he had noe declaration and Therefore craved a none suite and ye Co^rt Granted it.

EDWARD JONEINGS &
JAMES CHIFFORS pl^tff
JOSEPH HICKMAN Def^dt
upon attachment
The accon was called ye pl^tffs appeared ye Def^dt did not appear ye declaration was read and a bill of Two pounds thirteen shillings produced upon which ye Co^rt Granted Judgment upon ye whole paying ye Co^rt Charges

This Co:rt AdJorned untill y:e fourth hour in y:e after noone and mett againe according to AJornment

The Orphans Co:rt was called and adJorned untill y:e next day

Tho Bright pl:tff
Richard Bufington Def:dt } with Drawn
a Replevey

William Clayton pl:tff   This accon being called y:e pl:tf
Jeremiah Collitt Def:dt   appeared by his attorneys Charles
in an accon of Trespas   Pickering and John White and
and Ejectment defered   y:e Def:dt's appeared. David Lloyd
y:e Last Co:rt   in y:e behalfe of y:e Governour and
  alsoe y:e executor of Tho Brasie
and it was defered untill y:e next morning.

The next morning y:e afores:d accon was called againe and y:e declaracon was read And y:e matter being Largely debated concerning y:e way of Ejectment and the Courtt questoning the safty of proseeding in that way and maner Therefore the Court by y:e majority of voyses doe put by this accon desireing y:e ptys concerned to come to tryall according to y:e Constitucon of this Government and the shall bee fairly heard y:e Co:rt AdJorned untill y:e 8:th hour y:e next morning and mett againe according to adJornment

Philip Lambert was Bound over to Co:rt upon ye susspition of stealing goods from James Browne and William Clayton but nothing being fully proved against him he was discharged by y:e Co:rt paying his fees

David Lloyd pl:tff } The accon was called y:e Def:dt
James Sandilands Def:dt } aledged that y:e pl:tff hath not paid y:e fees of y:e former Courtt and it was refered to y:e Co:rt by both p:rtys to deside y:e difference which Co:rt ordered That David Lloyd shall pay y:e officers fees of y:e former Co:rt and if any Charges was Created by witneses or any other wayes y:e Def:dt shall pay them himselfe Therefore y:e prosced in order

to tryall; ye Declaracon was read the Def^dt Aledged that he had no sumons; the pl'ff answered that there was a declaration in time and noe need of a sumons because ye person is A Magisstrate; ye Def^dt Acknowledged to ye Declaracon but being not sumoned Craved a none suite; and after ye matter Largely debated ye Co^rt Granted the same.

John Nixson attended ye Co^rt for to pass a deed to John Parker but ye s^d parker appeared not to receive ye same

David Lloyd being Bound for ye appearance of Edward Eglinton att this Co^rt accordingly brought ye s^d Eglinton into open Co^rt and there delivered him into Cusstidoy of ye Corronor

MICHA THOMAS pl'ff ⎱ The Def^dt Confesst Judgment for
GEORGE FORMAN Def^dt ⎰ ye debt and Cost of suite

GEORGE FFORMAN pl'ff ⎱
EDWARD EGLINTON ⎱ Def^t ⎰ ye petty Jury was Called
and JOHN MADOCKE ⎰   and attested

Juriors

Robert Taylor   Randle Mallin   John Hood
Tho: vernon   Robert Burrow   Tho: Hood
Randle vernon   Tho: Minshaw   Wm Garrett
Robert vernon   Bartho Coppocke John Smith

The declareacon was read wherein ye pl'ff declaress for Thirty pounds and ye Defd^t plea is that ye have satisfied ye debt.

Evidences

John Child
Charles pickering
Joseph Richards
Roger Jackson
David Lloyd
William Tally

⎱ ye Jury finds for ye Def^dt with Cost of suite and Two pound damage John Wood foreman ⎰

The pl'ff Craved an appeall to ye next provinesiall Co^rt in Law and the Co^rt Granted ye same

ye Grand Jury p^rsentm^t

we of ye Grand Jury p^rsent Joseph Wood for that he on y^e

20th of ye 2d mo Last did absent himselfe forom ye service of ye Grand Jury

we also p'sent Humphrey Ellis for absenting himself from the service of ye Grand Jury this Co'rt

we alsoe p'sent Thomas Garrett for absenting himselfe from the service of ye Grand Jury this Co'rt

we alsoe p'sent Joseph Cuxson for absenting himselfe from the service of ye Grand Jury on ye 20th of ye 2d month Last

we also psent William Smith for absenting himselfe from ye service of ye Grand Jury on ye 20th of ye 2d month Last

we also psent Henry Barnes Joyner of this County for that about midnight Last he did sweare severall oaths Contrary to ye good and wholsome Laws of this province in that case made and provided   Caleb pusey foreman

we of ye Grand Jury psent Richard parker Caleb pusey Robertt Molder George fforman James Sandilands John Hoskins Roger Jackson for selling of beare &c without Licence Contrary to Law

we alsoe psent Edward Eglinton for Breaking of ye stocks in the Towne of Chester and unlawfully Leting out a prissoner against ye peace of the King and Queen &c

       Caleb pusey foreman

Whereas ye Supervisor of ye Township of Chester made psentment of severall persons that have neglected their service at high ways and that some opposed ye mending of ye Bridge over ye Trench that Carrys the watter to the Mill and ye Co'rt Considering ye same ordered that ye owners of ye sd mill shall repaire and uphold ye bridg at ye Mill over ye Trench and that ye Township shall Repaire and uphold ye Bridg that is over ye Trench that Leads to Wilham Woodmansies.

William Hauks appointed Supervissor for ye Towneship of Chichester for ye year insuing

The want of a prisson having been psented by ye Grand Jury it was this Co'rt debated Concerning ye Building of a new prisson and worke house for fellons and it was Agreed by y\ Co^rt that one should be builded Eighteene foot and Twenty six foot all Builded of stone and John Brisstow and James Sandilands are intrusted and Impowered by y\ Co^rt as near as y\ can to compute y\ Charges and make return of y\ same at y\ next County Co^rt

Whereas There was Complaint made to y\ Co^rt Concerning a way to y\ Landing at Calinhooke y\ Inhabittants there being at diferance about it; to end y\ diferance and to accomadate y\ Countrys Convenience The Co^rt ordered the Grand Jury to Lay out A Road and make return of y\ Same att y\ next County Co^rt

The Orphans Co^rt was Called againe: and John Child made complaint concerning the Orphans of John Brunsdone; whereupon y\ Co^rt Ordered that his widdow shall bring in to y\ next Co^rt an Inventory of y\ Goods and Chattles of her deceased husband

for as much as as y\ Estate of Georg Gleaves being insufficient for y\ bringing up of his Children and That it doth appear to this Co^rt that it was his desire that these p^rsons hereafter menconed should have y\ bringing up of them & being uncapable to mentaine themselves; Therefore y\ afores^d Co^rt as father of the poore in this Case have placed and put forth John Gleaves unto Bartholomew Copocke y\ Elder to serve until he be of y\ age of twenty two years; And pheby Gleaves unt Bartholomew Coppocke y\ yonger for y\ Terme afores^d

Hester Gleaves brought an appraysment of her Estate appraysed by Randle vernon Robt vernon Randle Malin being shee intendeth to marry againe: And y\ Co^rt Ordered John Blunston George Maris and Samuell Levis; and Caleb pusey to bee assistant unto them in y\ deviding of y\ afores^d estate wch was y\ Estate of Joseph Powell deceased according to y\ will of y\ deceased; And whereas y\ Estate of y\ deceased is made y\ worss by a Latter husband Geo: Gleaves by debts and other ways The Co^rt doth Order that y\ Land shall remaine to the Widdow and Children and not to be dissposed of but by y^e advoyce of y^e Orphans Co't

This Co't doth Adjorn untill y^e 1st 3^d day in y^e 1st mo next

Woley Rawson acknowledged a Deed in oppen Co't to Nathaniel Lamplue for a parcell of swamppey Land Lying in Chichester bearing date ye 6th of ye 1st month 1688

Thomas Merscor Acknowledged a Deed in oppen Co't to Joseph Cowburne for halfe an acre of Land Lying in Aston bearing date ye 7th day of ye Eight month 1691

John Wood by his Attorney John Blunston acknowledged a deed in oppen Co't unto Robert penall for Two hundred and fifty acres of Land and p'mises Lying in Edgment bearing date ye second day of ye Third month 1691

Ann Bunting Acknowledged a Deed in oppen Co't unto Samuell sellers for seventy five acres and a halfe Lying in ye Township of Darby bearing date the first day of ye Seventh month 1691.

petter Thomas acknowledged a Deed in oppen Co't unto John Parker for fifty Acres of Land and p'mises Lying in Spring towne bearing date ye 6th day of the Eight month 1691

Joseph Richards ye yonger Acknowledged a Deed in Oppen Co't unto Edward Cartter for Two hundred & fifty Acres of Land one hundred and fifty Lying in aston the s^d Land being for years bearing date ye 9th day of ye 4th month 1691

Ann freind Andrew ffreind and John ffreind acknowledged a Deed in oppen Co't unto David Lloyd for one hundred and Eighty Three Acres of Land Lying in Upland wth all ye housing and Improvements upon ye same bearing date the 27th day of ye Third month 1689

John Simcocke John Bristow and Randle vernan Executo's to Thomas Brasie Acknowledged a Deed in oppen Co't unto David Lloyd for a parcell of over-plus Land Lying in Ches^{tr} bearing Date ye 6th day of ye 6th month 1691

Isaac Whelden by his Attorney Joseph Need Acknowledged a Deed unto Samuell Levis for one hundred Acres of Land

Lying in ye Township of Darby bearing date ye Eighteenth day of ye first month 1691

Harman Johnson Acknowledged a Deed in oppen Co^rt unto Joseph Wood for fifty Acres of Land Lying in ye Township of Darby bearing date ye 6th day of ye 8th month 1691

Joseph Wood Acknowledged a Deed in oppen Co^rt unto Otter Ernest Cocke for ye aboves^d fifty Acres of Land bearing date ye 7th day of the Eight month 1691

Joseph Wood Acknowledged a Deed in oppen Co^rt unto Andrew Bone for seventy Acres of Land Lying in Darby bearing date ye first Day of June 1691

Otter Earnest Cocke Acknowledged a deed in Open Court unto Joseph Wood for sixty Acres of Land Lying in Darby bearing date ye Seventh Day of October 1691

Andrew Bone Acknowledged a deed in open Co^rt unto Joseph Wood for fifty acres of Land Lying in Darby bearing date ye 6th day of October 1691

Att A Co^rt held att Chester for ye County of Chester ye 8th and 9th Dayes of ye 10 Mo 1691

{ John Bristow p^rsident
John Simeocke
John Blunston
George Maris
William Jenkin
James Sandilands } Justices p^rsent

Geo: fforman Sheriff
Joshua ffearne Clerke

the Justices was called over Samuell Levis did not appear

The Grand Jury was called over severall did not appeare but afterwards appeared Except Evan prodra & Joseph Wood

The Constables was called over severall did not appeare which afterwards did appeare

p^rsentmt

the Constable of Darby presents that he found a bad peece of Eight in ye hand of Thomas fox who being Examined said he had it of Charles Whitticor

JOHN NIXSON pl'ff } John Child appeared as attorney to
JOHN MADDOCK Def^{dt} } ye pl'ff
in an accou of debt } the Def^{dt} appeared in his owne person
on award } Refered untill ye next morning

ABRAHAM INLOE pl'ffs } in an accon of Debt after some
CORNELIOUS DERICKSON } debate defered untill ye next
ANTHONY NELSON D^{tt} } morning

DAVID LLOYD pl'ff } ye pl'ff and Def^{dt} was called
JAMES SANDILANDS Def^{dt} } and both appeared

The Corronors Jury was called and the declaracon was read the Def^{dt} Denyes ye declaration and puts the pl'ff upon ye proofe of it

        The Jury Impanelled and attested

Edmond Cartlidge	Robert Taylor
John Smith	Bartho: Coppock Eld^r
Tho: Coates	Isaac Taylor
Tho: Worth	John Hallawell
Rich: Parker	John Hood
ffrancis Yarnall	francis Chadsey

The pl'ff produced a pattent which was read bearing date in 1669 and severall other papers was read, ye Def^{dt} produced four pattents and three paper Evidences and ye old draught of Upland.

Anthony Nelson being attested s^d as to ye bounds of ye Land of Neals Lawsons westerly came to the side of the backstow and forther saith not

William Woodmansie being attested saith he tooke ye Land that James Sandilands now claimeth of Isarell Helme and coming to see the bounds of the Land the said that ye run parted the Land in question and soe Long as he Lived upon it there was never noe alteracon of noe fences but Neales Lawsons Lads took away some of the fencing but soone brought the same againe

John Bailes being attested saith he plowed the Land fourteene years agoe as to the fence it is in the same place it was then and that Neiles Lawson told him severall times that att the Cherry tree at the side of the backstow was the bounds of his Land and the fence then seemed to be an old fence and further saith not,

The Jury finds for the Def^{dt} with Cost of Suite and two pence Damage Judgment was given according to verdite upon which ye pl^{t}ff Craved an apcale to the next provintiall Co^{r}t in Law which was granted paying all Cost and Charges according to Law if againe Cast.

| MARY BOULES pl^{t}ff
ALEXANDER DEVERICK Defd^t
in an accon of trespas
on ye Case | the pl^{t}ff and Defd^t both apeared ye declaration was red the Def^t put in his plea in writing |

ye Jury attested

Johnathan Kay	John Worell
Albert hendrickson	William Cloud
Robert Barber	Samuell Holt
Randle vernan	Will: Talley
petter Taylor	Joseph Richardsson
Tho: powell	peetter pceterson

The Jury finds for ye plaintiff with Cost of suite and two pence Damage

Judgment given according to verdite
p^{r}sented

Greetto ye wife of Harman Johnson was bound over to this Co^{r}t for inticeing the Negeros Belonging to James Sandilands to Conveay good from there Master and shee Received them but shee promising to bee of better behaviour the said James Sandilands did forgive hir; and upon her submision and solomn promiss to the Co^{r}t to doe soe noe more shee was discharged paying hir fees.

JOHN NIXSON pl^{t}ff was called againe ye pl^{t}ff apeared by
JOHN MADOCK Defd^t his attorney John Child and Excepted of by the Co^{r}t and ye s^d Child doth oblidge himselfe to stand and abide to the Judgment of the S^d Co^{r}t

The Declaracon was read and the Defd⁺ˢ Answer was that he owed nothing to the pl⁺ff The bond and Award was read And yᵉ same Jury attested as in The afores⁴ accon The Jury finds for yᵉ pl⁺ff wᵗʰ Cost of Suite and one peny Damage The Coʳt Granted Judgment according to yᵉ verdite

The Coʳt adJorned untill yᵉ seventh hour yᵉ next morning and mett againe ordered by this Coʳt that the sheriff Repaire to Radnor and Haverford with some Assistance to Colectt yᵉ Levies according to yᵉ time of Comencement forthwith to the End that yᵉ accounts may be made up to yᵉ satisfaction of the County in Generall and to make a true Returne thereof at the next County Coʳt

A petition Exhibited to this Coʳt by severall of yᵉ Inhabittants in and about Thornebery for a Cart way to Chester and yᵉ Coʳt Considering of yᵉ same; Ordered The Clerke to send an order to yᵉ Grand Inquest to Lay out a Convenient Road from yᵉ Towne of Thornbery to Chester

ABRAHAM INLOE
CORNELIUS DERICKSON pl⁺ffs
ANTHONY NELSON Defd⁺
{ Called again and pl⁺ffs and Defd⁺ both apeared The same Jury as before Except ffrancis Chadsey Instead of William Cloud

The Declaracon was read; the Defd⁺ˢ answer was that he had Dealing with Epharim harman and if this be a debt to him he doth not deny it; The Jury finds for yᵉ pltffs Three hundred and nine Gilders & two stivers with Cost of suite and two pence damage

The Coʳt gave Judgment according to verdite

Chester yᵉ 9ᵗʰ of yᵉ 10ᵗʰ mo 1691

yᵉ Grand Juryˢ pʳsentmᵗˢ

We the Grand Jury pʳsent Margeritt Alias Gretto Johnson wife of Harman Johnson husbandman Late of Chester for that yᵉ sᵈ Greeto Johnson did since Chester faire Last fellonyously Receive of Tobey Negro of James Sandilands one Bushell of wheat meale and alsoo two Bushels of wheate and some Candles it being yᵉ proper goods of James Sandilands Contrary to ye good and wholsom Laws of this province in that case made and provided.   Caleb pusey foreman

Wee of the Grand Jury doe find great Cause to present ye matter to This Co^{r}t as a great greivance to ye County and a great discoriagement to those that have been or may bee acttive for ye future in Catching of woulfes
   Caleb pusey foreman

Chester 8th of ye 10th mo 1691

We of ye Grand Jury present Charles Whitecor husbandman of the Towneship of Ridley for that he about Chester faire Last as alsoe about as alsoe about ye begining of ye seventh Month Last did disperse and pay away ffrauddulently base false and Counter Coyne in this province to ye great nusance thereof   Caleb pusey foreman

Wee of ye Grand Jury doe present Richard Thomson of Havorford for That about fifteene monthes since hee did Confess That hee made of one peece of Eight a dozen bites and passed them away and alsoe made Stamps for others; Contrary to Law in that Case made and provided
   Caleb pusey fforeman

Wee of ye Grand Jury for ye County of Chester in persuance to an order of Co^{r}t bearing date ye 14th of ye 8th month 1691; for to Lay out a Convenient Road from ye kings Road in Darby Towneship to ye Landing place at Calin hook in ye County afores^d and to End ye difference about some peare trees soposed to bee in ye road now wee having been at ye s^d place and carefully and deliberatly considered ye s^d matter have unanimously Agreed as followeth (viz) The s^d Road to begin at a corner stone near to an ash tree by ye Creek side at ye bottom of Mortton Morttonsons Orchard; then on a stright Line four perches to another corner stone being at ye Lower corner of s^d Morttons Orchard then continuing a stright Line Eleven perches and seven foot to a corner stone near ye uper End of ye s^d. orchard which s^d stone standeth in ye outtermost streight Line Menconed in Mounce pettersons Deed from Andrew Swanson Bone; Then continuing a Line at Thirty two foot distance The end of ye s^d Mortons house being Built before ye s^d road was agreed upon Standing about six foot in ye s^d Road Excepted from ye s^d mounce pettersons fence to ye end thereof; Then still continuing ye s^d Line about six foot wth in ye s^d Morttons Land to ye end of his fence still continuing ye s^d Line through ye woods to a tree with notches by ye road Agreed on among themselves to Darby: Then along ye severall corses of ye s^d road to ye kings road at ye Eastermost corner of Thomas foxes fence; Then turning westerly at Thirty two foot distance from The afores^d Line back againe on ye s^d severall Courses still continuing Thirty Two foot distance ye s^d Morttons house End Excepted; as afores^d; to ye cross way near ye s^d Morttons house; then upon a streight Line cross ye s^d way to a corner Stone standing at ye corner of ye s^d Mounce pettersons fence being alsoe ye corner of ye s^d cross road; from thence downe in a streight Line Eleven perches and 10 foot to another Corner stone standing by ye s^d mounce pettersons fence side making here ye road 32 foot from ye afores^d stone at ye Lower corner of ye s^d morttons orchard then down ye s^d Mounce pettersons fence 5 perches & 2 foot to a corner stone standing by ye Criple side & near ye corner of ye s^d Mounces fence from which s^d stone to ye first mentioned stone it is six perches & two foot broad   Caleb puscy fforeman

A Deed pased from William Cloud ye Elder to Robert Mackee for one Hundred Acres of Land Lying on a Branch of Namans Creek with ye buildings and improvements upon ye same bearing date ye seventh day of ye Tenth month 1691

John Simcocke Acknowledged a Deed in open Court to Thomas Browne for forty Eight acres of Land Lying in Ridley Towneship bearing date ye 8th of ye 10th month 1691

This Court AdJorned untill ye second Third day in ye first month next

Att a Court held at Chester ye 8th day of ye first month 1691/2 { John Bristow prsident
John Simcocke
John Blunston
George Maris
Samuell Levis } Justices prsent

George fforman Sheriff
Joshua ffearne Clerke

After proclaimation was made and silence Comanded the Justices of ye peace was Called over James Sandilands and William Jenkin did not appeare The old Constables was called and appeared & gave in theire presentments that all was well and was discharged and others Chosen in their Roome as followeth (viz)

ye names of ye Constables for ye year Insuing

ffrancis Litle for Chester
John Bartram for Darby
William Malin for uper providence
George Smedley for Midletowne
Joseph Kent for Springfield
Robertt vernan for neither providence
Josiah Taylor for Marple
John Holston for Edgmont
William Rowe for Concord
Nathaniell Richards for Aston
Henry Lewis for harford
Isaac Taylor for Thornbery
Walter Martin for Chichester
Ringnear petterson for Ridley
Samuel Scott for Burmingham

ROBERT EWRE & ELIZABETH his wife Pltffs
Against JOHN SIMCOCK JOHN BRISTOW
and RANDLE VERNON   Defdts
in an accon of ye Case

The Accon was called and the Pltffs did not appear & was refered untill ye after noone

A new Grand Jury Impanilled

Tho: Coeborne	Thomas vernan	Bartholomew Coppock Junr
Randle vernan	Petter Taylor	Richard Armes
David Ogdon	Tho: Minshaw	David Evans
John Kingsman	Will: Swaford	George Peerce
Geo Woodyer	Rich: Bernerd	John Lewis
John Sharples	Rich: Woodward	being sumoned to serve of
John kirke	James swaford	ye Grand jury did not ap-
John Marshall	John Howell	pear and was fined 10^s p^r
Tho: Coats		man excepting John Lewis
		of whom satisfacon was
		given to ye Co^rt and he
		was Excused

The Accon of Robertt Ewer was called againe in ye after noone

And John White and Charles Pickering appeared as Attorneys for Robert Ewer And Patrick Robinson and David Lloyd as Attorneys for ye Governo^r and ye Executo^{r}s of Thomas Brasie John Simcocke John Britsow and Randle vernan

The declaracon was read and ye Defd^{ts} Answer was ye Declaracon was not Leagall nor substantiall nor sufishent in Law to be Answered unto And after a great debate Concerning ye Leagallness and unLeagallness of ye Declaracon it was Refered to ye Court and ye Defd^t Craved a none suite and ye Court Considering ye same being but Just a Corrum ye Majority of which granted a none suite for that the Declaracon was Insofitient

Thomas Browne Supervissor for ye Township of Ridley for ye year Insuing

William Brinton Acknowledged a Deed in open Court to John Davis for fifty Acres of Land Lying in Burmingham bearing date ye 10th day of the first month 1690

ye Grand Jury p^{r}sentment
ye 8th of ye 1st mo 1691/2

we of ye Grand Inquest present Charles Pickering and James Standfield for that since ye Last Co^{r}t the did hunt take up and detaine for about Twenty four hours the swine of Daniell Humphreys and Humphrey Ellis to ye number about seven or eight: against ye Laws of this province in that case made and provided   Caleb pusey forman

William Cloud Acknowledged a Deed in open Co^{r}t unto Joseph Cloud and John Cloud for Two hundred Acres of Land Lying in Chester County with all ye Buildings and Improvements on ye same bearing Date ye 8th day of the 10th month 1691

An Assignment of ye same Deed from John Cloud to Joseph Cloud was Acknowledged in open Co^{r}t bearing date ye 7th day of ye 1st month 1691/2

John Blunston Acknowledged a Deed in Open Court unto John Roads for fifty Acres of Land Lying in Darby bearing date ye 2^d day of ye 1st mo 1691/2

John Mendinghall Acknowledged a Deed in Open Court unto George Maris for all his Land Lying in Concord with all ye Buildings and Improvements upon ye same at his decease bearing date ye 8th day of ye 1st mo 1691/2

John ffox & Thomas England acknowledged a Deed in Open Court unto Robert Langum for Seventy Acres of Land Lying in Midletowne bearing date ye Eight day of ye first month 1691/2

ffrancis Cooke by Michaell Blunston his Attorney Assigned over an assignment of a Deed unto John Blunston for one hundred Acres of Land Lying in Darby near to ye Landing ye Deed bearing date ye Last of November 1681 and ye assignment to francis Cooke bearing date ye 8th of June 1683 and this assignment bearing date ye 20th of ye 11th mo 1691

Thomas Hood Acknowledged a Deed in Open Co^{r}t by his Attorney John Blunston unto John Hood for fifty Acres of Land Lying in ye Towneship of Darby on the west side of Darby Creek bearing date ye Eight day of ye first month 1692

The Sheriff made return of an Execucon against Alexander Deuericks not to be found

James Browne Assigned a Deed over in open Co'rt unto Robert Jefreis for for sixty Acres of Land Lying in Chichester bearing date y" 8th day of march 1691

John Roads Acknowledged a Deed in open Courtt by John Blunston his Attorney unto Lewis David for one hundred Acres of Land Lying in y" Towneship of Darby bearing date y" second day of y" first month 1691/2

Richard Tucker Acknowledged a Deed in open Courtt by John Smith his Attorney unto Thomas Smith for one hundred Acres of Land Ly in y" Towneship of Darby bearing date y" fifteenth of y" second month 1691/2

Elizabeth Musgrove Acknowledged a Deed in open Court unto John fox for one hundred acres of Land Lying in Midletowne bearing date y" Eight day of y" first month 1691/2

The sheriff made return of an Execucon against John Maddock not to be found

y" Co'rt Adjorned untill y" 2^d 3^d day in y" 4th month next

The orphans Court was called and an Inventory of y" goods & Chattels of Thomas Brasic deceased presented to this Court to bee Entered & Recorded as followeth—An Inventory of y" goods and Chatles rights & Credits of Thomas Brasie deceased taken and Appraysed by Caleb pusey & Thomas vernan y" 29th of y" 7th mo 1690

	lb	s	d
Imprimis his wearing apparell.......	6	00	00
to plate butons	1	00	00
to a silver wach	3	10	00
to 1 paire of Iron racks	1	00	00
to a Steel Mill	0	08	00
to 1 Iron morter & pestill	0	10	00
to a Baking plate	0	12	00
to one drawing knife 1 falling axe....	0	04	00
to one grubing axe 1 paire of Chisils & 1 gouge	0	04	03
to one Inch borer 1 Lesser 1 Gimblitt.	0	02	06

to one Iron Spindle 1 Coopers ads....	0	04	00
to one fro 1 bill hook 1 hamer.......	0	02	09
to one paire of Iron trouses 1 truoll...	0	06	06
to 1 Copsa boult & 1 ads............	0	06	06
to 23 p Iron 1 Litle frying pan......	0	07	10
to 1 other frying pan & brandiron....	0	04	06
to 1 Iron driping pan 1 Thort saw....	0	14	00
to 1 Iron bar 1 Spitt 1 forke 1 paire of tongs 1 Litle pan 1 paire Taylors sheers	0	09	10
to 1 warming pan 2 Iron weges more Iron ware 3 stuyrips	0	18	00
to 1 Iron pott & hooks 1 brass pot one brass pan & som old brass........	1	16	06
to 15^d of old pewter	2	10	00
to 1 Litle Coper pott 1 Large gun 2 others	2	10	00
to 1 paire of Iron hanges 2 meale sives.	0	4	00
	£	s	d
to hempen Traises 1 dozen of trenchers one plater & one old bowle........	0	07	00
to 5 pound of harow tines 1 hour glass	0	03	06
to 1 bible in 2 volums..............	0	08	00
to 1 flock bed & boulster & 1 green rug	1	00	00
to 2 paire of boots 1 suit of green Cortaine and valones 1 Case of botles & Lumber	1	08	00
to 1 Leather belt 1 cane 1 halfe bushell 1 Earthen botle 1 paire of bellows one paile 1 plow share I pick prong.	0	09	06
to 1 bull & 1 heafer	4	10	00
to 1 sadle & bridle	0	11	00
to 1 old cortaine	0	03	00
to 1 feather bed & boulster.........	3	12	00
to 1 feather bed & boulster & pillow..	2	13	00
to 1 red rug 1 green 1 yellow 1 ash Collered rug	1	05	00
to 3 flaxen sheets & 2 pillow bears....	2	06	00

to 2 table Cloathes & 6 napkins......	1	10	00
to 1 paire of Canvis sheets 1 old one..	0	10	00
to 4 Cushons 2 axes 4 hatchets 1 paire of Large hooks 3 Laches & 2 spring Locks 2 box Locke 1 box & five heaters	2	06	00
to 3 Augers 1 marking Iron 1 paire of duftails 1 rest about 2^{lb} of old Iron 2 of small nails 1 Coffer 1 Coper and one brand Iron	3	04	00

Caryed to ye other Side

to one copper still & worme.........	10	00	00
to one small Iron pott & one brass skellitt	00	07	06
to one Iron pott	00	07	00
to two winscote Chestes	01	00	00
to one Cart sadle	00	02	06
to five Caps Lined with Calico & 8 gartt weebs	00	12	00
to one paire of Cart wheels and Cartt	01	00	00
to one paire of spitles and Case......	00	04	00
	£	s	d
to one paire of small brass scales.....	00	03	00
to 1 paire of stilliards	00	10	00
to 1 paire of hinges & other Iron things 1 broad hatchett	00	10	00
to 1 bay horse four pound	04	00	00
to a mare and Colt	05	00	00
to Cross mare and Colt............	05	00	00
to 3 hoggs and 3 sowes	04	15	00
	84	02	02

     Caleb pusey
     Thomas vernan
       his T mark

The Court AdJorned untill ye first Third day in ye Eight month next

---

Att a Court held att Chester for ye County of Chester ye 14th day of ye 4th month 1692

Justices:
- John Simcocke prsident
- John Bristow
- John Blunston
- George Maris
- William Jenkin
- Samuell Levis

Caleb Pusey Sheriff
Joshua ffearne Clerke

after proclaimation made and by the King & Queens Authority & in ye name of the Proprietor silence Comanded the Justices was called and all appeared

The Grand Jury was called over & all appeared Except Randle vernan and John Kingsman who after account given Concerning their absence the was Excused

philip Rumon supervisor for Chichester for ye year Insuing

Jeremiah Collitt declared in oppen Court that hee have received full satisfacttion of nathaniel Thornton on ye account of that Execution that was Levied upon his plantation

RICHARD CROSSBY pltff
JOHN CALLUERTT Defdt
in an accon of debt

The declaration was read and ye Defdt owned the Debt; and Confessed Judgement in open Courtt according to ye Declaration

JOHN HENDRICKSON pltff
MOUNCE PETTERSON Defdt
in an accon of slander
} withdrawne

JAMES BEALIFFE pltff
ROBERTT WAY Defdt
in an accon of Trover and Convertion
} withdrawne

Robertt Browne came into Courtt & acknowledged himselfe Gilty of Lying with a yonge woman and haveing ye Carnall knowledge of her Contrary to ye Law in that case made and provided, and Cast himselfe upon ye mercy of ye bench to doe what ye pleased with him; And the Courtt Considering the unlawfull act of unclainess seeing the woman is not to be found and ye s^d Browne Humbly submiting himselfe & promising for ye future to be carefull & doe soe noe more The Courtt have been pleased to show him mercey and doe fine him forty shillings to be paid into The sheriff before ye next Court and to be discharged paying his fees. And Thomas Browne Brother to ye s^d Robertt, doth Recognize himselfe in ye sum of Ten pounds for ye payment of ye afores^d fine and Charges &c

The Courtt AdJorned for one hour & mett againe

Robert Turner pl^{t}ff
Caleb pusey Defd^t
in an accon of Trespas on ye Case

The Declaration was read The Defd^t Appeared and had nothing to say why Judgement should not pass

The Courtt gave Judgement against Caleb pusey according to ye Declaration

The Court ordered that Every respective Township within this County for ye future from time to time shall within themselves appoint supervisors & fence vewers and make returnes of ye same to ye County Courtt from time to time.

Henry Barnes Joyner was called to ye bar to answer to Three P^{r}sentments for being Drunk and abusing Magisstrats where upon ye p^{r}sentments was read ag^t him who plead Gilty to them all And the Courtt gave Judgment that ye s^d Barnes should pay a fine of six pounds & Cost of suite &c, & remain prisoner untill payment; And alsoe to be bound to his good behaviour for one year and one day

Daniell Ryley was called to ye bar the Inditement was read ag^t him for stealing of a bell of Tho: Peersons horss and being asked whether he was Gilty or not Gilty he said Gilty but hoped hee should doe soe noe more; whereupon ye Courtt gave

Judgement That he pay fourteen shillings to ye party wronged and all Charges &c; and to be bound to ye good behaviour for one year and a day, and to remaine prissoner untill payment

Owen magdalion doth Recognize himselfe in ye sum of forty pounds for ye good behaviour of ye s^d Daniell Ryley to all ye Kings & Queens Leigs people and to pay all Charges according to ye affores^d Judgement

John Blunston attorney to William Shardlow of London acknowledged a Deed of feoffment in Open Courtt unto Robert Smith for two hundred Acres of Land Lying in ye Towneship of Darby bearing Date ye 10th day of ye 4th month 1692

Joshua ffearne Attorney to John Roads acknowledged a Deed of feofment in open Courtt unto William Jenkin Attorney to Ralph Lewis for one hundred & fifty Acres of Land Lying in ye Towneship of Darby bearing date ye 14th day of ye 4th month 1692

John Clewes Acknowledged a Deed of feoffment in open Courtt unto Joseph Edge for fifty acres of Land Lying in ye Towneship of Darby bearing date ye first day of ye second month 1692

John Bristow Attorney to John Nixson Acknowledged a Deed of feoffment in oppen Courtt unto John Parker for seventy Acres of Land wth plantation & Improvements bearing Date ye 4th day of ye 3^d month 1691

Joshua ffearn Attorney to Samuell Bradshaw Delivered a Deed of feoffm^t in open Courtt unto John Blunston Attorney to John Bowne for two hundred and forty Acres of Land bearing date ye 13th day of ye 4th month 1692

John Bristow & John Simcocke executors to Thomas Brassey Delivered a Deed in Open Courtt unto Andrew Jobe for one hundred Acres of Land Lying in ye Towne of Chester bearing date ye 12th day of ye 4th month 1692

John Blunston Attorney to William Shardlow of London Delivered a Deed of feoffment in open Court unto Thomas Worth for ye use of ye heires of Mathew Gratton being one hundred Acres of Land Lying in ye Towneship of Darby bearing date ye fourteenth day of ye fourth month 1692

Thomas Worth Delivered a Deed in Open Court unto John Hood for ye above said hundred Acres of Land bearing ye same date

ye Co^rt AdJorned untill ye 2^d 3^d day in ye 7th mo next

Geo: fforman Sheriff made return of an Execution ag^t Alexander Devericks att ye suite of Mary Boules that ye 13th of March 1691/2 he Apprehended and tooke in to Custidy ye body of Alixander Devericks after which ye s^d Devericks did satisfie ye Execution as witness my hand Geo: fforman

The new sheriff Calleb pusey made Return of an Execution ag^t John Maddocks att ye suite of John Nixon not satisfied onely four pound Ten Shillings Received.

The Grand Jury P^rsents ye want of a bridge at Walter fosits. Tho: Coeborne foreman.

Att a Court held att Chester for ye County of Chester ye 13th and 14th Dayes of ye 7th month 1692

{ John Bristow p^rsident
John Simcocke
George Maris   } Justices
William Jenkin } p^rsent
Samuell Levis }

Caleb pusey sheriff
Josh ffearne Clerk
proclaimation was made

After silence Comanded by ye King and Queens Authority ye Grand Jury was called over and all appeared. The Constables was called but William Rowe Isaac Taylor Walter Martin & Samuell Scott who was fined 10^s apeece

Robert Turner Admin^r of ye Estate of Christifull Taylor deceased Pl^tff Against Ralph & Dorothy ffretwell & ye Execut^rs & Adminis^rs of Ralph ffretwell deceased Defd^t In a plea of Trespas on ye Case

The Action was called and ye Pl^tff apeared by his Attorney Patrick Robinson.

The Defd^t did not Apeare; ye Declaracon was read; & a

Letter of attorney from Robert Turner to ye s^d Patrick was also read; and ye s^d Attorney produced ye Letters of Administration and Contractt in Open Court; and ye Court gave Judgment that this Accon be defered

ffrancis Chadsey Attorney to Denis Ratchford Acknowledged a Deed in Open Court to Thomas Green for 100 Acres of Land Lying in Concord bearing date ye 6th of ye Eight month 1691

The Court Adjorned for two hours and mett againe according to adjornment

PETTER BOYNTON Pl^{t}ff
JOHN MADDOCK Defd^t
in an Accon of
Scandle & defamacon

The Plaintiff & Defendant was called & both Apeared The Declaracon was read: The Defd^{ts} answer was that he never said such words

The was Impaneled
Juriors

Philip Rumon   John Worrell
Ellis Ellis   Albert Hendrickson
David Merideth   William Clayton
George Peerce   Tho: Marttin
John Worrilaw   Edward Cartter
John Bowetter   ffrancis Yarnall

Evidences
Joshua Jones
Ann Sandilands

The Jury finds for ye Plaintife with Cost of suite and two pence Damage

Judgement given According to verdite

ye Grand Inquest p^{r}sentm^t

wee of ye Grand Inquest doe p^{r}sent ye great want of a prisson

we do also p^{r}sent Richard Thomson for Ranging ye woods & for ye taking up of horses saying he was ranger but we find him not fitt for that honest Trust

we do also p^{r}sent Owen Magdaniell & Richard Thomson & Daniell Ryley for riding & ranging on first dayes as well as on other dayes & for fireing a pistill Late at night at John Callverts window to his and his wifes great afrightment

Tho: Coeborn foreman

we doe also p^rsent John Maddock for abuseing John Simcock & John Bristow being ye King & Queens Justices of ye peace for calling them a pack of roauges

Randle vernon foreman

We of ye Grand Inquest doe p^rsent Tho: Browne of Ridley for keeping of a Tipling houss & selling of rum without a Licence;   Tho: Coeburn foreman

we doe alsoe p^rsent petter Worrell ye yonger of Marple for takeing up and sadleing of John Shaws mare for his owne use & also for Cocking of hay on ye first day.

Tho: Coeburn foreman

we doe also p^rsent ye Cuntreys agrevance that John Bristow being head ranger hath Imployed Richard Thomson to take up a horse that was marked & hath marked him for ye Governo^r

Randle vernan foreman

we doe also p^rsent Richard Thomson now of Marple for taking & Converting a horse of Johnathan Heys to his own use; Tho: Coeburn foreman

we doe also p^rsent ye Towneship of Chester for want of a bridge at ye Kings Road at Calebs mill;

Tho: Coeburn fforeman

Richard Thomson & Owen Magdaniell was called to ye bar to answer an Inditement & submited themselves to ye Court & ye Court Considered the same and gave Judgment that ye pay three pounds a peece and all Charges Equally between them & to be bound to their good behavior for a year & a day

Richard Thomson was called to ye bar to answer to an Inditement for taking a horse of Jonathan Hays & Converting him to his own use and submited himselfe to the Court and ye Court Considered ye same & gave Judgement that he pay two ffould & all Charges & to be bound to his good behavior for a yeare & a day

The aboves^d Richard Thomson Exhibitted a petition to y^e

Court Concerning the aboves^d p'mises but their was severall things in ye pitition Concerning the horse that was proved to be false

Jacob Simcock Corronor of ye County of Chester Acknowledged a Deed in Open Court to Patrick Robinson Lawfull Attorney to Robertt Turner for Twenty two shares of ye Corn mill & saw mill and Implements thereof and ye Twenty two shares of ye Twenty two Acres of Land all in ye towneship of Chester bearing date ye 13th day of ye 7th mo 1692

ye Court Adjorned to ye Eight hour in ye morning & mett againe

whereas Complaint hath been made to John Bristow one of ye Justices of ye peace by William Clayton ag^t Henry Renolds for that ye s^d Henry Renolds did deny ye paym^t of one pound Eleven shillings altho ye s^d Clayton had a bill under ye s^d Renolds hand yett ye s^d Renolds denyed ye bill but afterwards by a writing under his own hand he owned ye bill but aledged that ye mony was paid in London, wch doth not appear as yett and this return being made to ye Court ye Court Considered ye same; and ordered that ye s^d Renolds shall pay ye s^d sum & all Charges; and if it afterwards be made appear that ye s^d money be paid in London; the said William Clayton is ordered hereby to repay ye same with all Charges.

Y^e Court Adjorned for two houres & mett againe according to adjornm^t

Isaac Warner and John Eldridge was called to ye bar to answer to a p'sentment of ye Grand Inquest for abusing John Simcock one of ye King & Queens Justices of ye peace in saying that hee was drunk and put themselves upon tryall

Jury

ye Jury Attested
Phillip Rumon
Tho: Massey
Isaac Taylor
Geo Peerce
Joⁿ Worrello
Joⁿ Worrell

Joⁿ Bowetter
Albertt Hendrickson
Will: Clayton
Tho: Marttin
Jonathan hayes
Randle Mallin

Evidences for y{e} Defd{ts}

John Hodskins	Joshua Jones
Mary Hodskins	ffrancis Litle
Geo: Simcock	y{e} Jury finds Isaac Warner
Susanah Simcock	Gillty of y{e} Inditement
James Browne	

whereupon Judgment was given that y{e} s{d} Warner shall pay a fine of forty shillings & all Court Charges & be bound to his good behavior

John Maddock was called to y{e} bar to Answer to a p{r}sentment of y{e} Grand Inquest for abuseing John Simcock & John Bristow two of y{e} King & Queens Justices of y{e} peace in calling of them a pack of Roaugs & y{e} Jury was called & y{e} s{d} Maddock did then in Open Court still afirm that y{e} s{d} p{r}tyes was two of y{e} greatest Rouges that ever came into America; whereupon y{e} Courtt gave Judgement that he pay a fine of five pounds and Cost of suite &c. The s{d} Maddock was also fined 5{s} for swearing

Thomas Browne was called to y{e} bar to Answer to a p{r}sent of y{e} Grand Inquest for Selling of rum & keeping an ordenary without Lisence but Submited himselfe to y{e} Court and the Court Considering y{e} same fined him five pounds and to pay all Cost of suite

Petter Worrell came into y{e} Court and Openly declared himselfe firmly bound by Recognes in y{e} penall Sum of 160 pounds for y{e} fines of Richard Thomson and all Courtt Charges and also for y{e} good behaviour of y{e} s{d} Thomson & Owen Magdaniell for one year & a day

frances worley was Attested declareth that y{e} horss which Richard Thomson took up & brought to John Bristow y{e} head ranger had noe Eare mark for hee felt w{th} his fingers on both his Ears very well becaus y{e} said he was a stray horss

Tho: Baldwin supervisor for y{e} Township of Chester for y{e} year Insuing

phillip Ruman supervisor for y{e} Township of Chichester for y{e} year Insuing

Ordered that all y{e} Inhabittants of y{e} County of Chester shall forthwith pay theire Levies that are behind and that a warrant be forthwith derected to the sheriff to Levie ye same

The Corronrs return of an Execution against Caleb pusey & Company at ye suite of Robertt Turner for ye sum of Three hundred & nineteene pounds eightteene shillings and seven pence half peney silver mony with Cost of suite by vertue of ye within writt upon ye 15th day of June 1692, I did take in execucon ye 22 shares of Land Corn & sawmill and Implements thereof belonging to ye within Caleb pusey and Company Cittuate in Chester County according to a schedule thereto Annexed & did Impanell & attest a Jury of twelve men to Apraise & vallue ye same according to Law for payment of ye debt & Charges wth in Exprest who did vallue & Aprise ye same att 550^{lb} Lawfull mony of Pensilvania according to the Apraisement und^r ye hands and seales of ye s^d Juriors dated ye 15th of June 1692 thereto also afixed and Jdid also in ye Courtt house of ye s^d County, notice thereof having been formerly given on ye 28th of July 1692 on ye 5th of August 1692, expose to sale 22 shares of y^e said corn and saw mills & Implements thereof & of Twenty two shares of y^e said Land at 378£ 2^s: 6^d in y^e p^{r}sence of severall persons & nobody haveing bid for y^e same, I adjudge the same to belong to y^e s^d Robertt Turner y^e Creditor for payment of his s^d debt of 310^{lb} 18^s: 7$\frac{1}{2}^d$ & of 11£: 10^s: 3^d Charges hee y^e s^d Robertt Turner haveing in open Court returned the sum of 46£: 13^s: 7$\frac{1}{2}^d$ to which y^e 22 shares amounted to over & above y^e s^d debt and Charges to y^e s^d Caleb pusey & Companie according to Law Conform to a Deed of sale thereof by me to him thereof made dated y^e 15th day of September 1692.

Jacob Simcock Corronor

George Willard Acknowledged a deed in open Court unto Reece hentt for one hundred & Twenty five Acres of Land Lying in newtowne bearing date ye 15th of ye 6th mo 1692

Albertt hendrickson acknowledged a Deed in open Court unto James Bails for Twenty Acres of Land Lying on ye South side of Chester Creek bearing date ye 14th day of ye 7th mo. 1692.

Thomas Bright assigned over a Deed in open Court unto Robert Huchinson for fifty Acres of Land Lying in ye Township of Concord bearing date ye 13th of ye 7th mo: 92

Patrick Robinson Attorney to Owen folke Acknowledged a Deed in open Court unto Samuell Levis for one hundred & fifty acres of Land Lying in ye Township of Darby bearing date ye twenty seventh day of ye fourth month 1692

ye Court Adjorned unto ye 1st: 3^d day in ye 8th mo next

---

Att an orphans Court held at Chester ye 1st 3^d day in ye 8th mo. 1692

John Bristow p^r sident
George Maris
William Jenkin } Justices p^r sent
Sam^ll Levis

ffrancis Litle Dep^t Sheriff
Joshua ffearne Clerke

William Vestall and his wife Relict of John Brunsdall Deceased was called and appeared and the Court Required the said William Vestall to give Security to the Court well and Truely to perform the Trust of Gardianship for the Children of the Deceased untill he hath pased his accounts in oppen Court and be discharged according to Law which accordingly he did

petter Baynton was called to give Security to this Court well & Truly to perform the Trust of Gardianship for two of the Children of James Sandilands Deceased but he making severall Aligacons in the matter it was defered untill the next Court he then making his Apearance

George fforman was called three times on the same Account and did not Apeare upon which the Court ordered that he be Sumoned to apear at the next orphans Court

By The Aprobation of this Court William Hill was Bound an Aprentice to Thomas withers untill he be of the age of Twenty yeares he being now Eight years of age Signed by the Clerke under the County Seal

This Court Adjorned until the first Third day in the first month next

---

Att a Court held at Chester for the County of Chester the 4th day of y e 8th mo 1692

John Bristow p rsident
George Maris ⎫
William Jenkin ⎬ Justices
Sam ll Levis ⎭ p rsent

ffrancis Litle Dep t Sheriff
Joshua ffearne Clerke

ISAAC WARNER pl'ff
JOHN PRUE Defd t
in an accon on y e Case
upon attachment in the
hands of James Baylis

After proclaimacon was made and silence Comanded by the King and Queens Authority the pl tff and Defd t was called and neither of them appeared this accon was defered by the Court untill the afternoone And then this accon was called againe and the pl tff did not appeare Thomas Withers appeared for The Defd t and desired a nonsuite but John Eldridge being being Attested declared that the pl'ff was gone over the River for an Evidence And the Court Considering that the weather was so bad that it was Impossible for any one to pass upon the River the thought fitt to Continue this accon untill The next Court; and it was Continued.

Henry Hastings for Abusing the Court was Comited into Custidy to Answer the Same But afterwards the s d Henry Hastings Exhibited a petition to the s d Court humbley submiting himselfe to their mercey being sory for what he had said and done and desired to be forgiven upon which the Court Considered the same and ordered that upon his now submiting and his promiss of good behaviour for the future he shall be discharged paying his fees

Robert Barber for many Reflecting words and abuses to the s d Court was ordered to be bound to his good behaviour and to appear to answer the same at the next County Court

Whereas the want of a prisson was presented the Last Court by the Grand Inquest and at this time the Court Considering the same have Agreed forthwith to build a prison and doe hereby order John Simcocke and John Bristow to take Care for the Building of the same And that the Sheriff Imediately take care to Levie the fines due to the publick in order to defray the Charge of the prison

Thomas Baldwin made Complaint that the Inhabittants of the Township of Chester being eight of them warned to appear to make a bridge upon the Kings Road at Ridley Creek Robert Barber Joseph Richards & George Simcock did not Appeare so that the work Could not be done; whereupon for there default The Court doth fine them five shillings a peece and orders that the Constable of the said Towne of Chester doe forthwith Levie the s^d fines for the making of the said Bridge

The Court Adjorned untill ye second Third day in ye 10th m^o next

---

Att a Court of quarter Sessions held at Chester for ye County of Chester ye 13th day of ye 10th mo and held by Adjrnment the next day 1692

John Bristow p^{r}sident
John Simcock
George Maris } Justices
William Jenkin } p^{r}sent
    Caleb Pusey Sheriff
    Joshua ffearne Clerke

The Grand Jury was called & Thomas Coeborn & Petter Taylor & Richard Bernnard did not appear but afterwards satisfaction being given to the Court Concerning theire neglectt the was Excused

The Constables was called & appeared & gave in their p^{r}sentments all well Except Nathaniell Richards Henry Lewis Sam^{ll} Scott & Nicholas Pile who was fined five shillings ℔ man nicolas Pile and nathaniell Richards afterwards Appeared & gave satisfaction to the Court & was remitted their fines

Robertt Turner Administ^r of ye Estate Christopher Taylor Deceased Pltff

Ag^t Ralph & Dorathy ffrettwell & ye heires of Ralph ffrettwell Deceased Defd^t

Continued ye Last Court & now called againe the pl'ff appeared by his attorney

The Defendants did not appear; this accon Continued till ye next Courtt

ye Co^{r}t Adjorned for two hours & mett againe

THOMAS WITHERS pl^{t}ff
ROBERT MAKEE Defd^t upon attachment } This accon Cast out for that the plaintiff Tooke out his prosess before the money was due According to the date of the Bond

John Neald Exhibited a petition to this Co^{r}t Concerning a Road Laid out by ye Grand Jury

Petter worrall ye yonger was called to ye Bar to Answer to a p^{r}sentment of the Grand Jury ye Last Court the P^{r}sentment was read he pleaded not Gilty & put himselfe upon Tryall ye Jury was Impanielled & Attested

Robert vernan
John Child
Will: Browne
John worrell
Randle Mealin
John Wood
Nathaniell newlin
Michaell Blunston
Andrew Jobe
Robert Cartter
John Bailes
Isaac few
} The Jury finds petter worrall the yonger Gilty of the p^{r}sentm^t Concerning ye mare Judgment Awarded that he pay all Court Charges & be Bound to his good behaviour to all the Kings Leige people for one year

ye Court adjorned untill eight ye next morning

Joseph Richards James Lownes Roger Jackson Robertt Barber George Simcock Exhibited a petition to this Courtt for a Road in Chester & the Court Considering the same ordered that the Grand Jury forthwith Lay out a road from the Dayall Post straight way to the Road for ye Convenience both of Towne and Countrey amake return thereof this Court

The 14th of ye 10th mo 1692

ye Grand Jurys Return of the Road in Chester

wee of the Grand Inquest by vertue of the within precept or order vewed the Conveniency for the Laying out the Road within menconed doe make our return as followeth as the same road or streett was Layd out by us Begining at the Dyall Post and so runing South Twenty Two degrees west to Low watter marke Then Begining againe at the Dyall Post affores^d Thence runing north Twenty two degrees East up to the Kings Road which said road or streett is to Containe Thirtye foot in Breadth and the affores^d Dyall Post is to be the western Bounds thereof

ye Grand Jurys p^rsentment

The 14th of the 10th mo 1692 wee of the Grand Inquest for the County of Chester doe p^rsent petter Worrall the Elder of Marple in ye County aboves^d That he about the Seventh month Last did feloniously take away Taned Leather from Owin Magdaniell of the same County Contrary to the Law in That Case made and provided   Thomas vernan foreman

MATHIAS VANDERHEDEN Pl^tff ag^t THOMAS BUTTERFIELD Defd^t in an accon on ye Case	The plaintiff & Defendant was called The pl^tff called Three times and did not Appear and the Defd^t appeared and Craved a nonsuite And the Court granted the same

Robertt Barber was called to answer to the order of the Last County Courtt for his severall Abuses and appeared and upon his Examination he still persisting in Contempt to the Courtt. The Court fined him Twenty shillings And to be still Bound to his good behaviour to all the Kings Leige people for one year and a day

Petter Worrall Elder was called to the Barr to Answer to a p^rsentment of the Grand Inquest the p^rsentment was read to which he pleaded not Gilty and put him selfe upon Tryall by the Countrey the same Jury Attested as in the Case of Petter Worrall the yonger

y⁰ 14th of y⁰ 10th mo 1692

wee of the petty Jury find Petter Worrall the Elder Guilty of stealing Taned Leather

John Child fforeman   Judgment According to verdite

whereupon the said petter Worrall finding himselfe Agrived with the verdite of the Jury Craved an appeale to the next provintiall Court in Law And the Court Granted the same paying all Cost and Damage if he bee againe Cast. Charles Pickering Came into Court and Acknowledged himself firmly Bound unto the King & Cheife propriat' in the sum of forty pounds That he the said Petter worrall shall prosecute the said appeale at the next provintiall Courtt and pay all Cost and Damage if he again be cast according to Law

JOSEPH KNIGHT pl'ff   ⎫
    ag'   ⎬ withdrawne
ROBERT MAKEE Defd' ⎭

Robert Ewer & Elizabeth his wife pl'ff ag' John Simcock John Bristow & Randle vernon Execut'ʳs of yᵉ Testament of Thomas Brasie Deceased Defd'ˢ noe body Appeared & soe the Accon fell

Yᵉ Grand Jurys Return of yᵉ Road to Thornbury

wee of the Grand Inquest the 7th day of yᵉ 8th month 1692 by vertue of an order of Courtt have Layed out a Road as followeth Begining at a marked tree by Edward Cartters which was marked by a formmer Grand Jury And so along a Line of marked trees to John Baldwins fence and then by Johns Consent through a Cornner of his feild and so along to a black oak being the Cornner of John Neilds Land and from thence downe to John Neilds feild and by his Consent over a Corner thereof and so through the Creek and up the hill by Gilbertt Williams Barn   Thomas vernan foreman

wee of the Grand Inquest yᵉ 13th of yᵉ 10th Mo 1692 do pʳsent Chester & Ridley for want of a bridge in the Kings road near walter fossits this being the Third time.

Thomas vernon, foreman.

John Neild Exhibited a petition to the Court Concerning the above said Road

Thomas Butterfeild Exhibited a petition to this Court his affores^d accon

George fforman Attorney to nathaniell Lukins Acknowledged a Deed in Oppen Courtt unto John Willis for two hundred & fifty Acres of Land Lying in Burmingham bearing date the 30th day of ye 7th month September 1692

ffrancis Litle Acknowledged a Deed of Morgage unto Richard Crossby for one mesuage in the towne of Chester with appurtenances bearing date the 10th day of the 10th month 1692

Caleb pusey Attorney to Clear Smith William Smith & Mary Smith heirs of William Smith Deceased Acknowledged a Deed of feofment unto Anthony Morgan of Darby for five hundred Acres of Land Lying in ye Township of Darby bearing date ye 15th day of ye 8th month 1692

Anthony Morgan Acknowledged a Deed in oppen Courtt of Efeofment unto Joshua ffearne of Darby for ffifty acres of Land Lying in the Township of Darby being part of the aboves^d five hundred acres bearing date the 7th day of ye 10th month 1692

Anthony Morgan Acknowledged of Efeofment in oppen Court unto Josias Hibard for one hundred Acres of Land Lying in the Township of Darby being part of the aboves^d Smiths Land bearing date the 7th day of ye 10th month 1692

Anthony Morgan Acknowledged a Deed of Efeofment in Oppen Court unto John Marshall for one hundred & ffifty Acres of Land Lying in the Township of Darby be the same more or Less being part of the aboves^d Smiths Land bearing date the 7th day of ye 10th month 1692

Anthony Morgan Acknowledged a Deed in Oppen Court unto Robert Scothorne for ffifty Acres of Land Lying in the township of Darby Bearing date the first day of the ninth month 1692

Rees Rotherrow Acknowledged a Deed in Oppen Court unto Thomas Rees for one hundred & Twenty acres of Land Lying in the Township of havorford be the same more or Less bearing date ye 12th day of ye 10th month 1692

Thomas Rees by his Attorney Joshua ffearne Acknowledged assignment of the affores^d Deed unto William Lewis of haverford bearing date the Thirteenth day of ye 10th month 1692

Richard Crossby Acknowledged one obligation unto ffrancis Litle for the performance of of ye aboves^d morgage bearing date ye 14th day of ye 10th Mo 1692

Nathaniell Thornton Acknowledged assignment upon Deed to Roger Smith for ffifty acers of Land Lying in Chichester bearing date the 24th day of ye 8th mo 1692

Joshua ffearne Acknowledged a Deed in Oppen Court unto his Brother Josias ffearne for one hundred acres of Land Lying in the township of Darby bearing date the Twelfth of the Tenth month 1692

Isaac Warner pl^{t}ff } wth drawne
John Prue Defd^t

ye Court adjorned to ye 2^d 3^d day in Eleventh mo next

Att a Co^{r}t held at Chester for ye County of Chester The 10th day of ye 11th Mo 1692

John Bristow
John Simcock } Justices p^{r}sent
Sam^{ll} Leuis

Caleb Pusey Sheriff
Joshua ffearne Clerk

John Hugg of west Jarsey came with a Complaint before Justices Bristow Against William Howard Laborer for goods stolne away from ye s^d Hugg of which The s^d Justices made Return to this Co^{r}t And the said Howard upon Examination did Confess That the Last Sumer he did Take & Carry away from ye s^d John Hugg all the goods which he is now Charged with which Amounteth to the Sum of Eight pounds Seventeene shillings And the Co^{r}t Considering the same ordered That the s^d Howard doe pay Thirty five pounds one shilling to ye party wronged And for satisfaction & payment of ye s^d sum according to ye Judgment The said William Howard hath in ye p^{r}sence of the s^d Co^{r}t bound himself a Covenaut Sarvant unto ye s^d John Hugg for ye Term of four years

At a Co͏ͬt held at Chester for yͤ County of Chester The 17͏ᵗʰ 18͏ᵗʰ & 19͏ᵗʰ days of the 11͏ᵗʰ month 1692

John Bristow
John Simcock
Sam͏ˡˡ Levis
George Maris

Justices p͏ͬsent

Caleb Pusey Sheriff
Joshua ffearne Clerke

William Hawks Exhibited a petition to this Co͏ͬt against Robert Makee for a debt due to him for worke done being made Appear before Justices Bristow By sufficient Evidence And yͤ same Returned to this Co͏ͬt with the acco͏ͭ which Amounteth to the sum of 1—12—6 which s͏ᵈ Acco͏ͭ The Co͏ͬt did allow of

Chester Court yͤ 19͏ᵗʰ of yͤ 11͏ᵗʰ month 1692 Wee yͤ Grand Inquest by yͤ Kings Authority in yͤ name of yͤ Propritery doe ꝑSent Elinor Arme of Springfeild for being with Child & having noe husband

Thomas vernan foreman

Chester Court yͤ 19͏ᵗʰ day of yͤ 11͏ᵗʰ month 1692 Wee the Grand Inquest by yͤ Kings Authority in yͤ name of yͤ Propriatery doe ꝑsent Thomas Poe and Sarah Buller for Comitting fornication

Thomas vernan

Whereas the Grand Jury have Taken into theire Consideracon yͤ necessity of a prison And of the defraying of yͤ Charge of yͤ County have unanimously Agreed to Lay a Levie for yͤ defraying yͤ s͏ᵈ Charges as followeth viz upon every male white & Black from 16 years to 60; 3͏ˢ: Every hundred Acres belonging to p͏ͬsons Resident: 3͏ˢ: And upon Every hundred Acres belonging to p͏ͬsons none Resident 4͏ˢ—6͏ᵈ And yͤ Co͏ͬt Considering of it Agreed to the same And doth order That forthwith warrants be Isued out to Levie The same in Every Township by the Respective Constables one moity to be paid at or before yͤ next County Court & yͤ other moity at or before yͤ 1͏ˢᵗ day of the ninth month following And that the Constables shall a townes meeting to make assesment for yͤ Levieing yͤ same And when an account is taken of males & Lands to return a dublicate of yͤ same to Chester or Darby where will be at both places for yᵉ Ease of yᵉ County Justices mett to receive yᵉ same upon yᵉ 13ᵗʰ day of yᵉ 12ᵗʰ mo next

John Maddock Acknowledged a Deed in oppen Courtt for fifty Acres of Land and housing planttacon & Improvements upon yᵉ same Lying in Neither providence called by yᵉ name of neither cutt bearing date yᵉ 10ᵗʰ day of yᵉ 11ᵗʰ mo 1692

At a Courtt held at Chester the 14ᵗʰ 15ᵗʰ & 16ᵗʰ days of the first month 1693

{ William Jenkin pʳsident
John Simcocke
John Bristow
George Maris
John Blunston
Samˡˡ Levis } Justices pʳsent

Caleb Pusey Sheriff
Joshua ffearne Clerke

After Proclaimation made & silence Comanded by the King and queens Authority & in yᵉ Propriatarys name the Grand Jury was Called over & Appeared, and gave in their presentment & was discharged And a new Grand Jury Returned by yᵉ sheriff was Impanelled

Robert Penall   David Larance   John Worrall
John Woralow   John Wood   Thomas Marttin
George Peerce   William Browne   Robert Chamberlin
Isaac few   Robertt Cartter   John Turner
William Malin   Andrew Job   nathaniell Richards

Thomas Pow Exhibited a petition to this Courtt

The said Thomas pow & Sarah his wife was called to the bar to Answer to a presentment of yᵉ Grand Jury for Comiting fornication who submited themselves to the Court And the Court gave Judgment That the said Thomas & Sarah doe stand at the Comon whiping post and for the officer to declare theire offence to the People.

And also fines them Twenty shillings and pay yᵉ Courts Charges

Robertt Turner Administr
of the Estate Christopher
Taylor Deceased   Pl'ff
    a't g
Ralph & Dorathy ffretwell
& the heires of Ralph ffretwell, Defd ts
Deceased

{ The Plaintiff Declared for six hundred pounds by his Attorney Patrick Robinson the Defendants not Appearing this accon ordered to be Continued untill the next Court

Mathias vanderheyden Pl'ff
    ag t
Thomas Butterfield   Defd t
in an accon on ye Case

{ The Plaintiff Declared for forty pounds upon a penall Bond The Defendants answer was that he Owed nothing to the plaintiff

But the Court Considering The same gave Judgment the Defendant shall pay to the Plaintiff seven pounds Twelve shillings but if the s d Defendant shall make good payment of five pounds two shillings the plaintifs Attorney is willing to abate the rest the Defendant paying all Court Charges this Court and the former Court also

The Courtt Adjorned for two hours and mett againe according to Adjornment

Richard Bufington Pl'ff
    ag t
Robert Makee   Defd t
upon attachment
} Continued

William Hawkes Pl'ff
    ag t
Robert Makee   Defd t
Continued these two
Courts

Richard Crossby   Pl'ff
    ag t
Joseph Richards yonger Defd t
} withdrawne

Thomas Withers Pl'ff
    ag't
Robert Makee Defd't } Continued
upon attachment nether
Pl'ff nor defd't appeared

The Court Adjorned untill eight in ẙ morning and mett againe

Robert Ewre & Elizabeth Pl'ff
his wife
    ag't
John Simcock John Bristow
& Randle vernon Execut'rs Defd'ts
of ẙ Testament of Thomas
Brasie Deceased

The Accon was called and the Declaration was read Patrick Robinson appeared Attorney for ẙ Defendants

And after some debate Concerning ẙ Declaracon the Defd'ts Attorney Aledged that the Declaracon was uncertaine as to the day month & yeare of the Deceison therefore Craved an Abatement where upon it was Left to the Court to determin the matter and the Court Considering the same Ordered that the cause shall be brought on to Tryall

The Defd's Attorney desired a Coppy of the Deed of Gift & a Coppy of Govern'r Penns Letter and hee would com to Tryall & it was granted

The Defd's put in their plea in writing

The Petty Jury Impanelled and Attested

Philip Rumon	Nathaniell Parks	The Jury find for
William Browne	Petter Dix	the Defendant with
Randle Malin	Thomas Minshall	Cost of Suite and
Robertt vernon	ffrancis Chadsey	two pence Damage.
Benjamin Mendinghall	John Mendinghall	Judgment Accord-
Joseph Baker	John Bailes	ing to the verdite

The Plaintiff Craved an Appeal to the next Provintiall Court in Equety which was Granted by the Courtt he paying all Cost and Charges as the Law derects

Robert Ewer and Thomas fairman doth Recognize themselves Joynty & severally to the Cheeife Propriatory his heires or assignes in the sum of five hundred pounds to prosecute this Appeal at the next provintiall Court to be held at Chester and to pay all Cost & Charges if againe Cast.

The Co^{r}t Adjorned to ye morow morning

ALEXANDER DEVERICKS Pl'ff
a^{t}g
EDWARD & ELIZABETH PRICHETT Defd^{ts}
in an accon of Scandell &
Defamation

The accon was called both Pl'ff and Defd^t Appeared; the Declaration was read wherein the Pl'ff declareth for fifty pounds Damage

The Defd's Answer was that the Declaration is a pack of Lyes

The petty Jury Impanelled & Attested but after some debate Concerning the matter the Defd^{ts} wife could not be there and he wanting his Evidences therefore both partys agreed to Continue this accon untill the next Courtt

John Clewes and Elinor Arme now his wife was called to the Bar to Answer to a p^{r}sentment of the Grand Jury for Comiting fornacation; who pleaded Guilty and submited themselves to the Court whereupon the Court gave Judgment that the p^{r}tys shall pay a fine of fifty shillings downe or give good security to the Sheriff to pay it within six months; and that the s^d Elinor shall stand at the Comon whiping post for one quarter of an hour with a paper upon her Breast thus I heare stand for an Example to all others for Comiting the most wicked & notorious sin of ffornacation

Whereas the Grand Inquest hath at severall times p^{r}sented the want of a bridge over Ridley Creeke and the same being dangerous and detrementall to the Countrey doe fine the supervoiser of Chester and the supervoisor of Ridly five pounds apeece

Ralph Lewis supervoiser for Havorford for ye year Insuing

The Court Adjorned for two houres

Wee of the Grand Inquest for ye County of Chester present Sam^{ll} Noyes for being drunk and behaveing himselfe disorderly to the breach of the peace on ye 12th of this Instant being the first day of the weeke in time of worship

George Pearce foreman

Sam^{ll} noyes was called to the Bar to answer to the above^{sd} presentment and being found Guilty the Court fined him Twenty shillings and to pay all Charges and to be bound to his good behaviour untill the next Courtt

Andrew Robinson Acknowledged a Deed in Oppen Courtt by his Attorney Patrick Robinson unto Daniell Williamson for five hundred Acres of Land Lying in new towne bearing date the 24th of the 9th mo 1692

Daniell Williamson Acknowledged a Deed of Morgage unto Patrick Robinson Attorney for Andrew Robinson for ye aboves^d p^{r}mises bearing date the 14th of ye first month 1692/3 the 15th of ye 1st mo

Robertt Turner by his Attorney Patrick Robinson Acknowledged a Deed in oppen Courtt unto George fforeman Attorney for Sam^{ll} Carpinter for the two mils at Chester and Implements bearing date the 14th day of the 7th month 1692

Sam^{ll} Carpinter by his Attorney George fforman Acknowledged a Deed of Morgage unto Patrick Robinson Attorney for Robertt Turner for the aboves^d p^{r}mises bearing date the 15th day of the first month 1692/3

George Simcock and his wife Susanah Acknowledged a Deed in Oppen Court unto Mathew Clemonson for five hundred Acres of Land Lying in Chester County near new towne bearing date the 7th day of ye 12th month 1692

William weaver Acknowledged a Deed in oppen Courtt unto Humphrey Scarllitt for one hundred & twenty five Acres of Land Lying in Chester County bearing date the Last day of the Twelfth month 1692

William Simson Acknowledged a Deed in Oppen Courtt

unto William Swafford for fifty Acres of Land Lying in nether providence bearing date the 14th day of ye first mo 1692/3

Humphrey Scarlett Acknowledged a Deed in oppen Courtt unto nathaniell Richards for seventy five Acres of Land Lying in Chester County bearing date the second day of the first month 1692

Joshua Hastings Acknowledged a Deed in oppen Courtt unto John Turner for two hundred & seventy Acres of Land Lying in Chester County bearing date the second day of the first month 1692

Joshua Hastings Acknowledged a Deed in Oppen Courtt unto John Musgrove for two hundred Acres of Land Lying in Chester County bearing date the second day of ye first month 1692

Charles Brookes Acknowledged a Deed in oppen Courtt unto Tho: England for one hundred Acres of Land Lying in Chester County bearing date the second day of the first month 1692.

Thomas Hood Acknowledged a Deed in oppen Courtt unto George Thomas for one hundred Acres of Land Lying in Newtowne bearing date the Thirteenth day of the first month 1692

William Trotter by his Attorney Samll Levis Acknowledged a Deed in Oppen Court unto Christopher Spray for fifty Acres of Land Lying in Darby bearing date the 12th day of ye 10th mo 1692

Thomas Pow Exhibited a Petition to this Courtt to which the gave noe answer.

John Hanam & John Palmer Exhibited a Petition to this Court a'g Robert Eyrs formerly Clerke of this Court for demanding fees of them sayin there is none due; And the Courtt Considering the same found that there was fees due and ordered that Execution shall goe forth against them if the will not pay without

There being a high way Layd out by ye Grand Jury Leading to thornbery and a Return made thereof and entered the Last Courtt but severall of the neighbourhood being dissatisfied therewith did petition this Court that the might have it Layd out more Conveniently unto which the Court gave way whereupon the make return to this Court that it shall goe through John Neilds feild by the Creeke And soe by a straight Line up the land of the orphans of John Dutton as it was marked as wee went along to the uper side of John Baldwins feild And hee to take downe two or three pannels of his fence and a slant to the Lyne and Along Baldwins Lyne about 20 perches and then as its marked to the old road.

This maketh voyd the former Entrey by order of this Court.

John Parker supervoisor for Ridley for the year Insuing

Richard Bernent supervoisor for Midletowne for the year Insuing

Thomas Masey supervoissor for Marple for ye year Insuing

Joseph Richards supervoisor for Aston for the year Insuing

Edmond Cartlidge & Richard Bonsall supervoisors for Darby for ye year Insuing

Wee of the Grand Inquest for the County of Chester held the 14th day of the first month 1692 doe present James Lownes and Susanah for fornacation   Thomas Cowborn foreman

The orphans Court having been called and Adjorned to this time was called againe Ad Caleb pusey in the behalfe of the widdow Routh desired of the s^d Courtt that she might sell fifty Acres of Land for the bringing up of her Children And the Court Considering ye same thought it Reasonable that it should be soe And Advoysed that she Apply her selfe to the Govenor^r and Counsell for their Approbation in the Case.

The orphans of James Sandilands made Choyse of their Gardians

Christian Sandilands came into Court and there oppenly made Choise of George fforman & Jasper yeates her Brothers in Law to be her Gardians and next ffreinds the performing what the Law in that Case Requires

Mary Sandilands Came into Courtt and there oppenly made Choise of George forman to bee her Gardian and next ffreind hee performing what the Law in that Case Requires

James Sandilands son of James Sandilands Deceased Came into Co^rt And Oppenly made Choise of George fforman & Jasper Yeates his Brothers in Law to bee his Gardians and next ffriend the performing what the Law Requires in that Case

The overseeress of the Estate of James Sandilands Deceased came into Court and desired in the behalfe of Jonass and Lidia orphans of the Deceased That According as the Law Requires the Execut^rs of the Deceased shall give sufitient security for the Estate of the s^d Orphans; and Petter Bainton being sucksesor of the Deceased who denyed to give security; But the Court upon Consideration thought Convenient to defer the matter untill the next Court at which time further care will be taken Concerning them And that the s^d Petter Bainton be sumoned in to the next Court

 this orphans Court adjorned to ye 18th day of ye 2^d mo next
 William Edwards Constable of Midle towne
 Thomas Menshall Constable of nether providence
 John Bartram Constable of Darby
 Petter Worrell Constable of Marple
 Richard Hayes Constable of Havarford
 Thomas Worrelow Constable of Edgmont
 Thomas Garratt Constable of Beathell
 Joseph Cocburn Constable of Chester
 Randle Malin Constable of upper providence
 William Browne Constable of Aston
 Benjamin Mendinghall Constable of Concord
 Evan Prodra Constable of Radnor
 The County Court Adjorned to ye 18th day of ye 2^d month next .

William Jenkins Acknowledged a Deed in Oppen Courtt unto John Ball for Three hundred Acres of Land Lying in the township of havorford bearing date the first day of the first month 1692/3

Att a Courtt held at Chester for y" County of Chester y" 18^(th) day of y" second mo 1693

George Maris president
John Simcock ⎫
John Bristow ⎬ Justices
John Blunston ⎪ p'sent
William Jenkins ⎭

Caleb Pusey Sheriff
Joshua ffearne Clerke

After proclaimation made & silence Commanded by y" King & queens Athority & in y" name of y" Propriatary; the Grand Jury was called over & Appeared

ALEXANDER DEVERICKS pl'ff
  a'g'
EDWARD & ELIZABETH PRITCHETT Defd^(ts)
in an accon of slander
and formation

The plaintiff was called Three times and did not Appear; the Defendant Appeared And Craved a nonsuite; And the Court Granted it him

THOMAS WITHERS pl'ff
  a'g'
ROBERT MAKEE Defd^(t)
upon attachment Continued this 2^d Court

RICHARD BUFFINGTON plaintiff
  a'g'
ROBERT MAKEE Defendant
upon attachment Continued this 2^d Court

WILLIAM HAWKES pl'ff
  a'g'
ROBERT MAKEE Def^(dt)
Continued this 3^d Court

The Grand Jury presents the want of a road from the township of Edgmont to the Limestone And from uper providence to the Limestone And from newtowne to Havorford mill.

The Court Considering of the s^d presentment, thought it nesesary; And so ordered that the Clerke give them an order to Lay out the same And to make Return thereof at the next County Courtt.

George Maris the Elder Acknowledged a Deed in Oppen Courtt unto his son George Maris the yonger for one hundred Acres of Land Lying in Springfeild bearing Date the seventeenth day of ye second mo 1693

ye Grand Jury return of a road to ye Limestone

According to an order of Courtt to us directed wee of the Grand Inquest for the County of Chester do make return of ye roads Laid out by us as followeth Begining at Chester road in Edgment at a marked Black Oak near Joseph Bakers Thence up ye ridge between Chester and Ridley Creek to a marked oake upon the Branch of Ridley Creek Thence over the barrons to a marked white oake on the Limestone hill

The Jurys return of a road from new towne to Havorford mill

Also begining in new towne at a marked white oake in Richard Bonsalls Land Thence to a marked white Oake in the Line between new towne and Radnor thence to a marked black oake in ye Meddow of Tho: Jones near Darby Creek Thence to a marked white oake near the fence of Evan Prodra thence near Ralph Lewis fence to a marked white oake at the Corner of David Larence fence thence to Havorford mill

          Geo Pearce foreman

this Court Adjorned to the second Third day in ye 4th mo next

---

Att a Court held Att Chester ffor the County off Chester the 13th Day of the 4th month June 1693

Mr George fforman on of the counsell president
Mr Peter Baynton
Jeremiah Collett
Thomas Weithers
Jonathan Hayes
Thomas Smyth
Justises present

Mr Joseph Wood sherif
John Childe Clark

After proclimation made the Justises Comision being Red they tooke theyr places on the Bench the Clarks comision being Red the Court was Called and AJorned tell the 22^d day of this Instant June 1693

1693 County Sesions
Att a Court held att Chester
ffor the County of Chester
the 22 of this instant June
according to A Jornment
and a Court of Common
Pleas held the 22 and and
and part of the 23 Day of
the same by AdJornment
  The laws being Red

Mʳ George fforman of the Counsell
Mʳ Petter Baynton — president
Jeremiah Collett
Thomas Weithers — Justices
Jonathan Hayes — present
Thomas Smyth

    Mʳ Joseph Wood sherife
    John Childe Clarke

 After Proclimation made & silence commanded In theyr Majesties names

 The Constables was Called and Attested
John Hodgkings Constable of the Towne of Chester
Joseph Couborn Constable of the same Township
Thomas Garratt Constable of Beathell
Benjamen Mendinghall of Concord
John Hurlbert Constable of Chichester
Samuell Scott Constable of Burmingham
William Edwards Constable of Middelltowne
David Morris Constable of Marple
Thomas minshall Constable of neither Providence
Richard Hayes Constable of havorford
Thomas Worriloe Constable of Edgment
Randell Mallin Constable of upper Providence
Evan Prodaro Constable of Radner
Joseph Stedman Constable of Springfield
Richard Woodworth Constable of Thornbury
William Browne Constable of Aston
Jenkin Griffith Constable of newtowne
John Radley Constable of westowne
Thomas Bradshaw Constable of Darbye

 The ould Grand Juery was Called and appeared and brought in theyer presentmen which is the 22th of the 4th month 1693.

wee of the Grand Inquest for the County of Chester Doe Present John Powell of Chester for being Drunke the 13th of this Instant and ffor swereing of oaths Allso ffor Attempting to Ride over severall Indian women and being with held Drew his knife thretned to rip them up: George Pearce fforeman where Apon the bench Dismised the Juery with thanks for theyr Care Aboute it whereupon the fforsaid John Powell being before summoned by the sherife by virtue of a summons Dated the 13 of this above s^d Instant Appeared before the bench and submiting himselfe wholey to the bench order was that he should be fined to pay 5^s ffor swering and 5^s for being Drunke and pay all Charges and to bring two sufficent men to be bound ffor his good behavior till the next County Court which two persons were Albert Hendrickson and John Beales whoe Did binde theyr selfs Joyntly and severly by theyr Recognicenes In the sum of fourty pounds to this Court for his good behavior towards All the Kings ledge Peopell till the next County Court

James Lowns and his now wife shusanah who was formerly present^{ed} by the Grand Inquest ffor commiting fornication who was sumoned to Appear to this Court he and his now wife shusana Appear^{ed} and submitted them selves to the bench order was that they pay 10 shillings for A fine and pay the Charges and be Dismised

The Grand Inquest that was summoned to Appeare Att this Court weare Called whose names are as folloeth

Thomas Couborn	Edward Beazer
Thomas ffox	Walter Martin
John Hood	Charles Whitaker
Richard Bonsall	Isacke Taylor: thornebury
Thomas Powell	George Thomas
John Colvert	William Coborne
William Hawkes	William Collett
Albert Hendrickson	Isack Taylor
Thomas Worth	John Mendinghall

Benjamin Mendinghall Exhibeted A petticion to this Court for a Roade way for the Inhabitants of the upper end of Concord and the Inhabitants of thornburg and thereabouts for a Cart Road to Chester towne the order of Court is that the Grand Inquest shall view the way from Gilbert Wollams land and If they see conveniant to lay it oute to Concord and thornbury and for the Rest of the Inhabitants there away

Thomas Couborn Exhibited A petition to the Court for a Roade way by Isack ffews and George Churchmans to com to Chester mill being theyr mark^{ett} for Corn, ordered by the bench that the Grand Juery shall view it and see if it be conveniant they lay it oute.

Ree sent of newTowne ordered to be supevisor for this yeare for that Township

John Childe Past A Deed of 300 Acres of land lying In westowne to William Cole Bearing date the same Day with the Sesions

PHILLIP YARNELL Plantif
MOSES MUSGROVE Defendant
in an Acction of scandell
and defamation
the Plantive and Defendant weare called & both Appearing they Joyne Issue
the Petty Juery being Called and Appeared

   the names of the Petty Juery Impaneled
Richard Parker: William fflower
Thomas Coates: Rogger Smyth
Robert Scothern: Thomas Garrett
Thomas Collier: Nickolas Pille
Richard Buffington: Thomas Baldwin
Robert Woodworth: Thomas Brown

The Decleration was Red

And the Defendants Evidences was Called & Attested: Elizebeth Woodyard being Attested Deposeth that the plantive Philip yarnell came to her ffathers house to the best of her knowledge and Asked whether she was a woman and she answered she was all one as other women she thought and he said y^t he would feele and she said that he should not and he said how should he know whether she was all on as other women If that he did not feele, since she was she that was to be his wife, and then he took her hand being stronger than shee and put Into his Codpise and would have her to feele his members how they went limber or stifer and the Deponant further saith that a nother night he y s^d Plantife came to her fathers house and then he Asked her sister Mary for to keepe her up and she said that she would doe what she could to do it and when she the Deponant did see him com in she ran oute into a nother Roome and Cacht hoult on the bed post and he followed her and Cacht hoult of her and lift her on the bed and they lay downe on the bed and she being Awake 3 nights before was very sleepy & she fell asleep and thought she might sleepe neare an hour or there abouts and as she was sleeping shee thought she felt her cloaths to goe up and her feete to move and she Awakeing Asked him how he could be soe wickedly and come from such a good meetting and then she Cryed bitterly And Att last he wept and Asked her for forgivenes and that he would kneele Downe on his beare knees to Aske her forgivenes and she said that she did not Desier any such thinge nor would never have any thinge to Doe with him more and saith further that when she Did Awake she Did happen with her arme to strike him and with her hand unawares she felt his members which Did a fright her very much & further saith not

John Joans being Attested Deposeth that when he was Att the Plantives house that the s^d Plantive asked what Peopell George Woodyard and his wife was and he said that they weare sivell People for ought he knew and the Plantive said that he would Goe try his Dafter Elizebeth and see what he could Doe with her and that If that hee could not prevaile with her he would serve such a trick that she was never served In her life before and further saith not

Mary Woodyard being Attested saith that the Plantife Did forse her sister Elizebeth Upon the bed shee Did see it and went away because she thought that he was an honest man

Sarah Smedlye being Attested Deposeth that she did heare Philip yarnell confess that he had been foolish in soe much that somthing scattered from him which was his seed and that she hard Elizebeth Woodyard say she did not know what was In his mind

John Worolo Being Attested for the Plantive saith that he and the Plantive Philip yarnell came to George Woodyards house together and that he did see the plantive and the two Girls and another man whose name is John Golden Asked Elizebeth whether Philip yarnall Did goe to forse her or no and she said no Its was ods betwene A mans breaking A house and Atempting to do it.

John Golden being Attested Deposeth as the Aforsaid John Woroloe Did before ffrances Yarnell being Attested for the Plantive Deposeth that he went A longe with his Brother Philip yarnell to George Woodyards house and saith that he asked George Woodyard to let them com face to face and the ould woman said she should not unless an officer came because he came to trapan them and the Girls said that he would never a forst her nor Did not know whether she was man or woman and After they came oute of the house that George Woodyard said he would not a had his Dafter to a made words about it

The verdit of the Juery is we of the Petty Juery Doe ffind ffor the Plantive Cost of sute and two Pence Damage Richard Parker fforeman } heare Apon Judgment Is Granted According to verdit

The Defendant Moses Musgrove thinking himselfe Agreeved with the verdit by his Attorney George Stroude Pettioned to A Court of Equity

Mr Joseph Wood High sherif Attorney for John Roads Past a Deed of fivety Acers off land to John Hood the land Lying and being In Darby township being part of John Blunstons late purchased (?) land.

Robert Scothern Attorney ffor Robert Smyth Past A Deed to John keirke for fivety Acers off Land the Land lying in Darby township

Joseph Wood sherif Attorney ffor William Gregory Past A Deed of one hundred Acers of land unto John Wood Attorney for Daniell Hibert the Deed bearing Date the 12th Day of June 1693 the Land lying In Darby towneship

Robert Scothern Past A Deed of fivety nine Acers of Land unto John Wood the Land Lying In Darby towneship

Thomas Weithers Plantive
And
Robert Mekee Defendant
} In An Action of Dept, The Plantive and D e f e n d a n t being both Called the Plantive Appeared and the Defendant Did not Appeare

the Plantives Decleration being Red and this being the third Court and the Defendants not Appearing Judgment is given by the Court for the Plantive to his Dept which is four pounds ten shillings with Cost of suite

William Hawkes Plantive
Robert Mekee Defendant
} In an Action of Dept. The Plantive and Defendant being Called the Plantive Appeared and not the Defendant and this being the fourt Court and the Defendant not Appearing, Judgment is Given by the Court the Plantive shall have his Dept which is the sum of one pound twelfe shillings and six pence with Cost of suite

Richard Buffington Plantive
Robert Mekee Defendant
} In an Action of Dept. The Plantive and Defendant being both Called, the Plantive Appeared and not the Defendant and this being the third Court and the Defendant not appering Judgment is Given by the Court that the Plantive shall have his Dept which is one pound six shillings & three pence with Cost of suite

Philip Yarnell Plantive
Elizabeth and Mary
Woodyard   Defendants
} In An Action of Scandell and Defemation.   with Drawn

This Court of Common Please AJornes tell the 12 day of September next ensuing

The Court of Equity held the 23th Day of June 1693 Att Chester

Moses Musgrove Plantive
Philip Yarnell Defendant
} After Proclamation made, Silance commanded The Plantive and Defendant being Called they both Appeared and the Court AJorned to the house of Justis Peter Baynton And Accordingly they mett And After the heareing of Both parties the Decree of this Court is that the Plantive and Defendant shall Pay Equally All the Charges of the Court of Common Please And that the Defendant Philip Yarnell shall pay All the Charges that Accrues to this Court of Equity

---

Att A Court of Quarter sesions held Att Chester ffor the County of Chester the 12th day of September 1693 And Alsoe A Court of Common Please held the 13 Day of the same
} Justices there Present
Petter Baynton President
Jeremiah Collett
Thomas Weithers
Jonathan Hayes
Thomas Smyth

Joseph Wood Sheriff
John Childe Clarke

After Proclemation made Silence commanded In theyr majesties names the Constables were Called and Appeared and the Grand Juery was Called and Appeared

William Ratew Exhibited A Pettion to the Court he haveing served oute his time and his master Nathaniell newland Turning him of without Cloaths fiting for a sarvant to have the Court ordered that his s^d master Nathaniell Newland shall Pay to his sarvant William Ratew on new hatt one new Coate

& A new Westcoate A new paire of Breeches and Drawers and A new paire of stockings and a new paire of shoes; and ten bushells of wheate or fourteen bushells of Indian Corne and 2 howes and on ax

Thomas Worth of Darby Attorney ffor Henery Gibbens of the same Past A Deed of twenty two Accers of land to Richard bonsall Attorney for John Wood of Darby, the Deed beareing Date the sixt Day of August 1693

John Wood and Jeane: by theyr Attorney Richard Bonsall Past over A Deed of twenty two Accers of land Lying In Darby Township unto Henery Gibbens by his Attorney Thomas Worth the Deed bearing Date the sixt Day of August 93

Joseph Wood high sherif of the County Attorney ffor Thomas Paskell Delivers A Deed for four Accers of medowe unto Samuel Sellers the Deed bearing Date the ninth Day of the seventh month 1693

ffrances Little Delivered A Deed of morgage to Justis Collett a torney ffor Mr George fforman Counselor and Jasper Yeates Gardians for James Sanderlens the Deeds bearing Date the fiveteenth Day of August 1693 ffor All his houses and Tennements In the Towneship of Chester with all priviledges belonging to the same ffor the sum of 36 pounds to be paid on the 15th Day of August in the yeare 1695: and If Payment be made then its to Returne to the said francis Little or his heirs executors administrators or asigns the fforesaid Justis Collett Delivered the Counter Part unto the saide ffrances Little In open Court

William Curtis and George Chandler and John Garrett ffor being Abetters to A match of wrestling Att the house of John Cox in the Township of Ridley weare Called to the bar And they submiting themselfs to the bench order is that they behave themselfs well ffor the ffuture and Pay theyr Charges and be dismist

Allsoe John Cox was Called to the bar for his suffering such unlawfull Exersise Att his house

September the 12th 1693 The Grand Juery by the kings and

Queens Authority Presents John Cox of Ridley Township ffor keepeing A Disorderly house of Entertainment there being lately A Revell and men have A busied them selfs to Drunkenness and ffighting and Abused themselfs and others to the Terrors of the Inhabitants thereabouts and therefore dangerous ffor strangers to goe to the house or Pass by.

Thomas Coeborne fforeman

John Cox being Againe Called to the bar to Answer the Presentment of the Grand Juery he submiting himselfe to the bench the order is that he shall Pay All the Charges that Dos Acrew Att this Court and to find two sufficent men for to be bound for his keeping A sevill house of Entertainment for the future the two Persons that Are his sureties are Joseph Kent and Andrew ffrind who doe Recognise themselfs Joyntly and severally to this Court In the sum of fourty Pounds of good and Lawfull mony of Pennsilvania

Samuell Scoole being Called to the bar to Answer ffor his being consarned A boute John Powell being In the Cannow with him when he was Drowned order is that he bring to men to be bound for his Good Behavior tell next Court And for his Appearance there to Answer

The Persons who doe stand bound ffor Samuell Scooles Appearance Att the next Court Are Robert Barra and John Clues who doe bind themselfs Joyntly and severally In the ffull sum of fourtye Pounds for his Appearance Att the next Court.

A Trew Return of a Road layd oute by the Grand Inquest the 21st of the 6th month 1693

According to Court order This Road begins Att A hickery marked with five noches A pon the land of John kingsmans Land In the Towneship of thornbury and soe throw the land of John kingsman to the Land of Benjamin Mendinghall Leying in Concord And then a long the land of Benjamin Mendinghall to the land of William Hiskock And then throw the land of the fore said Hiskock to the land of Nathaniell Newland And soe A Cross Part of the Land of Nathaniell Newland to his Plantation fence And then A Crose his Plantation Down to his barne end and up the Lane from his barn End and throw the Rest of his land to the Corner of Robert Chamberlins and soe Down the said fence as It now stands to the ould Roade Againe to the Tract of land that was formerly Thomas Brassies and soe throw that Tract of land to the Land of Mary Mores and so throw the land of Mary Mores unto Gilbert Woolliams and soe throw the land of the said Woolliams to A small hickery standing by the Roade side marked with five noches and there Ending

wee of the Grand Inquest according to the Courts order have viewed the land of Isack ffewes ffor a Road way for Thomas Couborn to George Churchmans and to Caleb Pusyes mill and we find it not conveniant to lay oute A Roade In that place neither Doe we find it conveniant to lay oute a Road upon Isack ffewes Land for Thomas Couborn

John Powell of the Township of Ashtown In this County was Drownded In Chester Creek the fifth Day of August 1693 Joseph Wood Coronor summoned A Juery The verditt of the Juery is: that they Doe find that the death of John Powell was wholey and solely an Accident and no wayes by any forse or violence used A pon him or A gainst him the 6 of August 1693 the names of the Juery Are As ffolloweth Joseph Richards senior foreman Joseph Richards Junior John Nixson John Beales, Charles Brooks: John Maddock, John Clues, Henery Hollingsworth Rogger Jackson, Allexsander ffinloe Timothy Atkinson Isack ffew: James Lownes.

The said John Powell Dying without will one Samuel Powell of Philadelphia being found to be nearest kin to him the Governour William Markham Esquier Granted him A letter of Administration to the Estate of John Powell and the Coronor by the Courts order Delivered It to him and to John Parsons whom he made Choyse of to Receve It in Posseion for the s^d Samuell Powell

Att the Court of Common Please the sheriff made Returne of three Executions Levied Apon the Estate of Robert Mekee on for Thomas weithers for the sum of four Pounds ten shillings with Cost of suite and one for William Hawkes for the sum of one pound twelfe shillings and six pence with Cost of suite and one ffor Richard Buffington for the sum of one pound six shillings and three pence with Cost of suite All Levied Apon the second day of August 1693 And Appraised the same Day by A Juery who was Attested by Justis Collett: they Apraised the Plantation with all the Premises belonging It being on hundred Accers of land lying in The Township of Beathell in the County of Chester: Appraised Att ffourteen Pounds: by the Juery whose names are as ffolloweth: Robert Eyre: James Browne, Tho Garrett: Henery hastings, William Clayton George Chandler, John Garrett Henry hames, Robert Jefferis William flower John Neals, Roger Smyth.

The sherif made Returne of an Execution that he Levied In the hands of Richard Crosby for what was in his hands of the Estate of George Andross ffor the sum of Eleven Pounds ten shillings with Cost of suite which is one pound ten shillings wh: makes the whole sum thirteen pounds for Mr George fforman Levied the 3^d day of August 1693 and Its fully satisfied sence

CORNELIAS JUSTESON Plantif And ANDREW FFRIND Defendant In An Acction of scandell and Defemation: the names of the Petty Juery

the Plantive and Defendant both weare Called and Appeared and the Dccleration was Red and they Joyne Isue the Juery was Called

John Bartram	John Hollaway	William Tally
Thomas Hood	William Smyth	Richard Bufinton
Edmund Cartlidge	John Hendrixson	James Hendrixson
Joseph Need	Matt: Morten	James Bayles

The verdit of the Juery is wee of the Petty Juery Do find it for the Plantive with one shilling Damage and Cost of suite John Bartram fforeman

WhereApon Judgment Is Given According to the verdit of the Juerey

Thomas Longshore of the County of new Castell Plantive Against nathaniell Wattmore Defendant In An Acction of Dept for the sum of 6^{lb}: 14^s } the Plantive was called and the Defendant they were both called and Appeared and they Referred It to the bench And After they heard both Plantive and Defendand they order that the Defendant Pay unto the Plantive the sum of four pounds fourteen shillings and six pence with Cost of suite

Nathaniell Newland ordered to be supervisor for the Township of Concord for this yeare

Robert Turner Plantive as Administrator to the Estate of Christopher Taylor Deceased Against the Esteat of Ralph and Dorithy ffreetwell Defendants this being the ffourth Court as It has been Called and none Appearing for the Defendants: the Decleration was Red and Alsoe A letter of Administration of Robert Turner for the Estate of Christopher Taylor And Alsoe the Articls of Agreement betwen Ralph ffreettwell and Christopher Taylor Deceased was Red And none Appearing for the Defendant: The Court Gives Judgment for the ballence of the Accounts which Appears to be the sum of ffive hundred and fourty Pounds seven shillings and nine pence, with ffive Pounds Damage and Cost of suite Against the whole Esteate both Reall and Personall of Ralph and Dorithy ffreettwell as heirs Exceutors & Administrators of Ralph ffreettwell Deceased, Alsoe It was ordered by the Court that whatsoever sum or sums of money Could be made Appeare was Paid towards the Iland of Tinicum was to be Allowed of & to be Paid Backe to the said Ralph frettwell or his heires or Assignes

Petter Dix for not standing to the Award of the Justis of A peace but would bring it to Court Judment was there confermed and he orderd to pay all the Charges that Did Acrew

Richard Crosby came into Court and acknowledged full satisffaction for the morgage of ffrances Little house at Chester

Att an orPhants Court held Att Chester ffor the County of Chester the third Day of October 1693
Thomas Powell made his complaint Consering the Estate of his Brother Joseph Powell Deseaced In the behalfe of the orphans of his Brother

The Justises there Present was
Mr George fforman
Petter Baynton   President
Jeremiah Collett
Thomas Weithers
Jonathan Hayes
Thomas Smyth

Joseph Wood Sherif
John Childe Clark

The order of Court is that John Blunston and George Marris and Samuel Levis and Caleb Pusye Appeare Att the next County Court there to Give an Account to the Court how the Estate of Joseph Powell Is Divided or Disposed of.

Samuell Levis being Called Att the request of Joseph Wood high sherife and after Examination Samuel Levis Did then Promise to give security to the next County Court ffor the Estate of Joseph humphrye Decesed which is the sum of thirty nine Pounds and seven pence or to Deliver up the Effects In to the Courts hands This orphans Court Ajornes to the first third day of march next

Att A Court of Common Pleass held the third day of october 1693 the Justices as A bove said there Present

Andrew ffrind Plantife and Andrew Robinson of West Jersey Defendant was Called and the Defendant Exhibeted A Peticion to the Court by Reason of his being of the Assembly he could not Apeare, the order of Court is that the Action be continued till the next Court

Robert Langhum Exhibited A Pettion to the Court for his Custom of the Country he haveing served Eight years and had nothing Allowed him the Court ordered him to Appeare Att the next County Court

The Court ordered that the Township of Chester shall helpe the Townshipe of Ridly to make a foote bridge Att Walter fosetts over Ridlye Creeke within twelfe Days time After this Court.

The boyes that Mauris Trent Brought In to this Country were Called to be Judged by Court Caleb Pusyes boy Alexsander Ross A Judged by the Court to be Eleven years of Age and to serve tell the Age of one and Twenty and to have the Custom of the Country and be Discharged from his serviitude by the said Caleb Pusye, Richard buffintons boy Deniell Mack Deniell was A Judged by the Court to be ffourteen years of Age and to serve tell he is twenty one years of Age and the said Richard Buffinton is ordered to pay him the Custom of the Country and A Discharge from his servitude.

Thomas Weithers boy James Hercules A Judged to be thirteen years of Age And to serve tell he is twenty one years of Age and then to be Allowed the Custom of the Country and A Discharge from his servis by Thomas Weithers, Nickoles Piles boy: George Leacy A Judged to be twelfe years of Age and to serve tell he is twenty one and to be Allowed by his master as the aforesaid.

Jeremiah Colletts boy Alexander mccany A Judged to be fourteen years ould and to serve tell he is twenty one years of Age and to be Allowed as the A fore said by his master Jeremiah Collett

William Colletts three boys Magnis Simson A Judged to be Eleven years of Age and to serve tell the Age of twenty one and to be Allowed by his master as the Rest of the boys James Canide and James Driver both William Colletts sarvants were A Judged to be fourteen years of Age and to serve tell they are Twenty one years of Age and to be allowed As the Rest by theyr master William Collett

Ann and Petter Baynton Plantives Against the estate of George Anderos Defendant by an Atachment In the hands of Richard Crosbye the Cause was Called and Continued tell the next Court of Common Pleass ffor the sum of 10^{lb} 18^{s} 0^{d}

Henery Raynolls Plantife Against the Estate of George Anderos Defendant by an Attachment In the hands of Richard Crosbye, ffor the sum of fourty three Pounds. The Cause was

Called and Continued till the next Court of Common Pleass. This Court of Common Pleass AJornes to the Twelfe Day of December next

| Att a Court of quarter ss held Att Chester ffor the County of Chester the 12th Day of December 1693 | Mr Petter Bainton President Jeremiah Collett Thomas Weithers Thomas Smyth Jonathan Hayes | Justices Present |

Joseph Wood sheriff
John Childe Clarke

After Proclimation made and silence Commanded In theyr MaJesties names: the Constables were Called And Appeared And the Grand Inquest was Called And Appered: Samuell Scole Appeared being bound Att the last Court and nothing more Apeareing Against him he is Discharged by Proclimation Paying the Charges: Robert Langum sarvant to Caleb Pusy formerly his Pettion was Red Againe Att this Court for the Custom of the Country he haveing served Eight years and his Indenturs being Brought in Court spetifiing that Att the Expiration of his Time he should have it: the Justices Considering of ordered that his s^d master Caleb Pusy to Pay him the Custom as the law Allowes: only Jonathan hayes on of the Justices would not consent; but the Rest Did that he should have it.

Thomas Hoape being Bound Over to Appeare Att this Court was Called and Appeared And by his suerties Owen Mack Daniell and William huntly Is bound for his Appearance Att the next Court of quarter sesions Mary Martin was Called And Appeared And being Examined wheither she was with Childe by Thomas Hoape and shee Denied that she was with Childe The order of Court is that shee Appeare Att the next quarter sesions And ffrances Baldwin Doe Recognise himselfe for the Appearance of the said Mary Martin the next qua^{rt}: SS: The Court AJorned ffor 2 hours: And Meett Againe According to A Jornment John Joans: Josia Taylor; Thomas

Marcy was Called and Attested to Give in theyre Evidences to the Grand Inquest and Alsoe John Shaw & David Ogden and Daniel Williamson were Attested and Gave in theyr Evidence to the Grand Inquest And the Grand Inquest Brought in theyr Presentment which is as followeth. Chester County December the 12th 1693 The Grand Juery by the King and Queens Authority Presents John Bristow ffor Takeing and new brand marking of A horse that was Brand marked and Eare marked before and Converting him to his owne use Tho: Coeburn fforeman: Witneses they that were Attested who sets theyr names to the presentment ordered that [they be] summoned to the next Court

The Court A Jorned to the house of Justis Baintons

And mett According to AJornment The Grand Juery presented the the want of A prison for the County And they have given in theyr Judgment that on hundred and ffivety Pounds will Defray the Charge: The order of Court Is that there shall be A Levye fforthwith for the Reasing of the some for the Defraying of the s^d Charge

John Neales Exhibited A pettion to this Court for the Custom of the Country This being the second Court he haveing served his tim faithfully and his Indentures being brought In Court and Expresses the Custome of the Country to be Paid him The Courts order is that his master Robert Taylor shall Pay him the s^d Custome his master Robert Taylor being called and asked where he had paid any thing to him s^d no nor would not: only Justis Hayes Dos not Give his Consent to it but all the Rest does order it.

John Cock being bound over to Answer Att this Court and nothing more Appearing Against him he is discharged Paying his Charges: and good behavior for the future.

Att a Court of Common Please held the 13th Day of December the Justices as before s^d present. Ann And Petter Baynton Plantifes Against the Estate of George Andros Defendant: by an Attachment In the hands of Richard Crosby ffor the sum of 10£: 18ˢ: 00ᵈ the Cause was Called this being the second Court and the Defendant George Andros not Appearing Its Continued tell next Court

Henery Reynols Plantif Against the Estate of George Anderos Defendant by an Attachment In the hands of Richard Crosbye ffor the sum of fourty and three pounds: the Cause was Called and the Plantif not Appearing Richard Crosby Craved A non suite which the Court granted

ANDREW ROBERSON of West Jersy Plantif: JOHN COCK Defendant In an action of scandell } the Cause was Called and both Appered and Declerd they were agreed only the Defendant was to pay the Charges

William Collett of Concord Asigned over a sarvant boy whose name is James Driver unto Thomas Worolaw of Edgment tell he is of the Age of Twenty one years ould.

Charles Brooks Passed A Deed of on hundred and ffivety accrs of land lying in the Towneship of Ashtown unto Robert Chamberlin of Concord the Deed bearing date the 12ᵗʰ Day of December 1693.

Robert Langum Past A Deed of seventy Accrs of land with houses orchards and All Appurtents thereunto belonging unto William Edwards the Plantation lying in Middeltown the Deed Bearing Date the 12ᵗʰ Day of December 1693

Thomas Boweter Past a Deed of on hundred Accres of Land unto Charles Thomas of which hundred 50 Accres Is on sarvants Rent and the other is on Penny Accre the Deed bearing Date the 12ᵗʰ Day of December 1693 the land lying in the Towneship of Edgment

The widdowe Routh Past a Deed of 50 Accrs of land to John Beals the land lying in the Towneship of Chester the Deed bearing Date the 13ᵗʰ Day of the tenth month 1693

Samuell Levis Did Pass a Deed of on hundred Ackers of Land to Joseph Need the land Lying in Darby Township: the Deed bearing Date the 11ᵗʰ Day of the tenth month 1693:

And Joseph Need Past A Deed to Samuell Levis for ninty Ackers of land It lying In the Towneship of Darbye bereing Date the 11th Day of the tenth month 1693

George Simcocke by his Attorney Thomas Smyth Past A Deed to Samuell Levis for fivety Ackers of land lying in Darby Township the Deed beareing Date the 21st day of the ninth month 1693

George Simcocke by his Attorney Thomas Smyth Past A Deed unto. Joseph Wood for on hundred And twenty Two Accers of land lying in Darby Township the Deed bearing date the 24th Day of the ninth month 1693.

George Simcocke by his Attorney Thomas Smyth Past a Deed to John Wood his Bro: in law ffor a Plantation of 29 Ackers of Land with All Appurtenants the Land lying in Darbye Towneship the Deed beareing Date the 16th Day of November 1693

James Swaffar Past a Deed of Two hundred and ffivety Ackers of Land to Jeremiah Collett the land lying by Ridley Creek bounded by George Woodyards Land the Deed beareing Date the 13th Day of December 1693

ffrancis Little Past A Deed of his houses and land and lot which he had In Chester Towne unto Petter Baynton Justis of the Peace the Deed Bearing Date the 13th Day of December 1693

Allixander Deverix Exhibeted A Pettion to this Court ffor to have some thing Allowed him for his time that he was on Tinicum Island And the Court Considering thereof Did Allow him the sum of six pounds, whereof the said Allixander have Receved the sum of Two Pounds ten shillings towards it

William Rattew Exhibeted A Pettion to this Court Aboute 3 months Servitude which his fformer master William Collett Dos Demand, the Pettion being Red William Collett Desired the Court that It might be Refered tell the next Court and It was ordered that they Appear Att the next County Court

Samuell Levis was Called And he Appeared and the Court ordered that he Appeare Att the next orPhans Court and there to Deliver up the effects of Joseph Humphry or to Give sufficent security to the Court

George stroud ffor speaking some words Against Justis Weithers was Brought before Justice Baynton and being Examined he Desiers that he may Appeare before the whole bench Att his Request Justis Baynton Granted It) and when the Court was sett he was Called and Appeared And submits himselfe to the bench: And the order of the Court Is that If he behave himselfe well towards the maJestrats and All other of the kings leige Peopell for A year and A Day and Pay the Charges he be for this Time Discharged

Mr George fforeman Acknowledged ffull satisfaction ffor the mortgage of ffrances Littls houses and Land Att Chester Town that was made over to him and Jasper Yeats as Gardiens of James Sanderlens ffor the sum of thirty six pounds which was fully satisfied to the fore named.

The sheriff made Returne of An Execution that he levied one the estate of Ralph and Dority ffretwell heires exceecutors & Administrators of Ralph ffretwell Esqr: late Deceased:: obtained by Robert Turner administrator of the Estate of Christopher Taylor Deceased: ffor the sum of ffive hundred and fforty pounds seven shillings and nine pence with ffive pounds Damage And Cost of suite Against the whole Estate both Reall and personall of the fore said Ralph and Dority ffretwell heirs exceecutors administrators of Ralph ffretwell Esqr late Deceased

Wee whose hands are hereunto subscribed being summoned the Twenty sixth Day of the seventh month 1693 To serve upon the Jury as Appraisers to the estate of Ralph and Dority ffretwell heirs exceecutors administrators Assigns of Ralph ffretwell Esqr late deceased levied by way of exceecution by virtue of A writt Directed To the High Sherif for the same purpose being mett apon the Island of Tinicum a pon the Twenty ninth Day of the same Instant have According to our Attest Given us by the High Sheriff To make A True And conscionable Appraisement of such Goods lands and Chattles as should be Brought before us have Appraised the said Island of Tinicum with all the goods houses orchards Gardins and Chattles belonging to the same Att the vallue of ffive hundred and seventy pounds Tenn shillings As wittnes our hands and seals this Twenty ninth Day of September 1693.

Thomas Worth	John Bartram
Richard Bonsall	John Wood
John Smyth	Joseph Need
John Hood	John Hallowell
Thomas Hood	Charles Whitaker
Edmund Cartlidg	Richard Parker

Joseph Wood sheriff

Att A Petty Sesons held Att Chester the 26 Day of December 1693 Att the house of Peter Bayntons And haveing seriously Considered of the presentment of the grand Inquest ffor the building of the Prison And It being that which the law made by the Representativs of the

Jeremiah Collett
Thomas Weithers
Jonathan Hayes
Thomas Smyth
} Justices present

Josheph Wood sherif
John Childe Clark

County and Province Requiers to be Don Did Apoynt A nother Sesons to be holden the 8th Day of Jenuary Att the house of John hodgskins Att Chester where they meet According to Apoyntment And there Did make An Aseasment ffor the Raiseing of the sum of one hundred and ffivety pounds for the Defraying of the Charge Att the True vallue of 2 pence pr pound uppon the Real and Personall Estates of All the Inhabitants of this County seasable by the ffirst Act of the new lawes All ffreemen 6^s pr he^d: And there Did Att the house of John Hodgskins Constitue and Apoynt and Authorise Joseph Wood high sherif of the County to be Collecter ffor the said levie to be gethered by the ffirst Day of the 3 month next: Counsellor fforman being then Present with the fforenamed Justices

Att An orphants Court held ⎫ Mʳ George fforman President
Att Chester ffor the   ⎪ Jeremiah Collett   ⎫
County of Chester   ⎬ Thomas Weithers   ⎬ Justices
the 6ᵗʰ day of   ⎪ Jonathan Hays   ⎭ present
march 1693/4   ⎭ Thomas Smyth

                                         Joseph Wood sherif
                                         John Childe Clark

    Humphry Johnson Being Bound to Apere Att this Court of orphants to Give In An Acount of the Estate of Lawrance Routh Deseased: was Called And Appeared And Brought In An Invetory of the Apraisement of the Estate of Lawrance Routh but not being Authentick nor haveing noe Apraisors hands to the A praisment was not Excepted of by the said Court where A pon the said humphry Did Ernestly Request the Court to Grant him A little longer time the Court Considering the same Did Grant him liberty tell the 13ᵗʰ Day of this month

    Samuell Levis Gave In Band Att this Court ffor the Estate of Joseph humphry Deceased.

    Thomas Powell Appeared and Brought In A Coppy of his Brother Joseph Powells will Deseased and Complayned that It was not ffullfiled the Court considering thereof ordered that he Appear the 13ᵗʰ Day of this month untoe which time this Court Doe AJorne

---

The orphants Court Court held ⎫ Mʳ George fforman President
Att Chester ffor the County   ⎪ Jeremiah Collett   ⎫
of Chester A Cording to   ⎬ Thomas Weithers   ⎬ Justices
AJornment the 13ᵗʰ Day   ⎪ Jonathan Hayes   ⎭ present
of March 1693/4   ⎭ Thomas Smyth

                                           Joseph Wood sherife
                                         John Childe Clark

    Humphry Johnson was Called And Appeared And Brought In A Inventory of Estate of Lawrance Rouths Deceased with An Apraismᵗ A praised by Caleb Pusye Randell Vernon: Robert Carter Dated the 10ᵗʰ Day of the first month 1693/4

of the Estate Reall and Personall of Laurance Routh of the township of Chester Deceased being As ffolloweth

The Inventory of Lawrence Rouths Estate

	£	s	d
ffirst his wearing Apparell	02	10	00
Itm 3 cowes & an old Decayed cow & calfe	11	00	00
Itm one paire of oxen Att.............	09	00	00
Itm A Cart and wheels	01	00	00
Itm ffor six swine big and little..........	02	10	00
Itm ffor 2 brass kettls & A skillett.......	01	02	00
Itm ffor A Iron kettle	00	10	00
Itm 4 old Pewter Dishes & a plate........	00	10	00
Itm ffor An old ffrying Pan & pot hanger..	00	03	00
Itm ffor An oxe Chaine	00	07	00
Itm ffor a box smoothing Irons & 2 heaters	00	03	00
Itm ffor 2 old Axes 3 Iron wedges.......	00	08	00
Itm ffor A Brass Chefindish & A Candelstic	00	04	00
Itm ffor A hatchell & Iron Bakeing Plate.	00	08	00
Itm ffor 3 old Augors & a old Grubing ax.	00	03	00
Itm ffor 2 old saws a adds Drawing knife And A Plaine Att	00	08	00
Itm ffor A steel mill & a old Clock........	02	00	00
Itm ffor A large lattine Dixcionary And some other old Books	01	05	00
Itm for A paire of ffire tongs 2 Glas bottells	00	01	06
Itm ffor A plowshere and Coulter.......	00	05	00
Itm ffor A horse Att	03	15	00
Itm ffor A mare & Coult & a Cow........	11	00	00
Itm ffor An old Trunck & A Sickell And some other Lumber About	00	06	00
the Totall sum of ye personall Estate is	48	18	06
Itm the Lands with the houses and orchards & All the Improvements	70	00	00

Wittnes our hands

Randall R varnon
<small>his marke</small>

Caleb Pusye

Robert Carter

An Account of the age of the Children of Lawrance Routh when he Deceased. Tho: Routh was A boute 6 years of age

Lawrance Routh was A boute 4 years ad ½ old

Rachell Routh a boute 2 years and ½ old

ffrances Routh Aboute 8 months old

The Depts of Lawrence Rout left to pay when he Deceased as followeth

	£	s	d
Itm to James Sanderlings	2	12	00
to Mary hickman for wages	2	00	00
to John Parker	2	12	00
for A Coffin for him	0	09	00
ffor other Charges for his Buriall	0	08	00
ffor Rent ffor the land	3	05	03
To Samuell Carpenter	0	09	00
	11	15	9
Paid oute of the Crop seuce the 26 day of the 10 month last as the Petty sesons was at Chester	00	08	00
Pay^d more Att Another time	00	10	00
Payd toe the Taylor	00	11	6
	1	09	6

Depts not yett paid

To Philip Rumon	01	15	00
To Caleb Pusye	01	15	00
To Robert Barber	00	09	00
Humphry Jonson Expended of his owne mony for family use	01	10	3
7 bushells of wheat for the Rent of the land	01	11	6

To Allice Tremaine	00	03	00
To William Brown for worke...........	00	03	00
	07	06	9

An Acount of laying oute of the mony for the 50 Acers of land sould to John Beals

To John Parker for worke	2	00	00
To John Parker more for worke	0	13	6
ffor ffour bushell of seed wheate	1	02	0
Goods as I Recev^d of John Powell for my familys use	03	03	00
ffor Iron work In the house Cart whels plow shers Coulter	00	13	02
In Blew linnen for my famlys use........	00	15	00
ffor A horse	03	15	00
To John Parker for work	00	06	00
more for my use and Children	01	10	04
	14	00	00
Pay^d to Charley Brooks	11	00	00

The order of this Court is that the s^d Humprhy Johnson Doe bring In security to this Court for the orphants Estate Above said and he the said humpry Johnson And John Beals Doe bind themselfs Joyntly and severaly In the sum of thirty seven pounds to this Court ffor the aforesaid Estate In a penall bond

Thomas Powell Appeared A gain A boute his Brothers orphants Estate and the Courts order Is that John Bristow Doe Collect It and bring it into the next orphants Court

---

Att A Court of Quarter sessions held Att Chester ffor the County of Chester the 13 Day of March 1694

{ Mr George fforman President
Jeremiah Collett
Thomas Weithers } Justices
Jonathan Hayes   Present
Thomas Smyth }

Joseph Wood sherif
John Childe Clark

After Proclimation made & silence commanded In theyr maJesties names The Grand Inquest was Called and Appeared Excepting two of them one being Ded and the other not being Cappable there was 2 Chosen In theyr Rome the 2 Chosen were Albert Hendrickson and William Couborn who were both Attested

The Constables were Called and new ones were Chosen: for the ensueing yeare Richard Woodworth Constable of upper Providence

John Willis Constable of Thornbury
Peter Thomas Constable of Springfield
Anthony Morgan Constable of Darbye
Randell varnon Constable of Neither Providence
Godwin Walter Constable of Concord [crossed]
Thomas Marey Constable of Marpoole
David Philip Constable of Newtowne [crossed]
John Cox Constable of Ridlye
Edmund Butcher Constable of Burningham
John Gibbous Constable of Beathell
John Morgan Constable of Radner
John Beales Constable of Aishtowne
Philip Yarnell Constable of Edgement
William Lewis Constable of havorford
David Ogdon Constable of Middletowne
Henery Hollingsworth and Isack ffew Constabls for Chester Township for this yeare
John Radley for Westtowne
George Stroud Concord
John Green Constable of Concord ded
Ree sent Constable of new Town

The Court A Jorns ffor 2 hours: the Court mett Againe According to A Jornment Thomas hoope was Called: and Appeared & Mary Martin was Called and Appeared and was Examined whether she was with Child by Thomas Hoape or not she saith that shee is not the Courts order is that thay Appeare Againe Anone

Ruben ffoord Exhibited A pettition to this Court ffor to have his Indenturs and the Custome of the Country of his master John Gibbons but he haveing no Part of the Indentures the Court tooke no more notis of It his Master John Gibbons by A Righting from under his hand Did A firme that he had formerly Delivered them to him in A note:

The Grand Inquest by the king and Queens Authority: ye 13th of March 1694 Presents Joseph Richards of Aishtown supervisor for not Cutting and Clereing the Roade way that leads ffrom Concord throw the s^d Township of Aishtonn: Thomas Conborne fforman: The Court orders Joseph Richards have an order to warne the Inhabitants of the Township of Aishtowne to make good the publicke Roads In the said Township.

Chester County March: 13: 1693/4 the Grand Juery by the king & Queens Authority haveing Perused the Account of the County Depts and Credit of the County of Chester that John Simcock & John Bristow prodused to us being Confirmed by the Grand Juery ffor the yeare 1692: Bearing Date ffrom A Court held the 18th of Jenuary the same yeare which was Confirmed by the said Grand Juery to the yeare 1690 last except some Accounts which are paid to this present yeare 1692 which may bee here After Intradused Subscribed by the A foresaid Grand Juery the A foresaid 18th of Jenuary: ffirst we ffinding this Account not to A gree with your warrants you Issued oute last which are A memorandum of the Depts that you charge us with being A bove three scoore Pounds les by youre owne Accounts then what you Charged the County in your warrents: 2 secondly the subscription of your Account sheweth that some are paid till the year 1692: we Desier you to make it Appeare to whom It is paid and how much It is. 3^{ly} Likewise wee Desier you to Give an Account what mony you Receved from the County one the three former levies ffirst the Tax of the Court house and Prison. 2^{ly} for the Tax of the woolves heads: 3^{ly} the Tax ffor the Court house and Prison Counsell and Assembly mens wages and Relife of the poore

&c which was In the yeare 1688: 4¹⁷: what mony there is behind In Arrears Due ffrom the County on the Non Resident land and others which have not Payd to these three Affore mentioned levies you haveing made the County Depter to you by these aforesaid levise soe that this account Is imperfect: ffurther we Desier that John Simcock & John Bristow make oute the Account In Answer to this presentment & the two former presentments ffurther we present John Simcock & John Bristow two make oute the Accounts In Answer to this presentment and the 2 former Presentments two the satisfaction of the Country Thomas Cocborne fforeman:

Walter Martin: Thomas Powell: John Colvert: William Collett: Albert Hendrixson: Richard Bonsall: Thomas Worth: John Hood: Charles Whitaker George Thomas: Thomas ffox: John Mendinghall: William Co*borne: Isack Taylor:

Thomas Hoap was Called Againe and Appeared and Mary Martin not being with Childe by him: the Courts order is that Thomas hoape be Clared by Proclimation he paying the Charges: which was Accordingly Don: the said Mary Martin was Called and Appeared And not being with Childe the Courts order is that she be fined five shillings for her lying and that shee Pay her Charges And be Discharged by the Court

John Bristow was Called to Answer the Presentment of the Grand Inquest ffor takeing and new Brand markeing of A horse that was marked before John Bristowe he Appears and Is willing to come to tryall. The Petty Juery as was Impanelled

John Bartram..	Mickell Blunston
William Garrett..	John Smyth
Thomas Brite..	John Worrılaw
Joseph Cocborn..	John kinsman
John Beails..	Henery Hollingsworth
William Mallein..	Humphry Johnson

the evidences as was Called was Josiah Taylor Being Attested Deposeth that there was A bay stone horse came Downe to Daniell Williamsons and that he had a little Cut of one of his Ears and that he had a Brand marke to be seen when he Did swett which Brand marke was F. S. which could not be seen withoute a Did sweett.

Thomas Marcy being Attested: Deposeth that he was the first that brought this horse Downe out of the woods and As he Brought this with other horses he as A came Downe with them he looked to see If he could see any mark that this same horse had and that when he came to the Indian ffields he Did see this horse Did Stumble and being In A sweett Did see that he was marked with F. S and and that the horse had a little Cut of one of his Ears but it was not to be seene but one mite ffeele it plaine

John Shaw being Attested Deposeth that there was a bay stone horse came Downe In theyr neighberhood and that a stayd there a boute a yeare and that was the horse that Richard Tomson Brought to John Bristow and that he was marked with to letters F. S. and that he did see it

Daniell Williamson Being Attested Deposeth that Thomas Marcy enquired of him If he Could tell what marke that horse had and A little time after he the said Deponant went to Darby with one of his owne and that this horse ffollowed him and as he Rid home againe he Did see this horse sweatt and then he could see the two letters F S: Brand marked on the said horse

Thomas Bright being Examined said that John Bristow Desiered him to looke one the horse to see If that he could perseve any mark that a had and he looked up and Downe and felt and that he Did thinke there was part of an S under the B which John Bristow had marked him with

The Petty Juery Brought In theyr verditt which is ye 13th of the first month

Wee off the Petty Juery Doe ffind John Bristow not Guilty: William Garrett fforeman

The Court Gives Judgment on the verditt and orders that John Bristow be Clered by Proclimation he paying the Charges: which was accordingly don.

Att A Court of Common Pleass held Att Chester ffor the County of Chester the 14th Day of March 1694

Mr George fforman President
Jeremiah Collett
Thomas Weithers
Jonathan Hayes
Thomas Smyth
} Justices Present

Joseph Wood High Sheriff
John Child Clarke

An And Peter Baynton Plantive Against the Estate of George Andros Defendant In the hands of Richard Crosby ffor the sum of ten pounds Eighteen shillings: Mr George fforman Appearing ffor the Plantives and this being the third Court and the Defendant not Appering nor none ffor him and the said Mr George fforman being Attested that there was none of the said Dept paid to his knowledge

The order of Court Is that the Dept be paid with 3 pence Damage and Cost of suite.

JOHN ORIEN Plantive Against MOUNCE and PETER STALKER Defendants } In An Action of scandell and Defamation

The Plantive was Called And Appeard and David Loyd Appeared for the Defft^s the Decleration was Red And Defence Attorney would Justify the Decleraton } The Juery was Called and Impaneled

The same Juery as was before Att the Quarter Sessions,) the evidences John Bartleson was Called ffor the Defendant: And he being Attested, Deposeth that he hard one Lacye say that the Plantive John Orien had taken A pigg ffrom A sow in the woods and that he Denyed that he had marked a pigg.

The verditt of the Juery is ye 14th of the first month 1694: wee of the petty Juery Doe ffind no Cause of Action William Garrett fforman the Court Gives Judgment there with.

Hance Urin Plantive Against } In An Action of scandell
Mounce Stalker Defendant } and defamation

the Plantive was called and Appeared & the Defendant Allsoe the Decleration was Red they Joyne Issue The Evediences being Called ffor the plantive: Catherin Morten Being Attested Deposeth that shee hard Mounce Stalker Call hance urien Rouge and say that he was A hog thife Aboute 10 days after the time of Crismas last past

John Orien being Attested Deposeth that he hard the said Mounce Stalker Call the Plantife A hog Thife and A Rouge and that he would prove him soe Garthright Orien being Attested Deposeth that shee hard the said Mounce say that the Plantive was A hog thife and A Rouge Walbera taton being Attested Deposeth that she hard Mounce Stalker Call the Plantive A hogg thife

The same Juery as was In the Causes before the verditt of the Juery Is ye 14th of the first month 94 we of the Petty Juery doe ffind ffor the Plantife Twelve pence Damage with Cost of suite

William Garratt fforeman

Henery Taton Being Attested ffor the Defendant Deposeth that when he was Constable that hance Urin had Taken A pigg from Mounce Stalker and that the pigg was put In A Barrell and that and that the Defendant brought the Deponant a warrent & he Did bring him before John Blunstone one of theyr MaJesties Justices of the Peace of this County and that the said hance was ordered to bring the pig A gaine to the said mounce and ffurther saith not

Judgment Is given According to the verditt

Lawrance Bartleson Plantive Against
Peter Stalker Defendant In an Action of Scandell and Defemation they were Called and they with Drew the action before the Juery were panelld

JOHN NEALE Plantive Against ⎱ In An Action of scan-
HENERY BARNES Deffendantt ⎰ dell and Defemation
David Loyd Appeared ffor the Defendant

The Decleration being Red the Juery As before named In the other Causes

John Ditton Evidence for the Plantive being Attested saith that he was Att the house of Thomas Powells and Henery Barnes was there and Deposeth that the said Henery Barnes Did say there that John Neale had A son in Meryland as big As himselfe and that he had brought a letter from him oute of Meryland

Jeremiah Collett being Attested: saith that he being Att the house of Caleb Pusie Did heare Henery Barnes say that John Neale had A son In Merryland but It was not by his wife:

Thomas Powell being Attested Deposeth that John Neales son In law came to his house and that Henery Barnes Asked him who It was and he tould him who it was And the said Barnes said that John Neale had A son In Merryland and that he brought A letter from him to John Neale

Caleb Pusie being Attested said that he hard Henery Barnes say that he had Brought A letter from one oute of Merryland that Called John Neale ffather: John Childe being Attested saith that he being Att the house of Caleb Pusies Did heare Henery Barnes say that John Neale had A son in Merryland that was not by his wife but by a nother woman

The verditt of the Juery is wee of the Petty Juery Doe ffind noe Cause of Action but the Plantive suffered A nonsuite before the verditt came In.

Caleb Pusye Past A Deed to Robert Lonshore Attorney ffor Thomas holmes ffor Two hundred and Eighty Acres of Land with All Its Appurtenants thereunto belonging Lying In the Township of Rydlye Bearing Date the 20th of Aprill 1693

John Simcocke Past A Deed to John kinsman ffor ffive hundred Aceres of Land lying in thornbury Township Bearing Date the 14th of March 1693/4

John kinsman Past A Deed to Elizebeth Hickman widdoe ffor Two hundred Acres of Land Lying and being In the Township of thornbury the Deed Beareing Date the 14th of March 1693/4

John kinsman Past A Deed to Joseph Edwards ffor one hundred Acres of Land Lying and being In the Township of Thornbury the Deed Bearing Date the 14th Day of March 1693/4.

BenJamin Mendinghall Past A Deed unto Joseph Edwards ffor fivetie Acres of Land lying and being In thornbyry Township the Deed Bearing Date the 14th Day of March 1693/4

Nathaniell Richards Past A Deed unto Richard Barnerd ffor one hundred And seventy ffive Acres of Land lying and being In the Township of Aishtown Beareing Date the 14th Day of March 1693/4

Henery Barnes Past A Deed ffor thirtye Acres of Land with the meadow lying by Ridly Creeke unto Robert Pennell and Randell Malling Atorneys ffor John Worell bereing Date the 14th of march 1693/4

Robert Wade Attorney ffor Peter Baynton Past A Deed unto Henery Holinsworth ffor the house and Land Att Chester Towne that was fformerly ffrances Littles the Deed Bearing Date the 12th of ffebuary 1693

Walter Martin Past A Deed to William Thomas ffor fourty Acres of Land being Part of that Tract of Land that the said Walter Martin Is settled one the Deed Bearing Date the 10th Day of ffebuary 1693

Joseph Wood high sherif Past A deed unto Samuell Levis ffor ffivety Acres of land lying in Darby Township the Deed Bearing Date the 26th Day of ffebuary 1693

Joseph Wood Past A Deed unto ffrances Yarnell ffor 35 Acres of Land lying in Darby Township the Deed Bearing Date the 12th Day of the first month 1694

Joseph Wood Past A Deed unto John Maris ffor 25 Acres of Land lying In Darby Township the Deed Bearing Date the 12th Day of the first month 1694

Robert Barber Attorney ffor Ann ffinch widdoe Past A Deed unto ABraham Beeks ffor one hundred Acres of Land lying and being In the Township of Edgment Beareing Date the 25th Day of the 10 month 1693

John Blunstone Attorney ffor Joseph Potter In England Past A Deed to George Thomas of Newtown ffor one hundred Acrs of Land lying in newtowne Beareing Date the 12th Day of the first month 1694

John Blunstone Attorney ffor the fforesaid Joseph Potter Past Two Deeds more one to Thomas Hood of Darby ffor ffivety Acres of land lying In Darby Towneship Beareing Date the 12th Day of the first month 1694

Another Deed to John Holleway ffor ffivety Acres of land lying and being In the Township of Darbye Bearing Date the 12th Day of ye first month 1694

Att A Petty Sessions held Att the house of John Hodgskins the 27th Day of the first month: 1694

Justices there present { Mr George fforman, Jeremiah Collett, Jonathan Hayes, Thomas Weithers, Thomas Smyth

There the Justices Did Constitute and Apoynt Joseph Wood to be collecter of the levies that is for the building of the prison which is After the Rate of two pence pr pound of the Reall and Personall Estates of All the Inhabitants In this County And six shillings pr head for All freemen In the Country which said levie is to be Gethered by the first Day of the 3 month next

Joseph Wood sherif
John Childe Clarke

And there John Bristow Did Deliver up the mony that he had In his hands of the orphants of Joseph Powell Deceased and Alsoe the bills Due from severall Parsons to the said orphants the mony he Delivered in to the hands of Jeremiah Collett (viz) the sum of Eight pounds sixteen shillins and nine pence which he Receved of these persons: of John Edge 2£ 2s 0d of William Mallin the sum of 3£ 12s 6d and of Richard Woodworth the sum of 3£ 17s 0d and of Bartholomew

Copock 0£ 9ˢ 3ᵈ and one pound four shillings besids which makes the fore mentioned sum 8ˡᵇ

A ffarther Account of what John Bristow Deliverd Into the hands of Jeremiah Collett

	£	s	d
A Bill of ffrancis Worly ffor A steare sould him for the sum of	3	00	00
A Bill Due ffrom John Madock for the sum of	2	05	00
A Bill due ffrom Thomas Powell for the sum of Eight	8	00	00
A Bill Due ffrom Robert Nailor for the sum of four pounds 4£	4	4	00
A Bill Due ffrom Joseph Kent for the sum of	2	11	00
A Bill due ffrom William Simson ffor the sum of	2	12	00
A Bill Due ffrom Thomas Browne ffor the sum of	3	00	00
A Bill Due ffrom Henery Swift ffor the sum of	3	05	00
A Bill Due ffrom Hester Powell for the sum of	4	00	00
A Bill Due ffrom ould Bartholomew Coppock for the sum of	5	00	00
	37	17	00
And the Eight Pounds sixteene shillings & nine pence	£ 08	s 16	d 9
which is on the other side the leafe makes in the whole	46	13	9

Att A Petty sesions held the 7ᵗʰ day Day of Aprill 1694 Att the house of Mʳ George fformans Att Chichester:

Lookeing over and Examining severall Accounts we find that the County Is Indepted unto severall Persons the sum of one hundred sixty and six pounds

George fforman ⎫
Jeremiah Collett ⎬ Justices
Thomas Weithers ⎬ ther
Thomas Smyth ⎬ present
Jonathan Hayes ⎭

John Childe Clarke

nineteen shillings and Eleven pence And that whereas A Levie was layd the 17th Day of y° 11th month in the yeare 1692 ffor the Defraying the Depts of the County (viz) Every meale white or Black ffrom 16 years ould two sixty should pay 3^s pr h^d And 3^s pr hundred for every hundred Acers of Land and 4^s & 6^d pr hundred ffor non Resident Lands And that there is part of the first moeity being Gathered by Caleb Pusye and we ffinding A nesseity of that first part two be Gathered two helpe two Defray the A fore said Dept of 166£ 19^s 11^d that whereas Caleb Pusye was Apoynted Collecter of the said levie which formerly he Did Receve part of Wee Doe Continnue him In said station untill the said moeity be Collected and two be fforthwith Gathered and two be Paid Into such Person or Persons as shall be hereafter Apoynted by the Justices

One the seventh Day of may in the yeare 1694 Mickell Isard now of the County of salem In West Jersy Came to Chester And before Jeremiah Collett: and Jonathan Hayes two of the Justices of the peace of this County Attested that the land that he sould formerly to Thomas Baldwin of this County was bounded by the severall Corses of the maine Run that leades throw the hed lyne of that whole Tract of land that was formerly the said Mickell Isards

Att A Court of Quarter Sesions Held Att Chester ffor the County off Chester the 12th Day of June 1694	Mr George fforman President Jeremiah Collett Thomas Smyth Jonathan Hayes	Justices there Present

Joseph Wood Sherif
John Childe Clarke

After Proclimation made and Silence commanded

In thire MaJesties names: The Constables weare Called And Anthony Morgan Constable of Darbye not Appearing was ffind ffive shillings.

Henery Holingsworth & Isack ffew weare Attested Constabls ffor the Towneship of Chester ffor this yeare: The

Grand Juery was Called And Appeared they Brought In theyr presentment as followeth

Chester County June y{e} 12{th} 1694 The Grand Juery by the king and Queens Authority Presents James Letort ffor Taking up A mare and two Coults of Danniell Harys and Brand marking the two Coults with his Brand marke Thomas Colbourn: fforman

Thomas Worrolaw was Chosen supervisor of the Roade ways ffor the Township of Edgment ffor one yeare

Nathaniell Richards preferd A pettion to this Court ffor to have A Road way to his house haveing been eight or nine years In this Country and haveing now noe setled Road way to his house: The order of Court is that the Grand Inquest Goe and lay him oute A Roade way where they shall see most Conveniant

The Inhabitants of the Towneship of Radner pettitioned to this Court ffor A Roade way to be layd out for them ffrom the middle of Theyr Township To the scoolekill: ffoard And the Court orders the Grand Inquest to lay oute A Roade way ffor them where they shall see most Conveniant

Richard Armes presented A petticion to this Court Consarning A sarvant boy that he had Run A way thirteen times and for what Charges he had been Att ffor the Takeing of him up and for the loss of his time: The Court Considering of It desierd him to stay tell they had spoken with John Joans of Philadelphia Aboute him he being the boyes Gardian and that he should have an Answer the next Court

names of The Grand Inquest for this yeare 1694, Phillip Rumen John kinsman

Richard Armes	John Jerman	William Garratt
Michell Blunstone	Nickolas Jierland	William Smyth
Daniell Humphry	Morrice Lewellen	William Huntly
David Morriee	Petter Peterson	Swan Boone
Nicholes Pille	William Browne	William Thomas

The Inhabitants of the Towneship of Radner petitioned to this Court for A Roade way to be laid oute for them to the foord over the scoole Creeke And the Court considering of the same order is that that the Grand Juery goe and vew It and If they see Conveniant to lay It oute for them.

Nathaniell Richards Petitioned for A Roade way to his house his way being stopt order Is that the Grand Juery goe and where they see most Conveniant to lay oute A Roade way for him

Att A Court of Common Pleas held Att Chester ffor the County of Chester the 13th Day of June 1694

Mr George fforman President
Jeremiah Collett ⎫ Justices
Jonathan Hayes ⎬ there
Thomas Smith ⎭ Present
Joseph Wood Sherif
John Childe Clarke

After Proclimation made and Silence commaded In theyr MaJesties names

JOHN FFOX Plantif Against ⎱ In An Acction of Dept
CHARLES THOMAS Defend^t ⎰ The Plantive & Defendant being Called & Apperd They Joyne Isue: the Decleration was Red and the Defendant pleads that he owed the plantif nothing: the Juery was Called and Apper^d as followeth

The petty Juery

Edmund Cartlidge	Thomas Hood	John Smyth
John Mairis	William Tally	James Baylis
Albert Hendrixson	Thomas Garrett	Henery Hames
Thomas howell	James Swafard	John Hodgskins

The verditt of the Juery Is: the 13th of the 4th month 1694: wee of the Petty Juery Doe ffind for the plantife two pence Dammage with Cost of suite John Hodgskins fforeman: where A pon Judgment is Granted one the verditt the plantive Remitting the pennalty of the bond: he has Execution Granted for the principell & Charges

EDWARD HURLBERT Plantf Agaist ⎰ In An Acction of Asalt
LACYE HOWMAN Defendant ⎱ and Battery and for Breaking his sword

The Plantif and Defendant being Called Appeared the Decleration was Red and the Defend' Denied that he struck the said plantive: John Cox being Called for An Evidence ffor the plantif & being Attested: Deposeth that he see noe blow struck by the Defendat Richard Taylor being Attested Deposeth that he was there all the time and that there was noe blow struck

The same Juery as above named: the verditt of the Juery is the 13th of ye 4th month 1694: wee of the petty Juery ffinds noe Cause of Action John Hodgskins fforeman: the bench Aquist with the verditt

JOHN BEALES Pl^{t}f: Against } In An Acction of Tres-
JOSEPH RICHARDS Junor Defendant } pas: the Accion was Called and a Defect being in the Decleration; the Defendant Craved A Referance tell the next Court and the Decleration to be amended.

WILLIAM COLLETT Plantif Against } In An Accion of Dept:
JOHN BRISTOW Defendant } the Accion was Called & the plantife and Defendat Appeared: the Decleration was Red wherein the plantive Declered for the sum of scaven pounds five shillings and three pence: the Defendat Denieth that he owes nothing in manner And forme they Joyne Issue Edward Beck being Called and Attested ffor the plantive Deposeth that the first parsell of Barly that they Carried Downe to John Bristow was 32 bushells and that the next loade that was Carried Downe was 35 bushells which was All oute of the same heape Edward Jannings being Attested Deposeth that he helpt to Carry Downe Another loade which was 32 bushells more which Edward Attested was the same barly

Robert Pyle being Attested Deposeth that he had six bushells of Barly of William Collett And that he sowed It and It came Indeferant and but Indeferant.

Edward Beazer being Attested Deposeth that William Collett came to him and Desiered him to goe see som barlye as was In the Roade & that which he Did see Growed Indeferant well

Joseph Cloud being Attested: Deposeth that he Did Carry some barly Into John Bristow it was 15 bushells and that he Did see some barly that had been moved to Another Please and that he Carried some there which John Bristow said was but Dirt but yet he tooke it ffor All. John Bristow Junior being Attested Deposeth that the first Parsell of Barly as his father bought and had of William Collett was Indefferant barly and Came pretty well and that the next parcell which was 35 bushells and a peck And they wett that and that It was Greate part of It Rotten and Did not come and ffurther said that when his ffather bought It It was by a sample that William Collett Brought and that when his father looked on it he Did see some Amongst It that had Red Ends And that his father said he was Informed that that was soe would not come And that the last loade came Indeferant well.

Rogger Walden being Attested Deposeth that he Did helpe William Collett to Carry In som barly Att harvest and that It was good ffor nothing.

George Peacocke being Attested Deposeth that he helpt to Rake and Cock som barly Att harvest for William Collett and that he herd him say that he should be undon by haveing soe much Rotten barly that he had and that some of the barlye As they were A pitching of it up the water Run oute of It.

Edward ffoord being Attested Deposeth that he was Att William Colletts Att harvest and that there was A boute 5 Cart loade In the barne before he came and that he was A helpeing of the getting A boute 16 or 17 loade of Barlye that was good and sound. George Chandler being Attested Deposeth that he was Att the mowing of A boute 6 or 7 Acers of Barly as was sound And that A nother time he câme there and Did see William Colletts peopell boyle som barly for his Cattle and that he Did heare William Collett say that he would not sell the worst because he should be thought Ill of If that he should Doe it.

The same Juery As was before In the other Causes.

The verditt of the Juery is the 13th of the 4th month 1694

Wee of the petty Juery Doe ffind ffor the Defendant with Cost of suite the Defendant Returning to the plantive 35 bushells of bad barlye malted which Is In the Defendants hands: John Hodgskins fforeman:

Judgment Is given one the verditt:

The Plantive ffinding himselfe Agreeved with the verditt Apeals to A Court of Equitye, which is granted

Richard Moore Petticioned to this Court for to have pay for the keeping of Ruebeen ffoord that lyeth sick Att his house And the order of Court is that he shall have five shillings A weeke Allowed him

A Deed Past by David Lewis Attorney for Howell James of Radnor for one hundred Acres of land unto David Evan the Deed beareing Date the 26th Day of the 11th month in the yeare 1689

Edward hurlbert was fined five shillings for swereing

A Deed Past by Joseph Wood As High Sheriff of the County of Chester unto Robert Turner of Philidelphia as Administrator to the Estate of Christopher Taylor Deseaced ffor the Island of Tinnicum with all the buildings and Improvements Thereunto belonging: the Deed beareing Date the Twelfe Day of June 1694

A Deed Past by Counsellor fforman Attorney ffor Thomas Holmes of Philidelphia unto John Cock of this County ffor To hundred and Eighty Accres of land with All buildings thereunto belonging lying In the Township of Ridlye the Deed Beareing Date the 25th Day of March 1694

A Deed Past by Thomas England unto John Pennell ffor one hundred Accres of Land lying by Chester Creek side the Deed beareing Date the 9th of June 1694

A Deed Past ffrom Robert Hutcheson to Thomas King of Concord for fivety Acres of Land lying In Concord the Deed beareing Date the 6th Day of June 1694

Joseph Cloud Past A Deed unto his Brother John Cloud for Two hundred Accres of land with the Improvements thereunto beloning the Deed bereing Date the 7th Day of the 10th month 1693

A Deed Past ffrom Thomas Merscer to William Browne ffor one hundred Acres of Land with All Its Appurtenants thereto belonging the Deed beareing Date the Eight Day of June in the yeare 1694 the land lying in Aishtown Township

The sheriff made Returne of An Exceeution that was Granted to Mr George fforman In the behalfe of Ann And Peter Baynton Against the Estate of George Andras By vertue of An Exceeution Derected to him to levie the sum of tenn pounds Eighteen shillings and 3 pence Damage with Cost of suite of the Estate of George Andros In the hands of Richard Crosbye the sheriff Demanded the efects of George Andros of Richard Crosbye who Denyed that he had any such efects In his hands

Att A Court off Quarter sessions held Att Chester ffor the County of Chester the 11th Day of September 1694

The Justices Commissions was Read
Mr George fforman President
Jeremiah Collett
Jasper Yeates   Justices there
Jonathan Hayes   present
Thomas Smyth

Joseph Wood Sherif
John Childe Clarke

The Constabls were Called over And Appeared: And David Phillip Constable of Newtowne ffor his Contempt and Refusing to Exceeute the office was ffined the sum of two pounds And ten shillings: And Ree sent Chosen to serve the office for this yeare.

The Grand Inquest was Called And Appeared:

Thomas Johns Presented A peticion to this Court consarning the Roade way that went throw his meadow And was very much to his Detryment And there being A more Couveniant way found Att the end of his meadow the order of Court is that the way shall goe there Att the end of the meadow.

Henery Hastings Attested Constable ffor the Towneship of Chichest' for on yeare. Thomas Reese was Chosen supervisor of the Roade wayes for the towneship off Havorford ffor one yeare Caleb Pusye & Thomas Varnon and Robert varnon weare Attested Appraisors for the County

The grand Inquest brought in theyr presentment which is as ffolloweth: the 11th of the 7th month 1694: wee of the Grand Juery A pon the Complaint of Ruth Colvert: Doe Present Owein Mack Daniell ffor laying violent hands uppon her shee sollemly Declereing before us that he sought to have Ravished her.

Wee Alsoe Present Josiah Taylor ffor being to ffamillier with the wife of Daniell Williamson: And wee likewise present the wife of Daniell Williamson ffor being to ffamilier with Josiah Taylor

Wee of the grand Inquest Do Alsoe Present the straightnes of the Passage betwext the houses of James Sanderlins In Chester Towne   Philip Romen foreman

Owen Mack Daniell being Called to the bar to Answer to the presentmen of the Grand Juery Consarning his offering Abuse to Ruth Colvert: And he Denied the Evidences was Called who was William Edwards and his son John who being Attested the said William Edwards being neare to the place where the said Owen would have forst her: herd A great Cry and his son John being with him Run and Came to the place first and he went After but saw Owen Mack Daniell and Ruth Calvert there but see no harme the said John Edwards being Attested Declareth that he and his ffather being neare to the place herd A great Cry and he Run to see what was the matter and when he came there he Asked w^t was the matter and he did see the s^d Owen Rise up and she Called him Dog and said that he would have forsed her: where a pon the said Owen submited himselfe to the bench: and the order of Court was that the s^d Owen should Receve Eleaven laishes one his Beare Back which was Accordingly Don and to pay all Charges And Alsoe to bring sufficient security for his good behavior for the future

The Courts order is that A pon the presentment of the Grand Inquest that Josiah Taylor be summoned to Answer it Att the next Court and Alsoe the wife of Daniell Williamson to Answer to the presentment of the Grand Inquest

Humphry Scarlett was Chosen supervisor of the hye waies for the Township of Aishtown for this yeare

ffrances Chadsey was Chosen supervisor of the wayes for burningham Township

John Childes: Eare marke is Two notches oute of the under height of the Right Eare And his Brand marke is C one the buttock.

The ffiveteenth Day of the seventh month Anny Domi 1697

Jeremiah Collett Assigned over the remainder of his sarvant Allixsander mackeenis Time To EPhram Jackson before Jonathan Heyes Justices of ye Peace

---

| Att A Court of Common Pleas held Att Chester ffor the County of Chester held the 12th Day of September 1694 | Justices there present Mr George fforman: on of the Counsell: president Jeremiah Collett Jonathan Hayes Thomas Smyth |

Joseph Wood shèriff
John Child Clarke

JOHN BEALES   Plt Against
JOSEPH RICHARDS Defendant Junior
Action of Trespas

The Cause was Called and the plantif and defendant both Appeared and After some Debate the Defendant Craved A Referance tell the next Court and the plantife Desierd to Come to tryall now, but the Def^t pleaded he was not Prepared Desierd It mite be Continued tell the next Court the Court orders the Def^t shall pay halfe Charges and that It shall be Continued tell the next Court

FFRANCES CHADSEY Pl^t: Against
JOHN NEALS   Defendant
In An Action of the Case

The Cause was Called And the plantife Appeard: and the Deft was Called three times but Appeared not nor none for him Continued tell the next Court

Charles Brooks Past A Deed to Thomas England ffor Eighty Accres of land lying in the Township of Aishtown bearing the 11th of September 1694

A Deed Past by John Childe Attorney ffor Samuel Carpenter: to David lewis of havorford ffor one hundred Acres of land lying In Havorford the Deed bearing Date the 18th Day of the 4th month 1694

Thomas Loyds name was in the Deed but he is deceased & not signed

A Deed Past ffrom David lewis of havorford to James James for 50 Acres of land lying in havorford the Deed bearcing Date the 12th Day of September 1694

A Deed Past ffrom Thomas Smyth of Darby to his Brother John Smyth for 50 Acrs of land lying In Darbye the Deed bearing Date the 10th Day of September 1694

A Deed Past ffrom Thomas Nossiter and Ann his wife to Joell Bayly for one hundred And ffivety Accres of land lying in the Towneship of midletowne the Deed bercing Date the 15th Day of the 12th month 1692

A Deed Past ffrom Robert Wade and his wife Lydia unto Jeremiah Carter for his Daughter Lydia for 50 Acers of land lying In Chester Township the Deed The Deed beareing Date the Eleventh Day of September 1694

A Deed Past ffrom Charles Thomas to Joseph Wood High sheriff Attorney for John ffox ffor A plantation Contayning on hundred acers of land lying in the Township of Edgment: the Deed bearing Date the 11th of September 1694

George Stroude In the behalfe of himselfe and Thomas Greene and John Green and Richard Moore Past of unto John Neale Articles of Agreement for the Consideration of the sum of thirteen pounds thirteen shillings and eight pence and six pounds thirteen shillings and four pence unto the said John Neales wife During both the naturall lifes of John

Neales and his now wife to be paid at four Equall Payments yearly thats to say Att the four ffestival Dayes thats to say the first Payment to begin on the 22 Day of December next and to be paid in silver mony Att some house within three miles of the Town of Chester In the province of Pennsilvania and soe the next Att ye 25th of march and the next att ye 24 of June ye next ye 29 of September. And soe to Continue Dureing the naturall lives of the s^d John Neales and his wife And the fore named George Stroud Delivered A Bond In the behalfe of the forenamed Thomas Green and himselfe and John Green and Richard Moore for the performance of the A fore s^d payment the bond was for Two hundred and fivety Pounds bearing Date the Twentieth Day of August 1694

John Neales Past over Articles of Agreement to Thomas Green for Two hundred Acres of land and A barne and severall other things mentioned In the Indenture the land lying In the Township of Aistown the Indentures bearing Date the Twentieth Day of August 1694 And Alsoe Robert Carter of the Township of Ashtowne and John Beal of the same have past over seaven bonds unto the fore named Thomas Green ffor to pay him or his heirs excecutors or Assigns the full and Just sum of ffiveteen pounds A yeare for seaven years and to be paid yearly one the 26th Day of March the first payment every yeare As every bond spetifieth the first payment to begin In the yeare 1696: and soe to Continue till the expiration of the last bond which endeth in the years one thousand seaven hundred and two which is for the Consideration of the s^d Thomas Greens Paying as a fore s^d to John Neales

---

Att An orphants Court held Att Chester the second Day of the eight month 1694

Counsellor George fforman President

Jeremiah Collett
Thomas Smyth } Justices Present

Joseph Wood Sherif
John Childe Clarke

Thomas Browne was Called to Answer ffor Detayning A Dept of the orphants of Joseph Powell And he promises to pay

It by the 25th Day of the tenth month next Ensueing. John Maddock and Henery Swift And Robert Nailor and William Simson they being All summoned to Appeare Att this orphants Court ffor Detayning the orphants mony: of the said Joseph Powell And they Doe All of them promise to pay it At or before the 25 Day of the 10th month next to Justice Collett whom this Court Dos Appoynt to Receve It.

Humphry Jonson & John Beals Appeared Att this orphants Court for to have the thirds belonging to his wife from the Estate of Lawrance Routh Deceased And the order of Court Is that shee shall have It Allowed. And the said Humphry Johnson Dos oblige himselfe to have the orphants of Laurance Routh to be Taugh to Read and Right

The Court orders that John Baldwin & William Brown Doe Give security to the orphants Court In the sum of Two hundred and ffivety Pounds

---

Att A Court of Common Please held Att Chester by AJornment the second Day of the Eight month 1694

Counsellor George fforman President
Jeremiah Collett
Jonathan Hayes } Justices Present
Thomas Smyth
Joseph Wood sheriff
John Childe Clarke

FFRANCIS CHADSEY Pl.t Against the Cause was Called And JOHN NEALS Defendant the plantif Appeared And the Defendant was Called three times and did not Apeare this being the second Court Its continued.

JOHN BEALS Pl'f Against the Cause was Called JOSEPH RICHARDS Junior Defendat and the plantif and Defendant Apeared and Joyne Isue: the Decleration was Red and the Defendants plea was to have the plantif prove his Tytle to his land and the Plantifs Patern was Red and Aproved of to be lawfull and good: Edward Carter was Called ffor an Evidence for the plantif and being Attested Deposeth that

John Beals and Joseph Richards had A Diferance between them About their fences and that William Brown and the Deponant went to see it and Did see that Joseph Richards had fenced up to John Beals fence.

William Brown being Attested for the pl^t: Deposeth that he went to see Joseph ffence how he had Joyned his fence to John Beals and that the said Joseph Did seeme to be very ffaier and said that he would Remove it In three weeks Time and that he would make good one halfe of the ffence and that the Plantifs Answer was that he would not yeld to It unles wrightings weare Drawen betwixt them.

The names of the Petty Juery

Bartholomew Coppock	Joseph Cookson
James Hendrixson	John Baldwin
John Smyth	Joseph Cloud
Ralph Dralcutt	Daniell Broom
John Neales	William Collett
Robert Pennell	ffrances Chadsey

the verditt of the Juery is this 2 of 8th month 1694 Wee of the Juery find for the Plantf thirty shillings Damage with Cost of suite Bartholomew Coppock fforeman

Judgment Is Given on the verditt only the plantife omiting the thirty shillings Damage which he did one the Account that he will move his fence and that they may live loveingly together for the future.

Joseph Wood High Sherif Past A Deed to Counselor fforman ffor Twenty five yards of land that was part of George Androsis land ffronting to Delwere River In Chichester Town next to Samuell Rowlands land and soe Runing the same Breadth Along the said Rowlands line the Deed bearcing Date the 24 Day of ye 7th month 1694 the which said land was Taken by an excecution that the fforesaid Counsellor George fforman had Against the Estate of George Andros And was levied thereon and Appraised by Twelve men of the neighborhood whose names are As followeth

Edward Bezer: Ephraim Jackson: Abraham Beaks: William Hues: James Browne: John Eyr: Phillip Roman: John Neall: Rodger Jackson: William Clayton: George Grist: Joseph Cloud Apraised the 26th Day of June 1694. Apraised at the sum of fourteen Pounds

Joseph Wood As High sherif of the County Past a Deed to Joseph Cloud ffor A plantation that was fformerly Robert Meekees which was taken by Excecution And Apraised by Twelve men one the second day of August 1693 Att ffourteen Pounds and being Exposed to seale afterwards non biding more then the s^d Joseph Cloud he became purcheser: the Deed bearing Date the 24 of September 1694

Att A Court of Quarter sessions held Att Chester ffor the County of Chester held the 11th Day of the tenth month 1694

Counsellor George fforman President

Jasper yeates
Jeremiah Collett
Jonathan Hayes
Thomas Smyth
} Justices present

Joseph Wood sheriff
John Childe Clarke

The Constables weare Called And Appeared save those that were not well

The Grand Inquest was Called and Appeared & brought In theyr presentments Consarning The Roade wayes: wee of the Grand Inquest ffor the County of Chester the 11th Day of the 10th month 1694 Doe present the want of A Bridle Roade between Chichester Creeke and Chester Creek: Phillip Roman fforeman. the order of Court is that the Grand Inquest forthwith lay it oute In the most Conveniants place they Can ffind

Wee The Grand Inquest being the Representatives of this County Doe Desier of this bench An Account Consarning the Taxes Reised sence you came into commision how It is Disbursted and how much the Remaynder is: Philip Roman fforeman

The Returne off A Roade laid oute by the Grand inquest ye 11th of the 10th month 1694. Between Radnor meeting house and the scoolekill ffoord begining Att the meeteing house and ffrom thence over A Runn in John Roberts land and soe A long by a line over the said John Roberts Land and from Thence by A lyne over John Morgans land ffrom Thence over A swamp in William Davis land ffrom Thence over the widdow Thomasis land ffrom Thence over William Thomasis land by his house & ffrom Thence over Edward Griffes land throw part of his Inclosier heding the swampe ffrom Thence over Thomas Davisis land A longe Above his house under the hanging of the hill and soe to the said ffoord of the scoole kill.

Allsoe We of the Grand Inquest laid oute A nother Roade between John Longworthyes house and A Roade fformerly laid oute between Chester and Radnor meeting house begining Att John Longworthys house Att A marked white oake and ffrom thence A long over David Evans land by his house ffrom Thence over Richard Cooks & John loids land ffrom Thence over William Davis land ffrom Thence over Even ollivers Land and from Thence over the widdow Jeane Moors land & ffrom Thence over Samuell Miles land and part of Richard Miles land ffrom Thence over part of Griffith Miles land and soe to Chester Roade

wee the Grand Inquest ffor the County of Chester hath perrused the Accounts for the building of the Prison and ffinding them ffaier steated allsoe ffinding the County in Arears to the Tresurer for want of the ould levies Alsoe wee ffinding A nesesity of the Raiseing of mony ffor the Relife of the poore and the ffinishing of the Prison and the Defraying of the ould Depts and ffor the wolves heads (viz) one penny pr pound of All the Reall and personall Esteats and six shillings pr hed one All ffreemen. The order off the Court is that It be fforthwith Gathered

wee of the Grand Inquest ffor the County of Chester Doe present the non payment of the ould Arears of the ould leavies fformerly levied. Philip Roman fforeman

Wee off the Grand Inquest ffind noe Cause of Presentment

against Nathaniell Tucker And Johannis Urin. Phillip Roman fforeman

Josiah Taylor Being Presented the last Court of quarter sesions was summoned To Apeare Att this Court and Daniell Williamsons wife Alsoe Josiah Taylor was Called And Appeared and the woman lying in he is ordered to Apper the next Court of quarter sesions

The Court orders that Goden Walter pay 10 shillings unto BenJamin Mendinghall of Concord ffor his Trouble and Time In serving the ofice of a Constable which was Goden Walters plese to Doe

---

Att A Court of Common Please Held Att Chester for the County off Chester the 12th Day of December 94

Mr George fforman President
Jeremiah Collett
Jonathan Hayes } Justices Present
Thomas Smyth

Joseph Wood Sherife
John Childe Clarke

OWEN MACK DANIELL Plantive Against
DAVID ROBERTS   Defendat
In an accton of Dept

The Cause was Called the plantif and Defendant Apeared
The Decleration was Red and they Joyne Issue
The Petty Juery was Called And Attested.

The names of the Juery Walter Martin: Thomas Marcy: Jacob Chandler: Nathaniel Richards: Bartholomew Coppocke: Thomas Minshall: James Swaford: Ralph Dracut: Walter ffossett: John Beals: John Worolo: Humphry Johnson: The verditt of the Juery Is ye 12th of December 94 wee Jurors Give the verd^t ffor The Defendant with Cost of shuite and Two pence Damage. Walter Martin fforeman. Judment Granted According to verditt

FFRANCES CHADSEY Plantive Against
JOHN NEALS   Defendant
In An accon: of Dept

this being the fourth Court its Continued tell next Court

JONATHAN HAYES Plantive Against }
JAMES WHEELER Deffendant:
In An Accion of Dept

The Cause was Called and the Plantive Appeared and the Defendant Appeared not And being Run Away And the plantive Proveing his Dept by four evidences that It was A Just Dept Due to him from the Defendant the Court Gives Judgment ffor the same being the sum of Ten pounds Eighteen shillings and six pence with Cost of sute to be paid to the Plantive

The ffour Evidences that were Attested for the proveing of the Above Dept Theyr names are as followeth Thomas sidebotom: Peter Worrell the yonger And Thomas Masey and Josiah Taylor who were the evidences to the bond

WILLIAM TALLE Plantive Against
DANIELL LINSYE Defendant
in An acction of A Tytle of land.

The Cause was Called and the plantive Appeared And the Defendant being sick his wife Appeared soe the accon Is Continued tell next Court.

John Hodgskins Attorney ffor Walter ffosett and Thomas varnon and Randell vernon who were Attorneys ffor ffrances Pusye In England: Pases A Deed unto Calep Pusye ffor 250 Accers lying In Chester County the Deed bearing Date the 11th Day of the Tenth month 1694.

It being formerly John Pusyes land.

William Swaford Pases A Deed To Randell Mallin ffor A plantation that lyes In upper providence for 50 Accers of land with all the Improvements on it The Deed beareing Date the 11th Day of the 10th month 1694

A Deed Pased by David loyd Attorney ffor Samuell Carpenter and Richard Hayes To William Roe ffor one hundred Accers of land with all the Improvements the land lying in the Township of haverford the Deed beareing Date the sixth Day of the sixth month 1694

Samuell Levis Appeared Att the Complaint of the sherif for the Refusall of Delivering the horse Bridle and sadle that was John Greens which was for the use of the County the Court ordered that he should Pay four pounds for the Countys use

Randell mallin and Joseph Edge Pased A Deed to Peter Tregoe ffor ffivety Accrs of land lying In Middltowne the Deed Bearing Date the 11th Day of the Tenth month 1694.

John Hodgskins Attorney ffor David Merrideth and his wife Mary Passes A Deed unto David loyd Attorney ffor Thomas Joans of upper Providence for one hundred and ffivety Accres of land lying in upper providence the Deed beareing Date the 31st of the ffifth month 1694

Joseph Wood Attorney ffor Edward Hundloke of Burlington Pases A deed to Jonathan Hayes Attorney ffor James Standfield ffor 500 accres of land lying in Chester County neare Darby Creek the Deed bearing Date the 1st Day of November 1694

The Court orders John Hendrixson to be supervisor off the Roade wayes ffor the Township off Ridley ffor this yeare And Alsoe orders the supervisor of the Township of Midletown To make the Roade wayes good In that Township forthwith

This Court orders that the 3 Appraisors of the County (viz) Caleb Pusye & Thomas varnon and Robert varnon be ffind fourty shillings for Refusing to Execcute theyr office of Appraisors being Attested the appraisors for this County

---

Att An orphants Court held Att Chester ffor the County of Chester the ffifth Day off Martch 1694/5 } Counsellor fforman Jeremiah Collett Thomas Smyth } Justices Present

William Brown & John Baldwin was Called and Appeared to Answer the Complaint off: John Dutton Edward Duton and Thomas Dutton:

The Court Allowed that John Neald & Mary his wife Att the Request of the orphans be Gardiens ffor the Above named

Complayna^{ts} And Doe Alsoe Allow Thomas Cartwright & Joell Baly: as security ffor John Neald And Mary his wife to the vallu of Two hundred and ffivety Pounds. And Its alsoe ordered the ould Gardiens Accounts be Paid and Cleared before us Att the Court by the new ones:

Thomas Cartwright and Joell Baly have Also Promised before the Court to be come bound ffor the Indemnifieng of John Beals & Robert Carter ffor the seaven bonds Given To Thomas Green ffor the value of one hundred and ffive pounds to be paid Att seven Payments

---

Att A Court off Quarter ssons: held Att Chester ffor the County off Chester the 12th Day off March 1694/5

Counsellor fforman: President
Jasper yeats
Jeremia Collett Justices
Jonathan Hayes Present
Thomas Smyth

Joseph Wood sheriff
John Childe Clarke

After Proclimation made The Constables were Called over ffor to bring In theyr Returns & they Return^d All was well and there were new ones Chosen for to serve for this next yeare: John Pennick Constable ffor the Township off Beathell Richard Barnard Constable for Aishtown: William Vestall of Burmingham: John Boyeter off Middelltowne: John worrola off Edgment: Joseph Edge: of Springfield: Daniell Broome of marpoole: of Darby William fflower off Chichester: moris Lewellin of Haverford Allixander Edwards of Radnor Robert Scothorn In the Room of Josiah ferne

Josiah Taylor and Mary Williamson was Called to Answer the presentment of the Grand Juery ffor being to ffamilier each with other: they appeare and will Travis it

David Loyd their maJesties Attorny: In that Case

The Petty Juery was Called and attested: Thomas Varnon John Worrolaw: Joseph Baker: Robert Barber: Randell mallin: Robert Varnon William Mallin: James Swafoord: John Beales: Thomas Green: Thomas minshall: Robert Carter:

The verditt of the Petty Juery is: wee off the Petty Juery ffinds Josiah Taylor & Mary William: Guilty of the presentment as they stand Presented: Tho: Varnon foreman, the 12th of ye 1 month 1694/5 Judgment was Given one the verditt

The order off the Court is that Josiah Taylor shall pay All Charges that Doth acrue on both and to Give In good security for his Good Behavior for Twelve months

ye 12th Day of ye 1: month 1694/5

Wee off the Grand Inquest ffor the County off Chester Doe present the want off a bridell Roade Betweene the broade Roade neare James Brown's house in Chichester and Chichester Creeke and from thence to Chester Creeke. The Court orders that it be fforthwith layd oute: wee doe Allsoe Present the want of A Bridge over Chester Creek neare to the mill. wee Allsoe present the want of a Roade from the meetting house In havorfoord To Chester Roade throw the Township of marpoole: Phillip Roman fforeman

Wee the Grand Inquest ffor the County off Chester Doe Present Henery hollingsworth ffor Infringing in setting his house Apon Part of the landing belonging to Chester which the former Grand Juery layd oute: Phillip Roman foreman:

Whereas there was A white man named Thomas Spencer and A Black man named Ned that was taken up for Run Aways and was brought before Counsellor forman and by him Commited to the sherif. And Richard Hollwell being Administrator to the Estate of John Ball Deceased of the County off New Castell came and Demanded the two persons being belonging to the Estate of John Ball: the Court ffinding them belonging too the said Estate ordered the sherif to Deliver the said sarvants to ye said hollwell he Defraying the Charges that was Due

Henery Hollingsworth was Called to Answer the presentment of the grand Inquest ffor the setting of his house one the landing: And David loyd Attorney for the sd Henery Hollingsworth Appeared And Pleaded not Guilty in manner and forme And Craved A Referance to the Governour and Counsell:

And the Court granted And Joseph Wood High sherif Is Appoynted to Appeare to Represent the County by the order of Court before the Governour and Counsell

A Deed Past ffrom Daniell Humphry Attorney for William kelly for Two hundred and Twenty Acres of land lying In havorfoord: unto Humphry Ellis the Deed beareing Date the second Day of the tenth month 1694.

Humphry Ellis Past A Deed to Daniell Humphry for twenty Acres and three quarters of land lying In Darby Township the Deed beareing Date the Eight Day of the ninth month 1694.

Att A Court off Common Pleass held Att Chester ffor the County off Chester the 14th Day of March 1694

Counsellor fforman: President
Jasper Yeates
Jeremiah Collett Justices,
Jonathan Hayes   Present
Thomas Smyth

Joseph Wood: sheriff
John Childe: Clarke

JOHN BUZBY: Pl^t: Against: ISRAEL TAYLOR: Defendant

JOSEPH TAYLOR: Plt: Against: ISARELL TAYLOR: Defendant

FFRANCIS CHADSEY Plt Against JOHN NEALS Defendant In Acco: of Dept } the Plantive and Defendant were Called And the Pltv. Appeared; but the Defend Appeared not and this being the fourth Court: the Court granted Judgment by Defalt: for the sum of three pounds with Cost of shuite

JOHN DONALLSON Plt Against PETER And ANN BAYNTON Deft In Accion of Dept } the Plantive shues the Defendants as Exceecutors of the last will & testement of off James Sanderlins Deceased: and shues for the Estate of Alixander Crager not yet Administred unto: David loyd Appeared for the Defendants and Counsellor fforman and Justices Yeats came of the bench: and Grifeth Joans Appeared for the Plantive and the Decleration was Red and they Joyn Issue: the Juery were Impaneld the same Juery as before: the Plantive Declores for one hundred and sixty

Pounds ten shillings and three pence that was Due from Alixander Craker: the Atorny David loyds Ple was not Guilty In manner and forme as Decleared Against.

The Petty Juery Brought in theyr verdit (viz) wee off the Petty Juery Doe ffind for the Defendant with Cost off suite and Twelve pence damage: Tho: varnon foreman

Judgment Granted on the vardit. The Plantive ffinding himselfe Agreevd Craves An Apeale the Court Grants it he paying All Charges thats Due According to law:

A Deed Past ffrom William Gabartis to Andrew swanson boone ffor Twenty one acres and halfe of land lying In Darby Township the Deed beareing Date the second Day of December 1694

A Deed Past by Henery Lewis to John Lewis and others ffor one hundred acres of land lying lying in the weltch Tract: the Deed beareing Date the 8th day of ye first month 1694

John Blunston Attorny ffor Edward Person Past a Deed to John Beathell ffor one hundred Acres of land lying In Darby the Deed beareing Date the first of ye 4th month 1694

A Deed Past by m^r Jasper yeats Attorny ffor Joseph Willcox and John Moore as Excecutors of the Estate of Charles Pickering: ffor four Thousand Eight hundred and seventy Eight Acres of land unto m^r Robert Turner and for the Company within mentioned The Deed beareing Date the thirtieth Day off Jenuary 1604.

A nother Deed Past by m^r Jasper yeats Attorny ffor Phillip James ffor Cartaine Tracts off land unto m^r Robert Turner and Company the Deed bereing Date the 4 Day of martch 1694.

A nother Deed Past by m^r Jasper yeats Attorny ffor Nicholes Pearce ffor Cartaine Tracts off land unto m^r Robert Turner and Company as in the Deed mentioned the Deed Beareing Date the fourth Day of Martch 1694.

A Deed Past ffrom John Ball to Lewis David ffor one hundred Acres of land lying in havorfoord the Deed Beareing Date the Twelft Day of Martch 1694.

A Deed Past by Henery Hollingsworth Attorny ffor William Roe: to George Stroud Attorny ffor Thomas Moore and William Vestell: ffor one hundred Acres of land lying in Concord the Deed Bearing Date the 12th Day off Martch 1694:

A Deed Past by David loyd Attorny ffor Henery Lewis To Richard Hayes: ffor fivety Acres off Land lying in havorffoord the Deed beareing Date the 12th of martch 1694.

A Deed off Gift Past ffrom Mounce Petterson to his son Peter Petterson ffor his houses And lands ffor the Considerations mentioned In the Deed: bereing Date the 14th Day of Martch 1694/5.

A Deed Past ffrom Counsellor fforman Attorny ffor James Craft: To Nathaniell Richards And Joell Baly ffor ffivety Acres of land lying in the Township of middelltowne the Deed Beareing Date the 7th of the seventh month 1688.

Isarell Taylor Came Into Court and Confest Judgment on ffour bonds to pay with the lawfull Interest and All Charges: where apon excecution was Referd tell the next Court of Common pleas to be held for the County:

A Deed Past by Robert Barber Attorny ffor John Ball Past to Ralph Lewis off havorfoord ffor one hundred Acres of land lying in havorfoord beareing Date the 12th of March 1694/5.

A Deed Past by John Neald and Mary his wife unto John Worrell: A Deed of mortgage for ffive hundred acrs of land with all the Improvements thereon: lying In the Township off Aishtowne: ffor one hundred and ffive pounds: the Deed bereing Date the 12th Day of March 1694

A Deed Past by Joseph Wood Attorny ffor Richard Tucker unto William Gabitas ffor thirty Acres off land lying in Darby the Deed beareing Date 12th Day of the sixth month 86.

A Deed Past by John Neald to Joell Bayly ffor ffivety Acres of land lying In the Township off Aishtown the Deed beareing Date the first Day of Martch 1694/5.

A Deed off mortgage Past ffrom Joell bayly unto John Nealds and his wife Mary for the Payment off ffive pounds A yeare Dureing the naturell lifes of the said John Neald and

Mary his wife and when the said John Nealds Dies then two parts of the ffive pounds is no more to be paid and If that his wife Dies then theres the third Part to sease to be paid as the Deed more Att large makes A peare the Deed Is for both the plantations of the said Joell baylye: bereing Date the second martch 1694/5

Rogger Smyth Past A Deed unto Humphry Johnson ffor ffivety Acres of land with All the Improvements there on lying and being In the Township of Chichester.

John Childe Attorney ffor Daniell Linsy Past A Deed unto William Talle succesor of John Johnson ffor the halfe of one hundred and ffivety acres of land lying and being In the Township of Chichester being sould by the said Linsy to John Johnson A boute seventeene years Agoe never tell now made over by A Deed bering Date ye 12th of martch 1694/5.

The sheriff made A Returne of the Apraisement off the goods of James Wheeler Takeng by Excecution Att the suite of Jonathan Hayes: Apraised by the Apraisors of the County we whose hands and seals are hereunto set being A praisors for this County have this Day Apraised severall goods and Chattls of the Estate of James Wheeler to the vallue of thirteen pounds eleven shillings and (viz) six swine a grind stone Att Two pounds ffiveteen shillings four Chaires and a Cart Att eighteen shillings one Plow & Irons Att one Pound: A Black horse and A heifer Att ffive pounds Ten shillings wheate oates and A Table Att one pound eight shillings A gray horse Att Two pounds In all A mounting to the sum Above mentioned: as wittnes our hands this thirtieth Day of December Annoqu Dom: 1694: Thomas vernon: & Robert varnon:

Ordered by the Court appon the motion oft Robert Turner Esqr: that whereas a Certaine writt off ffiery ffacas was awarded Att A Court held ffor the said County the 13th Day of September in the yeare 1693: ffor the leveing of a Cartaine Judgment then obtained by the said Robert Turner Against the Estate off Ralph and Dorrithy ffretwell ffor the sum of ffive hundred and forty pounds seven shillings and nine pence with ffive pounds Cost sustained: Directed to the sheriff off the s^d County: and when Demanded to make Returne to s^d Court to signifie how he hath excecuted ye same: there a pon Doth aver to this Court that the Inquision by him Taken and excecuted & levied Returne cannot make ffor that the same is Casually Lost and whereas a True Coppy off the Inquision Taken by the sheriff is made Appeare to this Court Attested by the hand of the Clarke off this Court: That the sheriff Cause and Requier the Juery to the Inquision to be taken According to the Coppy A fforesaid an Inquision under their hands and seals to Returne to this Court to be held for this County the 12th Day of June next to be enterd a pon Record.

There was seaven bonds Acknowledged by John Neald: Thomas Cartwright: & Joell baily unto Thomas Green ffor the sum of one hundred and ffive Pounds to be Paid ffiveteene Pounds a yeare the Twenty sixth Day of Martch yearly the first bond to Paid the 26th Day off martch in the yeare one thousand six hundred and ninty six and so yearely tell the last be Paid which will be compleated In the yeare on Thousand seven hundred and Two: every bond under the Pennalty of Thirty Pounds If not paid According two the time speatified to the said Thomas green or his orders by the a bove bound John neeld or Thomas Cartwright or Joell baily by they or theyr heiers Exceecutors admr^s.

The ffore mentioned Isarell Taylors Confession of Judgment on the four bonds to John Busbie and Joseph Taylor was on the Condition of theyr makeing over theyr parts one and to the Island of Tinnicum both the said John Busbie and Joseph Taylor to make over unto the s^d Isarell Taylor and his heirs All their parts and sheres In and to the foresaid Island Att the next County Court to be holden Att Chester ffor the County of Chester:

The Court AJorns to the next Day after the Riseing of ye Quarter ssons: held ye 11th day 4th month next:

Att A Court held Att Chester ffor The County of Chester the 11th Day of the ffourth month 1695 by A Jornment held the 12th Day:

M'r George fforman President
Jasper yeates ⎫
John Blunstone ⎬ Justices
Jonathan Hayes ⎪ present
Samuell Levis ⎭

Joseph Wood sheriff
John Childe Clarke

After silence Comanded In theyr maJesties names The Justices Commission was Read: And the A bove said Appered And the Grand Inquest was Called And Appeard: And the Constables were Called over and Appeard & Robert Barber was Attested Constable ffor the Towneship cf Chester In the Roome of Henery Hollingsworth.

George Pearse Constable of Thornbury, Joseph Edwards for Concord: John Stedman Constable ffor Rydlye Joseph Taylor Constable for upper Providence William Swaford for neither providence:

Capt: James Letort was Called to Answer the Presentment the Grand Inquest ffor Takeing up and marking to Coults and A mare of Daniell Harrys: And he pleaded not Guilty And: whereon the Juery weare Impaneled And Attested: whose names Are as ffolloweth John Steedman: Thomas Pearson: Peter wood: ffrancis Yarnell Petter lister Henery Hastings Thomas Bright: ffrancis Baldwin Thomas Baldwin William Tally James Swaford George Mayris:

The said Daniell Hary being Attested: Deposeth that there was A Taylor as went up To worke Att James letort and there Did see three mares of mine and to yong ones weare marked with letorts Brand marke with l. t and that they weare Tyed with with Indian Roapes and newly marked and I heareing of this went up to his house with A nother man and when we came there wee ffound the ould mare Tyed up to a bear In A oute house and after we went into the house and the s'd letort was not at home but his sarvant and they enquiered how that mare Came Tyed there & he would make no answer And they Enquierd ffor the to yong ons but Could not get any knowledge and then they went up and Downe and met with some Indians and they tould us where they weare & we mett with them & they two weare both Brand marked newly with the a foresaid brand marke

fflorance Imanuell being Attested Deposeth that when Daniell Hary came to him to have him the Deponant to goe Along with him because that I Could speake theyr languige I went A long with him and when we came we found the ould mare tyed with a Rope by the neck And we Enquiered ffor the Coults and the sarvant Denied them and then I went back and milked the mare and shewed the sarvant the milke and could tell by that that the Coult had sucked and then we went to the Indians and enquierd of them and they tould us wheare they weare and we brought them there & shewed them that they weare newly marked and wee went Againe on the morrow and then he Dennyed us haveing the mare and would A layd violent hands on me but I went And Cut the Rope that the mare was tyed with and tooke her Away and as wee went A longe wee mett with letort & his wife and she said them horses weare theyrs & whereapon I said to her it was not trew & I spoke to the other man to stay for I would speake with them & tould them that we would not keepe the horses but would put them In an officers hands and shee said It was best soe to Doe

the verdit off the Juery is wee of the petty Juery ffind James Letort Guilty According As he stands Presented: ffrances Yarnell fforeman.

The said James letort produseing A paper from the Governour william markham Esqr That he had been with the said Daniell Hary before him & y^t It was made up. The Court orders that the said letort pay all Charges and be Cleared Doeing soe noe more

Peter Lester Chosen supervisor ffor the Towneship of Springfild ffor this yeare.

Jacobus Hendrixson was Chosen supervisor ffor the Township of Chester for this year

David James being sarvant to William Jenkin & haveing served Eight years to him And Asigns the Court orders Att the sarvants pettion that the said William Jenkins shall pay to the said sarvant the Custome of the Country & Two pound Ten shillings In lue of Apparell. the Grand Juery Brings theyr presentment as ffolloweth ye 12th of ye 4th month 1695 we off Grand Inquest for the County of Chester presents hance uren of Darby for shouting a mare of Morton Mortonson of ye same Township the 10th Day of this Instant: ordered y^t he be sommo^d to answer it ye next County Court

The 12th day of the 4th month 1695 wee the Grand Inquest Doe Alsoe present Henry Barns ffor A buseing and strikeing Henry Hollingsworth in the exceeuting of the office of A Constable A pon the 8th Day of the 3^d month 1695: The said Henry Barns was Called and Appeared and And submits himselfe to the bentch: and the Court orders that the said Barns shall pay the Charges thats Due and behave himselfe well ffor the ffuture and soe be Discharged:

wee the Grand inquest Doe Alsoe present Patrick kelly and Edward Downing ffor Breach of the kings Peace to the sheding of Blood the seventh Day of the 3^d month 1695. They weare Called and Appeared and submits themselfs to the bentch and the order of Court is that they pay what Charges thers Due and behave themselfs peacablely for the ffuture and be Dischar^d:

The 12th Day of the 4th month 1695: Wee the grand Inquest ffor the County of Chester Doe Present Thomas Howell and Sarah his wife ffor A buseing and scandilesing Henry Hollingsworth and his ffamily In his house and the street a boute the 8th or 9th Day of ye 3 month 1695: Thomas Howell and sarah his wife Appeared to Answer the presentment They pleaded not Guilty: but afterwards Relinquishing their plea and submited themselfs wholy to the Judgment of the bentch: whereapon the Justices haveing hard all the Allegations of the said parties and the said Thomas Howell and Sarah his wife haveing Acknowledged In oppen Court that the Abuse &

scandellous expresions which they uttered Against Henry Hollingsworth & his ffamily weare the effects of theyr Passion and Grounded only Apon Reports ffurther Declearcing that they the said Thomas Howell and sarah his wife never knew any such thing by the said Henry Hollingsworth nor his ffamily as they scandellized them with nor Did nor Doe they Belive the said Report to be True Thereffore Its ordered by the Court that the said Acknowledgment & Recantation of the said Thomas and Sarah Howell be A ffixt or sett upon the Court house Doore of this County and that Paying the Charges thats Due they be Discharged of this Presentment

wee off the Grand Inquest ffor the County of Chester Doe present William ffreeman mason A workeman in this Towne of Chester ffor A Buseing and strikeing of Thomas Howell to the Breach of the kings Peace A boute the begining of this 4th month 1695.

the said William ffreeman was Called to Answer the presentment And he Appeard and Confest himselfe Guilty of the said presentment & submits himselfe to the bentch the Court ordered that the said ffreeman Behave himselfe well towards all the kings leige peopele ffor the ffuture and pay the Charges thats Due and be Discharged

A Deed Past by Joseph Wood Attorney ffor Oliver Roberts ffor three hundred Acres of land unto David Phillips the Deed beareing Date the 16 Day of June 1692. The land lying and being In newtowne

A Deed Past by William Brainton to Hue Harry and his wife ffor one hundred and ffivety acres of land the land lying and being In the Towneship of Burningham. The Deed beareing Date the 11th Day of June 1695.

Another Deed Acknowledged by William Brainton to John Bennett ffor one hundred Acres of land lying and being In the Towneship of Burningham the Deed beareing Date the 11th Day of June 1695:

Another Deed Acknowledged by William Brainton ffor one hundred and ffivety acrs of land being In to Tracts the land lying in Burningham the Deed beareing Date the Eleventh Day of June 1695

Daniell Humphry Acknowledged A Deed to David Morris ffor three hundred & thirty Acres of land lying In the Township of marpoole the Deed Beareing Date the tenth Day of June 1695

James James Acknowledged A Deed To Thomas John Evan ffor ffivety acres of Land lying In the Township of Radnor the Deed beareing Date ye 8th Day of June 1695

A Deed Acknowledged by Richard Barnard to Joseph Jarvis ffor a plantation being Two hundred Acres of land and all Improvements lying ad being In Middletowne the Deed Beareing Date the Eleventh Day of June 1695

George Pearse Acknowledged A Deed to William ffisher Attorny ffor Elizebeth Andros ffor one hundred and ffivety Acres of land lying In the Township of thornbury the Deed beareing Date the Eleventh Day of June 1695

Robert Barber Attorny ffor Thomas Thomson of Salem and ffor ffrances Worlye of this County Acknowledged A Deed To Charles Brooks ffor ffiveteen hundred Acres of land lying and being In the Township of West Towne the Deed bereing Date ye 11 Day of June 1695

Charles Brooks Pases the same Deed with the Asignement on the back side and Alsoe Another Deed ffor the same ffiveteen hundred Acres of land To Ralph Dracott the Deed Bearcing Date the 12th Day of June 1695: the land being Purchesed by Tho Brasy of the Propriator William Penn:

John Bevan Acknowledged A Deed to Jonathan Hayes ffor Two hundred and seventy ffive Acres of land lying and being in the Township of Marpoole the Deed beareing Date the 12th Day of the ffirst month 1694/5

Joell Baylee In the behalfe of Daniell Baylee Acknowledged A Deed ffor on hundred and Twenty ffive Acres of land to John Ridlye with meadow belonging to It the land & meadow lying In the Township of west Towne the Deed bereing Date ye 6 day of June 1695

Robert Wade and his wife lydia Acknowledged A Deed to Henery Hollingsworth for Twenty ffoote of land ffronting Chester streete over Against the Court house and soe Downe to the Creeke Called now [or new?] Chester Creeke: the Deed bearing Date ye 11th Day of ye 4th month 95

Joshua Hastings Acknowledged A Deed ffor one hundred Acres of land to John Sharply the land lying In the Township of Neither Providence the Deed beareing Date the Eleventh Day of June 1695:

Edward Beazer Acknowledged A Deed to George Grist ffor on hundred Acres of land lying and being in the Township of Beathell the Deed bereing Date the 11th Day of June 1695

Andros Johnson late of Amos land Acknowledged A Deed to Morton Mortonson of the same ffor Two hundred and seventy ffive acres of land lying and being In the Township of Ridly the Deed beareing Date the 12th Day of the first month 1694/5

Another Deed Acknowledged by Andros Johnson to John orchard ffor one hundred and thirty and scaven Acres of land lying In the Township of Ridlye the Deed beareing Date the the 10th Day of the fourth month 1695:

Joseph Edge Acknowledged A Deed to George James ffor ffivety Acres of land lying and being In the Township of Springfield the Deed beareing Date the sixt day of the second month 1695:

Joseph Wood Acknowledged A Deed to John Beathell ffor nine Acres of land lying in the Township of Darby the Deed Beareing Date the seventh Day of June 1695

John Blunstone Acknowledged A Deed to Joseph Wood ffor one hundred and Twenty Acres of land lying and being In Darby the Deed beareing Date ye Twenty ninth of May 1695

John Elliott Acknowledged A Deed to Joseph Wood ffor on hundred Acres of land lying in Darby the Deed beareing Date the seventh Day of June 1695

Joseph Wood Acknowledged A Deed to John Elliot ffor six hundred and ninety Acres of land lying in East Towne the Deed beareing Date ye 29th Day of May 1695:

John Elliott Acknowledged A Deed to Joseph Wood ffor ffivety Acres of land lying In the Township of Darbye the Deed beareing Date the ffifth Day of June 1695:

John Childe Attorney ffor William Huews and John Bezer Acknowledged Two Deeds to Phillip Roman for Two Tracts of land lying In the Township of Chichester the one Deed for ffiveteen Acres of land the other Deed ffor ffourteen Acres In one parsell or Tract. Alsoe A nother Tract of three Acres In the same Deed And Alsoe A nother Tract or parsell of land ffor A landing to Chichester Creeke begining by Thomas Ushers Gardien fence And soe Downe by the Cripells to A marsh that was fformerly Henry Raynolds marsh. The Deeds bearing Date the Tenth Day of June 1695:

John Bezer Attorny ffor His sister ffraneis Bezer Acknowledged A Deed to Phillip Roman ffor fforty Two Acres of land lying In the Township of Chichester the Deed beareing Date the second Day of the ninth month 1694

Att the motion of Isarell Taylor Consaring his ffore said Confession of Judgment upon those ffour bonds It is ordered by this Court that excecution be Defered untill John Buzby and Joseph Taylor make over theyr parts of Tinicum Island by A Deed Acknowledged In Court the same as Also that Interest upon those bonds Cease ffrom this Day untill the Deeds be Acomplished.

The Coppy of what came to the Justices from Philidelphia ye 8th of June 1695:

These are to Certifie the Justices of the peace for the County of Chester: that this Day came before me Robert Turner Isarell Taylor Joseph Taylor John Busbye in order to signe and seale writings Consarning Tinicum Island Robert Turner haveing all things Ready appertaining to the Conveying of the A foresaid Island to the said Isarell Taylor Joseph Taylor John Busby the two last (viz) Joseph Taylor and John Busby not procuring security according to promise To Robert Turner there could be nothing Done as towards the premises as alsoe Israell Taylor tendred to the aforesaid Busby and Joseph Taylor Three parcells of mony being the Consideration mony for their shears in Tinicum Island but for the a foresaid persons want of security nothing could be Done in relation to that Affaire to the truth of which I am A wittnes: Patrick Robinson.

I the subscriber was there present when the mony was Tendered as a bove said as wittnes John Redman sen^r:

Attested before me one of their maJesties Justices of the peace this 10th Day of June 1695 John ffarmer

Robert Wade Pettitioned to the Governour and Counsell Att Philadelphia ye 25th of May 1695

Att A Councell held Att Philidelphia 25th May 1695 William Markham, Esqr Governour

Samuell Carpenter	David Loyd	John Brinkloe
Samuell Richardson	Caleb Pusye	Richard Willson
Anthony Morris	George Marris	Griffeth Joans
Joseph Growden	John Donaldson	William Clarke
Phinius Pemberton	John Williams	Thomas Pemberton
William Biles	Richard Holliwell	Robert Clefton

Upon Reading the Pettion: with the Pappers Annext ags^t the Countie of Chester ffor the Grand Jurie of the said Countie theyr takeing away his propertie in Chester ffor A landing by virtue of the 100^d law of the province enacting that Each County Court in this province & Territories thereof shall Appoint and settle a sufficent Cart way to the most Conveniant Landing Place in theire respective Counties ffor publick use and benifitt. After A ffull Debate the Question was putt by the Governour wheither the said law Could Justifie the said Grand Jueries act and It was Carried in the negative: whereapon It was ordered by the Governour and Counsell that the said Robert wade nor his Asigns be no ffurther Troubled molested nor Disquieted in the Peaceable Possession of his propertie: Patricke Robinson Secryterie.

The Grand Inquest haveing Examined Jeremiah Colletts Accounts and ffinds them to be A True Account and ffinds him Indepted to the County the sum of Eighteen shillings and Eleven pence And the County to be Indepted unto Thomas Smyth the sum of Eight pounds nineteen shillings and four pence

The Court AJorns toe the first third Day In the 8th month next

---

Att A Court held Att Chester ffor the County of Chester the first Day of the eight month 1695

John Simcocke President
John Blunstone ⎱
Jonathan Hayes ⎰ Justices
George fforman ⎱ present
Jasper yeates ⎰

Joseph Wood sheriff
John Childe Clarke

The Constables weare Called and Appeared And Returned All well

The Grand Jury being Called and Appeared Brought In theyr presentment (viz) ye first Day of the eight month: 1695: wee the Grand Inquest for the County of Chester Doe present John Hendrixson ffor keeping of bad orders for Admiting of People of Takeing to much liquors to the Disordering of Divers persons In his owne house: by quareling and fighting: Philip Roman foreman

John Hendrixson was Called to answer the s^d presentment and Appeard and submitted himself to the bentch: The order of Court is that he sell noe more liquors for the future and be Discharged paying the Charges:

Hance Urion being presented the last Court by the Grand Inquest was Called and Appeared and submitted to the bentch ordered that he Doe soe noe more and pay the Charges And be Discharged. The Court A Jorned till To A Clocke In the Afternoone

The orphans Court was Called: the same Justices as a bove mentioned. There was A petticon of George Stroud In the behalfe of the Children of Richard Moore Deceased that the widdow of the said Richard Moore may Give in Security to the Court he Aferming the Esteat to be Appraised to neare three hundred Pounds: whereof A boute on hundred pounds In Dept: ordered by the said Court that shee Appeare Att the next orphans Court to Give security for said Esteate and Thomas Green Doe Recognise himselfe in the sum of one hundred pounds for her Appearance & y^t the Esteate be no wayes weasted in the meane time

The orphants of William Smith Deceased whose names are Mary and Elizebeth Smyth did come Into the Court and made Choyse of Anthony Morgan and their brother William Smyth for Gardiens the said Anthony Morgan Acknowledging that he have ten pounds In his hands of the two Girls mony: And William Smyth and Mary Smyth Did Acknowledge A Deed for five hundred Acres of land lying in Darby Township bearing Date the fiveteenth Day of the eight month 1692 to ye s^d Anthony Morgan.

Ree Sent Brought A boy whose name Is John Pollen and there the Court Did order y^t the said boy shall serve ye said Ree sent tell he be of the age of one and Twenty years. And the said Ree sent shall pay the said boy the sum of Twenty Pounds Att the expiration of his Time the boy being Ten years and a halfe now this Court. This orphans Court A Jorned tell the first third Day of the first month next

The County Court mett Againe According to AJornment.

The boys brought In by Maurice Trent was brought to the Court to be A Judged what time they should serve haveing no Indentures: Andrew ffraisor sarvant To Francis Baldwin A Judged to serve five years. James Johnson sarvant To Joseph Coeborn A Judged to serve five years. Henery Nickols sarvant To John Kingsman A Judged to serve Eight years. Robert fflatt A Judged To serve his master Maurice Trent Eight years. John Mackell fray A Judged to sarve his master Maurice Trent five years.

Owen Mack daniell Plantif: Against William Roberts & David Roberts & John Hopes Defendants In An Action Dept

Due on bond: John Moore Apper^d ffor the plantif: David Loyd for the Defendants: they Joyne Isue the Decleration was Red and the petty Jury was Impanield: whose names are as follows

Thomas Baldwin:	Henery Hames:
James Baylee:	Henery Hollingsworth:
Joseph Coeborn	John Holston
ffrancis Baldwin:	John Worrola:
William Talle:	Nathaniell Richards:
James Hendrixson	Philip Yarnell

the verdit: of the Jury is this 2 day of the 8th month 1695: we of the Jury Doe find for the plantif with to pence Damage
Henry Hollingsworth foreman

The Defendants thinking themselfs agreeved with the verditt they mutually both parties Agreed to pas by the verdit and to refer the whole matter to the Justices on the bentch: the said Justices Doe award David Roberts and John Hoope to pay downe to owen Mack Donall ffive pounds Att present and to Give their bonds for five pounds more to be paid six months hence and five pounds Twelve months hence and five Pounds Eighteen months hence In All Twenty pounds and Owen Mack daniell to pay All the Charges the fore named parties Giveing bonds with sufficent security

A Deed Past ffrom Ralph Dralcutt to George Williard for ffiveteen hundred acres of land lying in Wilstown the Deed beareing Date the first Day of October 95

Edward Downing being bound over to Answer Att this Court the Complaint of Elizebeth Rutter ffrancis baldwin sarvant that he did lye with her, the said Edward Downing denied And would Travis It the same Juery as A bove only James Swaford and Isack ffew In the roome of Thomas and ffrancis Baldwin that was objected against by the said Edward Downing: The verditt of the petty Juery Is as ffolloweth: wee of the petty Jury Doe ffind the prisoner Edward Downing not Guilty: Henry Hollingsworth foreman The Court orders that he be Cleared paying the Charges

Elizabeth Rutter being brought to the Court and her master ffrancis Baldwin Complained that she had Run a way and that he was Att great Charges In finding her, and what Time she was absent and for her misdemeniors the Court orders that shee shall serve her said master or his asigns the full time of one yeare and halfe after the expiration of her Indenturs After the expiration of her Indenturs If she behave herselfe well or other wise to serve halfe a yeare more which will be To years.

Samuel Noyes and henry Barns being bound over to Answer Att this Court for severall misdemeniors they weare Called and Appeared and submitted themselves to the bentch the order of Court Is that they pay all Charges and behave themselfs well for the ffuture and be Discharged.

Ordered that Execcution be Awarded Att next Court Against Isarell Taylor Att The suite of John Busbye and Joseph Taylor Apon the Judgment obtayned Against him Att the Court held the first month 1694/5 unless the said Isarell Taylor shew Cause to the Contrary In the meane time or Att the said Court

George Pecocke being bound to Appeare Att this Court to Answer what he had Don with A Girle whose name is Martha Rowell he goen with her to mary land and Apon the Attestation of George Oldfild and Richard Car that she was well in Mary land he was Discharged paying the Charges:

Dennis linch Appeareing Att this Court to Answer An Atteachment of Isarell Taylor by his goods and Chattls and the said Isarell Taylor not Appeareing and no Decleration filed the Court Grants A non suite and orders that the said linch have his Goods Delivered to him:

A Deed Past by John holston and James Swaford for one hundred Acres of land lying in Edgment to Moses Musgrave the Deed beareing Date the last Day of the seventh month 1695 And the said Moses Musgrove morgages the same Deed and land to the said John holston and James Swafard for the payment of sixty pounds

A Deed Acknowledged by Caleb Pusye to Thomas Cocbourn for A Plantation Contayning seventy five Acres of land lying and being In midletowne the Deed beareing Date the Tenth Day of the fourth month 1695

The Grand Jury Brought In their presentment: y" first Day of the eight month 95 wee the Grand Inquest for the County of Chester have perused the Accounts with the Dublycates of both the levies and finding them faire stated and alsoe the County In Arears Philip Roman fforeman:

The Grand Jury that was Sommond to Appeare Att this Court was Called And Appeard Walter Martin: John Hurlbert: Thomas Worrolaw: Henry Hastings: Humphry Johnson: William Thomas: Joseph Need: Mathias Morten: John Smyth: Thomas Cartwright: Nathaniell Newland: John Hodgskins: Morton Mortenson: George Willard: George Chandler: George Lowns: ffrancis Worlye:

Edward Dangger was Attested Geager And Packer and Culler of this County of Chester

Chester: y" 2^d of october 1695: wee the Grand Jury by the kings Authority ffinding that the County is in Dept by the accounts that the last Grand Jury presented that the County Tresurer is oute of Purse & others in the Consarns of the County Charge & that the prison is not yet finished & severall wolfs heads to pay for: we the Grand Inquest have taken it into our Consideration to lay an A seasement apon the County ffor to pay the Judges expences which is to be payd to Joseph Wood Sheriff of Chester County and what was Disburst by the said Tresurer of s^d County Consarning the building of the Prison and to ffinish the said County prison with as much expedition as may be and the said levie to be raised as followeth on All Reall and personall Esteats Att one penny pr pound and three shillings per head freemen: (viz) Every Acre of Clear^d land and being in Tillage Att one pound pr Acre and for every hundred Acres of Ruf land by the River at Ten pounds per hundred and for every hundred Acres in the woods Att five pounds per hundred: for All horsis and mares from 3 years ould & upward Att 3 pounds: for every Colt one yeare ould and upwards 20 shillings: for all Cows and oxen from 3 years ould and upwards 2£: 10ˢ: 00ᵈ: for all Cattle one yeare ould and upwards Att one pound ffor all sheep a yeare ould and upwards Att six shillings a peece ffor All meale negroes from 16 years ould and upwards to sixty Att 25 pound pr negroe for all ffemeall negroes from 16 years ould to sixty Att 20 pound per negroe: for Chester mill Att one hundred pounds,

Joseph Coeborn Att 50 pounds Darbye mill Att one hundred pounds hartfoord mill Att 20 pounds Concord Mill Att 10 pound.

Jasper Yeates for his Esteate And Calling 200 pounds
Caleb Pusye for his Esteate and Calling 100 pounds
Jeremiah Collett for his Esteate and Calling 30 pounds
Nathaniel Newlin for his Calling 20 pounds All ordinary keepers for theyr Callings 20 pounds ffor All handecrafts that follow noe plantation for Calling 3 shillings a peece subscribed by us this present Grand Inquest

---

Att A Court held Att Chester ffor The County The Tenth Day of The Tenth month and by AJornment the Eleventh and Twelft Days of yᵉ same 1695.

John Simcock President
Jasper Yeates
George fforman
John Blunstone
Jonathan Hayes
Samuell Levis
} Justices Present

Henery Hollingsworth Deputy Sheriff
John Childe Clarke

After Proclimation made & silence Commanded In his maJesties name: The Constabls were Called & Appeared: Thomas Marcy being supervisor ffor the Township of marpoole Returned by Daniell Broome: Richard Tomson and Joshua Morgan ffor not Appearing to Doe their labor one the Roade ways: The Court orders that they shall be fined According as the law Directs In that Case

The Grand Inquest was Called and Appeard Except Thomas Worrolaw being Ill Could not Appeare: Robert Barber: James Bayliss and his wife Jeane Bayliss: and James Swaford weare Attested to Give in theire Evidences to the Grand Jury of what they should Require

The Inhabitants of the Township of Radnor Presented a Petticion to this Court ffor A Roade way ffrom David Meredeths Plantation to havorffoord meeting house: sixty foote The Court orders that the Grand Jury laid oute the said Roade before the next Court.

A Deed Acknowledged by David Loyd Attorny ffor Daniel Humphris and Humphry Ellis: To David Lawrance Contayning sixty Acres and Another parsell of land Contay^g ninety Acres, It being In the weltch Tract the Deed beareing Date the thirtieth of September 1695: An Baynton and Thomas Howell and Rogger Jackson were Attested to Give in theire Evidences to the Grand Jury of what they should Require

A Deed Acknowledged by John Morgan Attorny ffor his Brother Evan Morgan To Henry Lewis of Havorfoord ffor Eighty Acres of land with Appurtenants the land lying In the said Township the Deed beareing Date the third Day of the Tenth month 1695.

A Deed Acknowledged by William Brainton Senior To John Willis and his wife hester ffor one hundred Acres of land lying in Burningham The Deed beareing Date the Tenth Day of the Tenth month 1695.

David James being sarvant to William Jenkin formerly brought his Indentures To the Court it was Red the Court Considering of them they ordered Att the Request of William Jenkin that It should Remaine till next Court to see If It Could be made up In the meane while

A Deed Acknowledged by Rees Rhyddurah To Morris Lewellin ffor Thirty Acres off Land lying In hartffoord The Deed beareing Date the Twentie sixth of 8th month 95

John Simcock senior Acknowledged A Deed To his son Jacob Simcock ffor nine hundred and fforty Acres of land lying in The Township of Ridlye the Deed Beareing Date the Tenth Day of the Tenth month 1695:

There was a boy that was brought in by Maurice Trent whose name Is John Robbinson brought To This Court to be A Judged: The Court orders that he shall serve seven years and a halfe from this Court: The said boy was ordered to serve his Time To Thomas Cartwright being his now master or his Asigns:

A Deed Acknowledged by Oliver Cope To Robert Pile ffor Two hundred and ffivety Acres of land lying in the Township of burningham The Deed beareing Date the Tenth Day of the Tenth month 1695

JOHN HINSON Plt^t: Against ⎫ In An Action of Dept:
ABRAHAM WARREN: Def^t ⎭ The Cause was Called
and the Defendant Confest Judgment that It was Due. The Court ordered that he should make sattisfaction by servitude: The said Defendant was Indepted To owen Mackdaniell: The order of the Court is that Owen mackdaniell shall have six pounds paid him by the said John Hinson And that the said Abraham warren Doe make sattisfaction to said Hinson for sum of six pounds by servitude And that the said owen mackdaniell Doe pay the Court Charges thats Due one the action between him the s^d owen and Abraham warren

JASPER YEATES Plantif: Against ⎫ The Cause being Called
ISARELL TAYLOR Defendant ⎬ And Continued Till
In An Action of Dept ⎭ next Court

GEORGE FFORMAN Plt^t Against ⎫ the Cause was Called And
ROBERT WHITE Def^t ⎬ Continued Till the next
In an Action of Dept ⎭ Court:

JOHN DONALSON Plt^t Against ⎫ The Cause was Called And
ROBERT WHITE Defendant ⎬ Continued Till next Court
In an Action of Dept ⎭

Mr MAURICE TRENT Plt^t Against ⎫ the Cause Called And
OWEN MACKDANIELL Def^t ⎬ the parties having
In an Action of Dept ⎭ Agreed with drawne

Joseph Wood sheriff Against } David loyd Attorny for
Peter yoakem Def^t } Joseph Wood Apperd and
John Moore Attorny for Def^t Apperd and Requested that
It mite be Continued till next Court Att which time the said
Defendant Is ordered to Appeare to Answer the said suite:

Robert Barber being the Attested Constable for the Township of Chester In the said County Apon his Attestation Does present: first that Edward Bezer & William ffreeman both of the said County yeoman one the Eleventh Day of the eight month last past at Chester in the County aforesaid Did make An Asalt upon him the said Robert as he was Exececuting his said office and him the said Robert they Did beate wound & evilly entreate Againsts the kings peace & Divers laws & statutes In that Case made and provided: Alsoe the said Robert Barber Does present apon his Attestation that Samuel Bishop John Garrett Allexander Graves Robert Jeffirs David Roberts John Thomas and Thomas Test All of the said County of Chester your Complainat Did Refuse to Aid on the said Eleventh Day of the eight month Aforesaid Att Chester & would not Asist the s^d Constable in keepeing the kings peace and In Apprehending the said Afraiors: Edward Bezer & William ffreeman as wittnes my hand Robert Barber ye 11th of the 10th month 1695

Chester the 10th of the 10th month 1695: Wee off the Grand Inquest ffor the County of Chester Doe ffor the king present: William ffreeman as wittnes my hand Robert Barber ye 11th Day off the 8th month last in and before the house of Samuell Bishop: Signed by 12 of ye Jury William ffreeman was Called to Answer to the s^d presentment of ye Grand Inquest And he submits himselfe to the mercy of the Bentch: the Court Considering of the same ordered that he pay All Charges thats Due and behave himselfe well for the future And be Discharged for this Time:

Edward Bezer was Called to Answer to the presentment Above said and pleaded not Guilty & put himselfe to be Tryed by God and the Country: the petty Jury was Called And

Attested: whose names are as ffolloweth: Robert Pile: Andrew Jobe Randell Malling John Worroll: John Cock: Joseph Coeborn: William Browne Robert Carter: Peter Wood: Thomas Lonshaw: John Willis James Browne: The verdit of the Jury is this: Chester ye 11th of ye 10th month: 1695 we of the petty Jury find Edward Bezer Guilty of the A fray according to the presentment. Randell Mallin foreman

The Court Gives Judgment that Edward Bezer pay all Charges thats Due and be have himselfe well for the ffuture and be Discharged for this time

Chester County December the 10th 1695: we the Grand Jury by the Kings Authority Presents Patrick kelly and Judith Buller ffor marying Against the law In that Case made and provided in this province the 2 of December: John Stedman prosecutor Walter Martin fforeman:

The Court orders that they be brought to the next Court To Answer the same And that they marry Againe In the meane Time According to law.

Chester County December ye 11th: 1695: Wee the Grand Inquest by the Kings Authority Presents Robert Roman of Chichester ffor practising Geomancy According to hidon And Divineng by A sticke: Walter Martin fforeman

Chester County December ye 11th 1695 we The Grand Inquest by the kings Authority Doe Present Robert Roman of Chichester And Ann Buffington the wife of Richard Buffington: the said Robert Roman Takeing the wife of Henry Hastings Away ffrom her husband and Children and Convaying her Away And the said Ann Buffington being Confederat with the said Robert Roman: Walter Martin foreman

The Court orders that they be sommoned to Appeare Att the next County Court

Chester County December ye 11th 1695: wee the Grand Inquest by the kings Authority Presents these ffollowing Books Hidons Temple of wisdom which Teaches Geomancy And scots Discovery of whichcraft And Cornelius Agrippas

Teaching negromancy: Walter Martin fforeman: The Court orders that as many of s^d books as can be found be Brought to the next Court:

Chester County December ye 11th: 1695: we The Grand Inquest by the kings Authority Presents Elexander Graves ffor An Asault and battery on Edward ffreeman A boute the begining of September last past: Walter Martin fforeman

Elexander Graves was Called to Answer to the presentment and submitted to the bentch the Court orders that he pay the Charges that Due and behave himselfe well for the future and be Discharged for this time.

Chester County December ye 11th: 1695 we the Grand Jury Presents Samuell Noyes ffor being Drunke A boute the midle of last month and likewise being a common Drunker Walter Martin fforeman: Samuell Noyes was Called to Answer to ye Presentment and was find ffive shillings which he promised to Pay.

Chester County December ye 11th 1695: we the Grand Jury presents John Hickman ffor swereing A boute the begining of this month Walter Martin foreman John Hickman was ordered to pay five shillings for his swereing

Chester County December ye 11th 1695 we the Grand Jury Presents Samuell Levis And William Garett ffor one Thousand Accres of land which is behind ffor these Levies ffollowing ffirst the levie to the Court house and prison 2^s 6^d pr hundred

The next 3^s pr hundred accres the next 1^s pr hundred the halfe levie 1^s 6^d pr hundred which comes to 4£ 0^s 0^d: likewise ffor 3 levies on Att 2^d pr pound and 2 levies Att 1^d pr pound which is 20^d pr hundred which comes to 00£ 16^s 8^d The whole sum being 4£ 16^s 8^d: Walter Martin fforeman: Samuell Levis Desired Time till next Court to bring In his Accounts the Court granted it.

Chester County December ye 11th: 95 we the Grand Jury Presents Samuell Levis ffor A horse and ffurniture belongin to the County Att 4£ 00ˢ 00ᵈ: which he Desires till next Court & It was Granted:

John Garrett & Samuell Bishop & Robert Jefferis Elixander Graves & David Roberts were Called to Answer to the Presentment of the Constable Robert Barber ffor Refusing to Asist him In the Exceecution of his office and they submit themselfs to the mercy of the bentch the Court orders that they pay their feese And Doe soe noe more and be Discharged for this Time:

A Deed Acknowledged by James Swaffar To Jeremiah Collett ffor Two hundred and ffivety Acres lying betwene Ridly Creeke and Crum Creeke In the County of Chester the Deed bareing Date the Eleventh Day of December 1695:

Ordered that Exceecution A pon the Judgment obtained by John Busby & Joseph Taylor Plantifs against Isarell Taylor Deft be Respited tell the next Court:

Whereas Lewis fferill being Brought to Answer the Complaint of John Hinson who being Attested in oppen Court Averrs that he being Constable In maryland had the said lewis fferill In Costody and Delivered him to Another Constable from whom he made his escape And Is by this Court Committed to the sherifs Costody there to remayne untill the maJestrate of Cissell or Talbott Countys In maryland Doe send theire request to the maJestrates heare for the sending Downe the sᵈ fferill to Answer his misdemeniors there or otherwise to be Discharged by Due Corse of law paying the Charges Due here

Chester County Credt:: An Account of what money was Receved by Walter Martin Tressurer of sᵈ County of the Constabls and others ffor the ffinishing of the Court House and Prison Att Chester: by A levie: Att one penny pr pound And three shillings pr head on All ffreemen: Receved the seventh of the ninth month 1695: the sum of seventy three pounds Twelve shillings And one penny:

Chester County Dept^r 1695 by An Account brought In by the said Walter Martin the Twelfth Day of the Tenth month 1695

Being ffor the ffinishing of the Court house and Prison and other uses Amounting to seventy three pounds Twelve shillings and A penny which said Accounts both of Creditt and Deptor Wee the Grand Jury of the s^d County have Examined and Doe ffind them to be True and perfect In wittness whereof wee sett our hands this 12th Day of ye 10th month 1695: Henery Hastings: George Willard: Morton Mortenson: Mathias Morten: Joseph Need: ffrancis Worly: Thomas Cartwright: John Smyth Humphry Johnson: William Thomas: George lownes: John Hurlbert: John Hodgskins:

Be It Remembered That one the Twenty ffifth Day of ffebruary in the seventh yeare of the Reigne of king William the Third over England & Anno Dom: 9 John Test of Philidelphia in the province of Pensilvania: M^{r}cht Came in his proper person into the Court of Common Pleass held Att Chester In the said province Before Jasper yeates John Blunstone & Jonathan Heyes: three of the Justices of the said Court: and Then and There Did Exhibit To the said Justices A Cartaine Information The Tennor wherof followeth in these words vizt: Chester: To the Justices of the Court of Common pleas for the County of Chester In the said Province of pensilvania In America:

Be It Remembered That John Test of Philidelphia M^{r}cht: who as well for The Lord the king & the Governour of the said Province as for himselfe Giveth the Court here To understand & to be Informed y^t Samuell Harrison of the province of West Jersey marriner after the five and Twentyeth Day of march 1664 and before the Exhibition hereof In A Cartaine ship or vessell Called the pensilvenia marcht Did import into the said [erased] or Colony of pensilvania sundry Commodities of the Groweth production and manifacture of Europe which were not bona ffide: & without fraud laden or shiped in

England Wales or Towne of Barwick uppon Tweed and which were not Carried ·Directly thence To these parts or places of the s^d Kings Plantations but from another place Against the forme of the statute in that Case made & provided: whereupon the s^d John Test as well for the s^d Lord the King & Governour as for himselfe Craves the advice of this Court In the premises & y^t the s^d Samuell Harrison may forfitt & loose the s^d Commodities being the Groweth production & manifacture of Europe laden & Imported as before s^d As Alsoe that the s^d ship or vessell one which the same were Imported with all her Gunns Tackell ffurniture Ammunition & Apparrell may be A Judged to be forfeited one third part thereof to ye said Lord the king one third part thereof to the s^d Governour and that the s^d John Test may have the other third part thereof according To the forme of the s^d Statute And that the said Samuell Harrison may come here Into Court to Answer in & upon the premises & pledges to present Jo^n Doe & Richard Roe: And the s^d Samuell Harrison in his proper person comes and Defends the force and InJuries when &c and saith that he is in nothing Guilty of the premises laid to his Charge in manner & forme as the s^d John Test who as well follows for the lord the king as for himselfe by his: Information afores^d hath above supposed and of this he puts himselfe uppon the Country and the s^d John Test who &c: in like manner: Therefore a Jury was to Come before the s^d Justices &c & the sherif Returns Twelve To witt: Richard Parker: Isarell Taylor: Peter Wood: Wm Coebourne: Isaac ffew: Jo^n Hendricks John Orchar John Hodgskins: Samuell Bishop John Worrolaw James Lownes & John Cocks: who being called Appeared and who to say the Truth of the premises being Chosen tryed and Attested say Apon their Attestation that the said Samuell Harrison is Guilty of Importing the s^d commodities in the s^d ship or vessell in manner and forme as the s^d John Test by his Information A fore said hath supposed: Ra: 35.

Therefore it is Considered that the s^d Samuell Harrison according to the forme of the s^d Statute shall forfit and loose all the said Comodityes Imported as afores^d As alsoe the s^d ship or vessell called the Pensilvania marchant one which the same were Imported with all her Gunns Takle ffurniture ammunition & apparell one Third part thereof To the s^d Lord the king one third part thereof to the s^d Govr and the other third part thereof to the s^d John Tests owne proper use and the afores^d Samuell Harrison m^r m^rcy &c:

Whereapon It was ordered by ye said Court that Jonathan Belch Henry Hollingsworth & William Coebourne should goe one board the s^d ship or vessell and make a True Apraisment of the same vessell with her Guns Tackle ffurniture ammunition and Apparell as alsoe of the goods therein upon* their Attestations under their hands and forthwith make returne to the s^d Court of their Doeings therein: In pursuance whereof they the s^d Jonathan Belch Henry Hollingsworth & William Coebourne Afterwards to witt the same Day yeare & place aforesaid Did accordingly returne here A Certaine Appraisement or valluation of the said ship or vessell Called the pensilvania marchant with all the Tackle furniture Apparell goods and Comodityes whatsoever which the water Bayliff of this province had formerly found therein and seized therewith and now A Judged to be forfeited as Aforesaid: by which It Appears that first the said ship Tackle ffurniture & Apparell are Appraised Att sixty pounds Alsoe Two Thousand of pan tiles att Two pounds Ten shillings alsoe eighteen barrells of Coales at ffive pounds Alsoe Two piggs of lead att Twelve shillings alsoe Tarr & pitch att one pound Ten shillings alsoe Two barrels of Beefe Att Two pounds alsoe Two barrells of bread att one pound fourteen shillings and Alsoe pork pease and ffish att fiveteen shillings In all A mounting to the sum of seventy four pounds & one shilling: whereupon It is further Considered by the same Court that the said ship or vessell Called the pensilvania marchant with her said Tackle ffurniture and Apparell Togather with the goods and Comodityes Aforesaid shall be Exposed To sale by the said Walter Bayliff whose bill of sale Duely made and Exceecuted shall not onely Convey the whole Right & Intrest of All former and present owners and possesors of the said vessell unto such person or persons as shall by the same: but Alsoe vest such buyer or buyers with an Absolute Right & property thereunto And that the said water Baylif shall have the money or price of the said vessell with her Appurtenances & comodities A foresaid before the Governour of this province within one month now next Ensueing To Render To witt the one third part thereof To our said Lord the king one third part thereof to the said Gover^r And the other third part thereof to the said John Test According To the forme of the said statute:

Att An Orphants Court held Att Chester for the County of Chester the 10th Day of march 1695/6

{ John Simcock President
George fforman
Jasper yeates   Justices
John Blunstone   Present
Jonathan Heayes }

                 Henery Hollingsworth Dep^{ty} sherif
                 John Childe Clark

The Widdow Moore was Called & Apeared and Brought her Brother Thomas Green who Became Bound with the s^d widdow Moore ffor the securing of the Estate of Richard Moore deceased that the orphants Esteate shall not be wasted or any ways Disposed of Tell they come of age.

     Hanah Powell and Mary Powell being the orphants of Joseph Powell Deceased Came Into this Court and there Did Chose Caleb Pusye to be theyr Gardian and next frind and Requested that the Efects that is In Jeremiah Colletts hands may be Deliverd Into the hands of Caleb Pusye for theyr use ordered by said Court that Jeremiah Collett Do Deliver up All the Efects of Joseph Powells that he have In his hands to Caleb Pusye

     Jeremiah Collett Came Into Court and promised for to Deliver It all up In to the hands of the said Caleb Pusye

The Court off Quarter ss: Called the same Justices as above Att orphants Court The Constables were Called And Apeared and Returnd All was well and new ons Chosen:

Robert Barber for Chester:
John kinsman Constable for Chichester
Joseph Richards for Aishtown:
Robert Eyre for Beathell:
John Palmer for Concord:
Thomas Everson Constable of Thornbury
William Brainton Junior for Burmingham
John Redmall for Middletowne
John Golden for Edgment
John Powell for Neither Providence
Edward Prichett for Rydlye
Robert Naylor for Darbye
Peter Worrall for Marpoole
Thomas Taylor ffor Springfild
Thomas Parre for Radnor
Samuell Robenett for Upper Providence
David Phillip for new Towne
John Richards for haverfoord
John Radly for Westowne

The Grand Jury was Called and Apeard and Brought In theyr presentments (viz) (Chester County March ye 10th 1695) we the Grand Jury Presents the Township of Aishtown for not Cutting and Cleareing the high way throw theyr Town from Concord to Chester: wa: Marten fforeman Humphry Scarlett being supervisor of that Township Appeared In Court And promised It should be Don:

Chester County March the 10th 1695 The Grand Jury by the kings Authoritye Present Grace for Committing Adultry with Richard Joans she not being his wife shee now liveing Att Joseph Coeborns In the Township of Chester Wa marten fforeman: Ordered that she be brought to the Court If shee be found In the County:

Chester County March ye 10th 1695 the Grand Jury by the kings authority present William ffreeman for comitting an A salt & Battery with a strainger that Came to Chester Town A bout a month Agoe wa: martin foreman ordered that he be brought to next Court to answer s^d presentment

Patrick kelly and Judith Buller was Called to Answer the Presentment of the Grand Jury the last Court and she being not well they were order to Apeare Att the next Court: Robert Roman was Called to Answer the presentm^t of the Grand Jury the last Court he A peard and submits himselfe to the bench. The order of Court Is that he shall pay five pound for A fine and all Charges And never practis the arts but but behave himselfe well for the future and he promised so to Doe where a pon he is Discharged for this time

An the wife of Richard Buffinton was Called To Answer to the presentment of the Grand Jury the last Court: and Answer was made she was Ill and Could not be heare: order that she apeare the next Court

The Court of Common Pleas was Called the same Justices as Before Att the other Courts

JOHN DONALLSON Pl^tf: Against ⎰ the Cause was Called and
ROBERT WHITE Def^t ⎱ Jasper Yeates Apeard for
accon of the Case   ⎱ the pl'f and the Defendant not Appearing: and being Continued on Court All redy the Decleration was Red wherein the plantif Decleres that the Defendant became Indepted unto the plantif In the yeare 1692 the sum of six pounds seventeen shillings and seven pence as by Account In Court was made appeare where Apon Judgment was Granted for the s^d sum of six pounds seventeen shillings and Seven pence: and Execeution Granted for the same

CALEB PUSYE Plantif: Against ⎱ the Cause being
RICHARD JOANS Def^t: accon of Dept ⎰ Called the plantif Appeard the Defendant was Called 3 times and Appeard not: where a pon the Decleration was Red the Plantif Declers

that the Deft became Indepted unto the plantif the sum of Two pounds fourteen shillings and five pence As by Accounts In Court made Apeare the pl't Attesting to the truth of his Account where Apon Judgment was Granted to the plantife for the s^d sum of To pounds fourteen shillings and five pence and Excecution for the same was Granted to ye plantif with Cost of suite

JEREMIAH COLLETT Pl^{t}f Against
RICHARD JOANS Def^t In accon of ye Case

The Cause being Called the plantif Appeard the Def^t was Called 3 times and Appeard not The Declereth the Defendant Is Justly Indepted unto the plantif In the sum of four pounds four shillings and 10^d halfe peny on the account of himselfe and his Brother Wm Collett Deceased to whose the plantif is administrator the plantif by his account produced In Court made A peare Where a pon Judgment was Granted for the s^d sum with Cost of suite and excecution ordered for the same:

JOSEPH WOOD Pl^{t}f Against
PETER YOKEM Def^t In accon Dept

the Cause was Called David loyd A peard for the pl^{t}f and the Def^t was Called 3 times and A peard not this being the second Court soe Judgment was Granted to the pl^{t}f by Defolt the Defendant not Appearing for his Dept

DENNIS REIGN Pl^{t}f Against
THOMAS SIDE BOTTOM Def^t

accion of scandell and Defemation with drawen

Richard Crosby pettioned to this Court for to have his Dept Due from George Andross being fivety two pounds: ordered that he have excecution Against the Estate of George Andros Excepting that part of the land that is allredy seased in excecution Att the suite of An Baynton excecutrix to James Sanderlands Decesed

MARGARET LONSHORE widdo: Pl^{t}f: Against
JOHN ARCHER ALIS ORION: & WILLIAM SMYTH
And EUSTA EUSTASON: Deftants in action of Trespas

the Cause was Called and the plantif and Defendants Apperd they Joyne Issue

The petty Jury was Called and Attested whose names are (viz)

Thomas Minshall	Randell Malling	John Mendinghall
John Worrola	Andrew Job	Randell Vernon
Isack ffew	Richard Woodward	John Worrall
George Pearce	Joseph Coeborne	Thomas Marcy

The Decleration was Red: the Defendants plea was that he would Profe the beast to be his:

Judeth Blake Attested Deposeth that she Did know the beast to be the Defendants from A Calfe and that It was the same beast Mathias Morten was Attested for the Defendant and Deposeth that the Defendant John Orcher Asked the Deponent to goe alonge with him to see the marke of the best and that he went and Did see that It was the very same marke as all the other of his Cattle had.

Lawrance Parker being Attested saith y^t he had the Calfe from the other side of the River and Brought It to this side and soe It went A way And that It had a white face with a Red spot In the white and that he Did see John Archer marke this same with his marke

John Elliott being Attested for the Pl^{t}f Decleareth that the Pl^{t}fs negroe Tould him that that beast was none of theirs but was there from A Calfe & that John Orien Did say that If shee had not published it he would shue her and further saith not

The verdit of the Petty Jury: Chester the 11th of ye first month 1695/6 wee men of the petty Jurey Doe find for the Defendant with Cost of shute And Two pence Damage: Randell Vernon fforeman

John Richardson of the County of new Castle and Thomas Weithers of this County haveing A Cartaine Differance Depending between them: Dos bind themselfs Each to other In the sum of one hundred pounds of lawfull mony of this province and that shall stand and A bide the Judgment and Determination of the maJestrates now one the bench to put a finall end to It:

The Decree of the Court of Equity In the A peall of William Collett: In the suite that was Between John Bristow and him: the Decree of this Court Is that ffrancis Chadsey who Is administrator To the estat of John Bristow shall pay six pounds To Jeremiah Collett who Is administrator to William Collett and that Jerem^ah Collett pay all Court Charges that was Due

George Churchman Past A Deed unto his kinsman John Churchman ffor ffivety Acres of land with all Appurtenances thereunto belonging lying and being In the Township of Chester the Deed bareing Date the ffifth Day of Jenuary 1695

A Deed Acknowledged by Thomas Hoape To William Brainton for one hundred Acres of land lying att the north end of Concord Bearing Date the Tenth Day of ye first month 1695/6

George Woodyard Acknowledged A Deed unto Joseph Phipps for Two hundred Acres of land lying In upper Providence the Deed Beareing Date the fifth Day of ffebuary 1695/6

Joseph Phipps Acknowledged A Deed of mortgage for the Above Two hundred acres of land for the payment of mony for the same the Deed bearing Deate the Tenth Day of March: 1695/6

There was A boy Brought To this Court To be A Judged whose name John Cuningham who was A Judged To sarve his master John Worrell or his Asigns the full Terme of Eight years from this Court And to pay to s^d sarvant the Custome of the Country and A Discharge from his servis

There was A nother boy Brought whose name is Lydias Dobie and was A Judged To sarve his master Jasper Yeates or his Asignes the full Terme of six years ffrom this Court and to be payd the Custome of the Country and a Discharge

A Deed Acknowledged by Phillip Yarnell To Thomas Worrola for To hundred Acres of land lying In Edgmont the Deed Barcing Date the sixth Day of march 1695/6

A Deed Acknowledged by Thomas Coates To Thomas Smyth ffor fivety Acres of land lying In Darby Township the Deed Beareing Date the 11th of march 1695

John Simcock Attorney for Henry Maddock Dos make over A Deed To John Worrell for three hundred And Eighty Acres of land lying in the Township of Edgement the Deed Beareing Date the 11 Day of ffebuary 1695

A Deed Acknowledged by Richard Crosby Atorny for John ffox for one hundred Acres of land lying in Edgement: To Thomas Boweter the Deed Beareing Date the second Day of march 1695/6

Thomas Coeborn Acknowledged A Deed To his son Joseph Coebourn for one hundred Acres of land lying in the Township of Chester the Deed Beareing Date the Tenth Day of march 1695/6

Thomas Coeborn Acknowledged A Deed To his son William Coeborn for one Hundred and ffive Acres of land lying In the Township of Chester the Deed Beareing Date the ninth Day of March 1695/6

Thomas Coeborn Acknowledged A Deed To his son In law ffrances Baldwin for one hundred Acres of land lying In the Township of Chester the Deed bereing Date the ninth Day of March 1695/6

John Worrell Acknowledged A Deed To Richard Woodward for Two hundred And ffivety Acres of land lying In middelltowne the Deed Beareing Date the ffiveteenth Day of ffebruary 1695

Richard Woodward Acknowledges A Deed of mortgage ffor the same Two hundred and fivety Acres of land To John Worrell the Deed beareing Date the third Day of march 1695/6

Edward Bezer Acknowledged A Deed To Edward Peancck

ffor Twenty five Acres of land lying and being In the Township of Beathell the Deed Bearcing Date the ninth Day of march 1695/6

Mr George fforman Brought In his Account of what the County was Indepted to him and his ffather law James Sanderlins: The County of Chester Depter:

	£	s	d
To Ballance of an account Given in:	7	7	6
To Ditto account James Sanderlins:	20	03	6
To Caish p^d P. Robinson for Ption in Counsell A Boute the Devision of the County	00	6	00
To my Expences	00	06	00
To Expences acc^t Green	01	02	2
october 94: Paid John Childe ffor Receving of Doctor Cox mony	03	10	0
To Jeremiah Collett for Cox levie	02	10	0
To Caish To Thomas Weithers	06	14	10
	42	00	00

Per Contra 1694 October: ℔ Caish of Doctor Cox 42£: 00^s: 00^d Chester County March ye 10th 1695/6 The Grand Jury haveing examined this account Doe ffind It to be a True and Just Account: whereunto they subscribd theyr hands Walter Martin fforeman

John Bezer: John Hendrixson and his wife ffrances Hendrixson Acknowledged A Deed unto John Childe ffor Two parcells of land lying between horwicks Run and midle Run with all the meadows marshes Cripls & swamps &c as mentiond In the said Deed Contayning one hundred Acres be it more or less: the Deed beareing Date the last Day of September 1695

RICHARD CROSBY Plantif ⎫ In an action of Dept
GEORGE ANDROSE Def^t ⎭

Chester ss Richard Crosby of the s^d County yeoman complains ag^t George Andros late of Chichester In the s^d County of A plea that he render him fifty two pounds fiveteen shillings which to him he oweth and unjustly Detaineth &c and whereapon the s^d pl^t saith that whereas he haveing formerly Exhibeted his complaint & taken oute process ag^t: the said George Andross thereapon Returnable to the County Court held at Chester In the said County on the ffourteenth Day of the Tenth month 1683 whereapon It was by the Justices of the same Court with Consent of both parties ordered that the matter Contayned In the said Complaint should be referred to the Determination of John Hastings and John Harden the then constituted peace makers for the said County who In pursuance thereunto having seriously Considered the premises Did Judge and award that the said George Andros his heires and Asignes should pay or Cause to be paid unto the s^d Richard Crosbye or his Assignes the full sum of Eighteen pounds of lawfull money of this province upon the Twentieth Day of that Instant December at the then Dwelling house of James Sanderlines at Chester the one halfe thereof In Redy money as A foresaid and the other halfe In good marchantable wheat or Rye at the common markett prise which s^d a ward was on the 17th Day of the s^d tenth month Ratified by the s^d Justices & Regestred In the same Court according to the 66th Chapter of ye the lawes of this Goverment Excecution Awarded thereapon Directed to Thomas Usher then sheriff of the said County who by virtue of the said Excecution haveing taken or seized the s^d George Andross Plantation Att Chichester Afforesaid Did Cause the said plantation to be A praized by the County appraisors who one the Eight Day of the fourth month 1686 Did vallue the same Att sixty pounds: And Afterwards to witt Att the first month Court then next ffollowing It was ordered that the said sheriff Thomas Usher and the pl^t: Richard Crosby should have power To sell and Dispose of the s^d plantation Remaining unsold for want of buyers became afterwards Attached as the Estate of George Andross In the plts hands To Answer the suite of George fforman who by the Judgment of the County Court held Att Chester aforesaid the sixt Day of the Eight month 1691 Did recover Against the said George Andross as well a Cartaine Dept of Eleven pounds Ten shillings as thirty shillings Cost of suite as by the Records & respective proceedings of the said severall Courts may more Att large Appeare And the said Richard Crosby In fact saith that he hath Discharged with his owne money the s^d Dept and Costs Recovered by the last recited Judgment being thirteen pounds which with the Eight pounds charges by him Recovered Against the s^d George Andros as a foresaid with the lawfull Interest thereof Amounts in all to the s^d sum of ffivety two pounds ffiveteen shillings for which he the s^d hath not as yett obtained any Exceeution or other remedy in that behalfe whereby action accrued to him the s^d Richard Crosby To require and have of the s^d Def^t: the said sum of ffivety Two pounds fiveteen shillings Currant money of pensilvania nevertheless the s^d Defendant though often required the Afforesaid ffivety Two pounds fivfteen shillings to the plantif hath not Rendered but the same to render hath Denyed and still Doth Deny to the plantiffs Damage of Twenty pounds and thereof brings suite &c. And now here Att this Day comes the s^d Richard Crosby and offers himselfe the third time Against the s^d Defendant of the plea a fore said and he sollomly called cometh not but makes Default Therefore It Is considered that the plantif shall recover Against the s^d Defendant his Dept Aforesaid & his Damages & Costs of suite to fifty shillings to him the s^d plt of his Assent by the Court here A Judged and the s^d Def^t In mercy &c. and that the s^d pl^t may have Exceeution against the s^d the Defendants lands & Tenements for the Dept Damages & Costs afores^d &c whereupon at the Request of the said pl^t: It is Comanded to the shriff of the s^d County of Chester that he seise the s^d George Andros messuage lands Tenements and plantation Aforesaid with Appurtenances and the same to the foresaid pl^t withoute Delay he Cause to be Delivered Att a reasonable prise for payment of the s^d Dept Damages and Costs rendring the over plush If any be to the s^d Defendant: To hold To him the s^d plt his heires and Assignes for ever according to the forme & efect of the acts of Assembly past at philidelphia on the first Day of June 1693 and Afterwards Aproved of & Ratified by the king in Councell and In what manner the s^d sheriff had Exceeuted the s^d writt he should make knowen here the ninth day of the fourth month next under his seale and the seals of them by whom the s^d messuage lands Tenements & plantation & premises should be Appraised &c.

Att A Court held Att Chester ffor the County of Chester the nineth & 10th dayes of the fourth month 1696

John Simcock President
Jasper Yeates
George fforman } Justices
Jonathan Heyes } Present
John Blunstone

Joseph Wood sheriff
John Childe Clarke

After Silence commanded In his maJesties name

The Constables weare Called and Robert Eyre Constable of Bethell not appering was ffined ffive shillings: the Rest of the Constables Appeareing Returned all was All well: Samuell Levis Being Called three times and he not Appearing In his place as MaJestrate was by the Court ffind Twenty shillings:

The Grand Jury was Called And Appered excepting Walter Martin whoe being very Ill could not Appeare the first Day of the Court: but appeard Afterwards

The Grand Jury Brought in theyr Presentments: viz) Wee the Grand Inquest for the body of this County Doe Present: John Kocks ffor selling licker and letting men be Drunk for neare three Dayes together in his house: Nathainell Newland foreman: John kocks Appeared In Court and Craved liberty tell the next Court and he would Travis the Presentment: It was Granted

Wee the Grand Inquest for the body of this County Doe likewise Present Barbara ffriend ffor Beateing and abuseing the wife of John Hendrixson that In nine Dayes she miscaried: Nathaniell Newland fforeman: order that she be summond to make her Appearance Att the next Court to Answer ye presentment

Wee the Grand Inquest for the body of this County Doe present Robert Woodward of the Township lower Providence for ffeloniously Takeing goods oute of the house of James Swafords of the Township of Chester: Nathaniell Newland fforeman: ordered by the Court that Robert Woodard be summoned to Appeare next Court to ans^r:

the 9th of the 4th month 1696: we the Grand Inquest Doe Present Peter Peterson of the Township of Darby and Jacobus vanculine of the Township of Ridlye ffor Runing A horse Race ffor A wager on the first Day of the week being the seventeenth Day of the Third month Nathaniell Newland fforeman: ordered by the Court that they be summond to Appeare Att the next Court to Answer s^d presentment

Chester the 9th of the 4th month 1696: Wee the Grand Inquest Doe present John Radley ffor workeing on the first Day of the week being the 17th Day of the third month Nathaniell Newland fforeman: ordered that he be summoned to Appeare heare at the next Court to Answer the s^d Presentment:

Chester ye 9th of the 4th month 1696: we the Grand Inquest Doe present John Hendrixson & Robert White & Henery Colman & Johanis ffriend for being Drunke for neare three Dayes Att John Koeks house And we Doe Alsoe present Isaac Blendee being one In Companie and Drunke with them In Companye above Nathaniell Newland fforeman: ordered that the s^d persons be sumond to Appeare Att the next County Court to Answer the s^d presentment

John Hendrickson prosecutor

Chester ye 9th of ye 4th month 1696: we the Grand Inquest for the County of Chester Doe Present the Township of Chester for not makeing A Bridge over the Creek Att Calebs mill: Nathaniell Newland fforeman: Wee the Grand Inquest Doe Alsoe Present Ridley and Chester ffor want of A Bridge Att Walter ffawsets Nathaniell Newland fforeman:

Chester the 9th of the 4th month 1696: We the Grand Inquest for the body of this County Doe present Phillip Davis ffor ffelloniously takeing of goods oute of the house of John Simcocke: Nathaniell Newland foreman:

Phillip Davis was Called to Answer the s^d presentment who said that he came to John Simcock and Did take some Cloaths away John Simcock Aledged that he the s^d Phillip Davis Did take away A new shirt and A new paire of stockings a westcoate and two fine neckloths and a Cannow: which was In all to the vallue of Two pounds: The order of Court Is that he shall Restore the same goods In as good order as they were or the full vallue which Is Two pounds and to Receve Ten laishes on his beare back and To pay all Charges thats Due: and be Discharged for this time: the goods or the mony to the vallue Is to be Returnd to John Simcock.

The Grand Jury made Returne of A Roade way laid oute by them (viz) Chester County May the Eight 1696: Laid oute by the Grand Jury a Roade from David Merrideths Plantation To Havorfoord meeting house by virtue of an order of Court beareing Date at A Court held the 10th: 11th: 12th: Dayes of December 1695 att Chester as followeth: Radnor Begining Att David Merrideths Plantation Att A small Red oake marked with five knoches by Stephen Bevins Plantation the plantation on the Right hand Thence throw Reece Thomas and Peter Edwards land To A Red oake marked with five knoches: Havorfoord: Thence Throw Morris Lewellins Land Thence Thorow Thomas Reese Land Between To Cornfields Thence Thorow George Painters Land Thence Thorow Rachell Ellises Land Thence Thorow Morris Lewellins land the house on the left hand straite from Thence to the Bridge one the Run that comes from Reese Ruthero his house on the left hand Thence Thorow John Bevins land Downe to Havorfoord mill Thence up to Havorfoord meeting House: Subscribed by us the fforesaid Grand Jury: Wa: Martin foreman

John Greene was Called To Answer the Abuseing of John Simcock and Jasper Yeats To of His MaJesties Justices of the peace for this County and he Apperd And Exhibeted A petition to this Court and put himselfe one the mercy of the Bentch the Court Considering of It and he promiseing never to Doe so any more but to behave himselfe well for the future: the Court orders that he pay all Charges that Due and be for this time Dismised:

David Morris Ree Sent & Thomas Joans were Attested to Give In their Evidences to the Grand Inquest:

Sarah ffreeman being bound over to answer Att this Court for som misdemenors and Samuell Noyes and Henery Barns being bound for her appearace they were Called and they answerd that shee was Att philidelphia and soe nere lying in that she could not be here this Court:

Patrick keelly and Judeth Buller were Called: and they Appeard not ordered they be summoned to Appeare the next Court to Answer the presentment of the Grand Inquest.

Chester County: June the 10th 1696: The Grand Jury by the kings authority Lay A levie at A penny pr pound: on the Inhabitants of the County of Chester one theire Estates Reall and personall and one ffreeman and others according To the law In that Case provided for the Defraying the woulfs heads that the County Is In Dept for which are not paid and ffor the Relife of the poore and other publicke uses of the County subscribed by us the present Grand Jury Walter Martin fforeman. ordered by the Court that warrents be Isued oute to every Respective Constable In the County for to Gather The said levie and To bringe It in the next Court to be held the 8th day of ye 7th ber next

Chester County June the 10th: 1696: The present Grand Jury of the said County: Charge an account on the land late Charles pickerings: now Robert Turners Samuell Carpenter Joseph Willcockes & company being five Thousand acres of land scituate and lying In the County of Chester being In Arreages Due to the s^d County on severall levies as ffolloweth: To the Court House and prison Att 2^s: 6^d pr hundred Acres comes to 6£ 5ˢ 0ᵈ: To the woulfs heads At on shilling pr hundred Acres comes to 2 10 0: To Court house and prison & Counsell and Assembly men and salirys and other publike uses Att three shillings pr hundred acres comes to: 7 10 00: and To A halfe levie Att 1ˢ 6ᵈ pr hundred acres comes to 3 15 00 These four Above mentioned levies Amounting to 8ˢ per hundred acres is 20 00 00 To three levies sence To the Building the new Court house and prison Att: 1ˢ 8ᵈ per hundred Acres 4£ 3ˢ 4ᵈ the Totall sum being Twenty four pounds three shillings and four pence: subscribed by the ffore said Grand Jury: Walter Martin fforeman: William Clayton will except of this Account If the Court will be plesed to Grant him an order of Court to Gather It Allowing Reasonable Charges for the gathering It: the said William Clayton haveing Due to ʰim Eighteen pounds: 1ˢ: 6ᵈ: pence for his ffathers sallerys and his worke on the old Court house and he will be Redy to Give an Account to the Court when he hath Receved It: the Court grants It him that he shall have an order from the Clarke for him to Recevi It and that he shall Give an account To the Court when he have Recev'd It:

The Court of Common Please Called the same Justices: and sheriff & Clarke as Att the Quarter sessions:

Robert Barber Attorney for Joshua Hastings Acknowledged A Deed for Two Hundred Acres of land and Premises To Robert Varnon the Plantation Lying In Neither Providence the Deed beareing Date the nineteenth Day of of the first month 1695/6

Benjamin Mendinghall Brought A lad to be A Judged by this Court the boys name Is William Johnstown: who was A Judged to serve his said master and Asignes the ffull terme of six yeares from this Court.

John Bennitt Brought A sarvant Boy to this Court to be A Judged what time he should serve who was A Judged by this Court To serve his master or Assignes the full terme of five years from this Court the boys name is George Robinson

Nathaniell Newland Brought A sarvant boy whose name is Thomas Robbinson To be A Judged by this Court who was by the Court A Judged to serve his s^d Master or his Assignes the full terme of Eight yeares from the 20th Day of May last:

John Hanum Brought a sarvant boy whose name Saundy Hunter To be A Judged by this Court who was A Judged by the said Court To serve his s^d master or his Assignes the full Terme of five yeares from the 20th Day of May last past.

Henery Worlye Brought A sarvant boy To this Court To be A Judged whose name Is Thomas Bullen who was A Judged to serve his master Caleb Pusye or his Assignes the full Terme of seven years from the 20th of may last past.

George Williard Acknowledged A Deed To Edmund Butcher for one Hundred Acres of land lying In the Township of Burningham the Deed beareing Date the ninth Day of June 1696:

William Thomas Acknowledged A Deed for Two Hundred thirty and three Acres of land unto William Lewis the land lying In NewTowne the Deed beareing Date the 23th Day of the third month 1696:

Jeane Sharply and her son John Sharply Acknowledged A Deed To Joseph Sharplye for three Hundred Acres of land lying in Midletowne the Deed Bareing Date the ninth Day of June 1696:

William Browne Brought A sarvant Girle To this Court To be A Judged whose name Is Jeane Gorden who was A Judged To serve her s^d master or his Assignes the full Terme of five years from the 20th Day of May last past:

Robert Carter Brought A sarvant Girle To this Court To be a Judged whose name Is Margret Chambers who was A Judged to serve her s^d master or his Assignes ffive yeares and A halfe from the 20th Day of May last past:

Samuell Levis and William Garrett were Called to Answer to the presentment of the Grand Jury Att the Court Held the Eleventh Day of December 1695 and they promiseing to

Appeare the last Court Held In the first month: and not Appeareing that Court nor this Judgment Is Given A gainst them by Default:

Thomas Worrolaw Acknowledged A Deed To John Golding for Two hundred Acres of land lying In Edgemond the Deed beareing Date the sixth Day of June 1696:

The Court orders Robert Barber and Henery Hollingsworth To Appraise the goods and Chattls of Thomas Longshaw Deceased and to take them In to Costody:

David Loyd Attorney for William Howell Acknowledged A Deed unto Richard Heyes for fivety Acres of land lying in the Township of Havorfoord the Deed Bearcing Date the ninth Day of June 1696:

Samuell Bowne Acknowledged A Deed To John Blunstone Gardien To John Bowne for Two hundred and fivety Acres of land lying In the Township of Darbye The Deed Beareing Date the Tenth Day of the fourth month 1696

SAMUELL ROWLAND Pl^{t}f: Against: the Cause was Called
WILLIAM FFREEMAN: Def^t: and Robert Barber
In accon: Dept Appeared for the
plantif: and the Decleration was Red wherein the plantif: Decleres for the sum of three pounds Two shillings and Ten pence: and none Appearing for the Defendant the plantifs accounts being In Court produced the Court Gave Judgment for the s^d sum with Cost of suite

JOSEPH COEBOURN Pl^{t}f Against the Cause was Called the
RICHARD JOANS Deft pl^{t}f Appeared and the
In accon of Dept Decleration was Red and
none Appeareing for the Defendant: the Plantif Decleres for the sum of one pound thirteen shillings and six pence to which account the plantif was Attested that It was A True and Just account whereapon the Court Gave Judgment for the said sum of one pound thirteen shillings and six pence with Cost of suite

JAEMES BROWNE Pl'f Against ⎫ the Cause was Called and
RICHARD JOANS: Deft: ⎬ the plantiff appeared the
In accon: of Dept ⎭ Decleration was Red and
the Plantif Declered for the sum of Two pounds nine
shillings and six pence to become Due to him: and none Appeareing for the Defendant: the Court Gave Judgment for
the same: with Cost of suite:

JOSEPH COEBOURNE Pl'f: Against: ⎫ the said plantif became
BENJAMIN SMYTH: Deft ⎬ bound for the Defend-
In an accon: of Trespas ⎭ ants Appearence Att
this Court and he the s^d Defendant not appeareing your pltf
Is thereby Damnified to the vallue of four pounds and

RICHARD CROSBY Pl'f: Against ⎫ The sheriff Returns, the
GEORGE ANDROSE Deft ⎭ Exceeution with an Inquisition Annexed where A pon the Court Gave Judgment
that the Plantif shall hould the messuage lands and Plantations late of George Androse As his ffree hold To him his
heires for Ever according to law: And the said sherift To witt
Joseph Wood now Returns here a cartaine Inquission Taken
before him Att Chichester afore s^d the second Day of June
Instant by the Attestation of Twelve good and lawfull men of
the neighberhood by which It remayns ffound that the s^d
George Androse was seized in his Demeasne as of ffee of and
In one messuage or Tennement with a boute thirty five acres
of land thereunto belonging scituate lying and being in Chichester afores^d Begining Att a Corner stone by the River
Delawere being the Corner of George fformans land Runing
thence north north west Three hundred Twenty Two perches
To A Corner white oake saplin Thence Runing A longe the
kings Roade eighteen perches To A Corner Red oake Thence
Runing south south East Three hundred Twenty Two perches
To A Corner stake Thence by the River Dellawere Eighteen
pertches To the first mentioned Corner stone being A boute
thirty five Acres more or less with the Appurtenances of the
vallue of fforty ffive pounds Ten shillings and being soe

Thereof seized It is ffurther by the s^d Inquission found that the said messuage land Tennement & plantation by the lawes and usage of this Goverment became lyable To be seised and sold for payment of the s^d Defts Just Depts All which said messuage lands & Tennements Plantation and premises with the Appurtenances the said sherif The Day of his Takeing of the s^d Inquission hath Caused To be Delivered To the s^d Richard Crosbye Att the prise of fforty five pounds Ten shillings a fore said for Payment of the s^d Dept Damages and Costs of suits afores^d To Hold To him the said Richard Crosbye his heires and asignes for Ever as by the said writt he was Commanded &c: Therefore It Is Considered that the said Richard Crosbye may hold the said messuage lands Tennements & Plantation: A fore said with the Appurtenances as his ffree hold To him and his heires and Asignes for Ever in part of the s^d Dept Damages and Costs According to the forme & effect of the s^d Acts of Assembly & known usage of this Goverment.

George Grist Acknowledged A Deed to Edward Pennick ffor thirty Three Acres and A third part of an acre of land: the land lying and being In the Township of Beathell the Deed bearing Date the Eight Day of June 1696.

John Golding Past A Deed of mortgage for ffivety Two pounds To Joseph Baker To be paid to the s^d Joseph Baker or his orders In the yeare of our lord one Thousand six hundred ninty ad nine on the ninth Day of the fourth month then the said John Golding Is to have his s^d plantation with all the premises To him and his heires Againe Returned the plantation lying In Edgemond being one hundred acres of land with all houses:: The Deed beareing Date the ninth Day of June 1696

Thomas England Acknowledged A Deed To Thomas Cartwright for one hundred and Eighty acres of land lying in the Township of Aishtowne the Deed bearing Date the Tenth Day of the fourth month 1696:

Edward Bezer and William Hues Acknowledged A Deed unto John Pennick ffor seventy four Acres of land lying In the Township of Bethell the Deed beareing Date the Tenth Day of the fourth month 1696:

Edward Bezer Past A Deed over unto George Grist for Thirty three Acres of land and one third part of an acre of land lying in beathell the Deed Bearing Date the 10th Day of the fourth month 1696:

Phillip Roman Acknowledged A Deed To ffrancis Chadsey for one hundred Twenty ffive Acres of land lying neare the Township of Concord the Deed beareing Date the ninth Day of ye fourth month 1696

Att A Court held Att Chester ffor The County of Chester the Eight Day of the seventh month Anno Dom 1696

John Simcocke President
Jasper Yeates
Jonathan Heyes } Justices
Samuell Levis } Present

Joseph Wood sheriff
John Childe Clarke

After Silence commanded In His maJesties name

The Constables were Called and Returned All was well

The Grand Jury were Called: & they Brought in theyr presentments viz) Chester County September the 8th 1696: The Grand Jury haveing Perused The County accounts and ffinding that severall Tracts of land have not Paid their Taxees but are behind severall levies some in the Township are behind and the upper part of the County some Tracts being behind Ever sence they have been surveyed and others part of the said levies. The ffirst Levie being In the yeare 1685 The levie To the Court house & Prison Att 2^s: 6^d: pr hundred Acres To the woulfs heads Att 1^s: pr hundred Acres: The levie To the Court house and Prison Counsell men and Assembly mens salaries & other publike uses Att 3^s pr hundred Acres the levie Att 1^s: 6^d: pr hundred Acres and four levies sence one Att 2^d pr pound & the other three Att one peny pr pound these four last levies Amounting To 2^s & one peny pr hundred Acres as may be hereafter made Appeare from Time To time by theire severall Accounts Charged one them being in Arreareges due to the said County as well appeare by perticular Accounts one severall Tracts of land: subscribed by us the present Grand Jury Walter Martin fforeman: & all the Rest set their names To It

Chester County September the 8th: 1696 The present Grand Jury of the said County Charge an Account one the sosieties Land being ffive Thousand Acres of land scituate and lying In the County of Chester being in Arrearages Due to the said County one severall lands as ffolloweth sence the yeare: 1685: ffirst the levie To the old Court house & prison Att 2^s 6^d pr hundred Acres: 6£: 5^s: 0^d The levie to the woulfs heads Att one shilling pr hundred Acres 2: 10: 0 The levie To the Court house and Prison Counsell men and Assembly mens salliaries and other publike uses Att Three shillings pr hundred Acres To A levie Att one shilling six pence pr hundred Acres: Comes to 11£: 5^s: 00^d These four Above mentioned levies Amounting To Eight shillings pr hundred Acres for four levies sence on levie Att 2^d: pr pound and the other 3 Att 1^d pr pound being 2^s: 1^d pr hundred Acres The Totall sum being Twenty five pounds: four shillings and 2 pence:

Chester County September the 8th: 1696 The present Grand Jury of the said County Charge an Account on the land of Griffeth Joans being 1920 Acres of land scituate and lying In the County of Chester being In Arrerages Due to the said County on severall levies as ffolloweth sence the yeare 1685 the first levie to the ould Court house and prison Att 2^s: 6^d pr hundred Acres the levie to the woulves heads Att 1^s pr hundred Acres

The Levie To The Court house and Prison Counsell mens and Assembly mens salliaries And other Publike uses att 3^s pr hundred Acres The levie Att 1^s: 6^d pr hundred acres These four Above mentioned levies Amounting To Eight shillings pr hundred acres ffor four levies sence on levie Att 2^d pr pound and the other three Att one peny pr Pound being To shillings & 1^d pr hundred Acres The Totall sum being: 9£ 13^s 6^d:

Chester County September y''e'' 8''th'' 1696 The present Grand Jury of the said County Charges An Account on the land of Thomas Barker Seabean Cole Humphry South Tom Moore Samuel Jobson In Company being four Thousand Acres of land scituat and lying In the County of Chester being In ARerages Due to the said County on severall levies as ffolloweth sence the yeare 1685 The ffirst levie to the old Court house and prison at 2''s'': 6''d'' pr hundred acres The levie To the woulves heads Att: 1''s'': pr hundred Acres the levie To the Court house and Prison Counsellmen & Assembly mens salaries and other Publike uses Att 3''s'' pr hundred Acres The levie Att 1''s'': 6''d'' pr hundred acres These four A bove mentioned levies Amounting To Eight shillings pr hundred Acres for four levies since one levie Att 2''d'' pr pound and the other Three Att one peny pr pound being: 2''s'' 1''d'': pr hundred Acres The Totall sum being Twenty pounds three shillings & four pence: subscribed by us the present Grand Jury To these before mentioned three Presentments Walter Martin foreman: Nathaniell Newlien: Joseph Baker: Thomas Woriolaw: Henry Hastings Moulton Moulttonson: George Wilhard: John Smyth: Humphry Johnson Mathias Morton: Thomas Cartwright: George Chandler: John Hoskins: Joseph Need: John Hurlbatt

Chester y''e'' 8''th'' of the 7''th'' month 1696 We the Grand Inquest for the body of this County Doe present Mary Moore for ffornication And haveing A Bastard Childe Walter Martin floreman.

Mary Moore being Called To Answer the s''d'' Presentment: Appeared and Exhibeted A Peticion to the s''d'' Court which being Red and she being very sorry for the same the Court Considering thereof And shee submitting her selfe to the mercy of the bentch: the Court orders that shee shall be omitted Corporall Punishment and that she shall pay forty shillings for A fine and the Charges of the Court and Give security for the bringing up of the Childe: and be Discharged for this time George Stroud became her security for the bringing up of the Childe:

The New Grand Jury that were somon^d to Appeare Att this Court were Called Andrew Jobe: Robert Pennell: George Woodyard: James Whitaker ffrancis Baldwin: John Holstone: Peter Taylor: Joseph Coebourne Randell Mallin: Phillip Yarnell: William Cloud: Issaac ffew: Robert Carter: John Bethell: James Cooper: Robert Scothorn Adam Roads John Martin: they Apperd And were Attested

John Radley being Called To Answer to The presentment of the Grand Jury the last Court he Appeared and Confesses To It the Judgment of the Court is that he shall pay Twenty shillings for A ffine and pay All the Court Charges and Doe soe noe more and be Discharged for this Time

John Hendrixson & Johanis ffriend & Henry Coleman & Robert White: were Called To Answer the presentment of the Grand Jury: they pleaded not Guilty: The Court orders that John Hendrixson pay five shillings for being Drunk and Robert White is fined ffive shillings: Henry Coleman Is Discharged: Maudlin Hendrixson was Called To ffind sureties for her good behaviour It being proved that she beate hur husband Charles Whitaker became her security

John kock being Called Appeared And noe proofe Appeareing Against him he is Discharged for this Time paying the Charges of Court:

Jacobus Vanculin & Peter Peterson was Called To Answer To the present^t of the Grand Jury they Confes Guilty & submits them selves to the bentch The Court gives Judgment that they shall pay 5^s: A peece for A fine and the Charges of the Court and be for this Time Discharged & to Doe soe noe more:

John Shard being Brought Into the Court To Answer the Complaint of Joseph Wood High sherif of the County for Abuseing of him In the execcution of his office: John Shard Appeared and submits himselfe To the bentch The Court orders that he shall humbly Acknowledge himselfe to the s^d Joseph Wood and pay the Charges of the Court and Doe soe noe more And be for this Time Discharged:

Robert Woodward being called to Answer to the presentment of the Grand Jury Aboute the Taken away of James Swafords goods he was Called three times and Appeared not In the Court: James Swafar Evidences were Called and Patrick kelly being Called & Attested: Deposeth that he was Att John Simcocks house that Day that James Swaford Declereth he lost his goods and that aboute four a Clock In the After noone the Deponant Did helpe the s^d Robert Woodyard over the Creeke & that the s^d Woodyard Tould your Deponant that James swafar had Given him the s^d Woodyard A Dram of Rumm & he s^d that he had Rather that he had Given him some small beare & further saith not. James Swaffar being Attested Deposeth that Robert Woodyards two sons was Att plow Att his house & that he the s^d Deponant had some busines Att Chester faire & that before they went he & his wife asked the s^d Woodyards sons where they lacked any thing before they went & they would helpe them To It before they went & they Gave them a Dram & when they came home Att night It being night: the next morning he looked Att A bottle of Rum & there was A Greate Dele of It gon And they Could not tell what was become of It & then they looked ffurther & his wife missed three yards of holland & four neck char . . . and A silver thimble. And afterward I mett him & he s^d he would goe to a wise man a boute them and After some time his son Richard came to me & would have me to meet him Att A wise mans house & there I should here of my goods: and After I Considered of it I answered I would not goe: & Afterwards I had a warrant for him & then he mett me & Asked me what was the Reason I was In such hast & that If I would stay two weeks he would give me A bill that I should have my goods In two weeks time. John Sharply being Attested Deposeth that as he was goeing Two James Swafars mett with Robert Woodyard and he Asked me to goe To James Swafards with him and I Did & I herd Robert Woodyard Promise James Swafard To Pay him forty shillings & on the morrow I writt the bill for forty shillings

& further saith not: Alse Howell being Attested Deposeth that Robert Woodyard went over the Creeke and A boute four A Clock he came back a gaine And Asked for some small beare & said that James swafard had Given him a Dram and he had Rather he had Given him some small beare for he was very dry.

John Cannide being Attested Deposeth that he came to Chester To Thomas Howells & mett with Robert Woodyard there who Asked the Deponant where he worked Att James Swafards & he answered he Did & the s^d Woodyard s^d that he Did not thinke that James Swafard would have sarved his sons soe as not to leave them any food or Drinke And said that he was In James Swaffards house After that they came A way and further saith not: The said Robert Woodyard being Called Againe three times & not Apper^d In Court: The Court Gave Judgment that James Swafard Recover A gainst the s^d Robert Woodyard the sum of six pounds with Cost of suite.

Jonathan Heyes made knowen To this Court how that some of Owen Mackdaniells neighbours Complained to him that the s^d owen had Arms which they were A fraid of & that one the severall Complaints he ordered the said Armes to be taken & brought to this Court & the Court ordered that the s^d Arms should be committed In to the sherifs Costody And Alsoe that the said Owen shall shall not hence forward Entertaine no straingers In his house To let them Abide there:

Att A Court of Common Pleas held Att Chester for the County of Chester the 9th Day of the seventh month Anno Dom: 1696:

The same Justices as Att the Quarter sssesions: & John Blunstone more.

Joseph Wood High sherif
John Childe Clarke

William Woodmansee Brought A sarvant boy to this Court whose Name is William Bruise who was A Judged To serve his s^d master William Woodmansee or his Assignes the full terme of Eight years from The 20th Day of June last past

John Joans Past A Deed To John Bennett Junior for five hundred Acres of land & premises the land lying In the County of Chester the Deed bearcing Date the last of August 1696:

Joseph Wood High sherif Past A Deed for one hundred Acres of land lying in Darby To Obadiah Bonsall the Deed Bercing Date the Second Day of July Anno: Domi: 1696:

John Simcocke Past A Deed To John Davis for one hundred Acres of land lying in Thornbury the Deed bearcing Date the Eight Day of September Anno Domi: 1696·

There was A Deed offered to be Past from Richard Apt Thomas unto William Thomas and there was A Cavitt Entred Against It that hindred the pasing of the Deed by Thomas John Evans & others:

ffrancis Chadsey Past A Deed To John Martin labourer for one hundred & Twenty ffive Acres of land and premises It being In the Township of Concord the Deed barcing Date the seventh Day of september Anno Domi: 1696.

David loyd Attorny for Howell James & William James Past A Deed To David Evan for Two hundred Acres of land lying In Radnor Township the Deed bearcing Date the fifth Day of September Anno: Domi: 1696:

William Davis Acknowledged A Deed To David Evan for fivetcene Acres of land lying in the Township of Radnor the Deed bercing Date the fourteenth Day of Aprill Anno: Domi: 1696:

John Simcock Past A Deed To Henry Swift for seventy Eight Acres of land lying in the Township of Rydlye the Deed bearcing Date the ninth Day of September Anno: Domi: 1696

David loyd Attorny for William Carter Past A Deed To William Clayton for one hundred Acres of land lying In Concord the Deed bercing Date the fifth Day of September Anno Domi: 1696:

Reynere Peterson Past A Deed To Walter ffaussett for ffivety Acres of land & premises lying In the Towneship of

Ridlye the Deed bereing Date the Eight Day of September Anno: Domi: 1696:

Margret Tress Pltf ⎫ In An Action of Trespass one the
Samuell Jerrome: Deft ⎭ Case the Plantife was Called & John Moore Appeard for the plantif And the Defendant Samuell Jerrom Came Into Court and Confest Judgment for the sum of Eight pounds & Cost of suite: he is committed Into the sheriffs Costody tell satti-faction be made for the ffore said sum & Cost of suite:

Jeremiah Collett Acknowledged A Deed To Josiah Taylor for ffive hundred Acres of land lying in Upper Providence the Deed beareing Date the 11th Day of June: 1696:

Owen Mack Daniell Pl'f ⎫ In An Action of Trespas
Henry Hames Deft ⎭ the Pltf & Defendat were Called and they Appeared: the Decleration was Red the Defendants plea is (viz) that he hath performed the Above mentioned Condition so ffar as by law he is obliged to and puts himselfe upon the Country: They Joyne Issue The Petty Jury were Called whose names are as ffolloweth:

Joseph Kent	George James	
Henry Swift	Peter Thomas	
Peter lester	James Bayliss	they were Attested
John Sharplys	Abraham Beaks	The Jurys verditt
Thomas Taylor	James Swaffar	
John Worrell	William Cocbourne	

The plantif & Defendant went out afterwards And Agreed It betwene themselfs:

This ninth Day of the seventh month 1696 Wee of the petty Jury find it for the Defendant with Cost of suite & Two pence Damage

John Worrall fforeman

Robert Wade pl'f in action of Dept Against the Estate of Thomas Longshaw Deceased In the hands of Henery Hollingsworth Deft: the Canse was Called and Continued tell the next Court:

John Watts of New Castell Pltf: In an action of Dept Against the Esteate of Thomas Longshaw Deceased In the hands of Henry Hollingsworth: Defendant: the Cause was Called and David Loyd Attorny for John Watts Appeared & the Decleration was Red & Continued tell next Court: Decleres for four pounds sixteen shillings: 11^d

David Loyd Acknowledged A Deed unto Jasper yeats ffor A lott of land being fforty four foote In Bredth Towards the street ffronting Delaware River and fforty foote backwards from the house the lott being formerly In the Possesion of Roger Jackson but never made over To him & therefore now made over unto ye said Jasper yeates by A Deed beareing Date ye Eight Day of september Anno: Domi: 1696:

John Simcocke Brought his Account: The County of Chester Deptor To John Simcock for Ballance of his Account To the yeare 1695: the sum of Twenty Eight pounds Two shillings: John Simcocke Deptor to the seale of the old Court house the sum of ffivety seven pounds By Ballance Remains Due to the County from John Simcock the sum of Twenty Eight pounds Eighteene shillings

The sheriff made Returne of An Exceeution Against William ffreeman Granted Att the suite of Samuell Rowland: that It was ffully sattisfied: Alsoe Another Exceeution Granted To Joseph Cocbourn A gainst Benjamin Smyth levied one A mare which s^d mare was A praised by the County Praisors Att four pounds Ten shillings Apraised by Thomas Varnon & Robert Vernon:

The sheriff made Returne of An Exceeution that was Granted To James Browne Against Richard Joans: levied A pon some wheate & some barly And Afterward Appraised by Thomas Varnon & Robert vernon Att the sum of four pounds: 10^s:

John Cocks Acknowledged A Deed To Richard Crosby for Eighty Acres of land lying in the Towneship of Rydlye the Deed beareing Date the seventh Day of the seventh month Called September Anno: Domi: 1696

James Standfield Acknowledged A Deed To Thomas Hope ffor one hundred Acres of land lying in the Township of marpoole the Deed bareing Date the Eight Day of the third month Anno: Domi: 1696

James Standfield Acknowledged A Deed To Henry Hames for one hundred Acres of land lying and being In the Township of Marpoole the Deed beareing Date the Eight Day of September Anno: Domi: 1696

Phillip Yarnell Acknowledged A Deed To Ephraim Jackson for one hundred and Twenty Acres of land lying and being In the Towneship of Edgemond the Deed beareing Date the Eight Day of the seventh month 96

Att An orphants Court held Att Chester for the County The sixth Day of the Eight month Anno Domi 1696 — John Simcock, Jasper Yeates, John Blunstone — Justices: Present

Henry Hollingsworth came Into the Court and Requested of this Court that he mite have order To place oute the orphant of Thomas Longshaw Deceased to a man thats comeing In to this province to live And Is A pewterrer: The Court orders that he shall be placed to that man If that he Settls In this province And that he goe one Tryall between this and the next Court & then be brought to the said Court to be held the Eight Day of the Tenth month next unto which Time this Court Doth A Jorne

---

Att A Court held Att Chester for the County of Chester the Eight Day of the Tenth month 1696: — John Simcocke President, John Blunstone, Jonathan Heyes, Samuell Leviss — Justices Present

John Childe Clarke & Dept Sheriff

After Procklymation made and Silence Commanded In his MaJesties name The Constabls were Called and Appeared & Returned All was well In All theyr presincks The Grand Jury

weare Called and Appeard and went forth: this Court A
Jorned tell after Dinner The lawes were Read In the Court

The orphants Court being A Jorned to this Time was Called: the same Justices as Att the Court of Quarter ssesions: John Childe Clarke: } the orphant of Thomas Longshaw was brought to this Court The Court orders that he shall goe To William Huntly Tell the next orphans Court.

Caleb Pusye Came to this orPhants Court and made Complaint that there was money In the hands of Thomas Powell of the orphants of Joseph Powell & y^t the Intrest were not paid the Court orders uppon some Considerations that Two years Intrest of the money should be ommitted: and the s^d Thomas Powell Promises to pay the money To ye s^d Caleb Pusye: this orPhants Court A Jorned To the ffirst third Day in the first month next

The Court of Quarter sessions mett Againe According To A Jorument The Grand Jury Brought In their presentments (viz) Chester ye 8th of ye 10th month 1696: wee of the Grand Inquest for the County of Chester Doe present The Towneship of Neither Providence for want of Repaireing the Roade by William Swaffars: Andrew Jobe fforeman:

Chester ye 8th of the 10th month 1696

Wee off the Grand Inquest Doe present Richard Crosbye for Abuseing some of the MaJestrates of this County Att the house of James Cooper in Darby by Calling of them knaves & perticularly John Blunstone whoe he the said Crosby Called the said Justice blunstone knave and Rouge adding he was one that had bought and sold us and Calling many of the Inhabitants Beggarly Dogs and ffooles: saying he & his son knew more of the mathamaticall arts then eny of us all pretending he Could tell fortunes and who had stole goods and Describe where they was: alsoe Calling the s^d Coopers kinswoman named Sarah Cooper Drunken whore saying she had Drunke her selfe blind: and Called the said Coopers wife whore adding he Did not Care for such A Sallaways whore

all which Is A Grose Abuse both To the liveing and the Dead
som of which beare & others when a live bore noe small
ffigure In this Province: Andrew Jobe foreman:

The Court orders that the said Richard Crosby be summoned
to Appeare Att the next County Court to Answer the s^d
Presentment of ye Grand Jury: James Cooper prosecutor:

Chester the Eight of ye 10th month 1696 Whereas severall
of the Inhabitants of the Towne of Radnor have Complained
for the want of a Roade settled and Confirmed by the Grand
Inquest according to the usuall way in other Places of this
province and It being very Conveniant that such A Roade
should be laid oute & settled soe that none shall Impead or
molest it betwixt Darby and Radnor Darby being Att present
the principle markett for Corne and we of the Grand Inquest
Doe Desire of the Justices that wee may have An order to
lay out such A Road as may be benificall for the use of the
Country Andrew Jobe fforeman: The Court ordered that the
Grand Inquest have an order to lay oute the s^d Roade In the
most Conveniant Place they Can think meett: the Grand
Jury had an order to lay it oute

Chester ye 8th of the Tenth month 1696 wee of the Grand
Inquest for the County of Chester Doos present the County
for want of bridges over Crum Creek Rydly & Chester Creeke
In the kings Roade according To law: Andrew Jobe foreman:

John Bennett made over A sarvant boy whose name Is
George Robinson To Richard Thatcher him his heirs & Asigns
for his full Time of serv . . .

Joshua Morgan: Edward Beck Sarah Magdaniell & John
Howell were Called upon their Recogniceences & Appeared:
& James Standfield being bound to prosecute the said persons
appeard by Jonathan Heyes his Attorny who haveing laid the
whole matter and produced the proofes and papers To the
Grand Jury: who Returned they Could find nothing A gainst
the said Persons: they the persons To Witt Joshua Morgan
Edward becke & Sarah Magdaniell & John Howell were Dis-

charged by proclimation & Paying their ffees: And the Court orders the said persons to have their Goods Returned to them Againe:

Robert Wade plantiffe: Against the Estate of Thomas Longshaw in the hands of Henry Hollingsworth Defendant: the Pltf brought his Account Into the Court & sollemly Declerd it was a True Accont being the sum of six pounds one shilling and six pence halfe peny which the Court gave Judgment for with Cost of suite: that Henry Hollingsworth should pay oute of the Estate of ye s^d Longshaw y^t he have in his hands:

John Watts of New Castell Pltf Against the Estate of Thomas Longshaw Deces^d in the hands of Henry Hollingsworth ye Defe^{t}d: the Pltf brought In his Account ffor the sum of four pounds & sixteen shillings And Attested to It that It was a True account The Court gave Judgment for the said Dept & Cost of suite that Henry Hollingsworth shall pay It oute of the Estete of the s^d Tho Longshaw that he have in his hands:

Jasper yeates made knowen to the Court that there was A Dept Due to him from the s^d Tho: Longshaw: the Court ordered that Henry Hollings should Pay the s^d Jasper Yeates his Dept oute of the s^d Estate of Tho Longshaw:

John Baldwin Pl^{t}f Against
George Peacock Deft ac dept
by Attachment of All the Efects y^s In the County of the s^d Peacocks: to make satisfaction The Cause was Called the pltf Appeard & the Defendant was Called three times and not Appear^d the pltf produced A bill from under the said Defendants hand and seale for five pounds that was Due the last Day of the Eight month last & the Defendant not paying his s^d Just Dept nor Appeareing To Answer for Detayning the same the Court gave Judgm^t that the plantife shall have Execcution Granted to him for the same with Cost of Suite

Joseph bushell Acknowledged A Deed To Edward Johnings for one hundred and fourty Aceres of land lying In Beathell with houseing and all as is mentioned In the s^d Deed beareing Date ye 16th Day of the ninth month 96

Edward Johnings made over A Deed of mortgage for the same plantation To the said Joseph Bushell for the payment of the mony And Alsoe A bond of Two hundred pounds for the performance the Deed of mortgage and the bond of Performance beareing Date the 17th Day of the ninth month 1696

Phillip Roman Assigned over A Grand Deed for one hundred & Twenty five Accres of land lying in the Township of Concord To John Mendinghall his heirs and Assigns for Ever the Deed spetifieng 250: accres but Its but the one halfe sould to John Mendinghall

Godden Walter Acknowledged A Deed To John Hannum of Concord for A Parcell of land lying and being one south west side of the maine brainch of Chester Creek y^t leads throw Concord Towneship the Deed bearing Date ye second Day of September Anno Domi 1696

John Blunstone Acknowledged A Deed To John Beathell & Samuell Carpenter ffor the Trench that leads the water throw his lands to Darby mill the Deed beareing Date the Eight Day of December 1696:

Robert Pile Attorney for Edward Bezer Acknowledged A Deed To Thomas England for one hundred and sixty seven Accres of land lying and being In the Towneship of Bethell with all houseing & buildings thereon as the Deed Expreses the Deed beareing Date the Eight Day of ye 7th month 1696:

Jonathan Heyes Attorney for James Standfield Acknowledged A deed To Thomas Massey ffor three hundred Acres of land lying in the Towneship of marple the Deed beareing Date the Eight Day of September Anno: Dom: 1696

Thomas Massey made over A Deed for Eight Acres of land and seven Eight part of An Acre of land unto Henry Hames the land being In Marple It being by way of Exchainge for the like quantity of land as by the Deed beareing Date the Eight Day of September 1696 may more Att large a peare:

Henry Hames made over A Deed To Thomas Massey ffor Eight Accres of land & seven Eight part of An Acre of land lying In the Towneship of Marple the Deed beareing Date the Eight Day of September Anno: Dom 1696

Henry Hames Acknowledged A Deed of mortgage for Two Tracts of land lying and being In Marple To Jonathan Heyes for the Consideration of the sum of thirty pounds the Deed bearing Date y*e* Eight Day of December: 96

The Court A Jorned ffor Two weeks

Att A Court Held Att Chester ffor the County of Chester The 22 day of the Tenth moneth Annoq Domine 1696: by A Jornment After proclimation made the Court Caled

John Simcock President
Samuell Levis } Justices
Jonathan Heyes } Present
Joseph Wood sherif
John Childe Clarke

JASPER YEATES pltf } In an action of Trespas
GEORGE OLDFILD Deft } uppon the Case

The action was Called and Continued tell the next Court

William Jenkin Attorney for lewis David and William Howell Past A Deed to Jonathan Hayes ffor Two hundred Acres of land lying by Darby Creeke the Deed Beareing Date the seventh Day of December 1696

The Court Appoynted Andrew Jobe and Henry Hollingsworth & James Whitaker To Appraise the goods of George Peacock Taken by Exceecution by the shirif att the suite of John Baldwin

THOMAS WITHERS Pltf } In an action of Dept the Cause
ANTHONY WOOD Deft } being Called the plantif Apper*d* and brought his bond In to the Court from under the Defts hand and seale ffor Twenty three pounds thirteen shillings and three pence

The Deft being Called and not Appearing the Court Gave Judgment for the same with Cost of suite a pon the goods and Chattls of y*e* s*d* Deft as should make satisfaction for the same If not (: found on the) body of the said defendant.

Thomas sidebottom being brought before the Justices by virtue of a warrant for suspition of ffellony was Commited to the sheriff: and Brought Daniell Williamson & Thomas Taylor whoe Recognis themselfs To our soveraine lord the king In the sum of forty pounds for the Appearence of the said Thomas sidebottom at the next County Court to Answer the said Complaint:

Randolph Croxen Acknowledged A Deed To Thomas Powell ffor A boute Eight Acres of land lying In the Township of Upper Providence the Deed bereing Date the second Day of December 1696

Att An orPhants Court held Att Chester ffor the County of Chester the nineth Day of the ffirst moneth 1696/7

John Simcocke
John Blunstone
Jonathan Heyes
} Justices Present

Joseph Wood sherif
John Childe Clarke

There was A petticion Brought To this Court of the orphants of William Smyth Against Anthony Morgan The Pettion was Red: and the Court Considering of the same Requested Joseph Wood to Appeare And speaks To It In behalfe of the said orphants the next orphants Court. This orphants Court orders Henry Hollingsworth To Take Care of and To place oute the orphant of Thomas Longshaw as he see Conveniant

Jeremiah Collett Delivered the Estate of the orphants of Joseph Powell that he had In his hands To Caleb Pusye And Alsoo there was fiveteen shillings Allowed To the sheriff and six shillings to the Clarke of thet Esteate of the orhpants.

A Jorned to ye Court of quarter sessions to be held in ye 7 month next

Att A Court held Att Chester ffor The County of Chester the nineth and 10th Dayes of March Anno Domi: 1696/7

John Simcocke President
John Blunstone
Jonathan Heyes
Jasper Yeates
} Justices Present

Joseph Wood sheriff
John Childe Clarke

After proclimation made and silence In his MaJesties name: The Constables were Calld And Returnd All well and: And new ones Chosen. Joseph Edge Constable of Chester John Ditton for Aishtowne Robert Jeffers for Chichester Richard ffarr for Concord. Peter Dix for Bruningham: Abraham Beakes for Edgmond. James Sharplies for neither Providence John Hendrixson for R . . . The Remainder of the Constabls: John Hood Senior ffor Darbye: Henery Hames for Marpoole George lowns for Springfield John Steven for Radnor Richard bond for upper Providence Daniell Williamson for new towne David lawrance for haverfoord John Boyater for Middletowne in Roome of Thomas Martin Isaac Taylor for Thornbury:

Richard Crosby was Called To Answer to the presentment of the grand Jury the last Court: he Appeared: the presentment being Red: the Petty Jury were Called and Attested whose names are as followeth Walter Martin John Beales: Henery Hollingsworth: Peter Wood: John Hurlbatt: ABraham Beaks: David Lewis: Samuell Milles: Peter Lester: William Huntly Thomas Massey Barthollomew Coppocke Senior

The Evidences were Called And Attested: BenJamin Clift Declereth that he hard the fore named Richard Crosby Call John Blunstone one of his Maiesties Justices of the peace of this County Rouge Att the house of James Coopers In Darby And Call the said Coopers kinswoman whore And said that shee had Drunke herselfe Blind & was a Drunken whore: And Alsoe that he Called the said Coopers wife whore and that he Did not Care for such a Sallaways whore

Christopher Spray Being Attestd Deposeth that he hard the said Richard Crosby as was presented Call the said Coopers kinswoman whore and Calld the said Coopers wife sallaways whore And that he Called the said John Blunstone A Pittyful sorrowfull ffellow and that he had sold us and now was goeing to Redeeme us Agen: The Jury Brought virdit wee of Travis Jury Doe ffind Richard Crosby Guilty In manner And forme as he Is Inditted: the 9th of the first month 1696/7:

Walter Marten fforeman: Richard Crosby Appeard And submited himselfe To the bench and the Court ordered that he shall pay All the Charges thats Due and be Discharged for this time.

Thomas Sidebottom being bound over to this Court Appeared And the Court ordered that he pay five shillings for A fine and All the Charges thats Due and be for this time Discharged:

Jonathan Taylor: was Called and Apperd and the Court orderd him to pay five shillings for A fine and be Discharged for this Time:

Jacob Taylor and his sister Martha Taylor for some misdemeniours was Brought to this Court and they Acknowledgeing themselfs In fault and submitting themselves to the mercy of the bench the Court orderd them to pay all Charges thats Due and behave themselves well for the future (and five pound fine the Girle Martha to pay) and be for this time Discharged

The Court orders this Present Grand Jury To lay oute A Roade way for A Cart from Walter ffauscetts to Darby Bridge: forthwith

The Court orders Ellis Ellis supervisor for the Township of havorfoord to Cutt and Cleare the Roade way that leads to the limestone hill from Darby Township: Throw harfoord that he Cause the Inhabitants forthwith to Doe it.

David Loyd Attorney for Samuell Robbinson Past A Deed unto William Lewis for seventy Accres of land lying in New Towne the Deed beareing Date the 4th day of the 12 moneth 1696/7

David Prise Acknowledged A Deed unto Harry Reese for Three hundred Accres of land lying in Radnor the deed beareing Date the sixth day of the ffirst moneth 1696/7

Joseph Wood High sheriff Attorney for his Brother John Wood Past A Deed unto Bartholomew Coppock senior Attorney for Petter Britten for A plantation being Eighty nine Accres of land lying between Darby and Springfield the Deed beareing Date the 27th Day of the 12th moneth 1696/7

The Grand Jury Brought in theyr presentment: viz Chester the 10th of the first moneth 1696/7 we of the grand Inquest for the County of Chester: Doe Present Richard Tomson of marple Blacke Smith and Josiah Taylor of the same Towneship for Assaulting and violently Beateing the body of Edwerd Beck labourer one the third of this Instant to the breach of the Peace and Dishonour of the kings Crowne & Dignity being in the night season Andrew Jobe fforeman: The Court orders that they be summond to Appear Att the next County Court to Answer to ye s^d presentment:

Chester ye 9th of the first moth 1696/7 wee of the grand Inquest for the County of Chester Present Richard Crosby of Middle Towne In the s^d County of Chester for saying Att the house of Joseph Wood in Darby A boute three weeks sence: that the Grand Jury weare All perJured Rouges and that he would prove it Alsoe he the said Richard Crosby useing thretining words saying that If Either sherif or Clarke Came to Gather the County levie of him he would be the Death of him Andrew Jobe fforeman: the Court ordered that Richard Crosby be sumond to answer to the said presentment the next Court:

Thomas Smyth of Darby Acknowledged A Deed To his Brother John Smyth for fifty acres of land lying in Darby the Deed beareing Date the nineth of the first moneth 1696/7

Robert Neilor Attorney for Daniell Hibbett Acknowledged A Deed To Richard Parker for fifty Acres of land lying in Darby the Deed beareing Date the first Day of ye first month: 1696/7

Robert Neilor Attorney for Daniell Hibbett Acknowledged A Deed to William Bartram for fifty Acres of land lying in Darby the Deed beareing Date the first Day of the first month 1696/7

Robert Scothorne Attorney for George Wood Past a Deed To John Wood for four hundred and thirty five acres of land lying in Darby: Dated the seventh moneth 1696

John hood Attorney for John Bartram Past A Deed to John

Bartram the yonger for one hundred and ten Acres of land lying In Darby the Deed beareing Date the nineth of the first moneth 1696/7

Ralph Lewis Acknowledged A Deed To Ellis Ellis for thirty Acres of land lying in harfoord the Deed Bearcing Date fifth Day of March 1696/7

David Lloyd Acknowledged A Deed To John Sharply for A lott In Chester Greene being fourty foote ffront towards the River the Deed bearing Date ye 10th of ye first month 1696/7

Randell Mallin Acknowledged A Deed To Richard bond for Two Acres of land lying in upper Providence the Deed beareing Date the 22 Day of December 1696

William Woodmansee Acknowledged A Deed To Jeremiah Carter for A Roade way A Cross the said William Woodmansees land To A nother Tract of the said Jeremiah Carters land the Deed beareing Date the nineth Day of ye 1 moneth 1696/7

There being vakentcy

See In the yeare 1688 In this book for some Deeds that was Acknowledged Att the Court held for the County the 9th & 10th Dayes of the first moneth in the yeare 1696/7

INDEX

Owing to the varied nationalities of the Swedish, Dutch, English and Welsh settlers in Pennsylvania, together with the general illiteracy of the time, much diversity in the spelling of names will be found in the early court records. Aside from the fact that with some the father's first name became the surname of the children we find that Orion became Archer, and the descendants of Neales Lawson took the name of Friend. Few would recognize the name of Mendenhall in Mynar or Minall. Some attempt has been made to represent the later accepted forms in this index

Only one reference is given to a name on the same page.

ERRATA

Page 57: For Garnall read Yarnall.
Page 65: For Foreinam read Foreman.
Page 119: For Starnfield read Stanfield.
Page 239: For thoro, line 15, read there.

ADAMS, Samuel, 212.
AKRAMAN, John, 3, 4, 5, 10, 11, 12, 13, 14.
ALDRETS, Evert, 46, 47.
ALLEN, Nathaniel, 10, 12, 13, 19, 20, 22.
ANDERSON, John, 7, 8, 10, 13, 14, 159, 224.
    Justa (Justice), 13, 43, 44, 46, 47, 48, 53, 54, 132.
    Lassey, 10, 12.
ANDREWS, Elizabeth, 350.
    George, 20, 32, 33, 34, 36, 37, 38, 39, 43, 44, 45, 46, 69, 71, 75, 89, 110, 231, 237, 241, 297, 300, 302, 303, 315, 327, 333, 372, 376, 377, 378, 386.
ARCHER (ORION), Garthright (Gertrude), 316
    John, 372.
ARMES, Elinor, 276, 280
    Richard, 174, 254, 322
ASHCOM, Charles, 38, 40, 62, 74, 77, 89, 90, 92, 186, 200, 214, 232
ASHTON, John, 33.
ASTON, George, 34.
ATKINSON, Timothy, 296
BAILY, Daniel, 350.
    Joel, 57, 58, 108, 330, 339, 343, 345, 350.
BAINES, Elinor, 122, 138, 145, 168.
    William, 122, 138, 145, 168.
BAKER, Joseph, 64, 67, 70, 71, 72, 86, 101, 112, 114, 117, 123, 127, 143, 183, 199, 279, 286, 339, 387, 390.
    Samuel, 84, 89, 97, 98, 99, 105, 115, 186.
BALDWIN, Francis, 81, 153, 192, 234, 239, 301, 346, 355, 356, 357, 375, 391.
    John, 55, 83, 119, 174, 186, 192, 199, 232, 233, 273, 283, 332, 333, 338, 400.
    Thomas, 59, 147, 237, 266, 270, 289, 321, 346, 356.
BALL, John, 284, 340, 342, 343.
    William, 18.
BANKSON, Andreas, 3, 10, 15, 19.
    Hendrias, 8

INDEX 409

BARBER, Robert, 96, 104, 114, 123, 129, 136, 151, 156, 157, 160, 165, 185, 216, 232, 237, 249, 269, 270, 271, 272, 309, 319, 339, 343, 346, 350, 360, 362, 370, 383, 385.
BARBERY, John, 61.
BARKER, Thomas, 390.
BARNARD, Richard, 75, 77, 78, 117, 233, 254, 270, 283, 318, 339, 350.
BARNES, Henry, 162, 175, 178, 192, 194, 199, 221, 244, 317, 318, 348, 357, 382.
  John, 27.
BARRA, Robert, 205.
BAROON, Michael, 11.
BARTLESON, John, 26, 60, 70, 315.
  Lawrence, 316.
BARTRAM, John, 41, 59, 64, 67, 70, 71, 74, 75, 95, 151, 173, 214, 215, 216, 223, 253, 284, 297, 306, 313, 406.
  William, 406.
BAYLIS, James, 163, 164, 174, 259, 267, 269, 297, 323, 356, 360, 395.
  Jeane, 360.
  Mary, 163, 166.
BAYNTON, Ann, 300, 302, 315, 327, 341, 360, 372.
  Peter, 70, 72, 103, 217, 263, 268, 284, 286, 287, 293, 299, 300, 301, 302, 304, 305, 306, 315, 327, 341.
BEAKES, Abraham, 154, 319, 334, 395, 404.
  Samuel (?), 187.
  William, 209.
BEALS, John, 46, 52, 97, 117, 125, 126, 142, 151, 164, 194, 214, 215, 216, 230, 248, 271, 279, 288, 296, 303, 310, 311, 313, 324, 329, 331, 332, 333, 336, 339, 404.
BEALIFFE, James, 259.
BECK, Edward, 324, 399, 406.
BELCH, Jonathan, 368.
BENNETT, Edward, 77, 154, 155
  John, 86, 164, 183, 194, 195, 349, 383, 394, 399.
BEST, Mary, 111, 162, 164.
BESTRASOR, Richard, 178, 206.
BETHEL, John, 342, 351, 391, 401.
BEVAN, John, 109, 350, 381.
  Stephen, 381.
BEZER, Anne, 169, 196, 231.
  Edward, 34, 38, 41, 46, 57, 63, 64, 67, 70, 71, 86, 96, 103, 105, 107, 108, 116, 118, 121, 128, 146, 151, 152, 169, 180, 196, 197, 208, 216, 223, 224, 229, 231, 288, 324, 334, 351, 362, 363, 375, 387, 388, 401.
  Frances, 352.
  John, 23, 28, 32, 34, 73, 116, 179, 180, 352, 376.
  William, 121, 169.
BIASE, William, 116.
BILES, William, 3, 6, 8, 353.
BISHOP, Samuel, 362, 365, 367.
BISSE, Mary, 111.
BLACKWELL, Gov. John, 154, 161.
BLAKE, Edward, 146, 156.
  Judith, 373.
BLENDEE, Isaac, 380.
BLUNSTON, John, 26, 32, 35, 37, 39, 40, 42, 43, 44, 45, 49, 51, 52, 55, 56, 57, 61, 63, 64, 69, 70, 74, 75, 77, 84, 86, 87, 90, 91, 95, 96, 101, 105, 107, 108, 119, 122, 127, 128, 133, 138, 140, 145, 146, 149, 152, 155, 173, 179, 180, 181, 182, 183, 184, 185, 186, 196, 218, 223, 224, 225, 228, 229, 230, 241, 245, 246, 247, 253, 255, 256, 259, 261, 277, 285, 291, 296, 310, 319, 342, 346, 351, 354, 359, 366, 369, 379, 385, 393, 397, 398, 401, 403, 404.
  Michael, 26, 37, 38, 57, 64, 70, 71, 75, 121, 151, 233, 255, 271, 313, 322.

BOLES, John, 5, 7.
BOLTON, Edward, 156
BOND, Richard, 404, 407
BONDSON (Bonsall?), Richard, 37
BONSALL, Obadiah, 394
    Richard, 70, 119, 128, 214, 215, 216, 283, 286, 288, 294, 306, 313.
BOONE, Andreas (Andrew), 7, 12, 200, 224, 247.
    Andrew Swanson, 251, 342.
    Swan, 322.
BOULSTON, John, 17.
BOUND, John, 140.
BOWATER, John, 117, 143, 149, 150, 263, 265, 339, 404.
    Thomas, 151, 233, 303, 375.
BOWLES, Mary, 162, 175, 249, 262.
    Thomas, 80, 101, 102, 108, 109, 114, 118, 122, 123, 124, 128
BOWNE, James, 196.
    John, 140, 261, 385
    Samuel, 385.
BRADFORD, Thomas, 146
BRADSHAW, John, 100, 105, 106, 113, 148
    Samuel, 38, 55, 92, 95, 96, 110, 119, 261.
    Thomas, 92, 95, 97, 110, 120, 121, 149, 164, 194, 232, 287.
BRASSEY, Thomas, 22, 23, 25, 28, 32, 59, 88, 94, 120, 122, 127, 129, 132, 138.
    167, 179, 182, 190 221 234, 242, 246, 254, 256, 261, 273, 279, 296, 350.
BREALY, Isaac, 178
BRENSON, Daniel, 4, 6.
BRICKSHAW, Isaac, 60, 192, 199.
BRIDGMAN, Richard, 88.
BRIENTNALL, David, 55, 56, 58
BRIGHAM, Charles, 6
BRIGHT, Thomas, 242, 268, 313, 314, 346.
BRINKLOE, John, 353.
BRINTON, William, 64, 67, 71, 88, 95, 97, 116, 119, 141, 254, 319, 360, 370, 374.
BRISTOLL (Bristow?), John, 64, 65, 66, 67, 68.
BRISTOW, John, 75, 76, 80, 83, 90, 91, 96, 103, 105, 107, 108, 114, 118, 120, 121, 122, 124, 127, 128, 130, 132, 133, 136, 138, 145, 146, 150, 151, 153, 157, 158, 159, 160, 161, 168, 173, 176, 179, 184, 185, 196, 197, 199, 202, 213, 218, 224, 225, 228, 230, 234, 236, 240, 241, 245, 246, 247, 253, 254, 259, 261, 262, 264, 265, 266, 268, 269, 270, 273, 275, 276, 277, 279, 285, 302, 310, 312, 313, 314, 319, 320, 324, 325, 374
    Thomas, 82
BRITTON, Canawell, 25, 36, 68, 140.
    Peter, 405.
BROOKS, Charles, 234, 282, 296, 303, 310, 330, 350.
BROOKSHAW, Isaac, 60, 192, 199.
BROOM, Daniel, 333, 339, 359.
BROTHERS, Robert, 80, 102, 109, 162, 175
BROWNE, James, 3, 4, 5, 8, 9, 15, 16, 18, 23, 24, 26, 27, 32, 36, 37, 42, 43, 54, 57, 59, 63, 65, 66, 67, 68, 71, 74, 75, 77, 79, 80, 87, 96, 98, 99, 106, 111, 116, 125, 126, 129, 133, 139, 140, 142, 148, 150, 151, 153, 162, 167, 168, 192, 204, 205, 206, 207, 217, 232, 242, 256, 266, 297, 334, 340, 363, 386, 396
    Robert, 260
    Thomas, 138, 192, 252, 254, 260, 264, 266, 289, 320, 331
    William, 36, 46, 50, 63, 105, 125, 126, 135, 137 224, 271, 277, 279, 284, 287, 310, 322, 327, 332, 333, 338, 363, 384
BROWN-JOHN?, Thomas, 103 (See John.)
BRUCE, Arthur, 121.
    William, 393.

BRUNSDEN, Alice, 116.
  John, 245, 268.
BUCKINGHAM, John, 210.
  William, 96, 129, 146, 153, 186.
BUCKLEY, John, 73, 110, 154, 208.
BUDD, Thomas, 14, 136, 149
BUFFINGTON, Anne, 157, 158, 363, 371.
  Richard, 3, 5, 7, 18, 26, 27, 34, 35, 46, 48, 56, 79, 98, 105, 110, 118, 119, 129, 136, 148, 156, 157, 158, 181, 185, 186, 187, 226, 242, 278, 285, 289, 292, 297, 300, 371.
BULLEN, Thomas, 384.
BULLER, Judith, 363, 371, 382.
  Sarah, 276.
BUNTING, Ann, 246.
BURROWS, Robert, 75, 78, 117, 146, 199, 202, 243.
BUSHELL, Joseph, 52, 64, 67, 70, 71, 95, 109, 130, 182, 223, 400, 401.
BUTCHER, Edmund, 311, 384.
BUTLER, John, 175.
BUTTERFIELD, Thomas, 68, 272, 274, 278.
BUZBY, John, 341, 345, 352, 353, 357, 365.
CADMAN, Henry, 161, 221.
CALVERT, Jane, 82.
  John, 45, 49, 50, 55, 56, 57, 58, 82, 119, 127, 136, 137, 200, 259, 264, 288, 313.
  Judith, 81.
  Ruth, 328.
CANIDE, John, 393.
CANTWELL, Edmund, 6, 15, 17, 18, 21, 22, 47, 48.
CANUTE, Morton, 111. (See Knewtson.)
CAROLUS, Andrew, 114.
  Lawrence, 12, 13, 23, 25, 26, 32, 43, 44, 46, 47, 48.
CARPENTER, Samuel, 281, 309, 330, 337, 353, 382, 401.
CARR, Richard, 357.
CARRE, Andrew, 29.
  Priscilla, 29.
CARTER, Edward, 23, 24, 28, 30, 38, 78, 81, 86, 109, 112, 119, 120, 123, 124, 164, 181, 194, 214, 224, 230, 235, 246, 263, 273, 332.
  Jeremiah, 117, 135, 152, 227, 330, 407.
  Lydia, 330.
  Margaret, 192.
  Mary, 166.
  Robert, 183, 226, 237, 271, 277, 307, 309, 331, 339, 363, 384, 391.
  William, 304.
CARTLIDGE, Edmund, 35, 41, 55, 64, 78, 80, 92, 97, 120, 121, 143, 248, 283, 297, 306, 323.
CARTWRIGHT, Jean, 192.
  Thomas, 112, 163, 186, 192, 195, 339, 345, 358, 361, 366, 387, 390.
CHADS, Francis, 28, 40, 55, 62, 63, 70, 76, 80, 91, 105, 126, 147, 149, 150, 159, 167, 204, 207, 209, 226, 248, 250, 263, 279, 329, 332, 333, 336, 341, 374, 388, 394.
CHAMBERLIN, Robert, 93, 129, 277, 296, 303.
CHAMBERS, John, 211, 212.
  Margaret, 384
  Stephen, 35, 37, 41, 45, 62.
  William, 112.
CHAMPION, John, 4, 5, 18, 22, 24.
CHANDLER, George, 138, 145, 196, 204, 297, 325, 358, 390.
  Jacob, 71, 90, 105, 108, 112, 128, 139, 162, 169, 199, 209, 216, 217, 223, 227, 229, 233, 234, 336.

CHANDLER, Jane, 140.
　　John, 134, 140, 141, 149, 153, 162
CHARD, John, 100
CHEVERS, James, 157, 241.
CHILD, John, 10, 11, 12, 13, 26, 33, 34, 35, 37, 45, 48, 55, 59, 65, 67, 72, 75, 78, 81, 103, 112, 125, 129, 151, 154, 156, 158, 162, 173, 195, 209, 210, 211, 243, 245, 248, 249, 271, 273, 286, 287, 289, 293, 299, 301, 306, 307, 310, 315, 317, 319, 320, 321, 323, 327, 329, 330, 331, 332, 334, 336, 339, 341, 344, 346, 352, 354, 359, 369, 376, 379, 388, 393, 397, 398, 402, 403.
CHURCHMAN, George, 89, 94, 96, 104, 108, 139, 159, 184, 233, 289, 296, 374
　　John, 374.
CLARK, John, 129.
　　William, 162, 353
CLAUSE, Christian, 10, 12, 18, 21.
　　Margaretta, 21.
CLAYTON, Joseph, 60, 156, 161.
　　Prudence, 52, 54.
　　William, 3, 4, 6, 8, 9, 10, 11, 12, 14, 19, 22, 23, 25, 28, 36, 46, 52, 66, 71, 116, 135, 136, 139, 149, 164, 179, 181, 184, 204, 229, 230, 234, 236, 242, 263, 265, 297, 334, 383, 394.
CLEMENSON, Mathew, 281.
CLEMENT, Timothy, 87
CLEWES, Elinor, 276, 280.
　　John, 103, 240, 261, 280, 295, 296.
　　Richard, 134, 165, 175, 177, 215.
CLIFT, Benjamin, 404.
　　Samuel, 14.
CLIFTON, Robert, 353
　　Thomas, 46, 63, 105, 115.
CLOUD, John, 255, 326.
　　Joseph, 255, 325, 326, 333, 334
　　Robert, 63, 64, 65, 66, 67, 70.
CLOUD, William, 25, 26, 31, 32, 36, 43, 49, 52, 57, 63, 64, 65, 67, 70, 72, 90, 91, 97, 112, 115, 116, 117, 164, 194, 249, 250, 252, 255, 391
COATES, Thomas, 76, 96, 101, 248, 254, 289, 375
COBB, William, 5, 7, 12, 28, 36, 40, 102.
COBOURNE, Joseph, 131, 133, 153, 216, 227, 239, 246, 284, 287, 313, 355, 356, 359, 363, 370, 373, 375, 385, 386, 391, 396
　　Thomas, 15, 16, 19, 20, 22, 23, 24, 26, 28, 33, 49, 64, 67, 70, 71, 72, 87, 89, 94, 96, 97, 120, 132, 133, 181, 183, 216, 225, 239, 254, 264, 270, 283, 288, 289, 295, 296, 302, 312, 313, 322, 358, 375
　　William, 74, 75, 97, 104, 117, 132, 174, 195, 216, 225, 239, 288, 311, 313, 367, 375, 395.
COCK, Cox, Erick, 8, 9, 10, 11, 12, 13.
　　John, 5, 10, 11, 12, 13, 19, 20, 31, 294, 295, 302, 303, 311, 324, 326, 363, 367, 376, 380, 391, 396
　　Lassey (Lawrence), 3, 4, 6, 7, 8, 10, 11, 15, 16, 19, 21, 22, 31, 68
　　Mouns, 8, 9, 10, 19, 20.
　　Otto Ernest, 3, 6, 8, 9, 10, 12, 15, 19, 25, 26, 28, 29, 32, 33, 232, 247.
　　Peter, 5, 115
COLE, Sabean, 300.
　　William, 289
COLEMAN, Anna, 3
　　Henry, 4, 7, 26, 380, 391.
　　Lassey, 102, 130.
COLLETT, Jane, 90
　　Jeremiah, 15, 16, 19, 20, 22, 23, 27, 31, 34, 36, 38, 39, 40, 41, 42, 43, 45, 46, 49, 51, 52, 55, 57, 58, 61, 62, 63, 64, 69, 71, 77, 78, 79, 80,

87, 88, 90, 107, 108, 112, 113, 130, 136, 139, 142, 147, 148, 151, 159, 160, 162, 187, 195, 206, 211, 212, 225, 226, 230, 232, 236, 237, 240, 242, 259, 286, 287, 293, 294, 297, 299, 300, 301, 304, 306, 307, 310, 315, 317, 319, 320, 321, 323, 327, 329, 331, 332, 334, 336, 338, 339, 341, 354, 359, 364, 369, 372, 374, 376, 395, 403.
   John, 78, 84.
   William, 75, 76, 78, 84, 88, 119, 141, 148, 149, 155, 162, 164, 175, 194, 216, 224, 227, 288, 300, 303, 304, 313, 324, 325, 333, 372, 374.
COLLIER, Edward, 66.
   Thomas, 139, 149, 289.
COOPER, James, 391, 398, 399, 404.
   Sarah, 398.
   Thomas, 70, 76, 108.
COMPTON, Jonathan, 138.
CONWAY, Patrick, 209, 210, 211.
   Philip, 208, 210.
COPPOCK, Bartholomew, 69, 74, 77, 86, 87, 89, 90, 91, 96, 105, 107, 108, 118, 120, 121, 122, 124, 128, 137, 138, 145, 146, 155, 168, 173, 175, 179, 180, 182, 184, 195, 220, 221, 243, 245, 248, 254, 320, 333, 336, 401, 405.
   Ellen, 148.
   Margaret, 148.
COOK, Arthur, 150.
   Francis, 192, 255.
   Richard, 238, 335.
COOKSON, Joseph, 44, 75, 78, 117, 195, 230, 244, 333.
COPE, Oliver, 361.
CORNELIUS, John, 5, 26.
CORNELL, William, 53.
CORNUTE, Morton, 54, 108, 110.
COX, 114. (See Cock.)
   Doctor, 376.
CRAFT, James, 343.
CREGAR, Alexander, 341.
CRISPIN, Silas, 15, 16, 19, 20.
CROSBY, Richard, 33, 34, 36, 37, 38, 39, 43, 44, 45, 46, 56, 65, 68, 71, 72, 75, 80, 83, 89, 91, 103, 104, 114, 117, 122, 127, 132, 166, 200, 241, 259, 274, 275, 278, 297, 298, 300, 302, 303, 315, 327, 372, 375, 376, 377, 378, 386, 387, 396, 398, 399, 404, 405, 406.
CROSS, John, 221.
   Richard, 221.
   Thomas, 19, 20, 22, 72, 118, 119, 139, 186, 192, 203, 209, 220, 232.
CROXEN, Randolph, 403.
CUNNINGHAM, John, 374.
CURTIS, William, 294.
DALBOE, Lawrence, 3, 4, 5, 6, 7, 11, 16, 17, 19, 22, 50.
   Peter, 4, 8, 9, 11, 17, 20, 24, 216, 240.
   William, 11, 51, 216.
DANIELL, Eusta, 8, 19, 23
DANGER, Edward, 358.
DART, Samuel, 4, 6.
DAVID, Davis, John, 254, 394.
   Katherine, 126.
   Lewis, 256, 342, 402.
   Philip, 381.
   Thomas, 335.
   William, 238, 335, 394.
DAWSON, Emanuel, 123.
   Nathaniel, 114
DAY, John, 26.

DELAGRANGE, Arnoldus, 26, 28, 30, 33, 40.
    Margaretta, 29.
DENNING, Philip, 96, 103
DERRICKSON, Cornelius, 248, 250.
DEVEREUX, Alexander, 227, 249, 256, 262, 280, 285, 304.
DICKS, Peter, 75, 78, 88, 279, 298, 404.
DILLION, William, 220.
DOBIE, Lydias, 374.
DONALDSON, John, 341, 353, 361, 371.
DOWNING, Edward, 348, 356.
DRACOTT, Ralph, 148, 188, 200, 202, 226, 228, 231, 333, 336, 350, 356.
DREWITT, Morgan, 3, 4, 5.
DRIVER, James, 300, 303.
DUCKETT, Thomas, 88.
DURBOROW, Hugh, 104, 105, 183.
DUTTON, Edward, 338.
    John, 283, 317, 338, 404
    Thomas, 338
DYER, Robert, 64, 65, 67.
DYMOND, Richard, 21, 23, 24, 25.
EAVENSON, Thomas, 127, 128, 140, 146, 370.
EAYR, John, 234, 334.
EDGE, John, 75, 78, 80, 89, 101, 108, 119, 124, 152, 221, 319.
    JOSEPH, 89, 108, 123, 261, 338, 339, 351, 404.
EDWARDS, Alexander, 339.
    Joseph, 318, 346.
    John, 328.
    Peter, 381.
    William, 117, 284, 287, 303, 328.
EFFINGALL, Abraham, 56.
EGLINTON, Edward, 32, 34, 240, 243, 244.
ELDER, Thomas, 31, 32
ELDRIDGE, John, 147, 157, 166, 173, 184, 187, 265, 269
ELFRETH, Josiah, 156.
ELLIOTT, John, 228, 351, 352, 373.
ELLIS, Ellis, 203, 405, 407.
    Humphrey, 230, 244, 255, 341, 360
    Rachel, 381
    Widow, 238
ELY, Joshua, 49, 50
EMPSON, Cornelius, 126, 237.
ENGLAND, Philip, 201, 220
    Thomas, 234, 255, 282, 326, 330, 387, 401.
ENOCH, Harmon, 20, 24.
ERICKSON, Peter, 3, 4, 5, 19, 21, 23, 24, 184.
EUSTASON, Eusta, 93, 372.
    John, 4, 11.
    Mouns, 6, 7, 51, 93
EVANS, David, 254, 326, 335, 394
    John, 350
    Mary, 156.
    Nathaniel, 10, 11, 12, 13, 20, 22, 23, 24, 26, 32, 52, 66, 78, 81, 83, 91, 96, 106, 118, 166, 167, 194, 199.
    Thomas John, 394.
EVERTS, Brantie, 46
EWER, Elizabeth, 253, 273, 279.
    Robert, 236, 253, 254, 273, 279, 280.
EYRE, Anne 72, 73, 104, 162, 163.
    John, 234, 334.

INDEX 415

EYRE, Robert, 25, 32, 34, 35, 37, 38, 39, 40, 42, 43, 44, 45, 49, 51, 52, 55, 57, 61, 63, 64, 67, 69, 72, 73, 74, 76, 77, 86, 87, 90, 91, 92, 96, 102, 103, 104, 105, 107, 108, 112, 113, 116, 118, 121, 122, 124, 128, 129, 133, 138, 145, 146, 155, 161, 162, 163, 164, 168, 173, 174, 194, 282, 297, 370, 379.
FABRUSHES, Jacobus, 12, 15, 19, 21, 22, 23, 24
FAIRMAN, Thomas, 8, 10, 15, 17, 19, 22, 29, 280.
FARMER, John, 353.
FARR, Richard, 72, 75, 125, 404.
FAUSETT, Walter, 50, 56, 60, 76, 78, 81, 86, 89, 112, 115, 120, 127, 128, 147, 164, 182, 194, 200, 221, 224, 226, 230, 234, 239, 262, 299, 336, 337, 380, 394, 405
FEARNE, Joshua, 26, 32, 36, 37, 89, 91, 96, 105, 107, 108, 109, 110, 118, 121, 122, 124, 128, 133, 138, 140, 144, 115, 146, 155, 169, 180, 182, 185, 196, 199, 201, 213, 218, 223, 224, 225, 228, 229, 230, 236, 241, 247, 253, 259, 261, 262, 268, 269, 270, 274, 275, 276, 277, 285.
Josiah, 275, 339.
FENWICK, Major, 29.
FERILL, Lewis, 305.
FEW, Isaac, 97, 159, 227, 271, 277, 289, 296, 311, 321, 356, 367, 373, 391.
Richard, 20, 22, 26, 33, 38, 60, 104, 107, 108, 110, 120, 123, 176.
Susana, 107.
FINCH, Anne, 91, 319.
FINCHER, Anne, 64.
FINDLOW, William, 91.
FINLOE, Alexander, 296.
FISHER, John, 57.
William, 350
FISKE, Casper, 8, 19, 23.
FLATT, Robert, 355
FLOWER, William, 289, 297, 339.
FORD, Edward, 325.
Reuben, 312, 326
FOREMAN, George, 13, 15, 16, 26, 27, 56, 59, 65, 67, 68, 69, 71, 75, 77, 85, 88, 94, 95, 97, 98, 99, 105, 107, 114, 118, 119, 124, 130, 131, 136, 139, 147, 148, 160, 161, 168, 173, 179, 181, 182, 196, 199, 200, 208, 213, 217, 218, 224, 225, 228, 230, 231, 234, 236, 237, 241, 243, 244, 247, 253, 262, 268, 274, 281, 283, 284, 286, 287, 294, 297, 299, 305, 306, 307, 310, 315, 319, 320, 321, 323, 326, 327, 329, 331, 332, 333, 334, 336, 338, 339, 340, 341, 343, 346, 354, 359, 361, 369, 376, 377, 379, 386
FORREST, Walter, 16.
FOULK, Owen, 268.
Sabrant, 31.
FOX, John, 59, 82, 156, 178, 194, 220, 255, 256, 323, 330, 375.
Thomas, 97, 120, 121, 139, 247, 252, 288, 313.
FRAMPTON, Elizabeth, 94.
William, 56, 94.
FRAZER, Andrew, 355.
FREDERICK, Michael, 21.
FREEMAN, Edward, 364
Sarah, 382.
William, 340, 362, 371, 385, 396
FRETWELL, Dorothy, 262, 271, 278, 298, 305, 344.
Ralph, 262, 271, 278, 298, 305, 344.
FRIEND, Andrew, 78, 85, 86, 88, 93, 94, 96, 101, 102, 103, 104, 105, 115, 118, 122, 134, 160, 173, 174, 182, 185, 206, 215, 233, 240, 246, 295, 297, 299
Anne, 156, 160, 174, 181, 185, 224, 240, 246.

FRIEND, Barbara, 379.
    Johannes (John), 92, 103, 104, 118, 122, 124, 160, 174, 215, 224, 227, 231, 240, 246, 380, 391.
    Richard, 41, 62.
    Sarah, 224.
    Susanna, 227, 231.
GABITAS, William, 146, 163, 342, 343.
GAMBLE, Francis, 150.
    Gideon, 156.
GARDINER, Thomas, 216.
GARRETT, John, 37, 294, 297, 362, 365.
    Thomas, 28, 49, 50, 52, 63, 71, 128, 244, 284, 287, 289, 297, 323.
    William, 97, 120, 121, 149, 232, 243, 313, 314, 315, 316, 322, 364, 384.
GIBBONS, Henry, 119, 228, 294.
    John, 46, 51, 64, 67, 70, 71, 92, 95, 147, 154, 159, 230, 311, 312.
GIBBS, Edward, 127.
GLEAVE, George, 60, 101, 108, 119, 197, 218, 220, 245.
    Hester, 197, 218, 223, 245.
    John, 245.
    Phebe, 245.
GOFORTH, William, 99, 103.
GOLDING, John, 154, 291, 370, 385, 387.
GOODSON, John, 100
GORDON, Jeane, 384.
GRATTON Matthew, 121, 261.
GRAVES, Alexander, 362, 364, 365.
GRAYBORNE, William, 50.
GREEN, John, 311, 330, 331, 338, 381.
    Richard, 162.
    Thomas, 105, 126, 167, 263, 330, 331, 339, 345, 355, 369.
    William, 48
GREENSELL, John, 8, 9, 10.
GREGORY, William, 101, 102, 195, 228, 292.
GRIFFITH, Edward, 335
    Jenkin, 152, 201, 287
GRIST, George, 334, 351, 387, 388.
GRICE, John, 12.
GROWDON, Joseph, 353.
GRUBB, Henry, 16.
    John, 7, 12, 18, 48, 122, 181, 208.
HALE, Thomas, 89.
HALL, Thomas, 86, 89.
HALLIWELL, Richard, 340, 353
HALLOWELL, John, 41, 80, 83, 92, 128, 143, 152, 237, 240, 248, 297, 306, 319
HAMBY, William, 111.
HAMMS, Henry, 136, 165, 297, 323, 356, 395, 397, 401, 402, 404
HANCOCK, Richard, 7.
HANKE, Luke, 149.
HANNUM, John, 72, 74, 76, 88, 116, 127, 132, 150, 195, 282, 384, 401.
    Margery, 77, 150
HANSON, Mouns, 8
HARDING, John, 26, 28, 30, 33, 37, 39, 44, 45, 49, 51, 52, 63, 77, 96, 106, 108, 179, 180, 377
HARPER John, 19, 20, 22
HARRISON, Francis, 69, 71, 87, 89, 90, 91, 97, 103, 104, 107, 108, 112, 118, 121, 122, 128, 140, 143, 146, 150, 155, 161, 168, 173, 182, 184, 185, 187, 196, 199
    Samuel, 130, 366, 367, 368.

HARRY, Daniel, 322, 346, 347.
    Hugh, 152, 349.
HART, John, 22.
HASTINGS, Elizabeth, 166.
    Henry, 3, 4, 5, 19, 20, 21, 22, 26, 32, 34, 41, 52, 57, 116, 217, 269, 297, 328, 346, 358, 363, 366, 390.
    John, 20. 33, 39, 66, 81, 117, 170, 377.
    Joshua, 20, 22, 23, 24, 25, 28, 30, 34, 39, 65, 68, 80, 81, 82, 87, 89, 101, 105, 109, 112, 120, 134, 146, 179, 180, 183, 186, 192, 199, 202, 203, 207, 208, 209, 230, 240, 282, 351, 383
HAWKES, Jane, 138, 166.
    William, 53, 54, 84, 105, 111, 124, 126, 134, 138, 140, 145, 149, 160, 162, 167, 169, 193, 196, 203, 207, 209, 214, 215, 216, 226, 232, 244, 276, 278, 285, 288, 292, 297.
HAYES, James, 109, 114, 123, 195, 206.
    Jonathan, 38, 55, 66, 89, 103, 119, 127, 128, 129, 141, 154, 159, 207, 212, 214, 249, 264, 265, 286, 287, 293, 299, 301, 302, 306, 307, 310, 315, 319, 320, 321, 323, 327, 329, 332, 334, 336, 337, 338, 339, 341, 344, 346, 350, 354, 359, 366, 369, 379, 388, 393, 397, 399, 401, 402, 403.
    Richard, 284, 337, 343, 385.
HAZELL, John, 6, 7, 22. 24.
HAZLEGROVE, John, 27.
HEADINGS, Lawrence, 6, 30, 31, 156.
HELME, Israel, 6, 9, 29, 30, 33, 232, 237, 238, 248
HENDRICKSON, Albert, 4, 8, 9, 10, 11, 12, 13, 19, 20, 22, 23, 24, 26, 32, 34, 41, 49, 55, 69, 76, 97, 102, 106, 108, 137, 151, 156, 157, 158, 162, 173, 199, 237, 240, 249, 263, 265, 267, 288, 311, 313, 323
    Andrew, 224.
    Frances, 376, 379.
    Hendrick, 216.
    Jacob, 217, 237, 347.
    James, 297, 333, 350
    John, 17, 33, 38, 60, 114, 123, 231, 259, 297, 338, 354. 367, 376, 379, 380, 391, 404.
    Maudlin, 391.
    Tatton, 224.
HENSON, John, 113.
HENT, Rees, 267, 289, 311, 327, 355, 382.
HERCULES, James, 300
HERMAN, Ephraim, 232, 250
HEWES, William, 3, 4, 5, 8, 9, 15, 16, 23, 24, 28, 35, 36, 45, 56, 61, 65, 68, 75, 334, 352, 387.
HIBBERD, Daniel, 292, 406.
    Josiah, 274
HICKMAN, Elizabeth, 318.
    John, 20, 51, 52, 70, 79, 160, 364.
    Joseph, 187, 241.
    Mary, 35, 309.
HILL, William, 268.
HINSON, John, 361, 365
HITCHCOCK, William, 116, 295
HOEMAN, Andrews, 7, 9. (See Homan.)
HOSKINS, John, 60, 76, 99, 117, 118, 122, 132, 136, 140, 153, 160, 174, 181, 201, 221, 227, 244, 266, 287, 306, 319, 323, 324, 326, 337, 338, 358, 366, 367, 390
    Mary, 166, 266
HOLLINSHEAD, John, 14.
HOLLINGSWORTH, Henry, 296, 311, 313, 318, 321. 340, 343, 346, 348, 351, 356, 359, 368, 369, 385. 395, 396, 397, 400, 402, 403, 404

HOLLINGSWORTH, Margaret, 82.
    Thomas, 200.
HOLMES, Jonas, 104.
    Thomas, 21, 92, 186, 200, 214, 215, 217, 317, 326
    Tryal, 214
HOLSTON, John, 77, 81, 114, 152, 226, 232, 253, 356, 357, 391.
HOLT, Samuel, 249
HOMAN, Andreas, 7, 9.
    Lawrence, 156, 224, 323.
    Matthew, 224
    William, 224
HOOD, John, 70, 232, 243, 248, 255, 262, 288, 291, 306, 313, 404, 406.
    Thomas, 146, 243, 255, 282, 297, 306, 319, 323.
HOOPER, Abraham, 162, 175.
HOPE, John, 355, 356
    Thomas, 228, 301, 311, 313, 374, 397.
HOPMAN, Hans, 7, 11, 17.
HOULSTEAD, Matthias, 15, 16.
    Mathew, 17
HOWARD, William, 275.
HOWELL, Alse, 393
    John, 96, 195, 238, 254, 399.
    Sarah, 348.
    Thomas, 323, 348, 349, 360, 393.
    William, 121, 155, 168, 173, 184, 238, 385, 402.
HUDSON, William, 167.
HUGG, John, 275.
HULBERT, Edward, 77, 79, 85, 88, 89, 90, 323, 326.
    John, 65, 68, 69, 78, 142, 146, 208, 287, 358, 366, 390, 404.
HUMPHREY, Daniel, 233, 255, 322, 341, 350, 360.
    Joseph, 49, 119, 128, 169, 290, 305, 307.
HUNLOKE, Edward, 338.
HUNTER, Saundy, 384
HUNTLEY, William, 301, 322, 398, 404.
HURST, John, 59, 60
HUTCHINSON, Mathew, 50.
    Robert, 268, 326.
IMMANUEL, Florence, 347.
INDIAN, Chato, 115
INGELO, Richard, 48.
INKHORNE, Andreas, 5, 9, 11, 19.
INLOE, Abraham, 248, 250.
IRELAND, Nicholas, 156, 322.
IZARD, Michael, 8, 9, 10, 12, 24, 33, 34, 55, 59, 129, 132, 321.
JACKSON, Ephraim, 329, 334, 397.
    Roger, 117, 120, 144, 201, 243, 244, 271, 296, 334, 360, 396.
JACOBS, Thomas 65, 67
JACOBSON, Hendrick, 225.
JAMES, Amy, 217
    David, 348, 360
    George, 351, 393.
    Howell, 117, 183, 234, 235, 326, 394.
    James, 238, 330, 350.
    Philip, 342.
    William, 394
JEFFERIS, Robert, 58, 256, 297, 362, 365, 404
JEGOU, Peter, 48.
JENKIN, William, 156, 157, 183, 241, 247, 253, 259, 261, 252, 268, 269, 270, 277, 284, 285, 348, 360, 402.

JENNINGS, Edward, 98, 103, 125, 241, 324, 400, 401.
    John, 71.
JERMAN, John, 153, 167, 174, 185, 233, 237, 322.
JERROME, Samuel, 395
JERVIS, Joseph, 350
JOB, Andrew, 165, 215, 261, 271, 277, 363, 391, 398, 399, 402, 406
JOBSON, Samuel, 390.
JOHN, Thomas-Browne, 103, 203, 206, 230, 231.
JOHNSON, Andros, 351.
    Anne, 112, 132.
    Charles, 18, 33,
    Clause, 14.
    Fop, 30.
    Greeta, 249, 250.
    Gurstow, 131.
    Harmon, 3, 18, 26, 102, 124, 247, 249, 250
    Humphrey, 307, 309, 310, 313, 332, 336, 344, 358, 366, 390.
    Jacob, 131, 224.
    James, 355.
    John, 5, 10, 12, 18, 24, 33, 35, 37, 43, 44, 74, 102, 106, 113, 121, 344.
    Margaret, 3, 111, 250
    Ringnea, 131.
    William, 34, 50, 61.
JOHNSTOWN, William, 383.
JOLLIFFE, John, 43.
JONES, Ellis, 238
    Griffith, 341, 353, 389
    Henry, 125, 126, 133, 260.
    Jane, 94, 95.
    John, 71, 195, 290, 301, 322, 394
    Joseph, 126.
    Joshua, 263, 266
    Josias, 186.
    Mary, 201.
    Richard, 370, 371, 372, 385, 386, 396.
    Thomas, 233, 238, 286, 327, 338, 382, 394
JUSTASON, John, 9.
JUSTICE, Charles, 206.
JUSTISON, Cornelius, 297.
KAY, Jonathan, 249
KEACH, Elias, 104, 112.
KEEN, Urin, 84, 90, 112, 120
    Villamchy, 21.
KELLY, Patrick, 348, 363, 371, 382, 392.
    William, 341.
KENNEDY, James, 300
    John, 393.
KENNERLEY, James, 19, 20, 22, 26, 33, 36, 44, 58, 74, 106, 117
KENT, Joseph, 253, 295, 320, 395
KERSEY, Thomas, 210, 211.
KING, Thomas, 38, 75, 88, 95, 146, 163, 233, 234, 326
KINGSMAN, John, 28, 36, 41, 42, 46, 52, 63, 92, 97, 115, 116, 117, 139, 164, 194, 201, 212, 217, 224, 234, 254, 259, 295, 313, 317, 318, 322, 355, 370
KINNISON, Edward, 149, 159, 176, 181
KIRK, John, 121, 139, 254, 292.
    Thomas, 226, 231
KNEWTSON, Morton, 21. (See Canute.)
KNIGHT, Joseph, 226, 273.

LACY, 315
  George, 300.
LAMBERT, Philip, 242.
LAMPLUGH, Nathaniel, 20, 52, 56, 65, 68, 75, 77, 91. 100. 106, 147, 182, 187, 203, 207, 209, 214, 246.
LANGHAM, Robert, 255, 299, 301, 303
LASIE (LAWRENCE?), Thomas, 97, 131, 176, 183
LAWRENCE, David, 164, 177, 183, 185, 194, 277, 286, 360, 404.
  Marcus, 19.
LAWSON, LAWRENSON, Lawrence, 13
  Annakey, 7
  Anne, 104, 115.
  Lassey, 4, 6, 8, 10
  Neales, 7, 8, 9, 26, 33, 41, 76, 85, 86, 104, 248, 249.
LEHMAINE, Philip Th., 36, 64, 68, 140, 232.
LESTER, Peter, 74, 76 101, 119, 220, 221, 346, 347, 395, 404.
LETORT, James, 322, 346, 347
LEVIS, Samuel, 64, 69, 71, 74, 77, 84, 85, 86, 90, 139, 169, 180, 182, 183, 185, 186, 196, 197, 199, 213, 218, 223, 224, 225, 228, 229, 230, 236, 241, 245, 246, 247, 253, 259, 262, 268, 269, 275, 276, 277, 282, 299, 303, 304, 307. 318, 338, 346, 359, 364, 379, 384, 388, 397, 402.
LEWELLYN, Morris, 174, 238, 322, 339, 360, 381
LEWIS, David, 66, 67, 326, 330, 404.
  Henry, 121, 253, 270, 342, 343, 360
  John, 121, 167, 174, 254, 342.
  Ralph, 261, 280, 286, 343, 407.
  William, 34. 80. 117, 127, 275, 311, 384, 405
LINSEY, Daniel, 7, 10, 109, 337, 344.
LITTLE, Francis, 108, 113, 122, 132, 138, 145, 147, 149, 157, 168, 174, 175, 211, 225, 253, 266, 268, 269, 274, 275, 294, 304, 305, 318
  Mary, 166
LLOYD, David, 134. 200, 201, 213, 224, 226, 239, 242. 243, 246, 248, 254, 315, 317, 337, 338. 339, 340, 341, 343, 353, 356, 360, 362, 372, 385, 394, 396, 405, 407.
  John, 335
LOCKE, Andrew, 173, 174, 175, 185, 237.
  Elizabeth, 151, 152
  Mouns, 118, 122, 124, 174, 175, 216.
LONGSHAW, Thomas, 363. 385, 395, 396, 397, 398, 400, 403.
LONGSHORE, Margaret, 372
  Robert, 215, 317.
  Thomas, 298.
LONGWORTHY, John, 335
LOUNDER, Peter, 116.
LOWNES, George. 220, 358, 366, 404
  James, 93, 271, 283, 288, 296, 367.
  Joseph, 72, 110, 220
  Susanna, 283, 288
LUCAS, Robert, 3, 6, 8.
LUCKER, Annakey, 21
LUKENS, Nathaniel, 113, 119, 147, 200, 231, 237, 274.
LYNCH, Dennis, 357
MACKDANIELL (McDONALD). Daniel, 300.
  Owen, 178, 179, 261, 263, 264, 266, 272, 301, 328, 336, 355, 356, 361, 393, 395
  Sarah, 399
MACKELFRAY, John, 355
MACKLEWAY, Andrew, 12, 21.
MECANY, Alexander, 300.

MACKEENIS, Alexander, 329.
MAGDALION, Owen, 261.
MADDOCK, Henry, 143, 375.
    John, 117, 161, 190, 221, 231, 234, 241, 243, 248, 249, 256, 262, 263, 264, 266, 277, 296, 320, 332.
    Mordecai, 120, 210, 215, 216, 221, 226, 233.
MAKEE, Robert, 252, 271, 273, 276, 278, 279, 285, 292, 296, 334.
MALIN, John, 117.
    Randal, 45, 65, 68, 78, 81, 89, 109, 112, 139, 151, 162, 199, 218, 222, 243, 245, 265, 271, 279, 284, 318, 337, 338, 339, 363, 373, 391, 407.
    William, 59, 77, 81, 108, 152, 253, 277, 313, 319, 339.
MANN, Abraham, 12, 21, 29.
MARIS, George, 35, 36, 37, 40, 42, 44, 45, 49, 51, 52, 55, 57, 61, 63, 64, 69, 74, 77, 81, 82, 86, 87, 90, 91, 94, 96, 101, 105, 107, 108, 118, 119, 120, 121, 122, 124, 128, 132, 133, 138, 143, 145, 146, 155, 161, 168, 173, 179, 180, 181, 182, 183, 241, 245, 247, 253, 255, 259, 262, 268, 269, 270, 276, 277, 285, 286, 299, 346, 353.
    John, 82, 318, 323.
MARKHAM, Gov. William, 8, 10, 19, 155, 179, 296, 347.
MARLE, Thomas, 186.
MARSH, John, 66.
MARSHALL, John, 254, 274.
    Neales, 18, 148.
MARTEN, Walter, 23, 24, 28, 34, 37, 43, 46, 52, 55, 64, 66, 67, 70, 71, 97, 115, 116, 117, 118, 142, 156, 157, 159, 164, 178, 182, 194, 207, 214, 215, 216, 253, 262, 288, 313, 318, 336, 358, 363, 364, 365, 366, 370, 371, 376, 379, 381, 382, 383, 389, 390, 404, 405.
MARTIN, John, 21, 23, 24, 46, 50, 55, 75, 77, 104, 109, 112, 114, 117, 123, 150, 151, 167, 168, 183, 200, 203, 204, 205, 206, 224, 391, 394.
    Mary, 65, 301, 311, 313.
    Thomas, 66, 75, 78, 83, 118, 119, 120, 134, 140, 167, 183, 186, 199, 216, 217, 263, 265, 277, 404.
MASON, Richard, 106, 109, 124, 147.
MASSEY, Thomas, 60, 92, 265, 283, 302, 311, 314, 336, 337, 359, 373, 401, 404.
MATHORK, John, 117.
MAYO, John, 132.
MAYOW, John, 112.
MATSON, Neales, 12, 18.
    Peter, 20, 24,
MENDENHALL, Benjamin, 74, 80, 83, 84, 119, 123, 129, 134, 146, 279, 284, 287, 289, 295, 318, 336, 383.
    John, 26, 28, 35, 37, 38, 41, 51, 55, 65, 68, 72, 74, 78, 81, 83, 92, 95, 97, 106, 115, 116, 117, 119, 123, 129, 156, 157, 183, 199, 225, 255, 279, 288, 313, 373, 401.
    Moses, 72, 75, 80, 83.
MERCER, Thomas, 94, 246, 327.
MEREDITH, David, 201, 263, 338, 360, 381.
    Mary, 201, 338.
MILES, Griffith, 335.
    Richard, 238, 335.
    Samuel, 230, 335, 404.
MINSHALL, Thomas, 26, 32, 33, 45, 49, 57, 78, 81, 128, 222, 223, 224, 233, 243, 254, 279, 284, 287, 336, 339, 373.
MODY, Moody, Charles, 49, 50.
MOLL, John, 11, 22.
MOORE, Andrew, 66, 105, 115.
    George, 48.
    James, 238.
    Jane, 335.

MOORE, John, 115, 342, 356, 362, 395.
   Mary, 296, 369, 390
   Richard, 326, 330, 331, 354, 369.
   Thomas, 72, 75, 78, 116, 132, 142, 152, 186, 192, 199, 343, 390
MORE, Nicholas, 29.
MORGAN, Anthony, 274, 311, 321, 355, 403
   Evan, 360.
   John, 311, 335, 360
   Joshua, 359, 399.
   William, 88
MORREY, Humphrey, 100.
MORRIS, Anthony, 353
   David, 214, 217, 238, 287, 322, 350, 382.
MORTON, Catharine, 316.
   Mathias, 221, 297, 358, 366, 373, 390.
MORTONSON, Morton, 5, 70, 76, 83, 101, 102, 120, 237, 251, 348, 351, 358, 366, 390.
MOULDER, Jane, 166.
   Robert, 42, 52, 54, 59, 69, 70, 79, 105, 110, 111, 115, 127, 185, 211, 244
MULICKAY, Erick, 14.
MUSGROVE, Widow, 117.
   Elizabeth, 166, 256.
   John, 282.
   Moses, 289, 291, 293, 357.
NAYLOR, Robert, 135, 199, 320, 332, 370, 406
NEALSON, NELSON, Andreas, 4, 15, 36, 88, 93, 215.
   Anthony, 33, 34, 248, 250.
   Annie, 115
   Carey, 5
   John, 112.
   Mary, 5
   Michael, 29.
NEED, Joseph, 94, 128, 201, 237, 246, 297, 303, 304, 306, 358, 366, 390
NEGRO, Tobey, 250.
NEWLIN, Nathaniel, 74, 91, 101, 128, 183, 271, 293, 295, 298, 358, 359, 379, 380, 381, 384, 390
   Nicholas, 35, 38, 55, 57, 59, 61, 64, 72, 106, 149, 154, 155, 161, 168, 169, 173, 181, 183, 184, 185, 196, 199, 213, 218, 224, 225, 228, 230.
NIELDS, John, 112, 119, 139, 190, 203, 207, 209, 215, 228, 230, 271, 273, 283, 297, 302, 317, 329, 330, 331, 332, 333, 334, 336, 338, 339, 341, 343, 345.
   Mary, 338, 339, 343
NICHOLSON, John, 132, 149.
NICKOLS, Henry, 355.
NIXON, John, 45, 50, 59, 86, 89, 91, 185, 231, 241, 243, 248, 249, 261, 262, 296
NOBLE, Judith, 13, 14.
   Richard, 4, 6, 7, 8, 10, 11, 12, 13.
NORBURY, Thomas, 49, 86, 101, 182.
NOSSITER, Ann, 330.
   Thomas, 4, 7, 8, 9, 10, 22, 26, 32, 33, 35, 39, 44, 49, 50, 330
NOYES, Samuel, 20, 97, 98, 105, 107, 281, 357, 364, 382.
OBORN, Mary, 169, 196
   William, 38, 40, 116, 169, 196.
OGDEN, David, 57, 74, 81, 89, 109, 112, 117, 146, 149, 150, 254, 302, 311.
OLDFIELD, George, 21, 22, 357, 402
OLIVER, Evan, 238, 335
ORION (ARCHER), Garthright (Gertrude), 316
   John, 92, 93, 99, 100, 315, 316, 351, 367, 372, 373
   William, 12.

ORMES, Richard, 174, 183, 254, 322.
OTTER, John, 19, 20, 22
OWEN, Griffith, 220.
OXLEY, William, 3, 4, 5, 8, 9, 10, 11, 12, 13, 14, 15, 16, 33, 35, 37, 41, 45
PAINTER, George, 381.
    Widow, 120
PALMER, John, 72, 76, 116, 132, 150, 282, 370
    Mary, 77, 150.
PARKE, Nathaniel, 65, 66, 68, 75, 76, 110, 132, 142, 156, 157, 279.
PARKER, John, 135, 243, 246, 261, 283, 309, 310.
    Lawrence, 373.
    Richard, 97, 120, 121, 139, 164, 194, 244, 248, 289, 291, 306, 367, 406.
    William, 3.
PARRY, Thomas, 370.
PARSONS, John, 296.
PASCHALL, Thomas, 294.
PATRICK, Zachariah, 126, 148, 187.
PEACOCK, George, 325, 357, 400, 402.
PEARCE, George, 65, 67, 105, 119, 128, 141, 183, 195, 203, 207, 209, 254, 263, 265, 277, 281, 286, 288, 346, 350, 373
    Nicholas, 342.
PEARSON, Edward, 123, 127, 214, 221, 228, 342.
    John, 139, 221.
    Margaret, 45, 49, 50.
    Margery, 148
    Thomas, 38, 45, 50, 53, 60, 84, 89, 127, 128, 182, 183, 211, 217, 221, 230, 260, 346
PEDRICK, Roger, 4, 6
PEIRCE, Anne, 6.
PEMBERTON, Phineas, 353.
    Thomas, 353.
PENN, William, 25, 161, 202, 203, 208, 214, 350.
PENNELL, Elizabeth, 221.
    John, 326.
    Robert, 75, 77, 119, 128, 214, 215, 216, 217, 246, 277, 318, 333, 391.
PENNOCK, Edward, 375, 387
    John, 339, 387.
PETERSON, Annakey, 19
    Andreas, 15, 16, 19, 23.
    Hance, 18, 78, 88, 240.
    Morton, 18.
    Mouns, 10, 11, 12, 13, 15, 16, 19, 20, 22, 40, 63, 70, 80, 83, 93, 99, 101, 114, 123, 124, 201, 224, 251, 252, 259, 343
    Peter, 92, 93, 101, 119, 123, 135, 164, 194, 224, 249, 322, 343, 380, 391
    Reynear, 19, 23, 224, 225, 253, 304.
PHILLIPS, David, 311, 327, 349, 370
    George, 164, 165, 196.
    Samuel, 78
PHIPPS, Joseph, 26, 27, 149, 179, 180, 374.
PICKERING, Charles, 78, 88, 132, 134, 186, 200, 214, 215, 217, 242, 243, 254, 255, 342, 382.
PITMAN, Richard, 3, 4, 5.
PLUMMER, 125.
POLLEN, John, 355
POPINJAY, Armgard, 30
POTTER, Joseph, 143, 152, 319.
POW, Sarah, 277,
    Thomas, 276, 277.

POWELL, David, 153.
　Hannah, 369.
　Hester, 320
　John, 154, 288, 295, 296, 310, 370
　Joseph, 55, 107, 223, 245, 299, 307, 319, 331, 332, 369, 398, 403.
　Mary, 369.
　Samuel, 296.
　Thomas, 45, 65, 67, 75, 78, 80, 84, 86, 101, 110, 183, 186, 197, 214, 218, 224, 232, 249, 288, 299, 307, 310, 313, 317, 320, 398, 403
PREW, John, 44, 124, 269, 275.
PRICE, David, 405
　George, 65.
PRIESTNER, Elizabeth, 156.
PRINCE, Aringard, 28, 29.
PRITCHETT, Edward, 37, 38, 42, 43, 72, 74, 76, 86, 97, 101, 103, 117, 131, 216, 224, 236, 280, 285, 370.
　Elizabeth, 280, 285.
PROTHERO, Evan, 226, 230, 238, 247, 284, 286.
PUMPHREY, Walter, 4, 6
PUSEY, Caleb, 37, 46, 56, 72, 78, 80, 81, 82, 89, 90, 94, 95, 105, 109, 117, 118, 120, 123, 125, 129, 130, 146, 149, 151, 157, 164, 180, 181, 182, 188, 189, 190, 192, 197, 203, 209, 212, 214, 215, 216, 217, 226, 230, 232, 234, 235, 236, 239, 244, 245, 251, 252, 255, 256, 258, 259, 260, 262, 264, 267, 270, 274, 275, 276, 277, 283, 285, 296, 299, 300, 301, 307, 309, 317, 321, 328, 337, 338, 353, 358, 359, 369, 380, 384, 398, 403
　Frances, 337.
　John, 337
PYLE, Nicholas, 83, 84, 150, 154, 162, 199, 228, 233, 270, 289, 300, 322.
　Robert, 34, 38, 41, 46, 52, 55, 57, 61, 63, 64, 71, 72, 74, 77, 83, 86, 87, 89, 132, 154, 169, 181, 182, 193, 199, 217, 223, 229, 324, 361, 363, 401.
QUIST, Neales, 101.
RADLEY, John, 155, 183, 287, 311, 350, 370, 380, 391.
RAMBO, Andreas, 14.
　Brita, 21
　John, 216.
　Peter, 3, 4, 5, 7, 8, 9, 10, 13, 52.
RAWLINGS, RAWLINSON, Hester, 166.
　Thomas, 58, 96, 97, 123, 129, 132, 147, 185, 196, 203, 207, 209, 226, 231, 232, 237.
　William, 77, 78, 148
ROSEN, RAWSON, Ebritta, 59, 135.
　Wolle (William), 8, 9, 10, 11, 12, 13, 14, 15, 23, 24, 26, 31, 33, 42, 43, 45, 50, 53, 59, 119, 134, 135, 164, 173, 246
REDMAN, John, 353
REDMEAL, Elizabeth, 235.
　John, 370.
REES, Harry, 405
　Thomas, 274, 275, 328, 381
REIGN, Dennis, 372.
RETTEW, William, 155, 175, 176, 293, 304.
REVELL, Thomas, 3, 8, 10, 15, 19, 23, 25, 28, 33, 67.
REYNOLDS, Henry, 3, 4, 5, 7, 10, 11, 13, 18, 25, 26, 27, 30, 31, 32, 33, 34, 37, 38, 41, 43, 45, 46, 49, 51, 52, 53, 54, 58, 59, 61, 79, 87, 110, 124, 125, 126, 127, 152, 159, 160, 184, 207, 208, 212, 265, 300, 303, 352
　Richard, 68, 156.
RHOADS, Adams, 92, 96, 101, 121, 156, 157, 199, 228, 391
　John, 140, 255, 256, 261, 291.
RICHARDS, John, 370.

RICHARDS, Jone, 158.
  Joseph, 22, 23, 24, 26, 34, 37, 41, 45, 64, 67, 70, 71, 72, 80, 92, 101, 105, 112, 125, 126, 129, 134, 140, 142, 147, 158, 164, 176, 177, 178, 183, 194, 195, 200, 201, 203, 209, 224, 226, 234, 237, 241, 243, 246, 270, 271, 278, 283, 296, 312, 324, 329, 332, 333, 370.
  Nathaniel, 158, 234, 253, 270, 277, 282, 318, 322, 323, 336, 343, 356.
RICHARDSON, John, 373.
  Joseph, 28, 34, 35, 109, 142, 249.
  Samuel, 353.
RIDGWAY, Richard, 4, 6, 129, 130
RILEY, Daniel, 260, 261, 263.
ROBERTS, David, 336, 355, 356, 362, 365
  John, 335
  Oliver, 349
  William, 355.
ROBINETT, Allen, 81, 96, 176.
  Samuel, 370.
ROBINS, Thomas, 130.
ROBINSON, Andrew, 50, 281, 299, 303.
  George, 383, 399.
  John, 361.
  Patrick, 186, 200, 214, 217, 254, 262, 263, 265, 268, 278, 279, 281, 353, 376.
  Robert, 26, 33, 201.
  Samuel, 405.
  Thomas, 125, 384
ROCHFORD, Dennis, 51, 52, 70, 116, 167, 179, 180, 263
ROMAN, Philip, 49, 62, 70, 91, 116, 121, 126, 138, 139, 145, 149, 153, 169, 186, 192, 196, 203, 207, 214, 215, 216, 230, 239, 259, 263, 265, 266, 279, 309, 322, 328, 334, 335, 340, 352, 354, 358, 388, 401
  Robert, 363, 371.
Ross, Alexander, 300.
ROUTH, Francis, 309,
  Lawrence, 150, 164, 194, 235, 307, 308, 309, 332
  Rachel, 309
  Thomas, 309.
  Widow, 283, 303
ROWE, William, 234, 253, 262, 337, 343.
ROWELL, Martha, 357
ROWLAND, Samuel, 65, 66, 67, 68, 95, 97, 105, 106, 113, 130, 134, 135, 175, 217, 333, 385, 396.
ROTHERROW, RHYDDURAH, RUTHERO, Rees, 274, 360, 381
RUDMAN, Richard, 58, 92.
RUDYARD, Thomas, 59
RUTTER, Elizabeth, 356, 357.
SALTER, Hannah, 7
SAMUEL, Hugh, 153
SANDILANDS, Anneka, 5, 34, 103, 166, 263.
  Christian, 283.
  James, 8, 9, 10, 15, 16, 17, 24, 25, 26, 27, 33, 35, 36, 39, 40, 41, 42, 44, 45, 46, 48, 49, 52, 53, 54, 59, 62, 68, 69, 71, 85, 90, 92, 101, 112, 125, 127, 132, 147, 149, 159, 160, 168, 173, 179, 181, 182, 183, 185, 195, 196, 197, 199, 202, 206, 209, 212, 213, 218, 221, 224, 225, 226, 227, 230, 231, 236, 240, 241, 242, 244, 245, 247, 248, 249, 250, 253, 268, 283, 284, 294, 305, 309, 328, 341, 372, 376, 377
  Jonas, 284.
  Lydia, 284.
  Mary, 283.
SANGER, John, 72, 75, 132, 149, 159, 176.

SARY, Thomas, 22.
SCARLET, Humphrey, 201, 281, 282, 329, 370.
SCHOLEY, Robert, 3, 4, 5.
SCOOLE, Samuel, 295, 301.
SCOREY, William, 188, 189.
SCOTHORN, Robert, 201, 274, 289, 292, 330, 391, 406.
SCOTT, James, 33, 34.
    Samuel, 253, 262, 270, 287.
SEARY, Thomas, 22.
SELLERS, Samuel, 119, 224, 230, 246, 294
SHARD, John, 107, 391.
SHARDLOW, William, 261.
SHARPLES, James, 404.
    Jane, 121, 138, 384.
    John, 45, 119, 121, 138, 164, 194, 195, 239, 240, 254, 351, 392, 395, 407.
    Joseph, 384.
SHAW, John, 264, 302, 314.
    Joseph, 211, 212.
SHORT, Miriam, 23.
SHUTE, William, 15, 16.
SIDEBOTTOM, Thomas, 231, 337, 372, 402, 405.
SIMCOCK, George, 120, 152, 167, 201, 225, 240, 266, 270, 271, 281, 304.
    John, 22, 23, 25, 28, 32, 34, 51, 57, 59, 61, 63, 64, 69, 75, 77, 83, 84, 86, 87, 88, 89, 91, 93, 94, 103, 105, 107, 108, 110, 113, 114, 115, 116, 120, 122, 124, 128, 138, 139, 140, 143, 145, 146, 149, 150, 155, 158, 161, 168, 173, 179, 182, 183, 184, 185, 186, 192, 218, 221, 224, 225, 227, 228, 230, 234, 236, 241, 246, 247, 252, 253, 254, 259, 261, 262, 264, 265, 266, 270, 273, 275, 276, 277, 279, 285, 312, 313, 317, 354, 359, 360, 369, 375, 379, 381, 388, 392, 394, 396, 397, 402, 403
    Jacob, 80, 83, 89, 95, 101, 105, 109, 117, 120, 135, 138, 143, 173, 221, 265, 267, 360
    Susanna, 225, 266, 281.
SIMONSON, Magnis, 300.
SIMPSON, William, 281, 320, 332.
SMEDLEY, George, 117, 253.
    Sarah, 291.
SMITH, Anne, 73, 104, 175.
    Benjamin, 386, 396.
    Clare, 274.
    Elizabeth, 355.
    Francis, 68, 71, 72, 73, 76, 84, 104, 116, 138, 163, 164, 168, 174, 175, 185, 231.
    John 57, 59, 92, 128, 134, 165, 212, 214, 215, 216, 231, 243, 248, 256, 306, 313, 323, 330, 333, 358, 366, 390, 406.
    Margaret, 107, 110.
    Mary, 274, 353.
    Robert, 84, 121, 152, 156, 201, 261, 292.
    Roger, 275, 289, 297, 344.
    Thomas, 57, 59, 63, 76, 96, 113, 114, 123, 156, 157, 199, 256, 286, 287, 293, 299, 301, 304, 306, 307, 310, 315, 319, 320, 321, 323, 327, 329, 331, 332, 334, 336, 338, 339, 341, 354, 375, 406.
    William, 59, 230, 244, 274, 297, 322, 355, 372, 403.
SOUTH, Humphrey, 390.
SOUTHBY, Robert, 71
SUMTION, John, 52, 53.
SPENCER, Thomas, 340.
SPRAY, Christopher, 282, 404.
STACY, Mahlon, 14.

STANFIELD, Francis, 60, 86, 92, 180
    Grace, 148.
    James, 38, 60, 92, 93, 99, 119, 134, 141, 146, 152, 156, 160, 164, 165, 175, 178, 179, 182, 185, 196, 199, 200, 206, 213, 215, 216, 220, 225, 226, 231, 232, 255, 338, 397, 399, 401.
    Mary, 165.
STANFORD, Anne, 6.
    William, 6.
STANYARD, William, 156.
STEEDMAN, Elizabeth, 127.
    John, 74, 110, 346, 363.
    Joseph, 45, 55, 66, 74, 156.
STEPHENS, Francis, 14, 18, 21.
    John, 404.
    Robert, 99, 100, 101, 103, 119.
STEPHENSON, Francis, 4, 6.
STEWARD, Peter, 135, 137, 147.
STOCKDALE, William, 208.
STOCKETT, STAWKETT, STALKER, Mons, 7, 8, 9, 10, 11, 12, 14, 19, 20, 26, 35, 36, 37, 315, 316.
    Peter, 315, 316.
STREATCHER, 125.
STRODE, George, 25, 26, 32, 35, 54, 55, 72, 75, 78, 80, 85, 86, 111, 113, 116, 127, 132, 134, 177, 178, 185, 235, 291, 305, 311, 330, 331, 343, 354, 390.
STUBBS, Joseph, 7.
SWAFFER, James, 102, 105, 109, 112, 125, 152, 156, 157, 162, 215, 216, 224, 226, 254, 304, 323, 336, 339, 346, 356, 357, 360, 365, 380, 392, 393, 395.
    William, 201, 254, 282, 337, 346, 398.
SWANSON, Andreas, 9, 100.
    Jacob, 30
    Swan, 3, 8, 10, 15, 19.
SWIFT, Henry, 134, 320, 332, 394, 395.
SYMES, John, 66.
SYMONDS, Daniel, 31.
TALLEY, William, 102, 103, 105, 106, 108, 110, 112, 113, 118, 121, 138, 153, 186, 192, 226, 237, 243, 249, 297, 323, 337, 344, 346, 356.
TATON, Henry, 316.
    Walbera, 316.
TAYLOR, Ebenezer, 3, 5, 6, 7.
    Christopher, 35, 40, 48, 49, 262, 270, 278, 298, 305, 326.
    Hannah, 128.
    Isaac, 174, 248, 253, 262, 265, 268, 313, 404.
    Israel, 341, 343, 345, 352, 353, 357, 361, 365, 367.
    Jacob, 405.
    John, 78, 81, 102
    Jonathan, 405.
    Joseph, 229, 341, 345, 346, 352, 353, 357, 365.
    Josiah, 174, 199, 238, 253, 301, 313, 328, 329, 336, 337, 339, 340, 395, 406.
    Martha, 405
    Mary, 222, 223.
    Peter, 48, 63, 89, 108, 128, 153, 183, 186, 192, 195, 214, 218, 222, 249, 254, 270, 301.
    Richard, 324.
    Robert, 32, 33, 37, 44, 45, 50, 60, 120, 128, 135, 137, 141, 152, 174, 220, 221, 243, 248, 302.
    Thomas, 117, 370, 395, 403.
    William, 34, 41, 42, 65, 68, 70, 221, 222, 223.

428 INDEX

TEST, John, 3, 4, 5, 8. 10, 15, 16, 17, 19, 20, 156, 366, 367, 368, 369.
    Thomas, 362.
THATCHER, Richard, 97, 115, 116, 117, 119, 139, 162, 183, 399
THOMAS, Charles, 303, 323, 330.
    George, 282, 288, 318, 319.
    John, 203, 207, 209, 213, 362.
    Micah, 226, 243.
    Peter, 61, 127, 246, 311, 395.
    Reece, 381.
    Richard ap, 394.
    William, 118, 184, 318, 322, 335, 358, 366, 384, 394.
    Widow, 335.
THOMSON, George, 23, 31, 32.
    Miriam, 49.
    Richard, 251, 263, 264, 266, 314, 359, 406.
    Thomas, 350.
THORNTON, Nathaniel, 53, 66, 89, 110, 124, 125, 139, 150, 151, 226, 230, 232, 240, 259, 275.
THRUMBALL, Samuel, 21.
TOBTON, Henry, 38, 60, 74.
    Hendrick, 221.
TREGO, Peter, 338.
TREMAINE, Alice, 310.
    Peter, 04, 192.
TRENT, Maurice, 300, 355, 361.
TRESS, Margaret, 395.
TROTTER, William, 149, 282.
TUCKER, Richard, 74, 92, 151, 256, 343.
    Nathaniel, 336.
TURBERFIELD, Mary, 165, 167, 173, 184, 194.
TURNER, John, 178, 179, 277.
    Robert, 40, 130, 188, 260, 262, 263, 265, 267, 270, 278, 281, 298, 305, 326, 342, 344, 352, 382.
URINE, Haunce, 60, 63, 70, 76, 80, 85, 92, 99, 101, 102, 177, 184, 224, 316, 336, 348, 354.
USHER, Sarah, 166, 168.
    Thomas, 25, 27, 28, 31, 32, 34, 35, 36, 39, 40, 42, 43, 44, 45, 46, 49, 51, 52, 55, 57, 61, 63, 64, 67, 68, 69, 74, 76, 77, 87, 89, 90, 97, 102. 106, 108, 110, 140, 150, 168, 180, 352, 377.
VANCULIN, Anne, 217.
    Jacobus, 380, 391.
    John, 74, 77, 84, 89, 90, 131, 227, 232.
    Renear, 84.
VANDERHEYDEN, Mathias, 18, 30, 31, 33, 272, 278.
VANDEVER, William, 18, 138.
VERNON, Randal, 28, 36, 40, 41, 45, 49, 56, 63, 64, 67, 68, 70, 71, 96, 120, 125, 128, 147, 157, 165, 180, 183, 186, 192, 199, 211, 218, 243, 245, 246, 249, 253, 254, 259, 264, 273, 279, 307, 309, 311, 337, 373.
    Robert, 28, 48, 78, 80, 108, 162, 222, 224, 232, 243, 245, 253, 271, 279, 328, 338, 339, 344, 383, 396.
    Thomas, 24, 28, 45, 74, 75, 78, 92, 99, 101, 108, 120, 129, 136, 139, 162, 202, 203, 207, 209, 232, 234, 237, 243, 254, 256, 258, 272, 273, 276, 328, 337, 338, 339, 340, 342, 344, 396.
VESTAL, William, 268, 339, 343.
VINES, 125.
WADE, Lydia, 65, 98, 166, 330, 351.
    Robert, 3, 7, 8, 10, 14, 15, 19, 22, 23, 25, 32, 34, 35, 37, 40, 42, 43, 44, 45, 47, 49, 52, 55, 57, 61, 63, 64, 66, 69, 77, 83, 85, 86, 104, 106, 116, 117, 175, 181, 182, 183, 185, 201, 212, 213, 318, 330, 351, 353, 395, 400.

WALDRON, Roger, 129, 132, 133, 325.
WALKER, Edward, 72.
　　Francis, 13.
WALLIAM, James, 48.
WALLIS, Thomas, 14.
WALTER, Edward, 96 (?), 147, 163.
　　Godwin, 85, 311, 336, 401.
WARD, John, 26, 27.
WARNER, Isaac, 79, 98, 105, 113, 126, 207, 208, 265, 266, 269, 275.
　　William, 3, 10, 11, 12.
WARREN, Abraham, 361.
WATERS, Edward, 96.
WATMORE, Nathaniel, 298.
WATT, George, 188.
　　John, 188, 189.
WATTS, John, 396, 400.
WAY, Robert, 78, 259.
WEAVER, Anne, 146, 158.
　　Anthony, 65, 72, 89, 94.
　　William, 158, 281.
WEIGHT, Samuel, 80, 102, 109.
WEST, William, 109.
WHARLEY, Daniel, 56, 130, 188, 189.
WHEELER, Gilbert, 14, 18.
　　James, 337, 344.
WHELDEN, Isaac, 246.
WHITACRE, Charles, 75, 84, 88, 93, 95, 110, 143, 218, 230, 247, 251, 288, 306, 313, 391.
WHITAKER, James, 216, 391, 402.
WHITBY, Thomas, 143.
WHITE, John, 28, 88, 200, 213, 214, 217, 242, 254.
　　Nicholas, 184.
　　Robert, 9, 361, 371, 380, 391.
　　William, 98, 103, 112, 195, 196.
WHITEHORNE, Thomas, 65, 70.
WICKHAM, John, 127, 135, 136, 137, 141, 147, 148, 152, 226, 231.
WILLARD, George, 55, 75, 97, 117, 119, 120, 141, 188, 215, 228, 267, 356, 358, 366, 384, 390.
　　Joseph, 24.
　　Susannah, 141, 148, 202, 203.
WILLCOX, Barnabas, 88.
　　Joseph, 342, 382.
WILLIAMS, Gilbert, 45, 52, 56, 273, 289, 296.
　　Dunck, 12, 15,
　　Henry, 48.
　　James, 48.
　　John, 46, 353.
　　Robert, 27.
WILLIAMSON, Daniel, 128, 233, 238, 281, 302, 313, 314, 328, 329, 336, 403, 404.
　　Mary, 339, 340.
WILLIS, Hester, 360.
　　John, 274, 311, 360, 363.
　　Margery, 58.
　　Thomas, 140.
WILSHERIE, Sarah, 42.
WILSON, Richard, 353.
WINCHCOME, Katharin, 20.
WINTER, William, 165.

WITHERS, Ralph, 25, 27.
  Thomas, 18, 32, 34, 35, 37, 38, 40, 41, 42, 44, 45, 57, 58, 74, 80, 106, 116, 187, 268, 269, 271, 279, 285, 286, 287, 292, 293, 296, 299, 300, 301, 305, 306, 307, 310, 315, 319, 320, 373, 376, 402.
WOOD, Anthony, 402.
  George, 26, 33, 37, 57, 70, 84, 89, 109, 121, 179, 180, 406.
  Jane, 110, 294.
  Henry, 92.
  John, 4, 6, 110, 123, 128, 156, 157, 167, 182, 195, 201, 226, 228, 230, 234, 235, 243, 246, 271, 277, 292, 294, 304, 306, 405, 406
  Jonathan, 230.
  Joseph, 93, 109, 112, 118, 122, 129, 138, 139, 145, 168, 196, 201, 215, 216, 223, 225, 230, 233, 236, 243, 247, 286, 287, 291, 292, 293, 294, 295, 299, 301, 304, 306, 307, 310, 315, 318, 319, 321, 323, 326, 327, 329, 330, 331, 332, 333, 334, 336, 338, 339, 341, 343, 346, 349, 351, 352, 354, 358, 362, 372, 379, 386, 388, 391, 393, 394, 402, 403, 405, 406.
  Peter, 346, 363, 367, 404.
  Susanna, 69, 230
  William, 35, 40, 44, 55, 57, 122, 223, 229.
WOODMANS, Thomas, 130.
WOODMANSEE, William, 3, 4, 5, 12, 22, 23, 24, 26, 37, 41, 45, 49, 52, 63, 88, 119, 124, 129, 141, 142, 153, 160, 174, 195, 209, 227, 230, 235, 244, 248, 393, 407.
WOODYARD, WOODWARD, George, 75, 78, 152, 186, 192, 254, 290, 304, 374, 391.
  Elizabeth, 127, 289, 291, 293.
  Mary, 290, 291, 293
  Richard, 125, 128, 129, 140, 167, 217, 254, 287, 311, 319, 373, 375, 392
  Robert, 129, 134, 154, 192, 199, 221, 289, 380, 392, 393
WOOLSON, Hanee, 10.
WORLEY, Francis, 266, 320, 350, 358, 366.
  Henry, 384.
WORRALL, John, 45, 50, 56, 65, 67, 108, 113, 117, 125, 129, 134, 139, 143, 152, 199, 231, 236, 249, 263, 265, 271, 277, 318, 343, 363, 373, 374, 375, 395.
  Peter, 146, 211, 217, 264, 266, 271, 272, 273, 284, 337, 370.
  Richard, 22.
WORRILOW, Ann, 240
  John 240, 263, 265, 277, 291, 313, 336, 339, 356, 367, 373.
  Thomas, 127, 147, 183, 199, 240, 284, 303, 322, 358, 360, 375, 385, 390
WORTH, Thomas, 26, 28, 32, 36, 37, 57, 64, 67, 70, 71, 75, 92, 96, 110, 119, 121, 151, 164, 194, 228, 248, 261, 262, 288, 294, 306, 313.
WROTH, James, 110
YARNALL, Francis, 57, 64, 66, 80, 81, 82, 83, 87, 146, 182, 214, 233, 248, 263, 291, 318, 346.
  Philip, 64, 94, 119, 289, 291, 293, 311, 356, 375, 391, 397
YEATES, Jasper, 283, 284, 294, 305, 327, 334, 339, 341, 342, 346, 354, 359, 361, 366, 369, 371, 374, 379, 381, 388, 396, 397, 400, 402, 403
YOKEHAM, Peter, 8, 9, 13, 15, 16, 17, 362, 372.

www.ingramcontent.com/pod-product-compliance
Lightning Source LLC
Chambersburg PA
CBHW020636300426
44112CB00007B/131